Religion and Profit

EARLY AMERICAN STUDIES

Daniel K. Richter and Kathleen M. Brown, Series
Editors

Exploring neglected aspects of our colonial,
revolutionary, and early national history and culture,
Early American Studies reinterprets familiar themes
and events in fresh ways. Interdisciplinary in character,
and with a special emphasis on the period from about
1600 to 1850, the series is published in partnership
with the McNeil Center for Early American Studies.

A complete list of books in the series is available from
the publisher.

Religion and Profit

Moravians in Early America

Katherine Carté Engel

PENN

UNIVERSITY OF PENNSYLVANIA PRESS

PHILADELPHIA

Published by
University of Pennsylvania Press
Philadelphia, Pennsylvania 19104-4112

Printed in the United States of America on acid-free paper
10 9 8 7 6 5 4 3 2 1

Library of Congress Cataloging-in-Publication Data
ISBN 978-0-8122-4123-5

In loving memory of
Gene E. Carte and Elaine H. Carte

and for Jeffrey

CONTENTS

NOTE ON TERMINOLOGY

Eighteenth-century Moravians went by a wide variety of names, some preferred by the group, some conferred upon them by outsiders. In the following work, the terms Moravian, Brüdergemeine, Renewed Unitas Fratrum, and Unity will be used interchangeably.

INTRODUCTION

ON THE EVENING of September 29, 1751, one of the Moravian missionaries stationed among the Delaware and Mahican Indians in the Lehigh Valley of northeastern Pennsylvania jotted down the events of the day. He wrote in German, the language of the international Moravian community, and he knew his diary would be circulated to members of the church throughout the world. The Moravians, a Protestant sect founded in 1727 by Count Nikolaus Ludwig von Zinzendorf and based in Germany, were key players in the rise of international evangelicalism. They established missions throughout the Atlantic world, and were especially attracted to Pennsylvania because of the profession of religious tolerance by the colony's Quaker founder, William Penn. When thinking over what to record, the missionary focused on the daily business of Gnadenhütten, the community whose spiritual care was in his charge. Several residents had departed that morning for a Moravian synod at Quittapahilla, in central Pennsylvania, while some of the "white Brethren" who stayed behind worked, despite the rainy weather, to make floats out of boards from the sawmill so that lumber could be sent downriver to the central Moravian town at Bethlehem. In the evening, he recorded, men from Bethlehem had arrived to transport the wood. They told their coreligionists that the Moravians' community ship, the *Irene*, had arrived in New York from London. The good news that her passengers were safely in Bethlehem after their long trip from Germany prompted members of the mission town to spill "some joyful little tears, and one heard some *Honnewe, Honnewe*," which was, according to the diarist, the Indian way of saying "dear Savior, dear Savior." Their friends secure, the Moravians rested comfortably in the knowledge that their missionary work among Pennsylvania's Indians, and their larger community, was progressing smoothly.

At the same time as the missionaries rejoiced, the comings and goings of the *Irene* were communicated in a very different form to a very different audience. As far as New York's merchants were concerned, the vessel was an ordinary merchant ship. That it was owned by a religious group mattered little to the dry-goods dealers who purchased space in her hull. That the Moravians used the profits gained through the *Irene* to support missionary work probably mattered even less to them. On October 3, a notice appeared in the *New York Gazette* announcing that the *Irene* would "sail with all Expedition" bound for London and Amsterdam, and that she "takes Freight at a reasonable Rate" and would depart "full or not." Some roofing tiles had been imported on the last voyage and were available for sale. These notices assured potential shippers that she was a reliable trading vessel that they could count on to transport valuable goods across the ocean.[1]

These two quite different accounts of the *Irene*'s arrival resulted from the confluence of two important trends in early modern history. The Moravians and their settlement at Bethlehem, Pennsylvania, sat at the nexus between them. The first was the rise of evangelical, revivalistic Protestantism, and it explains the presence of central European missionaries on the Pennsylvania frontier, as well as in New York, London, and indeed throughout the Atlantic world. Simultaneously, the growth of the transatlantic economy provided the means for the Moravians' material labors: wood from the sawmill became building materials for Bethlehem and neighboring settlements; the shops they helped build sold goods from Philadelphia and London alongside furs and tools procured closer to home; the roofing tiles imported on the *Irene* likely adorned some building in the growing port city of New York; advertisements and regular shipping patterns signaled the increasing maturity and stability of transatlantic trade. Taken together, jottings in a Moravian mission journal and advertisements in a New York newspaper illustrate how international evangelicalism and the developing market economy interwove in the mid-eighteenth century.

Yet the convergence of these two trends in the activities of the spiritually and materially industrious Moravians also signals something further: the ultimate intertwining of religious and economic concerns in the daily lives of early Americans. The "white Brethren" in Gnadenhütten were there to run the sawmill, but they worked alongside Indians who were part of the Moravians' far-reaching mission efforts. Many of the Europeans were themselves, at one point or another in their lives, missionaries bent on converting souls to Christianity. The town to which Gnadenhütten's lumber was sent, Bethlehem, was communitarian in 1751, meaning that its residents, bounded by shared religious purpose, functioned as a single economic entity. But this unusual economic model based on spiritual community did not prevent the Moravians from engaging in all sorts of entrepreneurial activity. In fact, it enabled them to make all that they could of the commercial advantages the eighteenth-century Atlantic world had to offer. Chief among their efforts was the *Irene*, a ship traveling steadily between North America and Europe, transporting members of the community alongside trade goods. The Moravians' religious and economic lives constituted a single web stretching from central Europe to the reaches of Pennsylvania's northern frontier. Trading ties begot converts, religious networks expedited financial relationships, and the production and sale of trade goods bolstered missionary communities. The Moravians' artisans and merchants, as they tanned leather, forged tools, or oversaw the loading of barrels of sugar into a ship, labored for the missions. For the Moravians, commercial success and spiritual well-being were inextricably connected.

The relationship between religion and economic life is one of the thorniest and most intractable topics people have found to argue about. It has provoked some of the most enduring historical scholarship of the modern era and simultaneously fueled some of the noblest jeremiads. At the crux of the dilemma is an elusive problem. Religion and the selflessness of true faith (particularly though by no means exclusively in a Christian context) appear to be in eternal conflict with the process of material accumulation that drives a market economy. And yet, though the conflict between religious faith and economic life seems inevitable, numerous exceptions leap to mind, where devout souls prospered, or wealth seemed to further religious ends. Mormon entrepreneurs and philanthropic billionaires offer two easy and common examples, not to mention the easy marriage between modern evangelical Protestantism and mass communications. For historians especially, the epic struggle between God and Mammon has generated a seductive and lasting narrative. At some distant time in the past, the argument runs, true faith kept selfishness in check. But since the birth of the modern era, a new "spirit" has taken over, vanquishing the better angels of human nature. This version of the past feels, as the saying goes, truer than truth, and yet, to quote another often-used phrase, the devil is the details. In daily life, the moments where religion was brought to bear on the economy were small, subtle, and frequent. Should a merchant take advantage of an ignorant buyer, or would the application of his business savvy violate his faith? Should a church's trustees use an innovative and complicated means of finance, such as a corporate structure? Should a missionary sell goods to prospective converts, potentially mingling commerce with the message he or she tried to convey? These were the nitty-gritty questions about the morality of economic life faced by religiously minded early Americans, and when they arose the idea of a grand historical conflict between religion and the market offered little clarity.

The story of Moravians in eighteenth-century Pennsylvania—their efforts to spread their Gospel among the Indians and Europeans of the area as well as their efforts to support their mission through engagement in the region's growing market economy—is another example of how difficult it can be to draw a clear distinction between religious faith and economic life. Indeed, the Moravians would have rejected the effort to find a meaningful separation, as their faith directly shaped their economic actions. Missionary work dominated Bethlehem and the lives of all its residents, so the story of the town's economy is also the history of its missions. In Bethlehem's communitarian years, between 1741 and 1762, town leaders determined almost every facet of life—from who would marry whom, to what career path each person would pursue—according to the needs of the missions. The missions also required a steady stream of cash. Saving souls was expensive work, after all, so leaders eagerly sought new business ventures to earn money. Missionary work thus made entrepreneurs of the Moravians.[2] Religious concerns shaped the town's economic life in a second way as well, beyond its missions. Like all major Christian groups, the Moravians worried about the moral implications of the search for gain, even as they never cut the church or its members off from the wider Atlantic economy. They decried worldliness, laziness, greed, thievery, and dishonesty in business. They saw these failings as sins and regulated their economy to keep it in line with their values. Town leaders consequently exercised close supervision over all business practice, and they worked to ensure that artisans and shopkeepers behaved in ways they considered appropriate. Spiritual consequences could flow from moral shortcomings in business. Together, the financial imperative of supporting the missions and the religious imperative to do it without falling into sin produced the Moravian economy of Bethlehem, a complex mix of the market and the moral.

Bethlehem's economy was neither isolated nor static. The choices Moravians faced when they worked to support their missions or regulate their own moral economic behavior evolved in response to the changes in the wider world of which the little town was only a part. Bethlehem existed within a larger Moravian framework, to be sure, but it also possessed deep connections to the many places where its merchants, artisans, and, above all, missionaries, worked. The events that unfolded in Bethlehem thus connect the histories of early evangelicalism, the growth of the Atlantic economy, and the violent course of native-white relations in the middle of the eighteenth century. They also reflect the tension between the international and the local in early American history. The Moravian church, also known as the "Unity," consisted of an extended system of towns, congregations, and missions that reached from its base in eastern Germany to Great Britain, Labrador, Suriname, the West Indies, and North America. Leaders in Germany and Pennsylvania coordinated movement throughout the whole, and members of the international community were in constant motion. Bethlehem was thus a key node in a wide network that ringed the Atlantic Ocean and reached far into the North American interior. Pressures in the Moravian Atlantic arose from many quarters, and its leadership, to which Bethlehem owed obedience, resided in Germany. Yet Bethlehem's history was also rooted in the Mid-Atlantic, because of its intimate relationship to missionary work. Events there equally defined the choices available to Bethlehem's residents. Over the sixty years between the town's founding and the end of the eighteenth century, Atlantic influences and local circumstances each played essential and competing roles in shaping Bethlehem's history.[3]

The Moravians founded Bethlehem in 1741, at the height of the Great Awakening, a wave of revivals that electrified Britain's North American colonies. Their actions were part of the sea-change in Protestantism brought on by the rise of evangelicalism (the Great Awakening's international progenitor), with its focus on heartfelt religion and actively spreading the Gospel.[4] The Moravians epitomized both of these trends, and they were key players in the wider movement. Bethlehem's purpose was from the first fundamentally missionary. Its location on the Pennsylvania frontier positioned it perfectly so that itinerant preachers and missionaries could reach both the region's European residents and its Indian population.[5] The economy the Moravians built reflected that mission as well: its shared household was designed to distribute resources efficiently so that everything possible could go to the missionaries' work. Yet even in its communal days, Bethlehem's residents shared many ties to their neighbors, and the line between what was a part of the communal "Oeconomy" and what was outside it was highly permeable. The Moravians' missionary activities did not meet with uniform success, however. Controversy arose among European Americans, particularly German immigrants, some of whom embraced the newcomers' energetic organizing and proselytizing, while others excoriated the Moravians as troublemakers.[6] By the late 1740s, as the fervor of the Great Awakening cooled, Bethlehem's Moravians changed course, turning more fully toward their Indian missions as the outlet for their spiritual energies. Meanwhile the followers they had gained among the Mid-

Atlantic's European population settled into a small denominational presence. In the 1750s, the community built its missions and its trading networks. The Oeconomy grew into a substantial institution and provided the basis for three distinct economic systems, linking Bethlehem to the frontier, its local economy, and Atlantic commerce. Each of these engagements demanded its own balance among shared religious goals, moral economic behavior, and profit.

Bethlehem's membership in both local and transatlantic communities came into sharp relief during the Seven Years' War and its extended aftermath. The course of those events reshaped every aspect of life in the town, led to the end of the town's communal structure, and ultimately reconfigured the way the Moravians' religious beliefs shaped their economy. The most acute local crisis came in 1755, when the mission at Gnadenhütten came under attack. Over the following three years, Bethlehem found itself on the front lines of the conflict between Pennsylvania and the Delaware Indians who had historically occupied the province. That fight was only a piece of the larger war, however, fought simultaneously between Britain and France, between native peoples and Europeans in North America, and, in the Moravians' European homeland, between Austrians and Prussians. As Bethlehem's leaders tried to cope with their theater of the war—a bitter, racial conflict—Moravians everywhere reeled from the financial crises that resulted when war ruptured the entire Atlantic system. During the early 1760s, as peace gradually returned in Europe, the church's European leadership moved to centralize and rationalize their international community, ultimately reconfiguring Bethlehem's place in the Moravian system, as well as the role of missionary work in Bethlehem's economy. Meanwhile, renewed racial conflict between whites and Indians in Pennsylvania further undermined the relationship between Bethlehem and its missions. Bethlehem's leaders carefully navigated this difficult terrain, but in the town that emerged from this era of dramatic change, religion took on a role in daily life very different from the one it had played before the war.

In the quarter century after the end of the Seven Years' War—years that included the American Revolution—Bethlehem's Moravians used their religious beliefs to form a new economy. Gone were the close ties to missionary work that had characterized the town's founding, and leaders and residents turned their attention to new, more individualistic pursuits. Religion remained central to the town's economic life, but, deprived of its missionary context, that economy took on a very different character. The Revolution, in which some but not all Moravians took a pacifist stance, further enhanced the role of individual conscience and moral life in the town's construction of the economy. By the end of the century, Bethlehem was a quiet place, separated by a thousand miles from its few remaining missions and by more than a half-century from its heady days of revival. Its economic leaders, and the leaders of the international Moravian church, pursued a strategy of privatization to support their ongoing religious work. The communal exuberance born of shared challenges and goals had faded, and the international network had become a quiet denomination.

Embedding the Moravians' religious and economic choices within the events of the eighteenth-century Atlantic highlights what is unique and historically specific about the group. Yet the Moravians' experiences also shed light on a wider story of how religion interwove with the economic life of early America, because, while the Moravians were distinctive, the challenges they faced and the framework they used to evaluate their economic choices were not. Though their exuberant and ecumenical evangelicalism ruffled more than a few feathers, the Moravians were quite traditional in their approach to economic matters.[7] They offered no religious or social critique to the economic systems within which they lived and worked, and their theological innovations never touched on matters of the market. Indeed, the Moravians offer an excellent example of how religion influenced economic behavior precisely because they did *not* provide distinctive teachings on the subject. Instead, they engaged the economy as they needed, in order to make money, and they employed the same traditions of Protestant Christianity that the vast majority of their neighbors in Europe and North America used to govern their actions. Moreover, that economy and the world it supported were profoundly interconnected, locally, regionally, and above all internationally. The Moravians serve as a reminder that no early American community can be evaluated fully in isolation from its larger context.[8]

To say the Moravians were not innovative in their religious approach to economic matters is in no way to suggest they did not care about morality in the marketplace, however. For the Moravians, as for most early American Christians, the material and the spiritual were at once locked in theoretical conflict and also permanently bound together in an intimate dance. European migrants brought this conundrum with them to the New World. Their Christian heritage taught that wealth was morally dangerous. At the most basic level, scripture proclaimed that it was so: the rich man was less likely to enter heaven than a camel was to go through the eye of a needle, the Bible taught, and the love of money was the root of all evil. But the realities of the material world also dictated that religious people, particularly the Protestants who had rejected the Catholic monastic and ascetic traditions, had to engage the economic world if they were to prosper, or even just survive. Religious and secular leaders alike sought to discipline greed, in part by regulating economic behavior they thought linked to avarice, such as charging excessive interest, or usury. Individuals who were concerned with the morality of their actions submitted their lives either to spiritual discipline by religious leaders or to their own brand of scrutiny, and, since the winning of daily bread was a major part of everyone's life and accounted for a significant portion of interactions between people, the danger of economic sins remained omnipresent. For religious people, using a Christian framework to evaluate material choices was a constant reality.[9]

The Puritans, Anglicans, Quakers, Lutherans, Moravians, and myriad other groups who immigrated to North America believed, in the context of their Protestant intellectual heritages, that the economic world was at best difficult to navigate. Yet the fact that one could not escape the material realities of life—whether one merely traded surplus crops or undertook to support a massive missionary project—meant that its dangers could not be avoided entirely. Instead, they had to be carefully managed. Some of the earliest histories of British America suggest that concern over growing worldliness and selfishness undermined hopes for a religious haven in the New World almost from the founding of the first Puritan colony. Edward Winslow wrote in 1624 that in Plymouth "religion and profit jump together" in New England, but only a few decades later Cotton Mather invoked the adage that "*Religion* brought forth *prosperity*, and the *daughter* destroyed the *mother*," when he described the Pilgrims' settlement that Winslow had lauded. Mather (and the many others who had enshrined that pithy saying into the language) believed economic success to be detrimental to true spirituality, and likely assumed that any community enjoying economic prosperity would necessarily lose some of its collective religious purpose and identity. Concern over a conflict between devout belief and economic success continued throughout the early modern period, and it was present among early evangelicals as it had been among their Puritan forbearers. John Wesley, the founder of English Methodism and a fellow traveler of the Moravians, wrote that "wherever riches have increased, the essence of religion has decreased in the same proportion." His prognosis was grim: "Therefore," he continued, "I do not see how it is possible, in the nature of things, for any revival of true religion to continue long." Evangelical theologian Jonathan Edwards addressed the developing early modern economy of the mid-eighteenth century directly when he rejected human intervention in the market as immoral. Protestant leaders throughout the seventeenth and eighteenth centuries thus shared a concern that wealth could undermine the spiritual safety of their communities.[10]

Many historians have interpreted these cautionary statements and fears of religious decline on the part of early Americans as signs that Protestant believers of the era rejected the growing market economy, thus providing evidence for an inherent conflict between traditional, community-focused, religious society on the one hand and the modern, market-driven, individualistic ethos that succeeded it. In the process such scholars transformed a persistent thread of Protestant life into a historical question of the grandest proportions. Max Weber, in his seminal *Protestant Ethic and the Spirit of Capitalism*, argued that once established, markets became forces unto themselves, making religion irrelevant to economic behavior and, because sustenance became no less significant for survival, also making religious devotion and practice less relevant to individual lives. Historian Perry Miller later famously applied Weber's findings to Puritan North America, and his powerful narrative came to symbolize for many the essential embodiment of the role of religion in American history: that it was utterly foundational in the country's Puritan origins, until it was lost to an unstoppable and amoral frenzy of buying and selling.[11]

Taken as a whole, the scholarship exploring the relationship between religion and the economy in British North America has offered American history a powerful and durable narrative based on assumed conflict between the two. It simultaneously gives causal force to the seemingly inexorable engine of capitalism and allows the nostalgic idealization of a harmonious earlier era of purer motives and greater spirituality. It is also supremely portable: historians have identified the turn to markets in each period from the founding of New England to the early republic. Yet while this argument of economic self-interest triumphing over religion may be persuasive in each case, the multiplicity of such cases, with communal and religious sentiments continually reviving just to be overwhelmed again by a new wave of market change, suggests that the persistent exchange between individuals' values and their material choices is more complex. It is this complexity that this book investigates.[12]

The Moravians' facile and simultaneous engagement in the lumber trade and international commerce, and the laments of Wesley and Mather about greed, each reflect significant aspects of the interplay between religion and economic life in the early modern Atlantic world. The former points to a wide terrain of engagement in the economy by religious people, the latter suggests why that engagement remained, and for many people remains, a matter that required thoughtful attention. Viewing the subject in this way suggests that many early Americans were engaged in a constant, unavoidable, and intimate negotiation between, on the one hand, Christian teachings that taught one to avoid the search for personal gain, to root out greed, and to comport oneself with honesty in all circumstances; and, on the other hand, the practical realities of material life in a dynamic economic world. The Moravians' choice to do whatever they deemed morally possible to make money so that they could fund their missions is one part of that history. It includes their careful monitoring of their own actions to ensure that nothing they considered unethical ensued. Beneath the "turn to markets" lay a broad and complicated history of practical, but meaningful, choices.

Despite this historical reality, a century of scholarship on conflict or collaboration between Protestantism and the development of a modern economy has provided neither clear answers nor even distinct questions.[13] More important, the subject itself may no longer be fruitful, because it masks a much more finely grained yet significant history. Countless negotiations between the religious and the economic occurred in the actions of individual merchants or families, and they were far too varied to fit neatly into a single model. They can, however, be surprising. In Bethlehem, the expensive nature of missionary work dictated that, for a while at least, there would be little conflict between religious priorities and the search for profits, not least because the same leaders coordinated both activities. At the same time, however, the Moravians subjected their economic lives to close scrutiny, ever wary of the moral pitfalls awaiting any tradesperson or merchant. The Moravians' experience was specific to their choices, but the lesson is significant nonetheless: there were times when religion and profit *did* jump together, but it was a complicated game of double-dutch. Daily transactions did not raise for the Moravians the specter of the clash of capitalism and Christianity, nor did they portend the impending doom of an impersonal economy. Instead, religious individuals grappled with immediate choices, such as whether to tell a buyer that goods were of low quality, or, in the Moravian case, to use the church's ship as a merchant vessel to increase its profits.

Bethlehem provides fertile territory to consider these issues for several reasons. It possesses arguably the deepest record base available for any early American town. Thousands of pages of diaries, council and committee minutes, account books, mission reports, spiritual autobiographies, and letters provide an astonishing level of information about daily life in town. These sources reveal in detail how the Moravians negotiated their economic lives.[14] Bethlehem is also apt for such a study because the town's fundamental purpose was at once religious and economic. As a base for missionary work, Bethlehem had to be economically productive, in a very real sense profitable, far beyond what was required to support its own residents. As a key juncture in a vast international network, it faced expenses connected to travel and communication that dwarfed what most non-Moravian Pennsylvania congregations encountered. Economics mattered in a way that cut to the core of the town's spiritual life.

The Moravians themselves provide further reason for studying the town. They were central players in the rise of international evangelicalism, a movement to revitalize personal, Protestant piety that dramatically reshaped European and North American Protestantism in the first half of the eighteenth century. They corresponded, disputed, and sometimes worked with other major figures of the day, from the Great Awakening's most famous itinerant, George Whitefield, to the influential John Wesley. They used some of the most sophisticated means of communication and financing available in the Atlantic world. Such efforts did not come cheap. Their far-reaching projects to spread the Gospel among non-Christians and to unify Christians were supremely and persistently expensive, driving the Moravians to engage the economy around them with all the tools they could find, from large-scale communalism on the Pennsylvania frontier to international commerce in ocean-going vessels. At the same time, however, the Moravians' core economic culture mirrored that of most early modern Protestants. They embraced private property and traditional social hierarchies, and they never sought to define themselves against other Protestant groups, either economically or religiously. In short, they kept deep records of economic engagements that—though on a larger scale and more linked to missionary work than was typical of most groups—were essentially similar to those found elsewhere.

Bethlehem's story attests to the flexible ways in which early Americans used their religious beliefs, goals, and perspectives to shape their economic choices. The varied intersections between these separate and yet inherently intertwined aspects of daily life suggest that early Americans did not simply welcome or reject either their Christian heritages or their economic futures. Quite the contrary, the two existed in fluid, persistent, and ever-changing combination, and negotiations between them were omnipresent, yet often minute and intimate. This is not the first study to identify such moments. The rich historiography of early America is replete with disparate examples.

Yet these stories, of Halle's Pietists, Quaker merchants, and entrepreneurial re-vivalists are too often seen as isolated examples, rather than evidence of an emerging approach to the subject of religion's role in economic life. Together, they point to a lasting exchange between religion and economic life, a phe-nomenon both local and international, with its own history of which we yet know only a part.[15] There is much left unexplored about how religious actors engaged their economic lives, most of it quite separate from the well worn, macrohistorical, and often sociological efforts to uncover whether Protestants embraced or resisted capitalism, a question for which more than a century of academic study has not offered a conclusive answer. The consequences of these many intersections for the character of the economy or the health of religious belief are only part of the story. The negotiation itself was a persistent reality for early Americans, constantly being reopened and altered by the many his-torical trends and events that shaped their lives. Its history sheds light on how they understood and navigated the most basic questions of their lives.

For the Moravians, as for many early Americans, those questions were a part of the central narratives of the eighteenth century: the rise of evangelical-ism, the growth of the Atlantic economy, the bitter rivalries between empires, and the struggle between Europeans and Indians for possession of the North American continent. The Moravians' missionary zeal compelled them to build a diverse, flexible, and expansive economic system, and it demanded that they engage all aspects of their Atlantic world. Over the decades between Bethlehem's founding and the end of the eighteenth century, the group navigated the chal-lenges of a changing religious environment and the perils of global war. All these factors shaped the way the Moravians understood the economy that supported them, and they responded in the only way they could, with unflagging atten-tion. "It is certain that God has been with us in our commercial ventures, and has blessed us in that realm more than we ever expected," wrote members of the Moravians' Commercial Council in 1766. "On the other side," the Council continued, "it is also true that Commerce, if it is not pursued precisely after the sense of Jesus, and if the spirit of the world comes into it, it is a most danger-ous thing, which can bring the fall of not only individual souls, but entire con-gregations."[16] The Moravians struggled with a tension—that ingrained tension between the material and the spiritual—that was hardly unique to their Atlantic experience. How they managed that tension reveals much about the way reli-gion influenced the economic lives of early Americans, and the way commerce in turn affected their reach for God.

CHAPTER I

The Pilgrims' Mission

IN THE PRESENT day, a large electric star sits on the hillside over the hulking, rusting mass of steel mills and railroad tracks that for a century dominated the life, economy, and even air of Bethlehem, Pennsylvania, a symbol of the town's desire to be known as the "Christmas City." To justify this claim, residents call on their colonial heritage as a communitarian religious enclave of the Moravian Church. Bethlehem's name is part pun—the Lehigh River that runs through town was also called the Lecha, and thus the Hebrew for "House on the Lehigh" became Beth-Lecha, or Bethlehem—but lore teaches that Moravian leader Count Nikolaus Ludwig von Zinzendorf christened the place on Christmas, just a few months after its founding in the spring of 1741. Either way, the name's biblical resonance signifies the deep religious sentiments of the Moravians and the shared sense of missionary zeal that animated them. Most European migrants to colonial America came to make better lives for themselves or their families, whether that meant finding a fertile piece of land to farm or the freedom to worship in their own way. The Moravians were different. They did not seek better lives for themselves as much as they believed they could bring a message of salvation to others, both their fellow European migrants and the Native Americans already living in the Mid-Atlantic.[1]

The Moravians rode into Pennsylvania at the beginning of the 1740s on a wave of ecumenical revivals and evangelical fervor that remade European and American Protestantism. Their leaders prayed, socialized, and corresponded with the formative figures of British evangelicalism, and even when they engendered controversy they catalyzed those around them into action. The Moravians sought nothing less than the rebirth of the Christian world, from Russia to the Ohio Valley and everywhere in between. Goodwill alone could not accomplish such a job, however. Missionaries needed food, a place to rest, a safe home where their children could be raised, books and hymnals, and, most of all, a dynamic community to sustain them in this daunting work. Bethlehem supplied all these needs to the Moravian missionaries who traveled in Pennsylvania, throughout the Mid-Atlantic, and even in the Caribbean. It was a sanctuary and a base for itinerant preachers perpetually on the move to spread the group's emotional brand of evangelicalism.

Bethlehem nurtured and supported the group's American missionaries, and it surged with the energy those "pilgrims," as Moravians called their missionaries, brought to their task. Because they believed it to be more cost-effective than forming many single-family homes, the people who built Bethlehem lived in a large, communitarian household. Those who stayed in town pooled their labor for efficiency's sake, so that they could maximize the number of pilgrims in the field at any one time. They shared dining rooms, dormitory-style housing, workshops, and ownership of buildings, tools, fields, and pastures, and they relied on their piety to render comprehensible all the sacrifices necessary to build a home in the rugged country of northeastern Pennsylvania. The missionary project thus led to Moravian communalism, the town's most distinctive economic structure and a deliberate endeavor that maximized profit for the sake of spreading the Gospel. Bethlehem's Oeconomy, its communal household, embodied the Moravians' devotion to their task, and within it missionary work provided a religious context for even the smallest economic choices. During its twenty-year history it was the base from which grew all other negotiations between the spiritual and the material among Pennsylvania's Moravians.

Evangelical Awakenings

The Moravians' energetic faith induced them to take on the staggering task of converting the world's peoples, a project that included the founding of Bethlehem. But the dedicated members of the Renewed Unitas Fratrum (or the "Unity" or "Brüdersgemeine," as they variously called themselves) were part of a larger international movement trying to revitalize Protestantism in the early eighteenth century. Collectively (though not always working together) these many groups, broadly known as evangelicals, transformed Protestantism.

In the two hundred years that followed Luther's Protestant Reformation, Europeans saw theological innovation cause controversy, warfare, and chaos. The state churches of England, Scotland, and the many German principalities struggled over doctrinal and ecclesiastical issues; Protestants in Catholic regions fought against the pressures of the Counter-Reformation; and much of Europe sank into the desperate and bloody Thirty Years' War (1618–1648), in which as much as thirty percent of Germany's population perished. Against this demoralizing backdrop, new movements intended to invigorate the experience of Christian life arose throughout Protestant Europe. English Puritans, who had been radicalized during their time in exile during the reign of the Catholic Mary I (1553–1558), preached a message of discipline and piety, free from the taints of worldly pleasures and the tarnish of corrupted institutions. The Puritans' Quaker compatriots interpreted the same message of spiritual renewal in very different terms in the seventeenth century, advocating individual communion with the Spirit of God within one. These British groups echoed similar developments on the Continent. In the small circles of the Labadists and the Inspirationists, radical ideas of personal piety flourished, but it was the Lutheran theologian Philip Jakob Spener who spread the movement of spiritual regeneration widely within the state churches of Germany. He published his *Pia Desideria*, or Pious Desires, in 1675, a work that advocated the revitalization of the German Lutheran church through personal piety. Spener's subsequent positions with the courts of Saxony and then Prussia reflected the widespread appeal of his thought. Through the efforts of his student, August Hermann Francke, Pietism, as the growing evangelical movement was known in Germany, became an institutional force in German Protestantism in the early eighteenth century, one that both encouraged and fed off the larger trends of Protestant renewal then spreading in central Europe.[2]

Francke sought the reformation of European piety through education. One of his most prominent students, and also one of the most problematic, was the Saxon Count Nikolaus Ludwig von Zinzendorf. Born in 1700, Zinzendorf was the son of an imperial count and the grandson, on his mother's side, of Baroness Henrietta Katharina von Gersdorf. Gersdorf took over responsibility for Zinzendorf's upbringing shortly after his birth, when his father died and his mother remarried another nobleman, leaving the infant Zinzendorf behind. The young count's grandmother brought him into the Pietist fold. She was one of the movement's patronesses, wealthy lay-women who financed Francke's establishments in Halle and played an impor-tant role in the extra-ecclesiastical development of European Pietism and revivalism generally. Zinzendorf grew up primarily in his grandmother's household and in the educational institutions at Halle, where he sat at Francke's table. But the child of established society and formal education rein-terpreted Francke's message of disciplined piety to suit his own temperament. Where Francke taught that spiritual rebirth required a life of self-examination, an intense and difficult process that was intended to be more akin to a painful struggle than to peaceful reflection, Zinzendorf believed he had been a *Kindergottes*, a child of God, since his earliest religious stirrings. No such struggle was needed, he felt, to bring him closer to God. Yet he also benefited greatly from his time at Halle, where he developed these ideas and built friendships with other like-minded members of the European elite, before his rejection of the necessity of the Pietist *Bußkampf* (struggle for redemption) and his leadership in the Moravian movement eventually divided him from Francke and the Halle fold.[3]

After completing his studies at Halle, the young Zinzendorf embarked in 1720 on a year of travel throughout Europe, which brought him into contact with a wide variety of religious and philosophical perspectives. In particular, his friendship with the French Jansenist Cardinal Louis de Noailles encour-aged in him the belief that there were true Christians in all confessions, even among Catholics—a dramatic statement for an eighteenth-century Protes-tant. To his disappointment, at the conclusion of his Grand Tour Zinzendorf faced an unwanted diversion from his religious path. His mother and step-father dictated that he go to Dresden and pursue a court career befitting his aristocratic station. While there, however, Zinzendorf's life took an unex-pected turn. His family's reputation for sheltering religious refugees led the leaders of a community of Bohemian and Moravian Protestants to seek assis-tance from his grandmother. Zinzendorf, then only twenty-two, granted per-mission for the little group to settle on his lands. They founded the town of Herrnhut and gave the young religious enthusiast a ready-made group of fol-lowers, if only he could win their allegiance.[4]

The events that brought the Moravian refugees to Zinzendorf are less co-incidental than they appear at first glance. The same spirit of religious revital-ization that nourished German Pietism in the early eighteenth century also gave fervor to Catholic Austria's Counter-Reformation and made the Haps-burg territories a less than hospitable place for Protestants living there. Efforts by those in Germany, the Halle Pietists especially, to support persecuted Protestants fanned the fires of confessional conflict and contributed to the stirrings of revivalism in Central Europe, particularly in nearby Silesia. Among those affected by these events were the members of the Unity of the Brethren, or Unitas Fratrum, a group in Moravia that traced its heritage back to the fifteenth-century reformer and martyr, Jan Hus. The Unity's adherents had been driven underground by centuries of persecution, but they managed to sustain a remnant through the generations nonetheless. A few among the Unitas Fratrum had even achieved fame in the wider European world. Jan Amos Comenius, a bishop and seventeenth-century educational reformer well known in Puritan circles, was even offered a teaching post in Massachusetts. His grandson, Daniel Ernst Jablonski, became court preacher of Prussia in Berlin. Jablonski was also consecrated a Moravian bishop in 1699, a fact that was significant within the Unity because it kept alive its tradition of apostolic succession. While Comenius and Jablonski moved in Europe's intellectual cir-cles, however, less famous members of the Unity struggled against the system-atic oppression and bureaucratic regularization of Hapsburg rule. In 1722, encouraged by the sympathetic response other Protestant exiles had received and led by the charismatic preacher Christian David, a few families fled to Saxony, and when they found a place to settle on Zinzendorf's lands, others soon followed.[5]

Herrnhut grew into a substantial but contentious religious enclave over the next five years. Its residents came predominantly from two sources. As the revivals stirring to the east spread through the region, so too did Herrnhut's reputation as a town of pious and devout souls. Many newly "awakened" in-dividuals traveled there, and some of them settled. In addition, news of the sanctuary for members of the Unitas Fratrum spread in that community's net-works, prompting more people to flee westward to Saxony. Herrnhut's rapid expansion brought its fair share of growing pains, however. Its more than two hundred residents divided into factions over liturgical and theological issues. Meanwhile, the town fell within the jurisdiction of the parish at Berthelsdorf, an adjoining town, and the energetic minister there pursued an orthodox Lutheran position. Some of the Moravians—members of the historic Unitas Fratrum—resisted this agenda, arguing instead that they were members of an oppressed Protestant people outside (and predating) the Lutheran fold.

Zinzendorf, who had only periodically intervened in these struggles in Herrn-hut's first years, moved in to take personal control of the situation in 1727.[6]

A series of important innovations marked the next few months and trans-formed Herrnhut's residents into the "Renewed" Unitas Fratrum—events the Moravians viewed in providential terms. In May of 1727, Zinzendorf used his seigniorial authority over Herrnhut to provide the town with a governmental structure designed to promote piety and bring order. The restructured com-munity had a board of elders that oversaw most secular and religious matters. It also had a series of religious groups, called bands, to encourage individuals' spiritual development. Later that summer, Zinzendorf happened to read an edition of Comenius's *Ratio Disciplinae*, a work detailing the history and order of the ancient Unitas Fratrum. Finding its tenets for preserving piety to be quite similar to what he had laid out for Herrnhut, Zinzendorf—never one to underestimate the possibility that divine power was working through him—came to believe that the ancient Unity had in fact been reborn in Herrnhut. A few weeks later, on August 13, the rest of the community joined him in this belief, when, during a particularly moving baptismal service, the group felt that its divisions were healed. The rejuvenated congregation moved forward confidently, despite not having solved definitely the issue of whether members were Moravian exiles, German Lutherans, or something new en-tirely. The group's wide array of names reflected that underlying ambiguity: it was variously known as the Renewed Unitas Fratrum, the Unity, the Brüdergemeine (or just the Gemeine) in German, the Moravians (in English), or most accurately, the Herrnhuter.[7]

Though the exact nature of the Brüdergemeine remained a thorny issue, the community developed a distinctive faith under Zinzendorf's tutelage, par-ticularly in the 1740s. The count preached a "religion of the heart," an antira-tional, antitheological style of piety built on the emotional surrender of the sinner to Christ's love in a joyous experience of "awakening" or rebirth. This focus on spiritual renewal placed the Moravians in the evangelical main-stream, even though some of the ways they expressed those beliefs seemed ex-treme to outsiders. Members sang and recited countless litanies, hymns, and poems designed to heighten their personal connection to the physical Christ suffering on the cross, the incarnated Savior at his most human. "Remember the bitter death of your son. Look at his five holy, red wounds which are in-deed the payment and ransom for the whole world," ran one of the church's central litanies. Graphic depictions of the Christ's wounds were both powerful and evocative. "Purple wounds of Jesus," the litany continued, "You are so succulent, whatever comes near becomes like wounds and flowing with blood." The vivid imagery of Moravian worship startled some, as did their radical Christocentrism—placing Jesus at the forefront of the Trinity and, opponents would argue, overlooking the key role of the Father and Holy Spirit. But theirs was an almost mystical faith of strong emotion that eschewed what they viewed as quibbles over theological trivialities.[8]

As they moved out from Herrnhut to found new communities and forge ties to Protestants throughout Europe, the Moravians' exuberance, flexibility, and phenomenal mobility put them at the center of the action. They were comfortable there. Their theology embodied the main principles of evangelicalism: they emphasized Christ in their worship and theology; the Bible formed a central part of their worship cycle; they viewed spiritual rebirth or "awakening" as the central event in one's life; and they possessed an urge to share the Gospel that few could rival. Moreover, life in Moravian communities appeared to be utterly God-centered, providing a model others could admire. Indeed, if that was their purpose, they succeeded admirably; when John Wesley, the future Methodist leader, arrived in the Moravian community at Marienborn, Germany, he commented (quoting Romans 5:5): "here I continually met with what I sought for, viz., living proofs of the power of faith: persons 'saved from *inward as well as outward* sin,' by 'the love of God shed abroad in their hearts'; and from all doubt and fear by the abiding 'witness of the Holy Ghost given unto them.'" But flexibility, and even sincere piety, had their limits, as the Moravians found when controversy followed them near and far. Unfortunately for Zinzendorf's hope of uniting the Christian world, the Moravians could not be all things to all people. Their flexibility appeared to some to be doctrinal error, and the resulting conflicts eventually led to fissures between the exuberant Moravians and their evangelical fellow travelers. During the early days of revival in the 1730s and 1740s, however, the charismatic count and his energetic followers seemed to be everywhere in the Protestant world[9] (Map 1).

Many separate trends, spiritual and intellectual, local and international, lay and élite, converged in the rise of international evangelicalism. People of all backgrounds seeking a new religious life flocked to great outdoor meetings where dramatic preachers taught a new kind of spirituality. Others chose to (or, sometimes, were forced to) move their families to places like Herrnhut, or even across the ocean to North America, so that they could devote their

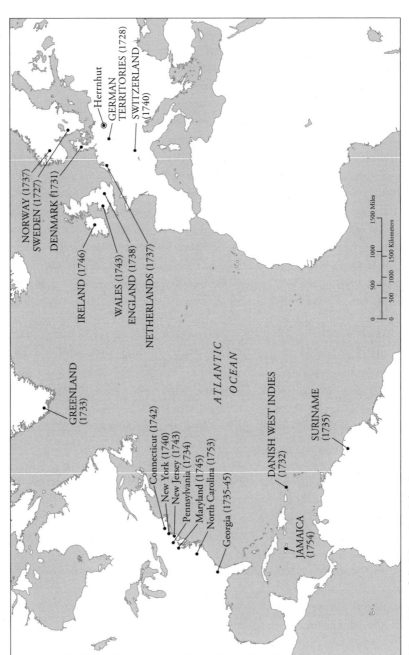

NORWAY (1737)
SWEDEN (1727)
DENMARK (1731)

Herrnhut
GERMAN
TERRITORIES (1728)
SWITZERLAND
(1740)

IRELAND (1746)
WALES (1743)
ENGLAND (1738)
NETHERLANDS (1737)

GREENLAND
(1733)

Connecticut (1742)
New York (1740)
New Jersey (1743)
Pennsylvania (1734)
Maryland (1745)
North Carolina (1753)
Georgia (1735-45)

ATLANTIC
OCEAN

DANISH WEST INDIES
(1732)

SURINAME
(1735)

JAMAICA
(1754)

0   500   1000   1500 Miles

0   500   1000   1500 Kilometers

Map 1. Map of the Moravian Atlantic.

lives to a revitalized piety. Leaders from many distant places and church communities tied these various centers together, through correspondence and through the belief that they were engaged in a shared project. Revivals in British America, Great Britain, and continental Europe thus built on each other through the careful labors of ministers, writers, and publicists. Their project was grand, and the renewal of Christendom seemed imminent. The cause was also political. Protestants believed their world to be under dire threat from an encroaching Catholic menace, and this threat informed their actions. When the archbishop of Salzburg ejected all Protestants from his district in 1730, a network of German and British clergy and philanthropists sprang into action to provide relief and guide the refugees to new homes. Through projects such as these, Protestants around the Atlantic consciously joined across the traditional boundaries of state churches in a shared effort with both religious and earthly dimensions.[10]

Some of the Salzburgers immigrated to Georgia, the new southernmost outpost in Britain's chain of American colonies, and the locus of a great deal of evangelical energy. Georgia's trustees, led by James Oglethorpe, had founded the province to provide a new start for wayward Protestants suffering either from persecution or from economic misfortune, and as a buffer between Britain's territories and Spanish Florida to the south. Olgethorpe's experiment eventually changed course when local colonists found the pull of slave agriculture too powerful to avoid, but preachers and ministers of many stripes, including the Moravians, took an interest in Georgia and made each others' acquaintance there. The Halle Pietists who had come to work among the Salzburgers rapidly came into conflict with the Moravians, and the groups' relations never warmed. More fruitful were the ties Moravians built in the budding circles of Methodism. When a party of Moravians journeyed across the Atlantic in late 1735, they shared passage with the young Anglican divines and future Methodist leaders, John and Charles Wesley, whose father was an acquaintance of Oglethorpe. As John famously recorded in his journal, he was amazed by the Moravians' calm through the rough waters their ship, the *Simmonds*, endured. "Now indeed we could say, 'The waves of the sea were mighty and raged horribly,'" wrote John, quoting Psalm 107, "They 'rose up to the heavens above, and clave down to hell beneath.'" During the storm, the Moravians' "great seriousness" and "humility" impressed Wesley. By observing them during the storm, he had hoped to see whether they were "delivered from the spirit of fear," as easily as they were from "pride, anger, and revenge." When he found them peacefully at prayer while their English shipmates were "trembling," he attributed it to the Moravians' powerful faith. For the next five years, Wesley followed the Moravians closely, turning to them for spiritual guidance, and even traveling to Germany in his spiritual quest.[11]

A fruitful period of cooperation among early evangelical leaders gave a similar cast to the evangelicalism that developed in continental Europe, Great Britain, and the British territories of North America. A small community co-alesced in London around the Moravians, the Wesley brothers, and George Whitefield, the famous itinerant minister. The Moravians and John Wesley together founded the Fetter Lane Society, an important evangelical community that remained within the Church of England in a formal sense, but adopted some of the key elements of Moravian practice. The fact that leaders within the community traveled extensively also contributed to the movement's coherence. These early leaders considered the wider Atlantic world to be their proper field of action. Wesley visited Germany after his American adventures, and the Moravians worked extensively in Britain, Europe, and North America. Whitefield journeyed incessantly, preaching in every British North American colony, and his contacts with the Moravians in Georgia led to a brief collaboration in that province and a second one in Pennsylvania. Networks of personal connections thus sustained and coordinated the emerging evangelical community.[12]

That community grew dramatically in the middle decades of the eighteenth century, and by the turn of the nineteenth evangelicals dominated the religious scene in North America. The Methodists and Baptists, relative newcomers in the denominational landscape, reaped the largest rewards, but significant evangelical factions among Presbyterians and Congregationalists also emerged. Evangelicals' focus on personal religious experience and their vibrant, revivalistic worship found a deep appeal within American society, and the older, more hierarchical Protestant churches, particularly the Anglicans, struggled to keep pace. The Moravians explicitly tried to avoid building a denomination, so institutionally they did not become major players in this triumphal story, but their early involvement was crucial nonetheless.

As it spread, evangelicalism permeated and, sometimes, divided the Protestant world. The revivals, renewals, and outpourings of faith triggered by these various leaders had dramatically different results, not least because they had very different styles and aims, despite a shared spiritual agenda. Wesley's

Methodists grew into a formidable denomination, while Whitefield never broke from the Anglican Church. The Moravians resisted any sectarian identity, but they were certainly viewed as a sect by others who found them controversial. Likewise, local circumstances mattered a great deal. Jonathan Edwards's early and well publicized revival in Northampton, Massachusetts, in 1734 and 1735 grew out of a particular congregation with generations of history, while the thousands who flocked to hear Whitefield experienced only the most passing form of community. Taken as a whole the local and the international intertwined to create a widespread, loosely coordinated, and extraordinarily diverse movement. The Moravians were often in the right place at the right time, bringing together these various groups. Their catalytic role depended on the theological flexibility and deep spirituality that allowed them to find common ground with most evangelicals. Internally, the energy that members of the Brüdergemeine drew from the spirit of revival propelled them throughout the Atlantic world, including to Pennsylvania, sharing the Gospel with anyone who would listen.

Spreading the Word

The same activist impulse that connected "awakened" Christians through extended networks and communities that crossed confessional and political boundaries prompted a new wave of missionary outreach to non-Christians and ultimately brought the Moravians to Pennsylvania to found Bethlehem. As in many things, the German Pietists offered the closest model for the Moravians to follow. From Halle, where Francke's institutions educated the children of Saxony and sent tracts and Bibles in numerous languages throughout eastern Europe, missionaries also went out to convert the peoples of the world to Christianity. Most notable of these was the effort at the Danish Indian colony of Tranquebar, undertaken in 1707. These German efforts paralleled those pursued by the Britons, also beginning at the turn of the eighteenth century, when the Anglican Society for Promoting Christian Knowledge and Society for the Propagation of the Gospel began outreach efforts to blacks, Indians, and generally unchurched European settlers in the New World. On the North American mainland, the somewhat limited seventeenth-century efforts of early Puritan missionaries in New England were reinvigorated in the eighteenth century by the likes of Presbyterian

Figure 1. Zinzendorf as Teacher of the Peoples, Johann Valentine Haidt, GS.583.
Courtesy Unity Archives, Herrnhut.

David Brainerd and Congregationalist Jonathan Edwards, who preached, respectively, among the Indians of the Mid-Atlantic and New England during
the middle decades of the century. The Moravian missionary effort was one
of the largest, however. It animated the Moravian community, made the
Brüdergemeine a presence throughout the Atlantic world, and inspired Bethlehem's foundation as a base for missionaries in the Western hemisphere[13]
(Figure 1).

The Moravians were in good company when they turned their attention
to missionary work, but they did it with a single-mindedness that was unique.
Zinzendorf believed that members of the "invisible church"—true
Christians—existed in all places and among all peoples. They were not, in
other words, organized into any single existing church, but could be found by
looking and preaching everywhere. He also believed that the Holy Spirit, and

not human action, was responsible for spreading Christianity and spiritual re-birth, and, further, that the Holy Spirit could and did save people of all races and from all religious traditions. Members of the Unity hoped to find these "First Fruits," individuals whom the Holy Spirit already had prepared for con-version, but they believed they took a very passive approach to such active work. They believed that the earthly missionary simply served the Holy Spirit, who guided the missionary to distant lands and then brought the potential convert to him when he reached the place of his work. Zinzendorf also di-rected that missionaries work only among those who came to them voluntar-ily, rather than coercing anyone to hear their message, because the Spirit had not yet readied the unwilling listener. Scripture provided appropriate models. Zinzendorf noted especially the story of Peter and the centurion, whom the Holy Spirit brought together, resulting in the first baptism of a Gentile (Acts 10). Peter's statement just before the centurion's baptism validated missionary work among those who had never heard of Christianity: "But in every nation he that feareth him, and worketh righteousness, is accepted with him." For members of the Brüdergemeine, sharing the faith was not about building their institutional church, but about fulfilling divine instruction. They be-lieved that they carried out the will of the Holy Spirit when they worked as missionaries, and this conviction lay at the center of their faith.[14]

The Moravians' beliefs about the process of conversion placed missionar-ies in a secondary role behind the Holy Spirit, but there was nothing passive or subdued about the way they undertook their outreach efforts. The Unity began considering missionary work almost immediately after its formation in 1727, because Zinzendorf, who had been raised hearing reports about the Halle missions to the Danish East Indies, had longed to undertake such a project since his youth. A different part of the world captured the Moravians' attention, however, and many of their early missions took them west, across the Atlantic. In 1731, on a visit to Copenhagen, the count met a slave, An-thony, from the Danish West Indies. After hearing the man's story, Zinzen-dorf saw opportunities for spreading the Gospel to what he viewed as some of the world's most spiritually destitute people. He reported what he had learned from Anthony to the Moravians in Herrnhut, and, within a year, the group's first missionaries set sail for the Danish island of St. Thomas, inaugurating decades of activity that yielded impressive results. Beginning in the 1730s, the mission effort unfolded in earnest, and the search for new mission fields guided the church's subsequent geographic development. Besides the West Indies, missionaries also reached Greenland (1732), Suriname (1735), South Africa (1736), and the Gold Coast (1736), among other places. In North America, the project in Georgia began in 1735, and when that effort failed, Bethlehem was founded in 1741.[15]

Missionary work was the heart of Moravian life, and its needs became the backbone of the Moravian economy. Construed to mean preaching both to non-whites and to "unawakened" Europeans (those who had not yet experienced a spiritual rebirth or were not churchgoers), these purposeful efforts gave the Moravians' earthly labors meaning. All of the group's subsequent actions, and certainly the history of its principal American town of Bethlehem, unfolded within that framework. According to the 1740 synod in Gotha, held on the eve of Bethlehem's founding, the "Plan of the Gemeine" (meaning the entire Moravian community) was "to preach Jesus the crucified to the hearts" of all people and "to make the word of the merits of the wounds of Jesus become [the Gemeine's] first and last thing and the motivation of all its doings from this hour until her end." Within this statement lay Bethlehem's animating spirit: town residents were dedicated to spreading the word of Christ to all they met, while simultaneously living extraordinarily God-centered lives. For the Moravians the ideal Christian balanced devotion with evangelical labor and looked outward as often as into his or her own heart.[16]

Pennsylvania provided the perfect territory for Moravian pilgrims, as the group's religious workers were called. Its formal religious freedom had long attracted the attention of German sectarians and Pietists, not least because William Penn had actively advertised among them when he began his American experiment in religious toleration. By the 1730s, the Delaware Valley had by nearly any measure become one of the fastest growing regions in British America, and the religious situation was as chaotic as any rapidly changing environment could be. Dozens of different sects competed for space in an open marketplace, and yet according to some religious observers the "Pennsylvania Religion" in fact meant no religion at all. Most of the colony's new migrants came in search of a better material life, and members of the continental Lutheran and Reformed churches did so largely without any ministerial oversight. To the chagrin of Henry Melchior Muhlenberg, whom the Halle Pietists sent in 1742 to bring order to the Lutheran wilderness, most of those passing as ministers were in fact little more than greedy charlatans. That the crusty Muhlenberg also placed Zinzendorf in this category did not change the underlying reality that Pennsylvanians who sought pastoral care had a great deal of freedom and very few options before them. Pennsylvania therefore looked like the perfect territory to the Moravians, both for what it had—a growing population of people seeking churches to join—and for what it lacked—a religious establishment that would determine what kind of church that would be.[17]

Moravian work in Pennsylvania began in earnest with a visit by August Gottlieb Spangenberg in 1736. Spangenberg, known as "Joseph" among other Moravians, was, after Zinzendorf, the most prominent member of the Brüdergemeine in the eighteenth century, and Bethlehem's principal leader between 1744 and 1762. Born in Germany in 1704, he received a theological education at Jena, then taught at Halle until he was fired in 1733 because of his growing connection to the Moravians. Almost immediately after joining the Unity he left for a missionary trip to the West Indies, and later he led the group that went to Georgia. From there, he visited Pennsylvania in 1736 as part of a scouting mission to find new territories for Moravian work.[18] His talent for organization and systemization served the Unity well for decades, and he used these skills when he described the opportunities he found in Pennsylvania, both among the Europeans and among the Indians. "There are two tasks for the Brethren," he wrote, "who will perhaps go there according to the will of God: The Gospel must be preached to the many thousands [of Europeans] who know nothing of it or who have an indescribable hunger for it; and the Awakened, who are eager for Fellowship, must be assembled into congregations." Providing pastoral care for the "unchurched" Germans was only the first of two jobs for the Moravians, however, though even that alone was "not the work of one" missionary, "but rather of many." In addition to the unchurched immigrants, Spangenberg continued, "There are the Indians, who would prefer not to live near the Europeans, and for whom perhaps the blessed hour [of salvation] has come."[19] These views, reported back to Zinzendorf in Europe, became the core of the Moravians' "Pennsylvania Plan," which consistently coupled attention for outreach to Europeans with the need to make the colony a site of the *Heydensache* (matter of the heathen), or work among the Indians. Though Bethlehem eventually became a major Moravian settlement, creating a town as such was less important to the Brüdergemeine in its planning than missionary work.[20]

Spangenberg's vision took a step toward realization in 1740 when one of the group's British connections, itinerant evangelist George Whitefield, hired the remnants of the Georgia effort to build an orphanage in Pennsylvania near the confluence of the Delaware and Lehigh Rivers, on a piece of land called the Nazareth Tract. The arrangement was practical rather than ecclesiastical. The Moravian group included carpenters whose skills Whitefield needed for the building, and no formal institutional connection joined the Moravians to the Anglican Whitefield. Happenstance thus determined the neighborhood of Pennsylvania where the Brüdergemeine first settled, but the Moravians seized on the opportunity because they had already chosen Pennsylvania as the next mission field in their great effort to spread the Gospel. Over the next few months, a few more of their coreligionists from Europe joined the migrants from Georgia in Nazareth. The Whitefield project was short-lived, however. Whitefield and the Moravians parted ways within a few months when they quarreled over the issue of predestination, which the Moravians, rooted in German Lutheranism, did not accept, and Whitefield, a staunch Calvinist, would not repudiate. Whitefield allowed the little group to stay on his land through the winter, but as soon they could the Moravians purchased five hundred acres to the south of Nazareth, at the spot where the Monocacy Creek ran into the Lehigh River.[21]

It is perhaps ironic—given that the Moravians had come to Pennsylvania in part to spread the Gospel to the Indians—that the tract they purchased lay within the confines of the Walking Purchase. In 1737, Pennsylvania's proprietors had swindled the Delaware Indians living in the region known as the "Forks of the Delaware," by forcing them to agree to the sale of a portion of land that could be walked off in a single day. The Europeans had cleared the route in advance and used runners rather than walkers, so that they claimed a vast territory that extended far north of Philadelphia and cut deep into the countryside west of the Delaware River. The land where the Moravians built Bethlehem fell within this territory, as did the Nazareth Tract, which the Unity bought from the financially strapped Whitefield in 1741. In the latter place, a group of Indians, led by chief Captain John, resided at the village of Welagameka. They appealed to the Moravians who sought to dispossess them, saying that their home included their burial grounds, orchards, and substantial cultivated lands. Regardless of the Moravians' feelings on the matter, however, the Delaware were facing substantial pressure from both the Pennsylvania government and the Iroquois to move away, and Captain John's group was forced out by the end of 1742.[22]

Bethlehem took shape quickly. In June 1741, seventeen Moravians moved to the Brüdergemeine's new home on the Lehigh. They envisioned their future town in terms of the Unity's mission to spread the Gospel. It was to be a base from which they could send out religious workers in many directions, to the Delaware and Mahican Indians to the north and west, as well as to German communities in Philadelphia, York, and Lancaster to the east and south. As they performed the hard work necessary to carry out their task, these first settlers punctuated their lives with religious observances tying them to their compatriots abroad, integrating the frontier settlement into the larger Moravian world. On September 5, the diarist for the new congregation recorded: "Today we had a blessed Day of Prayer: whereat the European letters just received were communicated. We felt the nearness of our Lord among our little group in a special manner."[23] Count Zinzendorf himself arrived in Pennsylvania a few months later and came to Bethlehem on December 21, 1741. His personal involvement indicated Pennsylvania's importance to the international Moravian church. The growing congregation, the new Bethlehem Gemeine, spent Christmas Eve together, celebrating with "an unusually blessed *Holy Communion*." Completing the festivities, Zinzendorf formally christened the town.[24]

The Pilgrim Congregation

Bethlehem's status as a missionary outpost had a profound impact on the town's economic order.[25] Moravians considered missionaries to be among the "pilgrims," esteemed individuals who were devoted to religious labors. Zinzendorf referred to Bethlehem as a *Pilgergemeine*, a relatively unusual appellation in the typology of Moravian settlements that highlighted the town's missionary purpose and invoked the highest circles of Moravian life. Translated literally as "pilgrim congregation," the term usually described Zinzendorf's own constantly moving household. It was formed after the count was exiled from Saxony in 1736, technically for encouraging peasants to leave the estates of other nobles, but in reality for being a religious troublemaker. Over time, Zinzendorf's pilgrim congregation came to comprise the count and his closest advisors, and in the highly centralized Brüdergemeine it became the focal point of all practical and spiritual life. In 1739, "pilgrim congregation" was defined as "a realm of Jesus Christ and an invisible college made of all workers who, because of the work of Jesus, have no specific place." The implication was that members of this select group had special callings and missions, beyond the specific circumstances of individual communities. Moreover, "a pilgrim congregation remains eternal but not in one place, but rather [goes] to 100, [or] 50 [other places], not with the intention of staying. General matters [of concern for the pilgrims] are to open lands, and to send people there."[26] The synod the following year in Gotha also emphasized the nomadic aspect of the definition when it stated, "a pilgrim people is that which is nowhere and everywhere at home." It was no accident that the Pennsylvania community, founded only a year later, was given the same appellation. Before leaving America, Zinzendorf advised in his Pennsylvania Testament that "Bethlehem should . . . merely stand, as long as it is alone, on the footing of a simple pilgrim congregation, united without name with all the children of God in Pennsylvania." In that moment, Zinzendorf was referring to the Brüdergemeine's political efforts to avoid becoming known as a new sect, be it as the descendants of the ancient Moravian church or otherwise, but by describing the town's residents as ambassadors in a larger ecumenical project, he strengthened the implication that Bethlehem was a locus for religious outreach.[27]

Nowhere was Bethlehem's status a pilgrim congregation more evident than in the brief exchange historians have generally used to identify the origins of its communal economic system, the Oeconomy. In June 1742, Zinzendorf presided over the division of the new town's residents into two roughly equal groups, the pilgrim congregation, here meaning the traveling members of the larger Bethlehem pilgrim congregation, and the house congregation (*hausgemeine*), the residents of Bethlehem. The creation of these two specialized subgroups officially institutionalized both Bethlehem's dedication to missionary work and the basis for what became the town's enormous shared housekeeping (*gemeinschaftliche Haushalting*). Everyone was a member of the larger Bethlehem pilgrim congregation and contributed to the mission project, but the distinction between laboring directly in the mission field and laboring to provide for those in the mission field gave a coherent structure to the whole endeavor. For Zinzendorf, however, the functional difference between those who spread the word of God personally and those who stayed in town paled next to the necessity that all members of both groups sustain the spiritual drive and focus required by the town's work. He admonished everyone to struggle for purity and ensure that Bethlehem be a model for piety in the New World, to maintain, in his words, its *Pilgersinn*, or pilgrim sensibility. That shared spirit animated the work that was to come for the two inter-

locking groups, and it helped to unite Bethlehem into one large pilgrim congregation, where everyone, whether doing laundry or preaching to Indians,
contributed to a shared task.[28]

Both groups had a duty to maintain the congregation's pilgrim sensibility, but in daily terms there existed an important division of labor. The house
congregation made the missionaries' work possible. Those who remained in
Bethlehem cared for the itinerants' children as well as their own, provided a
place of spiritual respite when needed, and ensured that missionaries would
not become financially dependent on the congregations they served. Count
Zinzendorf considered providing such support to be one of Bethlehem's central purposes, fearing that without material independence the purity of a
preacher's message might be corrupted by the demands of the people he
sought to teach. In 1743, just before leaving Pennsylvania, the count warned
against the consequences of taking payment for preaching: "that is the direct
way that you could make yourselves spiritual servants and slaves, as soon as
you let yourselves take money." Zinzendorf's philosophy linked Bethlehem's
communal economy to the Moravians' success as missionaries: for the pilgrim congregation to be effective, the house congregation had to be profitable. Indeed, if the house congregation supported only itself and failed to
produce sufficient surplus, its very purpose, sustaining the pilgrims, would
be threatened.[29]

Moravian missionaries fanned out across Pennsylvania and reached into
Maryland and New York. Some worked on building congregations in towns
or cities, while others gave real meaning to the appellation "pilgrims" by rang-
ing widely in search of souls to awaken. Bethlehem remained the home base
for all. "The pilgrim congregation will ordinarily rendezvous" there, wrote
Joseph Spangenberg in 1744, but otherwise "it moves around like a blessed
cloud, as the Wind of the Lord pushes it and makes everything fruitful." The
missionaries returned home frequently for spiritual and physical rest and renewal. As Sven Roseen, a Swedish-born Moravian, set out to work in the Blue
Mountains to the north he wrote that his "heart was still thankful for all . . .
mercies with which I had been blessed" among the Moravians, "compared
with which all my possible service could come to no consideration." Bethlehem remained a constant presence in Roseen's thoughts. On July 3, 1749, he
made a typical entry in his journal invoking the strong sense of community
he felt with those at home. "I awoke," he wrote, "rejoicing in the fellowship
of the Saviour, and of the friends in Bethlehem."[30] The missionaries' close ties

to the house congregation gave a deep spiritual meaning to the mundane labors of the latter group. Those who stayed home took comfort in the necessity of their earthly role to the town's larger religious purpose, and, Zinzendorf hoped, shared equally in a zealous pilgrim sensibility.[31]

The concept of a pilgrim congregation shaped Bethlehem's development far more fundamentally than the communal economy founded to support it. During the town's early years, for example, most strategic planning centered on the missions (to both Europeans and Indians) and the pilgrims that staffed them. Even Zinzendorf's travels while in Pennsylvania reinforced the idea that the new community was a base for spiritual endeavors and not itself a destination. He used the lion's share of his time in America traveling to visit potential new fields of evangelical labor, not helping to organize Bethlehem. He spent the first six months in Philadelphia and Germantown organizing and leading the controversial "Pennsylvania Synods," where he tried to unite Pennsylvania's religious groups in ecumenical fellowship under Moravian leadership. Only when broad-based hostility to that project led to its demise did the count return to Bethlehem, and then he almost immediately left again on a series of trips to learn about the Native Americans whom the Moravians hoped to convert. At no point did he spend any significant time concerning himself with the details of establishing the communal system that would support the town. This task he left to others with a more practical bent, reflecting his position that such matters were logistical, not spiritual, questions.[32]

The Oeconomy

The Moravians called their communal household the "Oeconomy." This was an apt choice, as the word's roots were indicative of the Brüdergemeine's approach to economic matters. The term derived from the Greek word meaning "household." Over time, it took on a host of implications that included the wise and thrifty use of resources and the "method of divine government of the world." All of these usages were appropriate for the Moravians' purposes. Maintaining a shared household of hundreds, such as the one found in Bethlehem, demanded thrift, order, and steady governance. The word had further connotations as well, however, which eighteenth-century readers encountered through the frequent reprinting, in many languages, of Robert Dodsley's *The Oeconomy of Human Life*. That book attempted to provide a neat structure to the duties and passions of man, and an exploration of the relationships between masters and servants, within families, and between man and God. "Oeconomy" thus implied a natural link between a practical, earthly household and a larger spiritual order. In Bethlehem, the "Oeconomy" was ubiquitous. It provided children's shoes, communion loaves, and coffins for the town's residents. The word appeared in countless letters, reports, and balance sheets, and it invoked the unique blend of religious spirit and pragmatism that characterized Moravian communalism. The Oeconomy's governors worked for maximal profits, and combined the labor of individuals into a common whole, building a system that reflected the Moravians' unusual devotion to evangelization and their pragmatic approach to material questions.[33]

The needs of missionary work led to the Oeconomy's founding, but it developed within the larger Moravian economic culture rooted in Herrnhut, the principal Moravian congregation town (*Ortsgemeine*) throughout the eighteenth century. Indeed, Bethlehem shared much with Herrnhut, despite the fact that the Saxon town never had an overarching communal structure like the Oeconomy. Most prominent was the two towns' shared dependence on craftwork and commerce. Home to around eight hundred residents by the time Bethlehem was founded in 1741, Herrnhut, like Bethlehem, had an economy based on artisanal work, rather than agriculture, and that precedent dominated Moravian economic practice. The preference for craftwork in Herrnhut came about at least in part as a matter of circumstance rather than planning. Perhaps not surprising in a place founded by refugees, matters of sustenance were handled rapidly in the first days after the settlers arrived in 1722, though those initial decisions had lasting results. Johann George Heitz, Zinzendorf's steward, selected a spot for the refugees on the road between Löbau and Zittau, a location not well suited for agriculture but in the path of a good deal of trade. By 1727, when the count gave the town a formal governing structure, most of Herrnhut's residents were earning their living as craftspeople, despite the fact that half of the three hundred refugees who had arrived from Moravia had been farmers in the old country.[34]

Zinzendorf certainly had other lands on which Heitz could have settled the newcomers had he wanted them to work as farmers, but neither the count nor his steward ever tried to shift Herrnhut's economic basis toward agriculture. Over the following decades, as the Moravians founded new communities, they never deviated from the artisanal and commercial pattern they had established in 1722. Eventually the Moravians' preference for artisanal work over agriculture became second nature. Leaders in Herrnhut wrote in 1761 that "the way of the Brethren-Peoples . . . is more to be urban, and to follow urban occupations, than to do farming and rural work." From the vantage point of experience, they continued, artisanal work was more convenient for a missionary community: "It appears to be more conducive for the affairs of the Savior and the benefit of the Unity," they wrote, "if many congregation towns are undertaken, in which appropriate trade and traffic and other urban [occupations] are pursued, than the enlargement of the agricultural economy would be." Artisanal and industrial work, in other words, were better suited to supporting the Moravians' form of expansive evangelicalism than agriculture.[35]

In the congregation towns, places historian Elizabeth Sommer has called "baptized towns," commerce coexisted with intense spiritual devotion, all under close church oversight. Indeed, these settlements were attempts to fill all aspects of life with the spirit of the Savior by merging town and congregation. The origins of the congregation town ideal dated to 1727, when, as mentioned above, Zinzendorf provided Herrnhut with two foundational documents, the Brotherly Agreement and the accompanying Manorial Injunctions. Although the former governed religious life and the latter worldly affairs, the documents gave Herrnhut's religious leadership, the Elders' Conference, jurisdiction over both the sacred and the secular. The two decrees together created a blueprint for Herrnhut that was designed to create a peaceful and harmonious town. They called for the rapid disposition of internal disputes without resort to worldly legal means, regulated commerce and the paying of debts, and prohibited dancing, gluttony, and excessive drinking at feasts. The Elders' Conference decided where people lived, what occupations they pursued, and what buildings went up, thus ensuring that Herrnhut developed in accordance with their vision of a congregation town. Yet that vision was not communitarian. Item seven in the Manorial Injunctions stated: "Each inhabitant of Herrnhut shall work and eat his own bread." Only shared responsibility for the enfeebled modified this rule that individuals labored on their own accounts. Thus, while Herrnhuters submitted to the authority of the Elders' Conference in almost all matters, they retained independent households and pursued their own fortunes.[36] Eventually, the difference blurred between Herrnhut as a town and the Moravian congregation that lived there. In 1728, the two documents were combined, further melding church and town into one entity and eliminating the possibility that Saxon authorities could interpret the statement of faith in the Brotherly Agreement as deviating from the state-sponsored Lutheranism. By the mid-1730s, when the Moravians began to settle new places beyond Herrnhut, the ideal of an exclusive Moravian town, one in which church and town were synonymous, and where artisanal rather than agricultural labor supported the inhabitants, had been firmly established.[37]

But Bethlehem was a pilgrim congregation, not a congregation town, and the distinction made all the difference. The needs of missionary work, and not the spiritual lives of the residents, dictated the town's organization and economy, and missionary work led directly to communalism. A shared household supported the greatest number of missionaries, and that simple fact justified the development of an economy that departed radically from the more standard Moravian model. Of course, Moravian communalism grew out of the habits of cooperation and close community that characterized the wider international church as well. Indeed, given the commitment to each other and to their faith that already united the dedicated missionaries before they came to Pennsylvania, they likely found it easier to build one large house than many small ones, faster to fence in one large field than many lesser ones, and more efficient to cook for a few large groups than to duplicate the effort in each nuclear family. But another driving motive was present as well: because the primary goal was profitability for the sake of supporting missionaries, efficiency and cost-effectiveness proved the greatest priorities. Moreover, sharing the work reinforced the idea that all labor, whether preaching to Indians or working in the dye house, contributed to the affairs of the Savior. Through the intimate tie between missionaries in the field and residents in Bethlehem, the Moravians' religious lives and their economic lives merged into one.

The communal model was a successful one, and after 1741 a steady stream of Moravians came to Pennsylvania from Europe to work in the missions and in Bethlehem. Though most spoke German—community records were kept in German until the 1860s—a significant number of settlers were of other nationalities, including a small number of blacks and a somewhat larger number of Indians. By the close of 1741, 131 people lived in Bethlehem. Just ten years later the number had swollen to 744. In 1753, more than 1,200 Moravians (including baptized Indians) lived in the Lehigh Valley area. Fifty-five percent resided in Bethlehem, while most of the remaining people lived in its daughter communities of Nazareth, Gnadenthal, Friedensthal, Christians-brunn, and Gnadenhütten. These six places collectively constituted the Oeconomy, and, though each had its particular character and responsibilities, leaders in Bethlehem coordinated the work of the whole in an ever more complex and ornate administrative dance.[38]

During the 1740s, the house congregation transformed Bethlehem from a forested riverbank into a substantial town. Construction proceeded with careful planning, so that builders addressed the community's most pressing needs first. They alternated large communal housing projects with the workshops necessary for economic stability. In addition to dormitories, the residential buildings included dining rooms, meeting rooms, and areas for craftspeople that required neither access to running water nor large amounts of space. The industrial quarter filled the little valley around the Monocacy Creek, stretching across the stream and a newly constructed millrace. It included six wooden buildings erected before 1745: a millwork, black smithy, tannery, gristmill, sawmill, pottery shop, and oil mill. In the next decade, stone structures replaced many of the early wood workshops. In order to keep pace with this ambitious building schedule, a combined saw and gristmill was built farther north up the Lehigh River at Gnadenhütten, an Indian mission, in 1747. Boards for Bethlehem now came floating down the river, while the mission used its new gristmill for necessary flour supplies. The town's farms and stables stretched north of the town center, toward Nazareth.[39]

As Bethlehem's house congregation grew, so did the pilgrim congregation. Semipermanent missions replaced traveling preachers, though the number of missionaries in the field still varied from year to year. In 1753, when the total Moravian population of the Lehigh Valley hovered around 1,200, there were 77 missionaries in the field. Of that number, ten lived in nearby Gnadenhütten. The remaining 67 were divided among the European communities of Germantown, Philadelphia, and Lancaster; Indian missions in western Pennsylvania and New York; and the two Caribbean missions of St. Thomas and St. Croix. St. Thomas was the largest single Moravian mission, with thirteen European Moravians serving a community of hundreds of slaves. In the majority of cases, however, a single married couple worked in a post, occasionally joined by a child who was too young for school in Bethlehem. The cost of maintaining the pilgrim congregation provided the Oeconomy with plenty of work.[40]

By its second decade, after thousands of hours of shared labor, the communal household clearly dominated economic life in Bethlehem. Spangenberg, Bethlehem's most astute administrator and a natural list-maker, thought more systematically than anyone else about the Oeconomy's complexities. While on a trip to Europe in 1751 he set down a series of ideas about the town he had built "as they occur to me one after another." The list, which he described as a set of general principles, offers an idea of how the Oeconomy functioned at its peak in the 1750s. The "whole Oeconomy is an institution for the better maintenance of that purpose which the Savior has for souls," he wrote, "And this is partly because we can lighten the loads of many brothers and sisters who otherwise would have it much harder, if they had to work for themselves, and partly because we can that much better take care of the affairs of the Savior."[41] Though Spangenberg more than any other person was responsible for building the Oeconomy, he stated that communal life had to be voluntary, even for members of the Moravian community: "it is a particular thing, and not advisable for all souls" to live in such a way. "It could bring as much damage to one as it was of use to another." In other words, Spangenberg believed communal life was hard, if rewarding. To his mind, no one should be compelled to join. This sentiment echoed the broader world of Moravian economic life, in which communalism held no particular status. The pilgrim congregation held a special place in the Brüdergemeine's life, but it was missionary work, and not communalism, that set it apart.[42]

Communalism never became a central facet of Moravian economic culture, but Moravian religious ideals created both the pilgrim congregation and the Oeconomy that supported it. Communalism was an expression of, not an ideal of, Moravian belief. All labor within the town had religious meaning. Spangenberg reminded Bethlehem's residents that they worked for God, for the community, and for missionary work. They were to ensure that "all Brothers and Sisters" go about their affairs "not out of duty, but rather with pleasure and gratitude for the Savior." This attitude was especially important among the various craft masters: "Put masters in each workshop who not only understand the work, but who are also inwardly devoted to the Little Lamb and the Gemeine." Work performed in the right religious spirit encouraged the members of the community to focus on God and was itself of great spiritual value. "We should take precautions against Idleness, in Pilgrims and in other workers," Spangenberg continued, "When one has to do with congregation-matters and matters of the soul, not only work but eating, drinking, resting, sleeping and the like all regularly take second place."[43]

The missionary endeavor required hard work on everyone's part. The group had a large financial task to accomplish, which included supporting itself, educating its children, maintaining missionaries in the field, and keeping up steady contact with Europe—itself an expensive proposition. Last, but certainly not least, Spangenberg invoked the most fundamental Protestant rationale for labor: "[They should do it] especially because it is the Savior's order and is good for a person, not only for one's body, but also for one's soul, when he works."[44] Spangenberg's comments drew on a long tradition that valued earthly labor as God's work, but in Bethlehem these words took on a special meaning. The tight connection between missionary labors and earthly labors in the Gemeine gave the town's economy, and its Oeconomy, a particular spiritual overtone.

The Moravians' religious fervor and the missions their devotion engendered provided the context for all their choices, not least the economic. The pilgrim congregation strove for economic efficiency, so its leaders were pragmatic and expansive in their policies, not ascetic or inward turning. Indeed, in 1746 one conference stated outright that the collective economy served practical, not spiritual, ends: "Our communal housekeeping is only out of need. It is no point of religion, much less of blessedness." It was useful, because "it is advantageous for the servants and maids of Jesus that many a one can be used who otherwise, through [the need to pursue] his own economy, would be hindered."[45] The Oeconomy, Bethlehem's most distinctive economic structure, was an outgrowth of that commitment to missionary work. The town's raison d'être was its pilgrims. All economic decisions flowed from that fact.

CHAPTER 2

Interconnected Worlds

LIFE IN BETHLEHEM's Oeconomy was distinctive, regimented, and deeply pious. Residents dedicated their lives to supporting missionary work and to the Savior. They also built one of early America's largest and most durable communal projects. The Oeconomy's success came from many quarters. Its hierarchical and authoritative government permitted an otherwise cumbersome system to function, but leaders' efforts had to be, and were, supported by the obedient acquiescence of the town's rank and file. Perhaps even more important to the Oeconomy's functioning was its pragmatism, however. Because Moravians were more interested in supporting missionary work than they were in challenging the nature of the early modern economy, their communalism was never economically absolute, and their members were never isolated socially.

Communal Bethlehem existed both within the larger Pennsylvania society and separate from it. Residents' lives revolved around the congregation's religious observances, the life cycles of its members, and the work required for maintaining the missionary effort. Nearly all decisions, from the minute to the deeply personal, were made by leaders concerned with furthering the Unity's shared interests. Yet, even as these factors made the Moravians unusual, to say the least, from the perspective of their neighbors and frequent visitors, Bethlehem quickly became a center of commerce and an important crossroads. The boundaries around the Oeconomy were permeable, and members of the Oeconomy shared much in common with their neighbors. Artisanal work stood at the center of Bethlehem's economy because it was simultaneously useful to the Moravians and profitable, but that sector required that customers visit the town's craftspeople on a regular basis. Evangelical labors too brought connections, and a steady stream of visitors to town even necessitated the building of several inns. Ties of friendship, kinship, and business thus softened the edges of the Oeconomy, linking those within to those without. Some such connections lasted only as long as a single transaction, while others residents sustained over decades. Bethlehem's Moravians therefore lived in two interconnected worlds at once. Their lives revolved around daily spiritual routines and missionary work in a way that was utterly distinct on the Pennsylvania frontier, and yet, even as communitarian missionaries, they still existed as part of, rather than in opposition to, their neighbors and the mainstream economy.

The Order of the Oeconomy

One of the definitions of the word Oeconomy is "domestic order," and Bethlehem was certainly a well-ordered place. The decision to join the community meant submitting oneself to the authority of church leaders, who coordinated the Oeconomy and oversaw each individual's spiritual development. Decisions affecting every detail of life—the distribution of work, choice of living place and marital partners, and even the most basic decisions about child-rearing—came from the community's leadership in Bethlehem or, occasionally, from church leaders in Germany. Within Bethlehem, the congregation was divided into many smaller groups, called Choirs, that joined people of like sex, age, and marital status, such as the Married People (sometimes subdivided into Married Men and Married Women), Widows, Single Sisters, Big Girls, and Little Boys. Zinzendorf believed that individuals of similar life experience shared common spiritual needs, and that praying together in these groups both enabled and deepened the individual's religious journey. The Choirs, each with its own living space and spiritual leadership, created a sense of family within Bethlehem, effectively breaking the large single household of the Oeconomy into manageable social units. Each Choir also had its own Elder, appointed by the church hierarchy in Herrnhut, who governed internal matters within the Choir. Together, the Elders' made up the influential Elders' Conference.[1]

Alongside this very real order existed an improvised and frequently changing oligarchy, which was just as characteristic of Bethlehem's early years. A small cadre of leaders, most of them members of the Elders' Conference, controlled almost all decisions in town, but they worked in and through a series of committees and councils. In practice this system ensured coherence in Bethlehem's organization and planning, and it met with remarkably little resistance. The Diacony Conference, for example, dealt with financial and economic matters, while the Helpers' Conference focused on the spiritual lives of individuals in the community. Both of these bodies met with some consistency, but religious and economic decisions were far too intertwined, and the membership of the various committees too overlapping, for those two entities to have had distinct administrative existence. As a result, meetings of each separate body were often sporadic, though meetings of the town's leaders in one capacity or another were near constant. Numerous temporary committees dealt with smaller or specialized issues. For the economic councils, which tended to function in an ad hoc fashion, expertise in a certain area led to membership. Rank-and-file Moravians retained a voice in the overall system through the Congregation Council (*Gemeinrath*), a group that theoretically included all communicants, but was more commonly a representative selection of men and a smaller number of women. But the Congregation Council, which only met occasionally, had more of an advisory role than anything else, modifying rather than shaping the policies of the key leaders. Dissent or disaffection within the Oeconomy rarely appeared in community records, and church leaders apparently faced no serious challenges to their authority or to the overarching communal system. Most likely, discontented individuals simply left. A self-perpetuating group of leaders thus determined most practical decisions. This high degree of centralization enabled the Oeconomy's leadership—synonymous with Bethlehem's religious leadership—to coordinate the intricate details of such a massive communal structure.[2]

A similar blend of system and spontaneity marked day-to-day governance. Bethlehem's temporal leaders relied heavily on the guidance of the Savior, and what they viewed as his direction reinforced their authority in the town. Divine assistance was more than figurative to the Moravians. In September 1741, Zinzendorf and other leaders in Germany, including Spangenberg, agreed to accept Christ's leadership in the role of Chief Elder of the entire Unitas Fratrum and to submit all important decisions to him. In 1748, they extended this divine leadership to the Chief Eldership of Bethlehem as well, symbolically increasing Christ's direct governance of the town and limiting that of Spangenberg, who had been the town's supreme leader before that.[3] Christ's opinion was discerned through the Lot. When a relevant question arose, leaders wrote a series of potential answers on slips of paper, and then drew one as an answer. Usually a blank slip was also included, allowing, the Moravians believed, Christ to reject the question altogether if it was not appropriate or timely. In this way they believed the Savior determined the actual course of Moravian affairs and ensured that they were following the right path. The Lot's choices, Moravians held, were not random but rather inspired by God, and its use increased the already intense sense of Christ's proximity that the group professed.[4]

All manner of questions were submitted to the Lot, but the Savior's approval was always required for marriages, admission to the Gemeine and to Communion, and the placement of someone in a missionary post. In other words, Christ's blessing was required for all decisions that changed a person's religious status within the community. Beyond these general rules, it is difficult to detect a clear pattern concerning when the Lot was employed. Moods seemed to strike particular conferences so that one day nearly every question was submitted to the Lot while another day saw similar decisions made without any resort to the Savior's opinion. On January 4, 1760, for example, the Diacony Conference decided, without mention of the Lot, "We must buy another five to six hundred bushels of oats." Two months later, the same council commented, "We will not be able to manage with our canvas," and decided, with the Lot's approval, to buy more. If there were religious differences between these two questions, both of which required purchasing necessary supplies for the Oeconomy, they were not recorded. On the other hand, the Lot was sometimes invoked when a problem became too difficult to solve within the conference. At the same meeting at which the mechanism was *not* employed when deciding to buy oats, the Diacony Council apparently disagreed about how to handle the community's horses for that winter, and "after lengthy discussion the Savior was asked" for the deciding vote.[5]

Religious observance in Bethlehem was highly communal and, like everything else, operated under the close direction of town leaders. Without the residents' intense religious sentiments, the source of their devotion to the community, it is doubtful that church leaders could have managed the Oeconomy as effectively or as profitably as they did. The Choirs determined the shape of religious life and ushered individuals through the life cycle. A child born into the community typically began her religious training in the nursery. From there, she moved to the Little Girls' Choir, then to the Big Girls, Single Sisters, perhaps the Married People's Choir, and finally, should life take its most usual course, the Widows' Choir. At each step along the way, she ideally would strive to grow closer to the Savior, aided by Choir leaders who understood her stage in life and her spiritual development. Benigna Zahm, born in Bethlehem in 1748, followed this typical path through her childhood. She was baptized in infancy, taking the first step on her spiritual journey. She described how her childhood in the Little Girls' Choir nurtured her relationship with Christ: "On February 26, 1760 . . . Br. Peter Boehler gave a memorable address on [the daily text] and an especial visitation of grace came upon the older children. The Holy Spirit showed us that some of the things that happened among us did not accord with the mind and heart of the Saviour." As the girls worked themselves into a state of distress about their spiritual lives, they turned to the leader of the Little Girls' Choir. This church worker was their teacher and spiritual guide, and she "recommended us in all our misery to the Saviour." Following her advice, Benigna found "forgiveness and absolution," and for the rest of her life she looked on that day as a pivotal moment in her religious development, not least because she was now ready to "really make use of the last year that I had to spend in the Children's Choir."[6]

The following year, Benigna, at age thirteen, passed three major milestones in a young Moravian's life, all of which were celebrated within the Choir. She entered the Big Girls' Choir on March 25, 1761, and she was formally received (*aufgenommen*) into the Moravian Gemeine the following December. That occasion overwhelmed Benigna: "My heart dissolved in shame and humility at my Saviour's feet. But I found that my longing had not been quite stilled." Benigna still wanted to join the *Abendmahlsgeschwister*, those Moravians who were admitted to Holy Communion (*Abendmahl*), and her wish was soon granted when she received permission via a drawing of the Lot. Benigna described her first taste of the sacrament: "on May 8 I experienced the indescribably great grace of enjoying, for the first time in Holy Communion, the body and blood of my Friend who was tormented for me, during which I was heavenly happy." Choir leaders played an important role in protecting this special privilege. Before all Communion services, Choir "helpers" interviewed each person in order to determine his or her spiritual state. Not infrequently, someone who had fallen away from a pure spiritual path refrained from the sacrament for some time, either voluntarily or by direction from the Choir helper, rejoining the communicants at the time she and her Choir helper found appropriate.[7]

Marriage, like admission to Holy Communion, was administered by Choir leaders, community elders, and the Lot, because couples played an important role in the church's mission. Missionaries and religious leaders, except those in the single persons' Choirs, were always married, a practical expression of the belief that husband and wife should support each other in their common labors. Eva Maria Spangenberg, for example, worked with her husband at Bethlehem's helm until her death in 1751. His second wife, Martha, then took on her predecessor's duties. When Spangenberg was unable to attend a meeting for some reason, the shorthand for his wife's name (the feminization of his name), "Spbgin," was jotted in place of his omnipresent "Spbg" in the list of attendees for a conference or committee session. Marriage proved especially important for those following a missionary call, and the church struggled over the years to find suitable partners for those in the field, particularly in the Caribbean islands, where the high death rate produced a steady stream of widows and widowers. Choir leaders from the Single Brothers and Single Sisters carefully suggested candidates for marriage with a mind to personality and to the tasks new couples would have to perform. These unions were then submitted to the Lot for divine approval, although the individuals themselves were permitted—even encouraged—to decline a proposed marriage that they felt was inappropriate.[8]

The final stage in a Moravian's spiritual life, death, was considered by the Unity to be a joyful reunion with the Savior. Shortly before the end, if its time could be anticipated, an individual recorded his journey through this world (sometimes called the *Sterbensleben*, or "dying life" to compare it with the eternal life to come) in a *Lebenslauf*, an autobiography that emphasized important spiritual events.[9] Those who ministered to the person in his final illness then finished this necessarily incomplete record. Johann Böhner, a missionary who served in the Caribbean for most of his long career, retired in 1778. His coreligionists finished his lebenslauf:

He rested then from active work, because his strength gave out, especially his hearing. Meanwhile, he busied himself constantly in one way or another, he translated some books of the Old Testament into Creole, although no real use can be made of it; he also dealt with this and that duty for the Gemeine; he had the Savior's work among the Negroes in his heart, and prayed diligently for it. His conduct among us was calm, loving, and edifying. The success of his two children in the Gemeine was near to his heart; he also had the joy of hearing that his daughter was married for the service of the Savior. In January 1785, his strength gave out markedly, and he himself believed that his pilgrimage here below would now soon end. After a sickness of several days, during which time he was mostly in slumber, he went home to be with Christ, his Lord, on the Lord's Supper day of January 23, with the beautiful [daily text], "I will stay in the house of the Lord forever, in his eternal rest." He was seventy-five years of age.[10]

Böhner had served his community as a missionary and lived to see his daughter follow his example. His life embodied the values that Moravian leaders hoped to instill in everyone, and the reading of his lebenslauf at his funeral highlighted his example for others.

Böhner's final days, as told by his peers, demonstrate the ebb and flow of daily life in Bethlehem in addition to telling the story of his death. The Daily Texts (*Losungen*), one of which so aptly marked the day of Böhner's death, were the touchstones of Moravian daily life and worship. Each year, Zinzendorf and other church leaders gathered to select biblical and liturgical passages for each day by Lot. The practice traced back to 1728, when Zinzendorf began closing each night's worship with a biblical "watchword" for the coming day. By 1731, the year's collected texts were being printed in a variety of languages for circulation throughout the Moravian world. Each day, in every Moravian town, home, and mission post, began with breakfast and the Daily Text, often read aloud with a short sermon from an elder or minister. Through the readings, people in widely separated places ensured they were all, quite literally, on the same spiritual page as their coreligionists throughout the world.[11] References to the Daily Texts punctuate almost all records left by eighteenth-century Moravians. After organizing the transportation of a group of migrants for Pennsylvania in 1742, for example, Spangenberg wrote in an open letter: "On the day of their departure from London, as they went under sail to Gravesend, the Text was: They that dwell under his shadow shall return."[12] Daniel Kamm, a Single Brother in Bethlehem, described how he felt when he first reached his new home: "I opened up to a Text, which said: but I will give you assured peace in this place. [Jeremiah 14:13] This the Savior also has richly granted to me." The texts unified the community, reinforced its sense of common purpose, and gave every day and every event a spiritual meaning.[13]

On a daily level, an unending series of worship services worked to tie the community together and renew the sense of shared purpose that was essential to the Oeconomy's functioning. After the morning blessing and reading of the Daily Text, days in Bethlehem fell into a rhythm of prayer services and work. Meetings and meals started and ended with hymns. Evenings were spent in communal services, including congregation services (*Gemeinstunden*) and evening services (*Abendstunden*), which included all the members of the congregation, and, short, quarter-hour, services (*Viertelstunden*) often conducted in the Choirs. The services themselves were frequent but brief and included a combination of sermons, liturgies, and song services (*Singstunden*), times devoted to singing hymns. While most of the community slept, a small number of "watchers" continued to pray through the night, so hardly a moment passed in Bethlehem without some expression of the congregation's devotion to God.[14]

Supplementing the daily routine of worship were two distinctive communal services that emphasized fellowship within the Bethlehem Gemeine and in the wider Moravian church. The most important of these was the love feast (*Liebesmahl*). During a love feast, members came together, either as Choirs or as a whole Gemeine, to celebrate in conscious imitation of the Agape of the primitive church. Participants sang hymns and liturgies and shared a simple meal of buns and coffee or chocolate (quintessential Atlantic world staples), enjoying each other's company and their common bond of religious devotion. Love feasts dotted the Moravian calendar, marking the comings and goings of important members and the anniversaries of important days in church history as well as in the Christian calendar. Each Choir also had its own festival days, marked by Love Feasts.[15]

While Love Feasts celebrated local community, congregation days (*Gemeintage*) emphasized the unified nature and mission of the international Moravian church. Once each month, congregants gathered to hear news from other Moravian congregations (*Gemeinen*) around the world. The constant communication between Moravian outposts, like the Daily Texts, allowed the geographically dispersed system to function, and its members to feel as if they were part of one entity. Each Gemeine and mission station produced a congregational diary, recording the major events of each day. These diaries were then abstracted into narratives, usually produced bimonthly. In Herrnhut, a busy group of copyists and editors gathered all this material together into a general record, called the Congregation Reports (*Gemein Nachrichten*), which were then recirculated out to all the various settlements. These reports, and other important letters, were the centerpiece of the Congregation Day. The Bethlehem Diary for Sunday, October 11, 1744, for example, recorded: "Today was a day of special blessing in Bethlehem. The regular services were held in the morning, and in the afternoon we observed our monthly *Gemein Tag*. In it letters and reports were communicated, which brought us blessing and gratification." Such celebrations were also used to mark important events in the community, like the welcoming of new members, or the reading of autobiographies for those who had recently passed on. They served the key function of binding together those in Bethlehem and joining them to other Moravians around the globe, both through information and through shared practice.[16]

The religiously focused lives led by Benigna Zahm, Johann Böhner, Daniel Kamm, Spangenberg, and the other Moravians in Bethlehem simultaneously emphasized personal relationships with the Savior and commitment to the Unity and its work. Ceremonies marking life-cycle events, including being taken into the community, admitted to Communion, and even dying were celebrated by the whole. In addition to these personal occasions, the Daily Texts, Love Feasts, and Congregation Days unified the group in its common goals. It must be remembered that religious life within town was only one of the two foci of Moravian attention, however. While those in Bethlehem worshiped and worked together, the missionaries whose letters they read on Congregation Days were also furthering Moravian religious goals. Providing practical support to the missionaries, an equally important part of Moravian religious life, meant building a fruitful economy at home.

Supporting the Pilgrims

The Oeconomy was, above all else, a labor arrangement. Because of its role supporting the pilgrim congregation, the house congregation—what became the Oeconomy—needed a system with the flexibility to allow individuals to respond to missionary calls and yet still bring in enough cash to keep the whole of Moravian work in America afloat, and this was no easy task. Friederick Cammerhof, a young Moravian bishop whose influence on Bethlehem was cut short by his early death in 1751, reported to Zinzendorf in 1748: "Our brothers and sisters who are traveling through the countryside or who are appointed to the care of posts here and there, in Tulpehocken, Warwick, Lancaster, . . . in the Jerseys and in New York," often returned to Bethlehem "with ripped stockings and shoes, because they have many rocky hills to cross."[17] The pilgrims were the core of the town's spiritual community, and the needs of the missions and missionaries determined a great deal about Bethlehem's economy, including the shape of the problems leaders had to grapple with as they built the Oeconomy and tried to turn a profit. The missions also defined the nature of work for the house congregation, by linking the earthly labors of those in town with the spiritual labors of those on the road.

For the members of house congregation, their hard work led to communal profit, and thus to participation in the missions. Their efforts fit within a wider Protestant context. Like their Lutheran and Reformed counterparts, the Moravians placed a high value on all forms of work as a means of living a Christian life. Count Zinzendorf believed that work was essential for existence. "One does not work only so that one can live," he wrote, "but rather one lives so that one can work, and when one has no more work to do, then one suffers or passes away." The schedule he envisioned for Herrnhut—including sixteen hours a day of labor—certainly gave concrete form to this idea. Zinzendorf, however, believed that his fellow Moravians should not see their toiling as a burden born of man's depravity. Although man's need to work had its origins in Adam's fall from grace in the Garden of Eden, he believed that Christ's redemption transformed earthly labors from a curse to a blessing. Thus, Zinzendorf taught, the true Christian, freed from worry, felt called to serve Christ through his work, not punished by God.[18] Zinzendorf also took pains to emphasize that no religious distinctions should be made between types of labor: what mattered was the spirit in which work was performed rather than the character of the task. "Dr. Luther said," reported Zinzendorf, "when a pious maid does the ordinary work of her hands, sweeping the room, feeding the cows, etc., she performs as blessed an act as does the priest before the altar. The Savior only sees with what heart and spirit one does something . . . that makes the most ordinary action as pleasing to him as the greatest deed."[19]

All Moravians served God equally through their work, according to Zinzendorf. The logical corollary to this belief was the position that every Moravian, whether in exclusive communities or living among non-Moravians, should be held to the same standards of diligence. If anything, those outside the closed Moravian communities faced a higher bar. "If, in true grace of heart, accuracy, punctuality, and cleanliness of the vessel are necessary anywhere, then they are necessary" in the world, among those not in towns like Bethlehem, wrote Zinzendorf, because those living in the world could more easily set a standard for the world. Similarly, a missionary who was newly arrived at a post should remember that his ordinary labors were as much a part of spreading the Gospel as his preaching. Hard work made one an example, the count argued, and the missionary should simply work diligently until those he sought to convert asked him about religion, since by ordinary toil he could create a reputation for himself as an honest and hardworking person. Those within congregation towns and those in ordinary towns, those on missions and those who pursued a trade, were all put on the same spiritual level through their labors, simultaneously elevating and equalizing all Moravians through their common effort.[20]

A devotion to work, no matter in what form, permeated daily life during the Oeconomy period, but always in the context of shared work for shared goals. For Bethlehem, where everyone was a member of the larger pilgrim congregation, missionary work gave meaning to all labors and sacrifices. Such a mindset was certainly fortuitous in light of the enormous task the Moravians faced—building a town large enough to house hundreds of people while simultaneously maintaining dozens of mission posts and itinerant ministers—and church leaders prided themselves on their congregants' productive labor. "We are therefore in favor of it when the Brothers and Sisters who are in the place can be quite industrious in order to give a hand to those who are in the field," commented Spangenberg in 1746. Everyone in town could be a part of this effort, he continued: "each child among us, when it is hardly four years old and spins or picks cotton for the pilgrims, serves the Gospel."[21] Notably, the Oeconomy functioned not by obliterating or devaluing individuals' labor, but by making people connect their own efforts with the good of the whole, and thereby making even the mundane a cause for spiritual celebration. "When I think of our dear Micksch," Bishop Cammerhof wrote, "and come to him in his stockyard and see how he handles his cows and calves and chickens and ducks, how he cares for his cows when they get their calves, and how he worries, day and night, that everything happen with blessing and according to the sense of the Savior, then truly can my heart joyfully thank the Savior."[22]

Though the Moravians believed that the labors of the house congregation were spiritually equal to those of the pilgrim congregation, the two groups were also linked in another way. Membership in either group was constantly changing, and Bethlehem's residents shifted easily between missionary work and tasks needed to keep the town going. The Oeconomy facilitated that movement by freeing individuals from many financial responsibilities, such as maintaining a household, caring for elderly relatives, and even raising children, and when town leaders rotated artisans between economic work in town and mission posts, they helped make missionary work an important experience in the lives of everyone in town, not just those on mission at any given point. Brother Micksch, the pious husbandman, worked as a missionary in Gnadenhütten. Abraham Boemper, a prominent resident in town, filled a post in Suriname before coming to Bethlehem to work as a silversmith.[23] Moving artisans in and out of Bethlehem caused disruption in the shops, but the community continued the practice nonetheless because Moravians valued the mission work more than economic stability. Examples are numerous. Johan Georg Geitner, a tanner, helped escort a Moravian community across the Atlantic as a church deacon. Shoemaker Edward Thorp served in Indian mission posts at Sichem and Pachgatgoch, as well as at European congregations in Philadelphia and New York City. The Lehnerts, Peter and Anna Maria, worked in the congregation at Macungie before returning to Bethlehem, where they were assigned to the community kitchen. The cumulative effect of this constant motion was to tie all Bethlehem's residents to the church's overall mission. Even those who never worked among the Indians, Pennsylvania Germans, or West Indians had to respond to the regular changes in Bethlehem's work force that came about because of the missions. The fluidity of the work force, combined with the economic fact that all the town's profits went to the missions, ensured that Bethlehem's artisans and shopkeepers were fully members of the mission effort.[24]

Of the adult men in town in 1752, 32 percent were ordained or worked in a missionary capacity at some point during their careers, and this number underestimates the importance of the experience more widely in the community, since married women shared the occupational postings of their husbands as a result of what the Moravians called *Streiter-Ehe*, or militant marriage.[25] Only married people could fill most religious offices (except, of course, leadership roles within the Single Brothers' and Single Sisters' Choirs), and a married couple shared whatever position to which they were appointed. Thus, when a mission post had to be filled, it was a couple, not a person, who went. Church leaders took note of this principle when they arranged marriages, urging the leaders of the Single Sisters' Choir to consider whether a candidate had a heart that was "completely willing, faithful, and devoted to the service of the Savior, whether she has a peaceful disposition, a cheerful being, and the other qualities necessary" for being a missionary.[26] Since women were included equally in mission plans, large numbers of married women, like Anna Maria Lehnert, participated in mission work among Europeans and Indians. Margarethe Jungman spent much of her adult life in the mission field. With her first husband she served in Shekomeko; in the company of her second husband she went to Pachgatgoch and then later to the Susquehanna Valley and to Ohio. In between these posts, however, she and her husband worked on the farm in Christiansbrunn, one of the little Oeconomy towns outside Bethlehem. Thus, though far fewer women than men were ordained, the experience of missionary work was certainly not limited to males. In this environment, individualized justifications for labor, while present, were submerged. It was spreading the Gospel that mattered.[27]

In economic terms, missionary work had the effect of depleting Bethlehem of dozens of healthy workers and exacerbating an already severe labor shortage in town. This was a complicated problem for Bethlehem's administrators. Generally speaking, new workers had to be new members, and, by design, few new people became part of the pilgrim congregation. Bethlehem's immigrants tended to come from other Moravian communities, usually abroad, and there were just not enough workers to go around. Moreover, those available were not always prepared or suited for the tasks they had to perform. Requesting more workers from Europe at a time when agricultural laborers were in short supply, Cammerhof noted: "If they are accustomed to farm work and understand it, then we can use them right away. If they are not yet used to hard work and know nothing of farming, then at least two years will pass before they can truly be used."[28] Cammerhof estimated that there were, in 1748, three hundred people living in Bethlehem, "from which the children, infants, pregnant and birthing women, and the sickly" had to be deducted. This group, "who cannot be counted on for work and help," totaled more than one hundred. Moreover, such people required attention: "you know already what kind of care 50 small children need." Nearly every industry suffered from the "lack of hands."[29]

Despite, or perhaps because of, the lack of sufficient labor, the Moravians built an artisanal economy in Bethlehem to meet the hefty price of their missionary work, drawing on their experience in Herrnhut. In a few years, they built a prodigious number of workshops. Thomas Pownall, a British colonial administrator and future governor of Massachusetts, recorded that during his 1754 visit he saw: "The Following Trades carried on by the Fratres [brothers] at this Settlement[:] Saddle-tree maker, Sadler, Glover, Shoemaker, Stocking-weavers, 4 frames going, Button maker Taylor & Women Taylor, Hatter, Ribband-weavers, Linnen-weavers, 6 looms in work, Woollen-weavers, three looms at work, Wool-comber, Dyer, Fuller, Dresser, Tanner, Currier, Skinner, Butcher, Miller, Chandler, Oil-maker, Baker, Cooper, Joiner, Carpenter, Mason, Glazier, Brick maker Stone Cutter Turner Potter Stovemaker Wheelwright Blacksmith, Gunsmith Nail-Maker Lock-smith, Pewterer, Tinman, Silver-smith, Clockmaker, Harnes-maker, Hemp dresser, Boat-builder, Surgeon, Apothecary." This impressive list formed the core of the Oeconomy's economy, and made Bethlehem a regional center for trades of all kinds.[30]

Artisanal work fit the demands of Moravian religious work in several ways. First, craftwork was well suited for the Oeconomy because it entailed fewer seasonal demands than agricultural labor, making it easier to move individuals in and out of the mission field according the Savior's wishes, as the Moravians viewed it, rather than because of the time of year. As noted above, work assignments in Bethlehem were rarely permanent, especially in the earlier years. Artisans were a part of the pool of potential religious workers, and church leaders (reinforced by the Lot) regularly posted them to missions. Unfortunately for the practical organization of the Oeconomy (though in keeping with the principle of putting missionary work first), such placements took precedence over economic needs, a fact that had frustrating financial consequences. As Cammerhof mused: "It is still a wonder of the Savior to me, when I look at it, that [the Bethlehem Oeconomy] still goes forward the way it does. The many changes of craft masters in this or that area that we have had to make, due to missionary plans or also sometimes because of spiritual reasons, often leave large gaps in many shops and the necessary regulation within [those shops]." Nonetheless, Bethlehem's leaders chose to deal with the problems created by missionary calls rather than choosing to exclude laborers from mission posts, segregating religious workers from those who worked for profit. Instead, they prioritized mission work over consistency in the Bethlehem work force, and dealt with the negative economic repercussions when they arose[31] (Figure 2).

Artisans provided flexibility to the Oeconomy's labor pool for the sake of the missions, but they were also able to do much needed work for the community itself. This internal work force was the second reason why artisanal

Figure 2. Thomas Pownall's 1754 image of Bethlehem, drawn from the south, emphasized the town's large buildings and regular lines. The Single Brethren's house dominates the center, while the industrial quarter sits off to the left, down a slope from the town's central buildings. Courtesy Moravian Archives, Bethlehem.

work fit the Moravians' needs well. In order to build a town out of the forest, the Oeconomy required the services of blacksmiths, carpenters, locksmiths, weavers, and tanners; having them be part of the cashless household was the most cost-efficient way to get the work done. The Moravians prized skilled labor and made use of those skills both internally and as businesses serving outsiders for profit. As Spangenberg wrote in 1751, "[We should] cultivate all crafts, particularly those that are indispensable to us, and useful to others, e.g., the tannery, wagonry, potters, etc., so that we will not only avoid paying money that we would otherwise have to, but also something will come into the coffers, and we will incur all the fewer debts." The workshops thus both saved and earned money for the pilgrim congregation.[32]

The cash that artisans earned from outside work was the third and most important reason behind developing this sector of the economy. Money was more useful to the Moravians than agricultural self-sufficiency would have been, because it could be used flexibly to support religious work at home and abroad. In 1770, several years after the Oeconomy had been dissolved,

Johannes Ettwein, who would become the town's leader during the Revolutionary War, made a rough accounting of its finances since 1741 "in order to prove," as he put it, "that their work had not been in vain, and that the income had been well used."[33] Ettwein estimated that £2,366 had been spent on journeys, the Society for the Furtherance of the Gospel (another means of funding missionary work), and the costs of circulating letters and the Congregation Reports throughout the international church. Some £2,350 had been lost in an attack during the Seven Years' War at Gnadenhütten, the Indian mission within the Oeconomy. Ettwein estimated that the missionaries had cost at least £1,000 pounds per year after 1747, totaling £14,000 during the last fifteen years of the Oeconomy period. This accounting, which admittedly was attempting to prove the financial importance of Bethlehem's contribution to Moravian religious efforts, posited that a total of over £18,700 had been spent on religious work during the Oeconomy period. To put this number into some context, a 1758 valuation of the buildings in Bethlehem came to £10,795. If Ettwein's accounts are to be believed, the Moravians likely steered almost all their profits into religious work.[34]

The trades were the main source of revenue for the Oeconomy. In 1752, this income from outside sources amounted to £1,036, with no single trade dominating. The most successful business that year was the saddlery (£121), followed closely by the tannery (£113). The least profitable business—unsurprising on the frontier perhaps—was the bookbindery, which brought only 18 shillings to the community till. The carpenters also fell in the bottom part of this scale (£6), most likely due to the Oeconomy's constant demand for their services, which left them with little time for outside work. The division between internal (for the Oeconomy) and external (for profit) work appears in the accounts for 1753–55 as well, indicating the importance of both aspects of the economy. The record also reflects the Moravians' ability to quantify in monetary terms the value created by the Oeconomy, an indicator that they understood their communal labors in financial terms. In those years, for example, the tailors did nearly nine times as much work for the Oeconomy (£248) as for outsiders (£29). Yet despite the amount of labor devoted to internal work, the trades remained profitable. During the period from December 1753 to July 1755, Bethlehem earned £1,102 more from the trades than it invested in them, and the various craftspeople also performed £2,500 worth of work for the Oeconomy in the same period. If the Moravians had been forced to hire outsiders for all these tasks, they would undoubtedly have incurred substantial debt, which would have hampered, or even halted, missionary work.[35]

Though not the focus of the Oeconomy's economy, agriculture was still important to Bethlehem, because it provided some of life's necessities. Everything the Moravians produced was something they did not have to buy, saving important cash resources for financing religious work. Nazareth, ten miles to the north of Bethlehem and second in population among the Pennsylvania Moravian communities, served primarily as an agricultural center, as did the other subsidiary towns of Gnadenthal, Friedensthal, and Christiansbrunn. In 1758, the year for which the best land accounting exists, the Moravian lands consisted of 11,407 acres, divided among Bethlehem (3,633 acres), the Nazareth Tract—including Gnadenthal and Christiansbrunn—(5,000 acres), Friedensthal (1,391), and Gnadenhütten (1,383). Combined, the church's estates equaled almost 18 square miles. This total, of course, included a large amount of land that was not yet cleared, as well as meadowlands, farmlands, and building lots.[36] In 1758, the Oeconomy produced 3,535 bushels of wheat, down from a peak of 5,034 bushels in 1756. The Moravians also dabbled in the grain market, buying 600 bushels of wheat while selling 310 bushels.[37]

Other products follow a similar pattern: the Moravians produced many but not all of the foodstuffs they needed for survival. They maximized agricultural production to the extent possible, and made up the deficit through purchases on the open market. They looked to agriculture neither for self-sufficiency nor for significant income. They sold enough to make a small profit and could have cleared more land had they wanted to, but there were several deterrents to investing in commercial agriculture on a wide scale. As Cammerhof noted, "even if we had something to sell, we are still too far from Philadelphia and New York, and have so much work for our carters, that we would not be able to [deliver it]." More significant than this objection, however, was the good fit Bethlehem's leaders found for the Oeconomy's needs in an economy centered on the skilled labor of artisans. Artisanal work allowed the easiest possible (although not easy) movement of individuals in and out of town on missionary calls, supported the town by saving money on their own internal work, and brought in much needed cash for the financial needs of the international Moravian church.[38]

The Limits of Communalism

A portrait of Bethlehem's internal communalism as serene and harmonious during the two decades of the Oeconomy (1741–1762) is surprisingly accurate. The community suffered from remarkably little strife between individuals, who might have chafed under its financial strictures and the authoritarian control of its leaders. There are two explanations for this. First, the group's shared religious commitment to missionary work gave purpose to the residents' sacrifices. The fruits of their labors were ever present, when Indians passed through town, when missionaries returned home, and when reports of mission places were read at communal services. Second, and equally important, Bethlehem's communalism was limited to the combined labor of its members. Residents worked for the Oeconomy, but they did not give over their private property to that system. Individuals continued to have the financial identities they had before arriving, preserving personal wealth, real estate, and other property in their own names. They could not benefit financially from their labors while members, whether working in a workshop or serving in a mission, but neither did they lose what they owned beforehand. That protection extended to social status as well. The Moravians made the same distinctions between the middling sort and people of quality that the wider early modern world did. As a result, the boundaries between living in the communal economy and living outside it were less harsh than one might at first assume, because personal wealth and social hierarchy persisted within Moravian Bethlehem, and softened the Oeconomy as an all-encompassing economic institution. This carefully negotiated form of communalism grew directly out of the Moravians' economic pragmatism, and it had visible consequences for Bethlehem's development.

The permeable boundaries of the Oeconomy were possible because Moravian economic culture was essentially a part of the dominant religious and economic cultures of early America. Combined labor of the kind present in Bethlehem was hardly commonplace in colonial economies, but the Moravians shared the general Protestant respect for private property, and it gave them an economic basis from which to communicate with their neighbors. This should hardly be surprising; the group had been founded by a member of the landed aristocracy and organized by seigniorial decree, after all, and Zinzendorf never forgot his wealth and status. The Moravians were in good company when it came to embracing an economy based on private property and social hierarchy. Seventeenth-century Puritans and eighteenth-century Quakers, as well as German Lutheran immigrants, all built their economic lives, and in some ways, their religious lives, around those concepts. Consequently, most religious groups, including the Moravians, concerned themselves with how properly to maintain and manage money without questioning either its essential presence or its unequal distribution. Historian Stephen Innes has argued that the Puritans "authorized a regime of private property and freedom of contract but endeavored to see that it was checked and balanced by moral witness and civic restraint."[39] If the Puritans in Massachusetts respected property rights, the Quakers who founded Pennsylvania a half-century later cherished them. William Penn financed his colony by selling large tracts of land to wealthy investors and encouraged the idea that the new territory offered economic opportunities as well as religious ones. Frederick B. Tolles based his analysis of Quaker economic practice on the idea that within that sect, "property rights were regarded as absolute," modified only by a belief in the importance of Christian stewardship, which dictated responsible ownership. Indeed, historian Barry Levy has argued that Pennsylvania's fecund countryside allowed financially strapped migrants from northwestern England to realize the domestic ideal of their faith. The ability to own, and pass on, private property in the form of land thus became a key component of Quakerism.[40]

Accepting private property led, almost inevitably, to differences in wealth among people, with those at the top of the social order wielding greater secular authority than those at the bottom. A hierarchically structured society was pervasive in the early modern world, and received the approbation of religious leaders and theologians. Luther famously upheld secular authority during the Peasants' Revolt, and the movement that took on his name accepted the "natural" orders and divisions within earthly society. John Winthrop viewed Puritan society as an organic body made up of unequal if interdependent parts, and a century later Jonathan Edwards described society as a place in which all have "their appointed office, place and station, according to their several capacities and talents, and everyone keeps his place, and continues in his proper business." Robert Barclay, the Quaker theologian, accepted social hierarchy despite the strong egalitarian impulse that existed within that group. After endorsing the "*mutual* Relation" between various groups in society and in the family, Barclay admonished: "Let not any judge, that from our opinion in these things, any necessity of *Levelling* will follow, or that all Men must have things in *Common*." In Philadelphia, wealthy Quaker merchants dominated both provincial and city government.[41]

The Moravians also accepted the hierarchical nature of secular society and the leadership it conferred on those of wealth and privilege. Individuals of aristocratic background held a strongly disproportionate number of leadership positions, particularly in secular (what the Moravians called "outward") affairs, and clothing ordinances passed in Herrnhut in the 1730s ensured that Brothers and Sisters would dress in ways that befitted their social origins. In Bethlehem, the differences between ranks were muted, but not eliminated. The Oeconomy created a functional equality and a minimum standard of living by providing like provisions to everyone, yet the social hierarchy and order that sustained eighteenth-century society continued to function within the Moravian enclave.[42]

The most striking evidence for the persistence of social hierarchy and private property in Bethlehem comes in the story of Timothy Horsfield, a wealthy individual whose story delineates the boundaries of the Oeconomy. Horsfield was a native of Liverpool, where he grew up as a member of the Church of England. He came to Long Island in 1725 and six years later married Mary Doughty, who had been raised a Quaker. A moment before he became her husband, Timothy also became her godfather, as she had to be baptized before being married within the Anglican church. Despite these ritual acts, however, Horsfield was not yet a devout believer. Two events in 1739 changed that, first when he felt himself moved by the preaching of George Whitefield and sensed the stirrings of evangelical religion in his life, and then later that year when he met Moravians Peter Boehler and David Nitschmann, who had traveled to New York from Georgia. According to Horsfield's lebenslauf, these "were the first [Moravians] that he saw, and who stayed with him." It was an important turning point in his life, and he "often recounted" how these men "made a special impression" on him. The Horsfields quickly came to play an important role in the transatlantic network of Moravian religious workers. His home on Long Island was "like an inn for the Pilgrims who traveled from the West Indies in the service of the Savior." Horsfield felt especially honored to include Count Zinzendorf among those who stayed with him, visiting him on the first night the "blessed disciple" spent in America.[43]

Horsfield served the church in a variety of ways during the 1740s from his home on Long Island. In 1743, for example, he helped secure the release of three missionaries who had run afoul of Connecticut authorities. On several occasions he facilitated cash transactions of several hundred pounds for the group, easing the flow of cash for his adopted brethren as they worked to establish themselves in Pennsylvania. In 1745, he placed his older two children, Timothy Junior and Elizabeth, in the Moravians' care at Bethlehem. Two years later, his younger son, Israel, joined them. In November 1747, after Horsfield visited Bethlehem, Bishop Cammerhof wrote Zinzendorf that "Br. Horsfield would prefer to be with his whole family in the Gemeine, and it will likely come to be[,] for now, however, he is still useful and needed in New York." For the time being, at least, Horsfield's practical service to the Moravians outweighed, in the minds of church leaders, his personal religious desires. The following year, Timothy Senior requested, and gained, admission to Communion. By April 1749, the next spring, Timothy and his wife Mary finally received permission to move to Bethlehem.[44]

The Horsfields moved to Bethlehem, but they did not join the Oeconomy. Instead, they occupied an ambiguous position on that institution's edges. Town builders constructed a house for the family, on the crest of the hill behind the cemetery. In 1753, around the time that Horsfield became a Justice of the Peace for Northampton County, his house was extended to include space, separate from his dwelling, for a store. The expanded building was half communal and half private—a blending that reflected Horsfield's position in Bethlehem—and it centralized much of the traffic coming in and out of town, welcoming both people in search of the county justice and those looking to buy sugar. Unfortunately, there is no extant evidence of discussions within Bethlehem about Horsfield's decision to move, or what we can assume was his preference to live in his own household rather than in a communal arrangement as his coreligionists did. The reasons for this decision can be inferred, however, from the complex economic relationship that developed between Horsfield and his new landlords. Perhaps because of some negotiations, or perhaps on his own initiative, Horsfield made his house on Long Island, to which he probably kept title, available to the Moravians, who turned it into a school. Horsfield paid an annual rent to the Oeconomy for his living space in Bethlehem, and he purchased most of his family's supplies, including coffee, grain, cloth, and even veal, from the Oeconomy. He continued to pay for his children's board and schooling as he had before moving to Bethlehem, another service that would have been free had he been a member of the Oeconomy.[45]

Horsfield's story adds an intriguing level of complexity to the cashless communal system. His purchases provided the Oeconomy with regular income even beyond the hundreds of pounds that he loaned to Bethlehem in the form of bonds at four percent, and such incidentals as the Love Feasts he provided to the Boys' Choir on his sons' birthdays. This arrangement raises the possibility that he remained outside the Oeconomy precisely *because* it was profitable to that system. Although it is also likely that Timothy and Mary wanted to maintain a greater level of independence than they could have had within the communal household, the beneficial results for the Oeconomy cannot be overlooked. Since membership in the Oeconomy did not require turning over one's funds to the church's coffers, the church did not automatically benefit merely by the addition of new, wealthy members to its ranks, but relied instead on their largesse. The Horsfields, however, who were outside the system, paid for their upkeep.

Not all members of Horsfield's household lived apart from the Oeconomy. His children were already living in the Choir system, and his slave, Josua, an Ybo whom Horsfield had purchased in 1743, "came to live in the Single Brothers' House." Bishop Cammerhof baptized Josua in 1750 and received him into Communion that same year, two years after Horsfield. Josua lived within the Oeconomy until his death in 1761, and, according to his lebenslauf, he kept a special place in his heart for his master: "he held Brother Horsfield especially dear, because it was through him that he came to know the Brethren and was brought to the Gemeine." Horsfield's move to Bethlehem did not fundamentally alter either his own economic position in the world or that of his slave, although both lived radically different lives in Bethlehem from those they had in New York. Josua did not gain his freedom, and Horsfield maintained his private property—in real estate, in financial assets, and in his slave. Indeed, Horsfield was one of the wealthier people in the area.[46] That the Moravian community in Bethlehem allowed this arrangement, even building his home, indicates an acceptance on its part of the economic structures that existed outside of the communitarian enclave— including slavery.[47]

Timothy and Mary Horsfield were the first family in Bethlehem to have a separate house built especially for them on community-owned lands, but they were not the only people in the area who participated fully in the town's religious life without joining the Oeconomy. The Ysselsteins, a family living on the south side of the Lehigh when the Moravians bought their tract on the northern bank, made their lands available to the church several years before selling the property to the Unity outright in 1747. James Burnside, a passionate Moravian from Georgia who worked as a missionary in Shekomeko and in Danesbury, Pennsylvania, after he came north, retired to Bethlehem in 1748 and purchased a small farm directly adjacent to the town on the west side of the Monocacy Creek. He, too, lived within the community, but separate from the Oeconomy, and, like Horsfield, he was also a justice of the peace.[48] This small group of individuals shared several characteristics that separated them from their fellows within the Oeconomy. To begin with, they first met the Moravians in North America, distinguishing them from those who joined the Brüdergemeine in Europe and effectively migrated as members of the Oeconomy. They also had British citizenship (something only a few community leaders in Pennsylvania bothered to acquire), giving them a stronger position within the colonial legal system and making them useful as community representatives.[49] Last, their families possessed economic resources that permitted them to remain independent of the Oeconomy. Though the Moravians did not require individuals to sign over their property in order to join, most members, including those who joined in America, simply did not have the resources to purchase independent farms. Hence, those who maintained an independent financial existence while still participating in the Bethlehem community tended to be better off and socially better equipped to navigate life in Pennsylvania than most of the town's residents were.[50]

In addition to the small group of people who remained outside the Oeconomy, those within the communal system also had a variety of economic backgrounds and resources. This diversity eased the sharpness of the distinction between those within and those outside Moravian communalism. Dozens of Oeconomy members maintained accounts with the Diacony, the financial arm of the Moravian church, and leaders frequently reminded them to draw up wills, lest they die intestate and create complications. In the meantime, however, a few pounds or shillings in a church account enabled members of the Oeconomy to buy the little things that made life a bit easier and a bit less uniform. For example, Johann Georg Geitner, a member of the Single Brothers' Choir, paid one shilling six pence to the store for two pounds of sugar on April 18, 1753. Account books remain silent as to why Geitner made this purchase or what he used the sugar for, but the presence of many such transactions during the communal period indicates that individuals within the community were occasionally acquiring things that the Oeconomy did not provide. That the church facilitated such transactions (it owned the store, after all) implies, at a minimum, tacit approval of the practice.[51]

On the other hand, some activities were not looked on so approvingly. A journeyman wheelwright got into trouble when he cut down trees from an adjacent farm. He had asked for permission for the impromptu logging, but that did not excuse his behavior in the eyes of town leaders. "He purposed to use the Boards in making himself a Chest," they recorded, while "the rest of the Wood he intended to lay by for odd Uses, alledging the Difficulty of procuring any such Thing from the Oeconomy." The irritated council clarified the "Nature & Situation of our present Oeconomy" to him, and explained "that Proceedings of that Kind, in acting for One's Self in such an Independent Manner, could not possibly be suffered as it tended to Confusion & Disorder." Though the transgressor was not permitted to keep his ill-gotten gains, a member of the commission was directed to find a chest for him, provided he really needed it. The Oeconomy's leaders did not want to permit what they perceived as outright wrongdoing, but they did not want the system's residents to suffer for lack of material goods either. The incident also served to reinforce the authority of the town's leaders in moderating such choices.[52]

The Oeconomy dominated the financial and working lives of Bethlehem's residents, but because the Moravians valued and protected personal property, it also existed within the larger web of the Pennsylvania and Atlantic economies. The wealthy had privileges that the poor did not, even if the more fortunate also chose to support the Oeconomy through loans and donations that extended beyond their labor. The Unity and its members owned slaves, and though the enslaved doubtless had better prospects than did their fellows who worked on sugar plantations, they still lacked freedom. But for most of Bethlehem's Moravians the calculus was less complicated. Residents both inside and on the fringes of the communal economy maintained independent financial lives, and though the Oeconomy pooled the labor of many, it existed as part of the larger web of early American economic culture.

Bethlehem's Neighborhood

Bethlehem was a part of the Mid-Atlantic economy and society, and its residents shared much with its neighbors. As businesspeople and as missionaries, the Moravians wove themselves into the fabric of the region's life. Nonetheless, town leaders still wanted to ensure that connections between the Moravians and outsiders followed the outlines of what the church considered acceptable, so they tried to channel congregants' relations with outsiders into safe areas, to protect the pilgrim congregation's internal peace, and also to guard its external reputation. They pursued two strategies to accomplish this task. First, leaders provided Bethlehem with a series of mechanisms for handling visitors so that they would be welcomed efficiently and yet not disturb what they should not, such as the congregation's religious ceremonies, or the decorum of the Sisters' Choirs. At the same time, church councils oversaw the behavior of those within the community as a way of monitoring relations with outsiders. The world could not be expected to live by Moravian standards, but Moravians could be.

Welcoming visitors to Bethlehem required basic infrastructure, and the Moravians built it soon after they arrived. They put a ferry across the Lehigh River to aid travelers and erected an inn, the Crown, to provide comfort. The Sun Inn in central Bethlehem and the Rose in Nazareth joined the Crown before the end of the Oeconomy period. Necessity had driven these steps. As Friedrich Cammerhof wrote to Zinzendorf in 1748, the Crown Inn "is useful to us in many ways and saves many in the Gemeine from unbearable troubles." The challenge was to staff the establishment with "brothers and sisters who are in all ways fitting to the task." The tavern was expensive, Cammerhof reported. "But we neither seek nor have profits," he added, "and we also sell only cider and beer to strangers and keep no rum." This last decision had been made at least in part because of the trouble of getting a license, but it doubtless made the Crown a more sedate spot as well, which would have pleased the pious Moravians.[53]

The visitors to the inn ranged widely, as did the Moravians' connections in Pennsylvania. In August 1761, a group of tourists from Philadelphia passed through, including the teenaged Hannah Callender. She reported that the Sun Inn offered "an elegant supper and diligent waiters," but the tone of her account indicated that she found the Moravians to be different from the folks she was used to, though they were nonetheless interesting. She wrote that the inn's profits went to the "common stock," suggesting that Moravian communalism attracted notice even in Philadelphia. Probably a more typical overnight visitor was Anthony Benezet, the Quaker abolitionist, whom Callender passed on her way to town. The Benezets were part of the wide circle of evangelical activists with whom the Moravians were acquainted and often did business. Anthony's father, John Stephen Benezet, a Huguenot merchant, entertained Zinzendorf when the count first arrived in Pennsylvania, and visited Bethlehem on several occasions. He housed Moravian travelers, used his funds to promote evangelical causes, and in addition to lending a substantial amount to the Moravians to help at Bethlehem, was also one of the subscribers for the building erected in Philadelphia for George Whitefield's preaching engagements.[54]

Some of the ties built through shared projects and commerce developed into more lasting alliances, such as those with the Benezets, that integrated Bethlehem into Mid-Atlantic society. Two of John Stephen Benezet's daughters married into the Bethlehem congregation during its earliest days, in ceremonies performed by Zinzendorf. Subsequent generations of Benezet women also married prominent Moravians (Anthony's niece married one of the Horsfield sons), but their choices to come to Bethlehem were likely personal and not coerced, reflecting continued ties between the Moravian and non-Moravian portions of the family. They became communicant Moravians and members of the Oeconomy, but their new faith did not require a renunciation of their old ties. One Benezet woman, Judith, remained among the Brüdergemeine until her death in 1786; another, who had married a Reformed preacher, presumably left the Moravian fold when he did and settled in southern Pennsylvania. Personal ties overlapped with financial relationships. For decades, the Brüdergemeine depended on the Benezet merchant house both for credit and as a source of goods, and Anthony Benezet played a key role in the relief effort aimed at helping those who fled to Bethlehem during the Seven Years' War.[55]

Of course, most of those who passed through the inn, or just crossed the ferry at Bethlehem to visit its shops, did not become long-term parts of the Moravian community. Yet there is no evidence that Bethlehem's leaders worried about ideological or moral contamination growing out of contact between Moravians and non-Moravians. This is particularly true in the town's economic governance, though perhaps it should not be surprising, given how much the Moravian economic system, based on efficiency, profit, and private property, resembled that of the wider economy around it. As missionaries, the Brüdergemeine viewed all interactions as occasions to spread the Gospel, either directly or through example, and outsiders were thus welcome. Strangers, as non-Moravians were called, regularly visited town and attended worship services; this was a prime reason why services were held in English on a regular basis. Hannah Callender, for example, recounted visiting as many as three different church services during her brief stay in Bethlehem. Even in the missions the Moravians welcomed outsiders. Itinerant Quakers who passed through the Indian mission in Pachgatgoch, Connecticut, were permitted to preach, though the mission diarist did record the Indians' tepid response to the travelers with some pleasure. On the other hand, the Moravians also believed that contacts with outsiders should be controlled so that order and decorum would be maintained. Adult men and married women could hold positions in the inns, or in businesses that welcomed customers. Children and unmarried women, however, could not. In addition, a particular person was appointed to give tours, handle questions from the curious, and keep unknown individuals from having too much freedom in town. The *Fremdendiener* (literally "stranger-servant"), as he was called, ensured that all proceeded smoothly. The job generally went to an older man whose character suited the position. It is doubtful that anyone thus chaperoned could have mistaken Bethlehem for an ordinary frontier town.[56]

The inevitability of personal, economic, and legal transactions with non-Moravians earned direct attention from the town's leaders. Zinzendorf, who believed in tackling issues head on, suggested that the pilgrim congregation find someone adept in Pennsylvanian law to aid the congregation, so that Bethlehem would stay on the right side of local authorities. This careful strategy persisted as Bethlehem grew. A standing committee, known somewhat ominously as the Commission of the Brethren, monitored all relationships with outsiders. It also made the extraordinary choice to keep its records in English, possibly because this increased the appearance of transparency, should a dispute arise. The Commission oversaw all kinds of issues that might affect the way neighbors viewed the Moravians, and it disciplined those who transgressed in ways that reflected poorly on the Unity. Many problems were minor, such as the mischievous behavior of a Bethlehem shepherd, a Brother Richter, who regularly seemed to find small items—a cow bell, a rod of iron— and put them to his own uses. The Commission demanded that he return his booty to its rightful owners, and, in one case, "ordered him to beg Pardon & say that the Brethren were exceedingly displeased with him for his Misbehavior & took not the least Part in it." The remedy suggests that the true crime had not been appropriating an abandoned item, but rather bringing shame to his community and congregation.[57]

The Commission's primary role was as a sort of legal gateway in and out of town. Quite regularly, individuals who lived in the region would petition to move to Bethlehem and to become members of the Oeconomy. The Commission interviewed prospective members to ensure they were not fleeing debts, servitude, or bad marriages. It also requested certificates from anyone who left the Oeconomy, attesting to a clean record between the individual and the town. Some, like William Lowther, stayed only briefly. He left in 1754, two years after being admitted. He gave as his reason that he was not "willing to give myself wholly over to our Savior, & consequently cannot be so obedient & subordinate to the Brethren in my work as I know I should be." Single women and widows found the arrangement more appealing, and some of the latter joined with their dependent children. Widow Boehlen, however, found the Oeconomy no more to her liking than Lowther had. She left again when she found that the Widows' Choir was in Nazareth, while the children were in Bethlehem. The leaders "expressed our Sympathy with her & told her she was at Liberty to return when she thought fit." On the other hand, Mary Penry, "a Single woman from Philadelphia," declared her decision to join in 1755, no matter what might come, and "she declared that if she might be permitted to stay she had much rather undergo any Hardships with the Sisters than go to Philadelphia again." But not everyone received permission to live in the Oeconomy. A man by the name of Brown declared his desire to join the Oeconomy, but his outstanding debts gave the Moravians pause. They asked him to "consider well of the Matter, whether it was his proper Calling from the Savior to live in Bethlehem or if he would not rather chuse to work for himself, in our Neighborhood & earn the Money he owes."[58]

By advising Brown to live on the periphery of the Oeconomy, the Commission suggested to him that he join the group of people who lived in fellowship with the Moravians, but were not fully integrated into the community. These individuals differed from the Horsfields, who were full communicant Moravians, in that their religious status was also peripheral. Some were employees, some were tenants. Some eventually became a part of the Oeconomy, others drifted away. Henry Strause, who lived for a while in Bethlehem, was asked to move to the satellite community at Friedensthal, where he might work "for Wages & have the Opportunity of conversing with the Brethren in Nazareth and Christiansbrunn." He appealed and gained the right to live in Christiansbrunn. An elderly couple made the journey in the opposite direction. They had been living in Gnadenthal, but were "sickly and weakly." Town leaders offered them a place in a house near Bethlehem, "for which a Lease or Agreement should be made with him." The couple willingly agreed, on the condition that their children remain in the Oeconomy in exchange for the interest on a small sum of money invested with the Moravians. These individuals rarely became central to the Moravian community, and make only a few appearances in the copious community records, but they demonstrate the Moravians' willingness to engage their neighbors in a variety of ways, both religiously and economically. There was no sharp line between insiders and outsiders.[59]

Over time, the steady trickle of individuals in and out of Bethlehem blended the Moravians into Pennsylvania's diverse community. Members sustained relationships with family who had not chosen to join, and town leaders supported those ties. Leaders discussed the poverty of one young man's mother, for example. They soon found that they were in part to blame: the young man had been assured when he joined the Oeconomy "that his Mother, with whom he had lived, should be assisted from Time to Time out of his Earnings, which not having been performed, at least not in the Manner he expected, he had thereby brought upon the Thoughts of leaving the Congregation." The Commission expressed its regret and offered to remedy the situation, but the man had already decided to leave. His younger brother, however, made the opposite choice, and stayed with the Oeconomy. The leaders also acted to preserve family relationships in another case, one that first came to light as part of what must have been a public quarrel between a couple. The husband, Leonard Schnel, was advised to "be cautious how he acted with his Wife so as not to hurt themselves, not bring Scandal, on the Congregation in whose Neighborhood he dwelt &c." That advice softened, however, when leaders learned that the Schnels had what they viewed as a serious problem. Mrs. Schnel did not want their son to be in the community's schools, though that was customary among Moravian families. The boy was sent home, over the "Reluctance" of his father, protecting family harmony before community conformity.[60]

Bethlehem's residents sustained a wide variety of relationships with Moravians living outside the Oeconomy and with non-Moravians, even as they pursued lives that differed markedly from the Pennsylvania norm. Travelers, acquaintances, and friends all passed through. The Moravians provided them with the customary accommodations and showed the curious around. Town leaders actively nurtured and protected these links, because they were essential to the town's economy and to the well-being of those living there, and also because they furthered the Unity's religious mission, by showing the Moravians' Godly way of life to Pennsylvania's many peoples. Members of the Oeconomy lived under a very different set of rules from those of their non-Moravian neighbors, but they did not turn their backs on them. Instead, Bethlehem's Moravians moved comfortably between their communal homes and their wider neighborhood, just as many of them slipped easily between German and English.

The Moravians carefully situated the Oeconomy in Pennsylvania society. They protected and guarded its borders, but they let it blend in as well. And yet devotion to the Savior, to the Unity, and to the missions shaped every aspect of Bethlehem's daily life, from the time one woke to the dormitory where one retired for bed at night. The needs of the missions determined marriages and work assignments, and the missions themselves gave meaning to labors within the community. The desire to evangelize and the need for money to support those efforts also forced the Moravians to look outward, for converts and for customers. But this was not difficult for the Brüdergemeine, which had always chosen engagement in the wider world over sectarian isolation. Through its residents' pragmatism and efficiency, Bethlehem succeeded in becoming one of the most successful communitarian ventures in the early American religious landscape, whether measured by economic security, duration, or population. Yet, because the Moravians' economic fortunes and choices were tied, at their very core, to the group's religious projects, as the latter evolved, the former had to change in response.

CHAPTER 3

Moravian Expansion in the Mid-Atlantic

BETHLEHEM STOOD AT the center of Moravian work in North America, but Moravian missionaries and itinerants were known more for their activities on the road than for their sturdy stone buildings and productive workshops. The 1740s, the high-water mark of the evangelical Great Awakening in America, saw a remarkable expansion and evolution of the Moravian presence on the continent. Yet that process was not smooth. The Brüdergemeine met substantial opposition to its efforts among European-American colonists, particularly from representatives of the European state churches, who saw the ecumenical Moravians as invading their territory and their congregations. Bethlehem's Moravians responded to the controversies and tumult by withdrawing from active work among "unchurched" Europeans in the region and turning their attention more intently to evangelical work among the Indians, and that project took center stage for the group in the 1750s. Their early efforts among European-Americans had a lasting impact, however. Though Count Zinzendorf never wanted his followers to form a lasting denomination—he sought rather the union of all Christian peoples— by the 1750s the Moravian presence in America had become just that, and a network of Mid-Atlantic congregations looked to Bethlehem for support. After mid-century, expansion gave way to stabilization. Moravians became a part of the religious landscape in North America. No longer the center of flashy controversies, they were increasingly known for their deepening contacts with Native Americans.

The Moravian Great Awakening

The Moravians arrived in Pennsylvania, not coincidentally, in the midst of the Great Awakening, a period of intense religious energy and controversy that lasted for a decade beginning in the mid-1730s. Indeed, the Moravians' outreach work played a key role in roiling the waters of that religious movement in America, as it did for parallel developments in Europe. The central issue in the Great Awakening was the spread of evangelical religion. Its emotional style, itinerant ministers, and emphasis on personal religious experience took hold in North America just as they had in Europe in the decades before. The powerful emotionalism and informal nature of evangelical gatherings threatened an older religious order. Jonathan Edwards's narrative of the 1734 Northampton, Massachusetts, revival was widely read on both sides of the ocean, and believers interpreted it both as evidence of true spiritual work and as a manual for further efforts. The Tennents, a famous ministerial family that was sympathetic to the cause, worked among Presbyterians in New Jersey and provided proof that the Awakening's transformation reached beyond erstwhile Puritan territories. George Whitefield's tours up and down the Atlantic seaboard, beginning in 1739, drew the attention of colonists who flocked to hear his dramatic and inspiring sermons. Itinerant preachers, including Moravians, traveled widely, challenging the boundaries between various denominations as well as the authority of the traditional clerical establishment. Ministers and church establishments quarreled over the qualifications necessary to become a member of the clergy. Settled pastors struggled to retain control over their congregations and to solidify often uncertain spiritual commitments made during moments of intense emotional turmoil. The result was an era marked by religious turmoil, intense battles over who had the right to preach and how they should go about it, and the widespread perception among religious observers that great things were afoot.[1]

Yet evangelicalism's message also brought divisions and controversies to American congregations. Individual Christians of many denominations drew a sense of empowerment from experiences of awakening or conversion. Leaders, most famously Gilbert Tennent, urged Christians to follow only ministers who had themselves been awakened. He warned that a "sad Security reigns" in the congregations of "natural" (unconverted) ministers, while only those who were "faithful," or awakened, were truly capable of leading a flock to God. He further argued that it was "lawful and expedient" for souls to follow their hearts to a pastor whose sermons they felt were truer, explicit permission for congregants to seek out those who preached in an evangelical style. Opponents worried about "enthusiastic" preaching designed to stir up the masses into emotional, and therefore unreliable, lathers, a situation they thought could only result in false conversions and doctrinal error. Only settled, properly trained, and respected clergy could ensure appropriate spiritual development, such opponents argued. Congregations and communities split over evangelicalism's experiential message, and the Presbyterian Church found itself in schism for nearly a decade. The Moravians, who paid little attention to doctrine and advocated an intense, even sensual relationship to Christ, fueled the fires.[2]

The Great Awakening was a time as much of division as it was of revival, and the Moravians found themselves squarely on one side of two key, related, issues that were each central to the conflict: clerical authority, which they undermined with their ecumenical message of Christian unity; and experiential, enthusiastic religion, which they preached to the horror of many more traditional ministers. For Zinzendorf, the field of potential souls was vast; the Moravians' task was to bring them together. The saved "have been awakened to life here and there through the word, through the voice of Jesus," he preached in Philadelphia in early 1742. "They comprise the invisible Gemeine in the world," and yet "they are not bound to one place, to one site, to one city or country."[3] The goal for the members of the Unity was to bring the "awakened" into fellowship with one another, an agenda that implicitly meant bridging the traditional boundaries denominations placed between themselves and other religious communities. Though the Moravians did not see this as a direct challenge to ministerial authority, which they accepted in principle, in practice it meant stepping on the toes of many religious leaders when they came into a town to preach. Second, the faith that Zinzendorf taught was based on a visceral, emotional attachment to the Trinity, and especially to Jesus. "The Father of our Lord Jesus Christ is our true Father and the Spirit of Jesus Christ is our true Mother. The Son of the Living God, his only born Son, is our true Brother and Husband," preached Zinzendorf in a sermon in Germantown, Pennsylvania. "And thus to be Godly," he continued, "means that you are so closely related to the religion which saves and to the Savior that he himself is your brother, your flesh and blood." For the count, "true religion" was to know—"to be as certain of this as that you are alive,"—that "The Son, the Brother, the Husband, must love our soul as our own soul, the body as his own body, because we are 'flesh of his flesh and bone of his bones.'" To accomplish this, Zinzendorf preached the "new birth," which would come about "through reflection on" the "deep humiliation" of Christ's sacrifice. Though the message of spiritual rebirth was garden-variety evangelicalism, the sensuality and physicality with which the Moravians described it repulsed some, even as it drew others to their fold[4] (Figure 3).

The Moravians became the lightning rods of the Great Awakening among German-speakers in the Mid-Atlantic.[5] There, the ruptures of the revivals came to a society that was already strained by large waves of immigration and a level of religious diversity rare in the eighteenth-century Atlantic world. To many European eyes, the cacophonous religious environment of the region in these years appeared chaotic and even potentially dangerous. Dozens of sects competed for congregants and for survival. Some, like the

Figure 3. Johann Valentine Haidt's depiction of the Moravians' "First Fruits," shows the first converts from each of the Unity's mission fields. Courtesy Moravian Archives, Bethlehem.

German Separatists and Mennonites, persecuted in Europe, had journeyed to Pennsylvania specifically for the religious freedom guaranteed by the colony's Quaker founder, William Penn. Others, such as the Anglicans and smaller numbers of Catholics and Jews, had come to participate in the colony's thriving economy, but also contributed their own religious voices to the clamor. Immigrants accustomed to membership in Europe's state churches often looked back across the ocean for religious leadership, but the church hierarchies there were not quick to respond. Immigrants in the German Lutheran, German Reformed, Dutch Reformed, and Swedish Lutheran communities struggled to get their European leaders to send authorized preachers to minister to them. In the absence of such ministers, a vacuum of religious leadership greeted many newcomers, and created space for ecumenical interlopers like the Moravians. Diverse as the region was religiously, it was also prime territory for evangelical revival. Scottish and Scots-Irish immigrants, generally Presbyterian, had brought with them the traditions of open-air communion festivals and revival seasons, both of which became integral to the American revival tradition. Those from some German-speaking areas had known the Pietist movement at home, and the messages of evangelical preachers consequently sounded a familiar note to them. When the state churches in Europe failed to provide adequate numbers of ministers to serve them, many turned to the eager and available Moravians for the religious leadership they sought.[6]

Zinzendorf believed that America, and particularly Pennsylvania, had a special religious future. In his eyes, its religious freedom and diverse population opened up possibilities for religious union that would be difficult or even impossible to achieve in Europe. "Now I am convinced of two truths," he wrote in his "Pennsylvania Testament." "The first is that America must necessarily be submerged in the blood of Jesus, but that also (this is the other truth) America must be treated in a different way from Europe." Working in America required different techniques from those that the Unity employed in Europe. For example, things that were "true martyr's tests" in Europe, were, in America, "not the deeds of heroes." Chief among the differences was the requirement that Moravians in America work not as part of a denomination, but simply as Christians. Church structures as they existed in Europe, Zinzendorf believed, would wither away in America. "As soon as there is freedom," he wrote, "the Savior needs no visible house." Moravian itinerants therefore theoretically avoided planting the seeds of their specific denomination—poorly defined as it was—but rather attempted to spread the Holy Spirit wherever it might go, eschewing and ignoring the structures of traditional religion. Indeed, Zinzendorf hoped to spread evangelical awakening even inside the various churches already established in Pennsylvania, hoping eventually to build a kind of pan-denominational union of true "Children of God." This mission would be possible, he believed, in Pennsylvania, far more easily than in Europe, where state churches and schismatic quarreling smothered the true faith.[7]

Armed with this mission, the pilgrim congregation set out to spread the Gospel and create a pan-Christian union in the Mid-Atlantic. It was that active agenda, rather than any particular belief, that incited controversy. Efforts proceeded in two directions, through the labors of the traveling pilgrim congregation in diverse areas throughout the region, and also through a series of ecumenical gatherings. The pilgrims, the Unity's preachers and teachers, were based in Bethlehem and preached countless sermons throughout the 1740s to German immigrants and English-speaking colonists. They dispersed across the region, thanks largely to the support that those toiling away in Bethlehem were able to offer. These pilgrims included a combination of settled ministers who worked—often with their wives—in one place for a longer period of time, and a small army of itinerants, who preached to whoever would listen and tried to spark communities into action or organization. By 1748 there were at least 132 Moravian missionaries and itinerants working in the field, and at least 112 of them worked among the German-speaking population. They believed that they sought merely to bring souls to Christ's invisible church of the saved, to make them children of God. They wanted North America to become Christian—and they defined Christian as their own faith—but they did not seek to make it Moravian per se. Though their listeners often did not appreciate the subtle distinction members of the Unity made between being Moravian and being preached to by a Moravian, the pilgrim congregation made a deep imprint in the Mid-Atlantic's religious communities. They preached in towns almost as dispersed as those Whitefield had reached, and they established communities from Maryland to Rhode Island. The Mid-Atlantic received the most attention, however, and itinerants were especially dense on the ground in Lancaster and Northampton Counties in Pennsylvania, as well as around New York City, Philadelphia, and in some parts of New Jersey.[8]

When itinerant Moravians preached in a particular congregation during the heady days of the Great Awakening, their evangelical message sometimes created or exacerbated conflict within those communities. Often they were invited and welcomed, but frequently by only a single faction within a particular congregation. Particularly dramatic were the problems Zinzendorf encountered in the poorly organized Lutheran community of Philadelphia. When chronicling this piece of the count's history, "Joseph" Spangenberg, one of the count's closest advisors and Bethlehem's most important early leader, later remarked, perhaps dryly: "If the count had handled himself according to worldly reason, he would have had nothing to do with the Lutherans of this land, as with other people who were only interested in their own religion."[9] Yet Zinzendorf held his identity as a Lutheran, which he never renounced, close to his heart. In 1734 he had, under a pseudonym, been examined in Sweden for Lutheran orthodoxy as a preliminary to being ordained. Shortly thereafter, theologians at Tübingen granted him a call to the ministry, saying that such a person as Zinzendorf should not have to wait for a call from a particular parish to become a minister. After these formalities, the count considered himself a Lutheran minister, although neither the Halle Pietists nor the leaders of German Lutheran orthodoxy recognized his credentials.[10]

Shortly after the count arrived in Philadelphia, according to Spangenberg's retelling, some of the city's Lutherans requested that he preach at a shared church where the Lutherans alternated Sundays with the local Reformed congregation. Zinzendorf alerted the leader of the Reformed church of his intentions, and then gave such a moving sermon on Palm Sunday that eventually (again, according to Spangenberg) "the service had to be stopped, for no one could hear or see any more because of the tears." Easter Monday, Zinzendorf received a "unanimous" call to be the Lutheran congregation's pastor. He accepted, with the understanding that when he was unavailable, another Moravian, Brother Pyrläus, would act in his place. To read Moravian accounts, this arrangement seems simple and straightforward, Zinzendorf was generally accepted as the called pastor of the Philadelphia Lutheran Church, and no one doubted his authority.[11]

Unfortunately, however, the situation was not as clear as Spangenberg suggested. Following the Moravians' version of subsequent events, on July 29, "during the observation of the Lutheran worship, some disorderly persons rushed in, and expelling Pyrläus and his hearers, took possession of the building in the name of the Reformed," despite the fact that it was the Lutherans' turn to use the church. To keep the peace, Zinzendorf later decided the best course of action would be to build a new church for the Lutherans at his own expense, avoiding conflicts over the building, and thus ending the affair for the Moravians.[12] But the Lutheran congregation itself had fractured over the issue of Zinzendorf's appointment, and it was the anti-Zinzendorfian Lutherans, not the Reformed congregation, who disputed Pyrläus' right to preach. Henry Melchior Muhlenberg, the talented Lutheran minister whom the Halle Pietists appointed to take charge of Pennsylvania's Lutherans, arrived shortly afterward. He also recounted the story, though from a very different perspective from that of the Moravians. At some point during Zinzendorf's tenure, according to Muhlenberg, "a few buttons of the sheep's clothing flew open and the other side of [Zinzendorf's] face was revealed, which made the sheep suspicious and scattered them." Once the Lutheran congregation had divided into two camps, each struggled to retain the trappings of authenticity that would give it the right to claim it was the legitimate Philadelphia Lutheran church. Muhlenberg continued his report, describing the Moravians as thieves: "Whatever each could snatch on the run he took with him. One had taken the church record book, another the alms bag, a third the alms chest, a fourth the chalice, a fifth the key, and so on. Afterwards a Lutheran deacon, Thomas Mayor, had put a lock on the church house." Subsequently, he recorded, Pyrläus and his followers (not true Lutherans in Muhlenberg's eyes, but souls the Moravians had seduced away from the church) broke into the shared building and preached on the day appointed for the Lutherans, which caused the uproar in which Pyrläus and his followers were "expelled," presumably not by the Reformed congregation, but by the anti-Zinzendorf Lutherans.[13]

The struggles among the Moravians, Lutherans, and Reformed in Philadelphia can be only imperfectly reconstructed, but Zinzendorf failed in his effort to lead the wider community. The conflict points to the tangle of issues at stake in the Moravians' efforts. Congregations in North America were often internally divided over the growth of evangelicalism, which the Moravians represented. Even if they could agree on what sort of faith they wanted preached, the shortage of authorized ministers and the presence of itinerants like Zinzendorf, who were willing to fill any pulpit, further heightened tensions. The squabbles between the Halle Pietists and the Moravians—begun long before in Europe—added fuel to the fire. The Moravians recoiled from the controversy, however, as evidenced by the fact that Zinzendorf constructed a new church for his followers. The new congregation was Moravian rather than Lutheran, which must have wounded the count's ecumenical sensibilities. The story replayed repeatedly across the 1740s in the many of the places Moravian itinerants traveled, and the result at the end of the decade was exactly what Zinzendorf wanted to avoid, the creation of a specifically Moravian community.[14]

The Moravians coupled the pilgrim congregation's labors with a second project, a series of ecumenical conferences, intended to organize Pennsylvania's Christians into fellowship with one another. Like the traveling ministers, this endeavor also offered the region's residents an image of the Moravians as evangelical activists, even meddlesome busybodies. Working with Henry Antes, a Lutheran businessman from Germantown, the count organized a series of religious conferences (called synods by the Moravians) that were intended, at least at the start, to minimize differences among Pennsylvania's many German religious groups. Their ultimate purpose was to encourage spiritual union, which for Zinzendorf meant creating a religious superstructure through which true Christians from all churches could come together as members of Christ's "invisible church."[15] Antes sent out the invitations, and on January 11, 1742, more than one hundred people attended the first Pennsylvania Synod. Virtually all the German religious groups in Pennsylvania as well as the Quakers were represented in the assembly, attesting to the widespread appeal of such an effort.[16]

Zinzendorf's hopeful plan was not to be, however. If the original goal of the synods had been to reduce strife among the various religious groups, in reality they did little beyond exacerbating preexisting quarrels and embittering much of the Pennsylvania religious community against Zinzendorf and the Moravians. Though the Moravians believed they preached an ecumenical message, others heard in their teachings an attempt to co-opt or absorb non-Moravian groups into the Unity's fold. The count's overbearing personality only added to the feeling. By the fourth synod, attendance had dwindled and the meetings had ceased to be conferences of delegates as much as they were gatherings of a religious community unto itself. Increasingly, Zinzendorf and the Moravians dominated the synods, and the assembled took for themselves the name of "the Church of God in the Spirit." Moravian practice guided the synods. Most notably, the Unity's custom of drawing lots on important questions—thereby leaving the choosing to God—became standard procedure. The goals of the new Church of God in the Spirit became more or less identical with those of the Moravian mission in America: to bring about a renewal of German Christianity through teaching and to bring the Gospel to the Indians. Furthermore, under Zinzendorf's guidance the Pennsylvania Synods came to correspond exactly with the count's own understanding of the path by which the Godly would come together to spread the Gospel and to prepare for Christ's return. Ultimately, the outcome of the meetings was deeply disappointing for Zinzendorf and the Moravians. The Church of God in the Spirit continued after 1741, but in a much diminished and predominantly Moravian form. Six months after the hopeful beginning of the synods, almost every German religious group in Pennsylvania had found more, not fewer, reasons to resent the Moravian presence in the colony.[17]

The controversies over the Moravians burned out at about the same time as the Great Awakening did, but the 1740s were difficult times nonetheless. The transatlantic evangelical community—insomuch as it had ever been unified—fractured, an inevitable byproduct of the turn toward institution building that developed after the first fires of revival waned. Zinzendorf and the Moravians, erstwhile leaders of sorts, became outliers and radicals in the eyes of many. They were, in short, that against which other groups could define themselves. The count's theological flexibility had once made them acceptable to many, but as people like Whitefield and John Wesley solidified their positions, the Moravians and their extravagant leader found themselves marginalized. Whitefield and the Moravians parted company over the concept of predestination in the early 1740s. Zinzendorf always considered himself a Lutheran, and would not adopt Whitefield's Calvinist position. On the other hand, he also could not accept Wesley's vision of sanctification, nor could the latter subscribe to what he saw as Zinzendorf's simplistic version of the soul's development. Presbyterian Gilbert Tennent, the lightning rod who had played a significant role in stirring the fires of revival in the 1740s, wrote a lengthy tract in 1742 denouncing Zinzendorf's theology, entitled "The Necessity of Holding Fast to the Truth." In it he argued that the Moravians threatened the Awakening by appealing to emotionalism for its own sake, rather than for the promotion of genuine conversions, and in doing so he used the Moravians to make his own positions appear more moderate. Across the Atlantic, the Moravians hewed a careful course in order to avoid political problems in the Lutheran territories of Germany, but even that did not ensure their welcome at home. Rumors began of dramatic and scandalous activities within the Moravian congregation towns, particularly Herrnhaag, which the group was forced to abandon in 1753. At the same time, controversy broke out in England, where the group had for years had much success, and where they had even gained an Act of Parliament granting them official legitimacy in 1749. The occasional ex-Moravian added to the fray. Pamphlet wars and exposés made for good reading, and the Brüdergemeine, with its aggressive expansion program and flamboyant leader, provided ready material.[18]

The Moravians failed in their plan to organize and unite North America's Christians during the Great Awakening. For the most part, they did not engage their opponents directly, and by the end of the decade they withdrew from many of their more controversial techniques. The Pennsylvania Synods lasted little more than a year, and the pilgrim congregation began to follow a more settled path, preaching to Moravian congregations rather than to large gatherings or in other churches. Through this process, the Moravian presence in the Mid-Atlantic matured and stabilized. Similarly, the furor of the 1740s also had the effect of spurring the European church establishments to pay more attention to German-speaking migrants in America. The Lutheran Muhlenberg made great strides among his flock, and Michael Schlatter, a Reformed minister sent from Holland, organized that church's hierarchy in 1747 and oversaw a rapidly growing number of congregations. By the end of the 1740s, the institutional void Spangenberg had found when he first came to the colony in 1736 was disappearing. The age of the itinerant had passed, and the Moravians became a permanent part of the Mid-Atlantic religious landscape.[19]

Tending the European-American Flock

By the early 1750s, the Moravian presence among Europeans in North America stabilized. With their work no longer the source of intense controversy, the community developed into a network of diverse towns, congregations, and missions. At the center of this world was Bethlehem, where the communal Oeconomy supported the ministers, teachers, and leaders who oversaw the rest. Bethlehem itself, after a period of turmoil caused by Spangenberg's brief ouster in the late 1740s, became a stable home to hundreds. The other towns of the Oeconomy, including the farming center of Nazareth and the adjacent smaller towns of Gnadenthal and Christiansbrunn, were more outposts of Bethlehem than separate communities and depended on the central town for nearly everything. The people living in Bethlehem and the "upper places," as the other Oeconomy settlements were known, were predominantly migrants from European Moravian communities, and they were deeply imbued with the spirit of the international Unity's evangelical project.

But Bethlehem and Nazareth, with their intricate Oeconomy and intense devotion to spreading the word, did not account for all of the Moravian presence in North America. The most tangible fruits of the itinerants' labors during the Great Awakening had been a series of congregations that looked to Bethlehem for denominational leadership. The communities of Lancaster County, Pennsylvania, including Lancaster, Warwick, and Donegal, serve as good examples. Itinerants had first traveled to the county, which had a large German population, in 1742. Zinzendorf himself visited and preached to a few large gatherings, including one at the Lancaster courthouse. These early visits resulted in two congregations. The first of the two, in the city of Lancaster, became the site of violence and controversy, when the Lutheran congregation there divided over the presence of the Moravian itinerant, Laurentius Nyberg. Within a few years, however, matters had settled down, and Lancaster hosted both Lutheran and Moravian congregations. By 1749, the Lancaster Moravians had a church, a school, and a parsonage, and they were served by experienced minister Abraham Reincke. The Moravians counted nearly one hundred people there as "attached" to the Unity—those whom, while not necessarily members or communicants, the Moravians considered in their spiritual care, and fifty children were pupils at the school.[20]

A few miles north of Lancaster lay the little town of Warwick, the site of the second congregation to come out of the area's revivals. The Moravians began preaching there early in the 1740s, and in 1747, George Klein, a sympathetic Lutheran and future resident of Bethlehem, donated land for a school and a congregation house in Warwick. In 1756, a second land donation resulted in the founding of Lititz, a new congregation town (Ortsgemeine). Lititz became an important satellite community of Bethlehem, and though it lacked the missionary functions that Bethlehem's residents embraced, it provided another locus for Moravian communal life in Pennsylvania.[21] In 1753, the church workers in Warwick also had oversight of a very small outpost to their northeast in Muddy Creek (now Reamstown), Pennsylvania, home to a small handful of communicants. Donegal, not much larger than Muddy Creek, lay to the southwest of Warwick, and it rounded out the Moravian communities of Lancaster County. The area was settled by Scots-Irish rather than Germans, and itinerant Jacob Lischy began a community there in 1745. It too became the focus of interdenominational strife, and the Moravians had to move to a second site. By the

1750s, however, Donegal developed into a small Moravian congregation, requiring the oversight of leaders in Bethlehem. Lancaster County's community of congregations was joined by several others. The Moravians built a presence to the west of Bethlehem, around Tulpehocken, Swatara, Quittapahilla, and Heidelberg; south into Maryland at Fredrickstown and Monocasy; and in southern New Jersey. These regional centers were the basis of a growing denomination, called "town and country churches" by the Moravians, and they received preachers and teachers from Bethlehem. They also supplied a steady stream of workers and apprentices to Bethlehem, as well as a variety of options (particularly in Lititz, after it was established in 1756) for those who no longer wished to live in the Oeconomy but did not want to leave the Moravian fold[22] (Map 2).

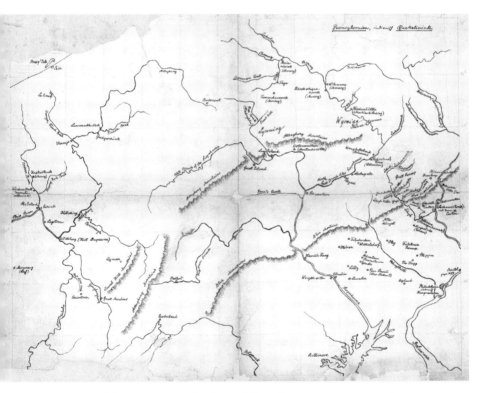

Map 2. Map of the Moravian Mid-Atlantic. The unknown artist attempted to include both Indian and European names for places. Ts.Mp.212.13. Courtesy Moravian Archives, Herrnhut.

Two other centers of Moravian work among European-American colonists deserve mention. The first, New York and New England, was going strong by the early 1750s. Though these areas never received the number of ministers or garnered the number of congregants that work in Pennsylvania, Maryland, and New Jersey did, they played a significant role in the larger community. Efforts in New York coincided with those in Bethlehem. Peter Boehler had first organized an informal and nondenominational worship group there in 1741. In 1744, at the height of the controversies over the Moravians, an Act of Assembly forbade the Moravians to preach or work among the Indians of that colony without a license, leading to the imprisonment of several missionaries. Tensions continued until the 1749 Act of Parliament recognized the Moravian Church throughout the British Empire. Even during the 1740s, however, New York City was home to an active community, including members from Manhattan, Long Island, and Staten Island. It served as a gateway to the American Moravian community. Important missionaries and evangelists, including Spangenberg, Zinzendorf, and Boehler, preached in the city while passing through en route to Europe or the West Indies, winning devoted and sometimes influential converts in the process. Moravians migrating to America typically came through New York (except the First Sea Congregation, an organized migration that landed in Philadelphia in 1742 after a stop in New Haven), and most letters flowed in and out of the port there. Although Bethlehem was undoubtedly the center of Moravian life in America, it depended on the New York community heavily. While the colonies north of New York remained largely unknown to the Moravians, a few scattered missionaries also worked among European-Americans there, particularly in Newport, Rhode Island.[23]

Last, but far from least, the Moravians also began a large-scale project in North Carolina in the early 1750s. On November 29, 1751, the Unity formally purchased nearly one hundred thousand acres of land from John Carteret, Earl of Granville, in the northwestern part of the province. They christened their holdings the "Wachovia Tract" (named after a Zinzendorf family estate in Austria), and they set about making it a profitable venture with typical energy. Over the next decades, the towns built there, the early Bethabara and the later Salem (now Winston-Salem) and Bethania, grew into substantial Moravian establishments. Much of the administration of Wachovia was handled from Bethlehem until the late 1760s, and the southern Moravians turned frequently to their northern brethren for laborers, financial assistance, and spiritual and political guidance. By the latter part of the eighteenth century, the two Moravian centers, in Pennsylvania and in North Carolina, rivaled each other in many ways, while they shared many familial, economic, and religious connections. In an important divergence from Bethlehem's origins, however, Wachovia was not initially intended as a base for mission outreach, though in the early nineteenth century Moravians there would perform very successful work among the Cherokee at the Springplace mission. Instead, the purpose of Wachovia was first to provide funds for the Unity and second to provide a safe haven for European Moravians, should one be needed. This fundamental difference from Bethlehem explains the striking differences, particularly in architecture, between Salem and Bethlehem, and also explains why Salem, when it was built, hewed more closely to the Herrnhut model of a congregation town.[24]

Zinzendorf had never wanted to build a denomination in North America, and yet by the early 1750s it was clear that his followers had done just that. Moravians in places as disparate as Bethabara, North Carolina, Lancaster, Pennsylvania, and Staten Island, New York, participated in an extended fellowship, followed the guidance of spiritual leaders from Herrnhut, and contributed in a variety of ways to the Unity's mission of spreading the Gospel. But at the center of it all remained Bethlehem, with its Oeconomy, its dedicated laborers who had committed themselves to the Unity's work, and its ongoing missions to Native Americans and in the Caribbean. Moravians in Bethlehem (or in the other closed communities at Lititz or in North Carolina) were not considered spiritually superior to those who lived in the town and country congregations, but they were following a particular calling, and they were more likely to become pilgrims, taking up the long and often difficult path of missionary work. Increasingly, that meant laboring among the region's native population.

The Indian Congregations

The Moravians were more successful, though not always less controversial, in their ventures to the Indians. In the years after the Great Awakening, those missions became the focus of the pilgrim congregation's labors in Pennsylvania, but the first efforts in that direction had begun even before Bethlehem was founded. Church leaders in Marienborn, Germany, sent Christian Henry

Rauch to New York to work among the Indians in 1739. Zinzendorf arrived in America two years later and, during his three tours of "Indian Land," visited what would be the principal arenas of activity for the group in the following two decades, including Mahican communities in the southern Hudson valley and Delaware towns nearer to Bethlehem, in Pennsylvania. In addition, he visited Iroquoia, a region where the Moravians established tentative ties though they rarely gained any converts, and Shamokin, a multiethnic native town in the Susquehanna Valley. Moravian work among Indians over the subsequent decades focused on these areas.[25] The missions took on a variety of forms. In some places, such as the crossroads town of Shamokin or the Delaware community at Meniolagemeka, missionaries worked among settled native communities, at the grace of native chiefs who tolerated them. In others, most notably at Gnadenhütten, northwest of Nazareth, missionaries and converts built new towns. The Moravians presence was felt in areas removed from the missions, however, because the native communities were themselves joined by networks of trade and kinship. Moravian work in one area was heard of and discussed in another. European Moravians, and the Indians who became part of the Moravian community, were, by 1750, a noticeable fixture in Mid-Atlantic frontier society, and they sometimes served as cultural intermediaries and interpreters in a region where increased contact was rapidly leading to more rather than fewer instances of friction, misunderstanding, and even violence.[26]

The Moravian missions found their greatest success among the Delaware and Mahican Indians of the Mid-Atlantic's river valleys. Both groups were part of the extended Algonquian language family, and both had long experience dealing with Europeans, who at times called them collectively "River Indians." When, in the early seventeenth century, the Dutch and Swedish arrived in (respectively) the Hudson and Delaware River valleys, the Indians living there quickly built trade ties with the new arrivals. Over the succeeding century, as more Europeans arrived, the Delaware and the Mahican both followed diplomatic strategies that allowed them to remain in their homelands, while simultaneously building economic and political links to the newcomers. In the Hudson Valley, the Mahican vied with the more powerful Mohawk for control of the fur trade market, but, by the third quarter of the seventeenth century, they lost that struggle and dispersed to eastern New England, the St. Lawrence region, and the Housatonic valley to the east. There they formed alliances with other tribes and created new communities. Through this strategy, and despite depleted numbers and continued epidemics, the

Mahican were able to stay in the regions they had long inhabited, and they remained important trade partners for the Europeans.[27]

The Delaware to the south followed a similar practice of flexible community formation, rooted in a cultural tradition of multiple and overlapping networks based on kinship, on lineage, and on local community. During the seventeenth century, they, like their Algonquian kin to the north, embraced trading opportunities with Europeans while also responding to the demographic crises brought by their new neighbors by regrouping and reforming into new communities. Again, as had happened to the north, war broke out between Indian groups—this time between the Delaware and the Susquehannock—as different tribes competed for control of the profitable fur trade with Europeans. By the end of the seventeenth century, rapidly increasing numbers of Europeans in the new colony of Pennsylvania substantially reshaped the political environment for the Delaware, who moved westward into the Susquehanna Valley and northward toward the Forks of the Delaware region. In the process, older Delaware groups reformed into new groups, continuing a time-tested strategy for survival. By the time the Moravians arrived in the Forks region in the 1740s, Delaware and Mahican Indians lived in an extended series of networks that stretched throughout the region. The advent of the Moravian missions as a new form of native community thus fit within a pattern already familiar to the Indians.[28]

Indian and European communities increasingly interwove with one another in the eighteenth-century Mid-Atlantic, though not always peacefully. By the mid-1740s, tensions between whites and Indians grew directly out of this intimacy. More than a century of disease, war, and incursions from Europeans had created impressive regional mobility, so that Indians shared a deep well of knowledge about Europeans and the challenges they faced in common. Indians subsisted from economies built around trade to Europeans, and those who lived close to the seaboard in particular had chosen to follow survival strategies that depended on continued contact with whites. The expansion of the European population, meanwhile, was dependent on trade links to Indians and a degree of military stability offered by the balance of power among three competing powers, the French, the British, and the Iroquois, each of which encroached on the region's northern and western borders. The inhabitants of the Mid-Atlantic frontier—whites and Indians alike—fought to protect an independent space between these competing forces, a fight that alternately threw them together and divided them into vying factions, so that the dense web of connections that tied peoples to one another in daily life was vulnerable to spasms of violence.[29]

This was the milieu in which Moravian missionaries labored, and they built a substantial community of converts. They proved particularly adept at the cross-cultural negotiation required in this difficult environment. Scholars attempting to explain the Moravians' success have emphasized the group's respect for Indian cultures. Missionaries learned indigenous languages, for example, enabling them to discuss the Gospel message ably with potential converts. In addition, they followed the strategy Zinzendorf had laid out, holding that setting a Christian example was as important as baptizing souls, which made their mission style frequently appear more amicable than aggressive. Their forthright yet persistent tactics made an impression on Indians who had become wary of all Europeans, whether traders, politicians, or preachers. One Mahican from Shekomeko famously reported that, though he had heard ministers speak of Christ before, Moravian Christian Henry Rauch reached his soul because he quietly and trustingly went to sleep shortly after arriving and introducing himself, thus showing that he did not fear immediate attack from his hosts.[30]

The choice to become Christian, or to live in a mission town in close alliance with whites, represented only one of the paths taken by Indians facing the economic, spiritual, and political challenges that generations of European presence had brought, however. To understand why particular Indians came to live among the Moravians thus requires answering two questions: first, why did natives see becoming Christian as an option, and second, what appeal did the Moravians in particular hold for them? The answer to the first question is at least partly political, even as it was often also profoundly individual and spiritual. Forming alliances with Christian missionaries entailed creating a new form of community, part of an ongoing process in which the Delaware and Mahican had long been engaged. Moreover, becoming more assimilated into European society offered a route for Indians to stay on the lands where they lived, and, they hoped, enjoy comparative harmony with their white neighbors. It also ensured continued access to the European trade goods that had become integrated into the native culture. Not all regional Indians took this path by any means—divisions within the Delaware over following an accommodationist strategy or a strategy of resistance were pronounced and grew over time—but certainly more than a few opted to hear the new message.[31]

A second explanation for the growth of Christian missions, and the

Moravian missions in particular, during the mid-eighteenth century is more spiritual. Christianity has often spread through individual conversions, and the sincerity of converts' beliefs should be given credibility. Moreover, a new native Christianity developed from the convergence of the Moravians' flexible approach to missionary work and the Indians' adoption and reinterpretation of the Moravians' evangelical theology. The Brüdergemeine's general distaste for formal theology made its message of Christ's love relatively easy to convey, and missionaries placed few barriers between themselves and the Indians they wished to convert. They spoke native languages, and lived—both men and women—among the Indians. They demanded little sacrifice in terms of the Indians' traditional culture. They did not, for example, try to disrupt the Indians' dependence on hunting or their styles of dress. The specifics of Moravian worship provided an added appeal. The blood and wounds theology that so shocked some Protestants may have resonated with Indian beliefs about redemption through torture. In addition, Moravian mission communities offered some new members, particularly women, the opportunity to assume leadership roles that had been threatened during the decades of extended dislocation Mid-Atlantic Indians had endured. The result was the development of a distinctively native Christianity that flourished among some Delaware and Mahican Indians.[32]

Though converts found in Moravian Christianity something they felt drawn to, those mission communities were embedded in a larger Indian society and culture, neither of which the Moravians sought to eradicate. Christian Indians retained ties to their extended families, kin networks, and tribes. Family members who had already become Christian provided routes for conversion for many Indians, but just as frequently Christian Indians felt the pull of non-Christian relatives. Often, individual Indians would move in and out of the Moravian community multiple times during their lives, a circumstance that testifies both to the sometimes complicated nature of native conversion, and to the persistence of other forms of community for those in the mission. Indeed, not a few Indian leaders, including the Delaware chiefs Teedyuscung and Papunhank, spent time among the Moravians, while continuing to act independently on behalf of their followers. Tribal identities often informed Indian choices, and even within Moravian missions interethnic marriages were less common than unions that respected and reinforced tribal boundaries.[33]

Moravian missions during the 1740s and 1750s took on a variety of forms. Some were little more than individual missionaries living within native communities. Shamokin, for example, was a substantial, multiethnic Indian town in the Susquehanna Valley. Most of its residents were Delaware or Shawnee, but it was also home to Shickellamy, an important Iroquois leader who represented his people's interests in the region. Shickellamy acquiesced to Zinzendorf's request to locate missionaries in Shamokin, and thus began a lengthy and sometimes fraught Moravian presence that lasted until the outbreak of the Seven Years' War in 1755. Missionaries never dominated Shamokin; they stayed at the permission of the Indians. On the other hand, they also succeeded in building some lasting relationships with Indians who appreciated that the Moravians labored alongside them and provided them with important services. Female Moravian missionaries acted as translators and as cultural intermediaries to native women to whom they ministered. Ultimately, though Shamokin never yielded a large number of converts, the Moravians came to know, and be known by, a great number of Indians through their work there.[34]

Meniolagemeka was the mission site in closest proximity to Bethlehem, a fact that meant it also faced a threat of European encroachment from the many Europeans moving onto the frontier. Like Shamokin, it was more Indian village than mission site, and the count had passed through during his stay in North America. In the years after the count's visit, there were sporadic contacts between the Delaware community and the Moravian headquarters, until in 1749 a well-known warrior from Meniolagemeka was baptized at Gnadenhütten. Later that year, Bishops Friederick Cammerhof and Nathanael Seidel visited the town, and shortly thereafter several prominent residents were baptized, including the chief, George Rex, his wife, and his grandfather. These conversions formed the nucleus of a mission community that lasted for several years. Because the town was only a day's trip from Bethlehem, and also close to Gnadenhütten, missionaries from those places served Meniolagemeka, until eventually, in 1752, a missionary couple arrived to stay. Yet the community at Meniolagemeka existed only precariously. The town lay on lands claimed by Europeans, and in 1754, the proprietors ejected the Indians. Those among them who still wished to live among the Moravians moved to nearby Gnadenhütten.[35]

A second set of missions developed in the northern Mid-Atlantic, multiethnic native towns dominated by Mahican Indians but also home to a variety of other eastern Algonquian groups. The oldest of those missions was at Shekomeko, in the eastern Hudson Valley. There, the early work carried out by Christian Henry Rauch, Martin Mack, and others flourished until 1746, when a series of conflicts with white and Indian neighbors led the Moravians and most of the Indian congregation to abandon the mission. Opposition to the missionaries at Shekomeko came from the same sources they had faced with their efforts to organize Europeans: many people found their emotional piety and their itinerant ministers to be nuisances or even dangerous. Meanwhile, the substantial number of Mahican who joined the mission engendered anger, both from whites who disliked any Indian presence on lands they planned to occupy, and also from other Mahican who rejected the Christian Indians' choices. Some converts chose to remain with the Moravians and fled south to the relatively new mission at Gnadenhütten, in Pennsylvania. Others, preferring to stay closer to their homes, went east to the missions at Pachgatgoch and Wechquadnach, while still others moved into nonmission native communities. Pachgatgoch managed to survive for nearly two more decades, but the central focus of Moravian mission work shifted south to Pennsylvania.[36]

Native Christians from both Meniolagemeka and Shekomeko converged at Gnadenhütten, a mission town created by the Moravians in the mountains north of Nazareth in 1746. Though it lasted only nine years, it was the pinnacle of Moravian missionary work in the Mid-Atlantic. It consolidated many of the Unity's missionary successes into one community, and became the nucleus of its future work in North America. In 1747, it was home to about thirty converted Indians. By 1753, more than 125 Indians and twenty white Moravians lived there, including both a significant number of religious workers (five married couples) and Single Brothers who worked in the Oeconomy sawmill built there. As in the other missions, the Indians came from a variety of backgrounds, and they were divided between Delaware and Mahican factions, even as the missionaries strove to create a common "Christian" identity. From Bethlehem's perspective, Gnadenhütten provided a steady stream of newly converted souls, considered proof of God's favor for Moravian religious work.[37]

Indian Missions Take Center Stage

Opposition to the Moravians' ecumenical project from Europeans in Pennsylvania, combined with success among the Indians, led to a shuffling of

Bethlehem's two arenas of religious work by the end of the 1740s, in essence a reprioritization in response to changed circumstances on the ground. Having run into significant opposition from European Americans (and European church hierarchies) in their project to organize Mid-Atlantic Protestants, Bethlehem's pilgrims deemphasized their work of organizing German Americans at the end of the 1740s, consolidated their gains among their European neighbors, and turned their missionary energies more fully toward working among the Indians. This evolution was powerfully visible at a synod held in Bethlehem in January 1749. Earlier efforts to cross or even eliminate denominational boundaries between the Moravian church and other American religious communities were downplayed, while the Unity's distinctive governing arrangements and the structures of its church organization were extended to those who had come to follow the group in America. Church leaders had recently decided to place Christ in the role of Chief Elder of the Moravian Church in Pennsylvania (an arrangement that had existed in Europe for some time), and by acknowledging this new organization those gathered at the synod also admitted that something deeper was changing. The Moravians' ecumenical efforts, and the "the Church Plan depending thereon" acknowledged the synod, "is somewhat Alter'd since the time our Br Lewis [Zinzendorf] was in the Country." Previously, the controversial "Pennsylvania Synods"—and ideally at least, all Moravian work among the Germans—had existed independently from the institutions of the Brüdergemeine, since theoretically the Moravians did not control the meetings. But future synods among European adherents were to be purely Moravian, even denominational, affairs. Moravian bishops would henceforth lead the synods in their authority as Unity leaders. The "door [would] not be shut against" those who wished to come inside the Moravian community, but the era of striving for ecumenical fellowship ended. Nonetheless, energy to spread the Gospel remained, and balanced the inward turn that occurred in the mission to European colonists. The community declared that evangelical work lay at the heart of its purpose. Members "from the Bottom of our Hearts own that it is our Plan & Calling, to catch the Souls of Men for our Lamb" and expressed their desires to carry this work out "amongst all & every Sort of religious Denominations, & all the Nations of the Infidels, to whom the Lamb orders us to go." This missionizing spirit, thwarted in one direction, now demanded a new focus.[38]

Fortunately, a likely mission field was already in hand. Immediately after concluding that the ecumenical outreach represented by the Pennsylvania

Synods had come to an end, the Moravians gathered at the 1749 Synod reasserted the importance of outreach to Indians who had not yet heard the Moravians' message, even as they also worried that some Indians among the faithful were now drifting away from the flock. They did so in language that resonated with the Moravians' distinctively graphic and sensual piety, emphasizing Jesus' blood and wounds.[39] "It is quite according to our Heart & Mind," the synod reported, "to lay hold anew in the Name of our Elder on such poor Sheep, as were many of our Indians who having run astray from the Lamb & his Wounds were plunged into various Confusions & Sins, & to forgive them all at once & to let them partake again of all the Happiness & Privileges of the Church." Moreover, as the synod report concluded a few pages later, the Moravians felt gratitude "When we consider what general Love towards our Brethren our Savior has wrought in the Hearts of the Children in this Country, which also in a remarkable Manner appears amongst the Indian Children, in quite Strange & remote Places," and had "Hopes in our Hearts that [Christ's] Side-Hole will be inhabited by many of them, & that the people of the Lamb will have from among them yet many Partners of their blessed Enjoyment." After relating the specific future plans for work at the missions in Gnadenhütten, Wechquadnach, Pachgatgoch, Shamokin, among the Five Nations, and at Meniolagemeka, the community's dedication to its labors finally took concrete form when synod participants described the presence of "14 Brown Hearts whom we, having overstreamed them with the Side Holes Flood, have conveyed deeply into his Side Hole." These new converts reminded the assembled onlookers of the importance of the missionary work the Moravians had undertaken.[40]

Over the following years, outreach to Indians and to other Europeans persisted, but those two "plans" took on very different forms. European-Moravian congregations settled into a larger denominational structure, while the Indian missions remained the site of active missionizing. At base, the distinction was racial: European-Moravians moved into the fold, Indian missions were, by definition, racial outsiders. As the chief Moravian town in America, Bethlehem's leaders oversaw the financial and ministerial development of each project. They accumulated reports and diaries on a regular basis and sent that information back to Europe. Although in principle Zinzendorf and the Unity administration oversaw all decisions, the constraints of great distance and Spangenberg's personal power within the church dictated that a great deal of responsibility resided locally in Pennsylvania. All missionary work began in the towns of the Oeconomy and radiated outward from that point. The communal household provided financial assistance to the missions at Gnadenhütten, Meniolagemeka, Pachgatgoch, and Wechquadnach. This mission network was sizable, and the lives of Bethlehem's residents were connected in many ways to the Indians who were within the fold. Taken together, the Moravians counted 267 people (including missionaries and Indians) in Christian Indian towns for a 1753 catalog of "those souls who are in the Brethren's care in America," and this number did not include those missionaries who were not in mission towns, such as those sent to Shamokin, nor did it count those non-European converts who had moved into European congregations, such as "Christian Anton der Neger" or his wife "Elisabeth Ind[ian]." who resided in Bethlehem[41] (Map 3).

Bethlehem's role as a pilgrim congregation at the head of missionary projects also extended beyond the North American mainland. Though missions to Native Americans were the most visible signs of the Unity's work in continental America after 1750, in the larger Moravian world that effort was dwarfed by its West Indian counterpart. Moravians had first arrived on St. Thomas in 1732, and, after a rocky start, the projects there became some of the international Unity's most successful. In 1753, the administrative leaders in Bethlehem counted 950 blacks under their care on that island (at all stages of connection to the church community up to and including communicants, and nearly all of them enslaved) and a further 151 on St. Croix. Fifteen white missionaries served this vast congregation. Over the following decade, efforts in the Caribbean would only expand, making that region increasingly important in Bethlehem's overall religious life. Missionaries regularly departed for the islands, and their children grew up in Bethlehem's schools. Bethlehem's leaders guided the missions' development and staffing. A conference held in the fall of 1750, for example, drew a Lot and determined that St. Thomas would "receive Johan Michlern as a smith," and then decided that "Hanisch should be ordained as a deacon for St. Thomas." These connections exacted costs too; in 1758, twenty-one people died in the Oeconomy congregations, not counting "the three single brothers in Surinam, Saremeca, and [St. Croix]." They may not have been included in the annual statistics, since they had been assigned elsewhere, but their loss was felt deeply nonetheless.[42]

Moravian leaders in Europe depended on Bethlehem's labors for the regular maintenance of those Caribbean missions and also for information about their progress, reinforcing the Pennsylvanians' role as a key hub of Moravian mission work. In 1753, Johannes de Watteville, a leading Moravian in Herrn-hut and Zinzendorf's son-in-law, reported that Bethlehem must serve as an intermediary for the sending of the Congregation Reports (*Gemein Nachrichten*), between Europe and the Islands, because there were no ships that ran directly enough to make any other alternative viable. Because it "had a more frequent

Map 3. Moravian mission fields at mid-century.

correspondence with St. Thomas," the Pennsylvania town had to undertake to "secure the Congregation Reports as well as the appendices in Bethlehem." That role continued, even through the difficult years of the Seven Years' War. On January 18, 1758, the Bethlehem diarist reported that "Br. Kuiper traveled back to New York, heavily laden with letters and reports for Europe, New York, St. Thomas, Jamaica, Berbice, Rhode Island, Pachgatgoch and Oblong." From Bethlehem's perspective, all these different mission projects were part of a single whole. Individual missionaries moved widely, depending on their specific skills, and might serve a white Moravian congregation one year and native peoples the next. In 1758, for example, Spangenberg reported that the Grubes, who had been serving both whites and Indians in Gnadenthal, had been sent to the Indian mission at Pachgatgoch in order to replace the Schmicks, who had themselves been called away to Berbice, in South America. Taken together, outreach efforts to North American Indians and to West Indian slaves created a powerful demand for the Moravians' spiritual energies, and the missions were an integral part of Bethlehem's daily life.[43]

By the early 1750s, Bethlehem's outreach work had fallen into a stable pattern. The controversies of the 1740s had largely passed. A dozen or so Moravian congregations of European-Americans from New York to Maryland looked to Bethlehem for leadership and guidance. A new, substantial project in North Carolina provided for a second center of Moravian life in America, as did the flourishing missions in the Caribbean. Closer to Bethlehem, work among Mid-Atlantic Indians had integrated the Moravians, if only partially, into the fabric of Indian society in places like Shamokin and Meniolagemeka. More substantial missions at (for a time) Shekomeko, Pachgatgoch, and then Gnadenhütten provided the basis for long-term work, especially among the Delaware, that reached to the end of the eighteenth century. All of the Unity's outwork projects in North America shared a common basis, however. Bethlehem's Oeconomy provided the financial and spiritual wherewithal that sustained missions, towns, and congregations. Indeed, as with the union of the house congregation and the pilgrim congregation evident in Bethlehem's earliest organization, the extensive mission project developed by the Moravians during the 1740s and early 1750s depended directly on an equally expansive economic project. In order to keep the missions growing and thriving, even through times of controversy, the members of the house congregation built a substantial economy that engaged all levels of the Atlantic economy and connected Bethlehem to distant ports, regional neighbors, and the Pennsylvania frontier.

CHAPTER 4

The Moral Parameters of Economic Endeavor

THE DESIRE TO spread the Gospel animated everything the Brüdergemeine did, from traveling to the Caribbean, to enduring controversy, to planting Bethlehem. The elaborate community they built could not be maintained, however, without a steady flow of cash. Missionary work was, at its very heart, expensive, and this imperative thrust the Moravians into the Atlantic economy just as surely as it sent them in search of new souls to awaken. At the same moment that Count Zinzendorf was attempting to bring Pennsylvania's Christians together in ecumenical fellowship, and even as the many members of the Bethlehem pilgrim congregation traveled out from their new town on their various missions, other Moravians were building what became an ornate and complex economic system designed to fund such far-flung religious work, a network stretching from the Mid-Atlantic backcountry to the great financial centers of Europe. Indeed, the Moravians' economic lives were the inevitable counterpart of their religious lives, and the two were tightly intertwined, reflecting, in many ways, the fundamental character of the eighteenth-century Atlantic world.

In the summer of 1742, while Zinzendorf toured Pennsylvania, the First Sea Congregation, a group of Moravians traveling from Europe to Bethlehem, arrived in Philadelphia. Like the thousands of other immigrants who arrived in the city that year, they disembarked from their ship the *Catherine*, at one of the wharves that lined the Delaware River. At any one time that summer the harbor sheltered at least a dozen vessels, most of them engaged in transporting goods between Philadelphia, New England, the West Indies, and

Great Britain. Countless small boats also plied the Delaware, so that the river was in constant motion. The Moravians had purchased the *Catherine* because they believed that traveling on their own ship would be more tranquil and harmonious than catching the first available means of transport, but the new arrivals were nevertheless treated to a bewildering blur of activity once they reached Pennsylvania.[1]

Philadelphia's busy waterfront resembled those of the other Mid-Atlantic cities. Merchants, dockworkers, clerks, and sailors busied themselves with the loading, unloading, counting, and exchanging of goods. Where there were sailors there were inevitably taverns and brothels, and the constant activity at these establishments gave the city a raucous cast, even as it was simultaneously the capital of refined British America. Certainly, had the Moravian newcomers heard of the poor nameless soul who "being in Liquor" drowned in the river and "sunk out-right" a few days after the Congregation arrived, they would have had that impression. The voices sharing and commenting on this rumor spoke in dozens of different accents and languages. Sailors in particular were a diverse group, hailing from Britain and the colonies but also from Africa, the West Indies, and South America. They mixed with the city's permanent inhabitants, who included more than a few African slaves owned by the local elite. In addition, Philadelphia was the entry point for a steady flow of indentured servants, many of them German-speaking and most of them probably a bit ill after a long and frequently unhealthy voyage. Visible testament to the region's hunger for labor, these newcomers passed through the city in great numbers. Most moved on to farm in the fertile regions around Philadelphia, but a few took advantage of the city's narrow alleys to make a break for it and find new futures in Pennsylvania.[2]

The goods heaped on Philadelphia's wharves were as diverse as the people who walked on them, though the cargo being loaded onto waiting ships reflected the colonies' subordinate yet vital position in the imperial economy. The Delaware Valley was a bread basket for the West Indies, as Pennsylvania's farmers supplied the sugar islands' slaves with grain. Pig iron piled up too, waiting to be transported to Britain. The list of goods coming in was more varied. Tools, cloth, books, clothing accessories and haberdashery, indigo, pepper, tea, coffee, and wine tempted visitors to the shops near the waterfront. The stacks of wares reflected the scope of the Atlantic economy just as surely as the people buying them did. Tea from China, cloth from continental Europe, sugar from the Caribbean, and spices from India made the early

American economy anything but provincial. Style, too, was international. Upstairs from one dry-goods shop on Second Street was a wig-maker who advertised a variety of "ENGLISH HAIRS of all sorts of Agreeable and natural colors." Residents of the city were ever aware of trends in Britain, and they demanded a steady flow of news and goods across the Atlantic.[3]

Yet Philadelphia remained a place where shops went by their proprietor's name, and personal connections were important. A shopkeeper who hoped to unload a quantity of tea and coffee told prospective customers via the *Pennsylvania Gazette* that he could be found "At the North-End of Second Street, next Door to Mr. Benezet's." The Moravian arrivals with the First Sea Congregation may well have paid particular notice to this advertisement in the *Pennsylvania Gazette*, as the Benezet family was well known to them. Huguenot merchant John Stephen Benezet was sympathetic to Zinzendorf's message and, as previously mentioned, hosted the count in his home during the latter's visit to Philadelphia. Nor was Benezet's name the only familiar item in the paper that day. A brief notice in German alerted readers that they could purchase reports of the Moravian-led efforts to create an ecumenical German community called the Congregation of God in the Spirit. Just beneath it another notice, this one in English, announced that B. Franklin had for sale a variety of stationer's goods as well as "grav'd Pictures of Mr. Whitefield," the great evangelical itinerant and the Moravians' former landlord at Nazareth. In this intricately woven economy, merchants financed revivalists, and the greatest revivalist of them all let his image be advertised for sale.[4]

Religious and economic development paralleled each other in the Mid-Atlantic and in the larger Atlantic world. Evangelicalism drew upon connections established by commercial-minded empires and adventurers. Journeys undertaken for religious purposes followed well-worn trade routes. William Penn traveled widely among Germany's sectarian community in the late seventeenth century in order to recruit settlers. Those initial German-speaking migrants and their many thousands of successors participated in the Penn family's twinned projects: a profitable proprietary and an experiment in religious toleration. Nor were the connections between the religious Atlantic and the commercial Atlantic present only in lofty ideals; they were part of the finely woven fabric of daily life. Migrants transported their capital, their aspirations, and their beliefs across the ocean, but they maintained ties to distant homes. In the international community that resulted, networks of ministers, relatives, and neighbors shared stories of the stirrings in their hearts, of friends and acquaintances who had been "awakened." Even more important, maga-zines, newspapers, and the business of print culture also spread the word. Those individuals, such as traveling ministers George Whitefield and John Wesley, publicist Thomas Prince, and printer Benjamin Franklin, who under-stood the power of the printed word to generate energy—hype—used it to transform an intensely personal religious experience into an anticipated, de-cried, everywhere discussed, and sometimes profitable cultural phenomenon.[5]

The Atlantic economy thus played an integral role in the spread of evan-gelical religion. The two phenomena were inextricably linked: the same spir-itual impulse that compelled the Moravians to travel from central Europe to the far reaches of the Western hemisphere touched thousands of other souls, from Saxony to Suriname, but the ships on which they traveled were financed by merchants and commodities, not prayers and hymns. In practical terms, religious individuals and groups who plied the waterways and roads of the mid-eighteenth century had to balance their moral sensibilities about eco-nomic behavior with their need to survive and, in the Moravians' case, spread the Gospel; their choices defined communitarian Bethlehem's broader eco-nomic context. The range of possible ways for religious belief to inform eco-nomic activity was quite broad, even for a group as purposeful about their activities as the Brüdergemeine. In some situations, profit and religion might "jump together," as when hard work for the community resulted in a better product, higher price, and more return to put toward missionary work. On the other hand, there were times when driving a hard bargain—charging the most the market would bear—might look like mere greed. From place to place, religion and economic life combined and recombined in a variety of ways, requiring that eighteenth-century Americans participate in a constant evaluation of moral and financial priorities.

Three economic networks extended outward from Bethlehem: interna-tional commerce, regional trade, and economic relationships with Indians. Each of these systems operated under its own set of rules, reflective of a par-ticular balance among three elements: religious goals, the Moravians' sense of moral economic behavior, and financial need. The first, shared religious goals, was easily defined. Missionary work animated the pilgrim congregation from its inception. Spreading the Gospel—and paying for spreading the Gospel—accounted, in one way or another, for the vast majority of the town's work. No matter how expensive missionary work was, however, the community's standards of moral economic behavior were also important, the second area of consideration. But though all could agree that moral behavior was required of congregants, defining what was correct in any given situation was a finely nuanced process, and a unique set of principles informed the group's market participation in each system. The third aspect of each trading network was the most straightforward: financial need. It was also ever present, though in a very different way from the group's moral standards or its religious mission. Making money was necessary, even good, and the Moravians' keen eye for opportunity, and willingness to shed the failing venture, shaped how they viewed all market behavior. The interplay among these three elements in each of Bethlehem's three trading networks defined how the members of the Oeconomy engaged the economy. Collectively, they indicate that the Moravians' approach to economic matters was at once careful and flexible, even as it remained intimately linked to missionary work.

International Networks

The Unitas Fratrum was an international group, and economic ties among the various branches of the church and to trading opportunities around the Atlantic were essential to its survival. Myriad lines of credit connected the central church apparatus in Europe to that in Pennsylvania. Money for transportation costs, publishing, missionary work, purchasing land, or buying essential items flowed back and forth. The deed for the Nazareth tract—a complicated tangle that occupied Bethlehem's leaders sporadically for years—was held in London, and church leaders in Europe regularly reassigned workers from one settlement to another. It is therefore impossible to describe Bethlehem's economy without reference to the Moravians' broader international economy. Arguably, this was the most seamless and uncomplicated of the ways that religion and economic factors balanced in Bethlehem's tripartite economic world. The members of the Brüdergemeine were able to pursue profit while also supporting missionary work in the international sector, because those profits could be steered directly into work among the "heathen."

Bethlehem's international economic engagement can be traced through multiple levels of economic participation, from the career of an individual merchant, New York's Henry Van Vleck, through the group's collective participation in international shipping, to the church's most creative economic endeavor, its Commercial Society. In each of these cases, the Moravians demonstrated a striking ability to merge religious and economic ends while simultaneously taking advantage of the Atlantic economy's most sophisticated and profitable mechanisms and sectors. The success of this system rested, however, on the preference Moravians demonstrated in the international sector for trading with one another when possible.[6] Conducting trade within the community, and thereby relying on those who were already subject to Moravian rules, allowed these projects to exist within safer moral territory. Moravian commercial agents thus found ways to blend the goals of profit and support for the missions quite neatly, by privileging intragroup commerce and creating a Moravian merchant community that was itself an important asset. This cooperative strategy enabled the group to sidestep some of the ethical complexities of trade and simultaneously to capitalize on the group's dispersal around the globe. The Moravians' international religious community therefore profoundly influenced their international trade.

The desire to work with Moravian merchants determined that New York, rather than the closer and politically more logical port at Philadelphia, dominated Bethlehem's trading links to the Atlantic economy. The choice is perhaps surprising, given Philadelphia's importance as a hub of international trade and the fact that the Moravians had faced governmental opposition in New York of a kind not found in the more legally tolerant colony to the south, yet two factors distinctly favored the northern site. First, early evangelical efforts in New York had yielded not only a small congregation but also several members from New York's merchant community. Second, New York had not been, as Philadelphia was, the scene of the Moravians' failed ecumenical efforts, which ultimately hampered organization in the Quaker colony. Religious ties, and therefore economic relationships, to Philadelphia were thus more missionary and transitory. Bethlehem maintained a congregation in the Pennsylvania capital, but economic ties were largely confined to a few non-Moravian merchants. Those limitations in Philadelphia, when compared to the many connections Bethlehem enjoyed with New York, were the primary economic fallout of the religious controversies that followed Moravian itinerants in the 1740s. The New York congregation on the other hand, reaped the rewards.

New York merchant Henry Van Vleck was Bethlehem's most important link to transatlantic trade. When goods needed to be shipped back and forth or bills needed to be paid, he coordinated these activities. Through his labors as a financial go-between, source of credit, warehouse and transport coordinator, and correspondent, he connected the frontier settlement to its region and to the larger Atlantic economy. At the same time, however, Van Vleck was not a member of the Oeconomy, and the church paid him for his services. He received payment from the Strangers' Store for transporting sugar, coffee, and tea, and bought at least one load of skins there. Indeed, he had multiple financial ties to the Oeconomy. "We are still in debt to Henry Van Vleck for around £70, which should be paid to him," reported William Smalling, one of the Bethlehem storekeepers, in 1757. When Van Vleck managed the finances of the Society for the Furtherance of the Gospel, one branch of the missionary apparatus, he was reimbursed for his expenses. On December 15, 1749, he earned ten shillings for freight on a load of books from London. The following March he received payment for some wampum that he had sent to Bethlehem for the use of the missions. In 1751, he was credited for cash he had advanced to a missionary on a journey to Pachgatgoch, a mission in Connecticut; a few months later he forwarded to the Society a cash gift from the Brethren in Germany to be used in the missions.[7]

Bethlehem's leaders recognized that a merchant's financial skills and connections could be invaluable to the Moravians. Van Vleck, for his part, would rather have removed to the quiet confines of the Oeconomy. In 1745, a few years after joining the community, the young merchant married, and the new couple were in agreement that "our intention [was] to go to Bethlehem." They were disappointed. "The Brethren advised me, however, to remain in New York and serve the Savior there," he later wrote in his lebenslauf. Church leaders needed him in the port where they could best employ his resources and skills. The delay later turned out to be financially fortunate from Henry's perspective, as his Moravian connections proved to be the foundation of his business. "Not long after [being told to stay in New York]," he wrote, "we were consigned goods by a merchant in England, who was in business with the [deceased Moravian merchant Thomas] Noble. I was doubtful about accepting them, but the Brethren said to me I should accept this opportunity from the hand of the Savior for my outward success. I did it and was happy, and said merchant as well as others trusted me all the more, whereby the Savior evidently blessed me, so that my credit was established in a short time."[8]

Van Vleck made good use of his Moravian-based credit and built a substantial career. In his capacity as a private merchant, he ran an importing and retail operation in the city. Like many other merchants, Van Vleck's business had several parts, including arranging for cargo to fill his outgoing ships, importing goods from Europe, and selling them in his store on Wall Street. He advertised the products he imported for sale "cheap for cash or short credit." In December 1757, for example, he posted a notice in the *New York Gazette and Weekly Post Boy* advertising dozens of different items, including textiles, spices, rope, and anvils. Two weeks later, the same advertisement ran again, this time with a further list of items that had been "Imported by Henry Van Vleck, in the *St. George* from London."[9] Van Vleck's shipping business network extended from New York to London, Bristol, and Amsterdam, and included both Moravian and non-Moravian business connections. Partnerships were an essential part of the merchant business, as the expense and risk involved in owning a whole ship was prohibitive for all but the wealthiest. Having an agent in New York who could tap into the larger merchant society was a valuable asset for the Moravians. Newspaper notices tie Van Vleck to at least seven ships in the transatlantic trade between 1748 and 1762, including the Moravian vessel, the *Irene*, for which he was a trustee. The *Concord*, a non-Moravian ship also linked to Van Vleck, was captained by Christian Jacobsen, one of the Moravian captains who worked on the *Irene*. Although he may only have contracted to import goods on some of these ships, he owned another boat, the *Mercury*, this time with Samuel Broome & Co.[10]

Van Vleck's career was representative of a group of Moravian merchants, nearly all of them in Europe, who served the church in a financial capacity and linked it to the Atlantic world but who rarely rose to the highest positions of leadership within it. Rather than reflecting ambivalence on the part of the church toward trade, however, this career path indicates the Moravians' recognition that specialization within the economy gave them more flexibility rather than less. In a fashion that paralleled the dynamics of Bethlehem's internal economy, these men used financial acumen in pursuit of profit in order to support the group's religious work. Moravian merchants literally embodied the church's flexible use of market structures to further its shared goals.[11]

Van Vleck epitomized the ability of Moravian fortunes and Moravian religious work to support each other. The same can also be said of the church's investments in transatlantic shipping, which grew out of the Unity's need for transportation across the ocean. The many members of the international Brüdergemeine were in nearly constant motion, crossing the Atlantic from England to New York, from New York to the West Indies, from Amsterdam to Greenland. Such travel brought the energetic Moravians into equally frequent contact with the seamier and riskier aspects of the eighteenth-century world. Travel was extremely expensive, ships were prone to disaster and did not run on schedules set by individual passengers, and fellow travelers might not maintain the high moral standards the Moravians demanded of themselves. The desire to protect themselves and their financial resources from the uncertainties of transatlantic travel effectively drove the Moravians into the shipping business. This preference for separation and security ran contrary to the Moravians' missionary impulse, but dovetailed perfectly with the prospect of efficiently concentrating on missionary projects where they would be most productive, rather than squandering money on travel.

Despite the clear need for transatlantic passage, the Moravians entered the shipping business gradually, and in a fashion that followed the church's needs rather than market opportunities. The Pennsylvania project required many people, and in their methodical way, church leaders organized mass migrations that protected their congregants from moral and financial hazards. The First Sea Congregation had included fifty-six people, mainly Married People and Single Brothers, and sailed on the *Catherine*, a ship purchased by the Unity specifically for that journey, from London to Philadelphia in June 1742. A Second Sea Congregation followed the first in the fall of 1743, this time comprising 115 members and sailing on the second congregation ship, the *Little Strength* (*Gemeinschiff*). Using their own ships protected the Moravians in three important ways. First, although the initial capital investment in buying a seagoing vessel was enormous, the price of any single journey subsequently decreased over time. Second, Moravian immigrants aboard their own ships avoided the debt that formed such a prominent part of German migration, and also avoided the individual indentures that would have divided the group upon arrival in America, interfering with its religious plans. Third, migrating as congregations—groups with leadership and pastoral care—shielded the Moravians from the dangerous and chaotic influences of rough port cities and irreligious fellow passengers. The regular rhythms of worship that prevailed on land continued at sea[12] (Figure 4).

In the case of the *Catherine*, the ship also transferred capital from Europe to America while it was bringing over the First Sea Congregation. Funds expended in Europe for the vessel went back into Moravian religious work, this time in America, when Peter Boehler, the minister in charge of the ship, sold the ship in Philadelphia. His instructions dictated that the *Catherine* be sold for no less than £400. The crew and captain were to be paid from that amount, £200 was to be given to the Society for the Furtherance of the

Figure 4. The *Irene*, the Moravians' Congregation Ship, sunk by French privateers in 1758. Sketch by Benjamin Garrison, Ts.Bd.2.1. Courtesy Unity Archives, Herrnhut.

Gospel (the Moravian organization which collected money for missionary work from both inside and outside the Moravian community), and any amount left over was to be used to support the new settlement at Nazareth, so that the capital used to buy the ship went back into in the work the new migrants were doing.[13]

On the heels of the successful *Catherine* venture, leaders decided to buy a ship for long-term use. Unfortunately, luck did not smile on that particular project. Nicholas Garrison, a ship's captain who had first met "Joseph" Spangenberg, Bethlehem's longtime administrator, in St. Thomas in 1736 and then traveled to Europe with Zinzendorf in 1743, bought the *Little Strength* in London. She transported the Second Sea Congregation safely to America, but on her return voyage, while carrying only a few passengers, Spanish privateers captured her.[14] Already the Moravians were probably using the ship for more than transportation. In June 1754, a Swedish visitor to Bethlehem reported being told about the loss, and the fact that the Moravians had attempted to have the ship returned, "as it was a great injustice to make a prize of a vessel which had been sent out for the sake of promulgating the Gospel to the world." The visitor was skeptical, however, and "inquired whether it had any lading." Upon learning that the ship "carried come brandy, sugar, etc.," he retorted, "do brandy and sugar belong to the promulgation and extension of the Gospel?"[15]

Neither discouraging loss of the *Little Strength* nor cynicism from contemporaries deterred the Moravians, however, who next decided to commission a ship, the *Irene*, at a shipyard in Staten Island. Although the process of building the ship was expensive, and church leaders disagreed about project details as they progressed, Spangenberg pushed the building forward under merchant Thomas Noble's direction. Noble died before the ship was done, an oddly fortunate event since it was ultimately the bequest he left Spangenberg in his will that paid for the *Irene*'s completion. She first sailed for Amsterdam on September 8, 1748. Over the next ten years, the ship made thirteen round trips, almost all of them between New York and London, many of them carrying new Moravian migrants to America, or church workers back to Europe, and always carrying letters and news between distant congregations. As with the ill-fated *Little Strength,* lost to privateers, she also became a trading vessel.[16]

Van Vleck was the principal agent for the *Irene* in North America, and the ship was also a significant part of his business. He was one of its trustees, and its captains, Nicholas Garrison and Christian Jacobsen, were both coreligionists. Since these men played important business roles in addition to piloting the *Irene*, their trustworthiness was crucial. On most of the *Irene*'s journeys, Van Vleck imported fabrics, thread, tools, and spices. In addition to importing goods on her, Van Vleck performed other services related to the ship's cargo. When she was in the harbor, waiting for a full load, he arranged for both "freight and passage" from his shop. When Jacobsen arrived in port, Van Vleck paid him for various items, presumably goods that the captain had taken on consignment in Europe. For example, on January 29, 1755, shortly before the ship sailed on its tenth voyage, Van Vleck paid Jacobsen "Fifty Four Pounds Currency being in full for a Trunk of Hose delivered him. I Say Rec'd in behalf of Mr. Thomas Lateward of London." Jacobsen later reported that he paid the money to Mr. Lateward in London that May. On the other hand, Van Vleck also paid for the privilege of using the *Irene* in his business, charging himself over £200 for freight in 1757.[17]

The ship's primary use remained to transport Moravians, and their letters and reports, across the ocean. In this way, the investment furthered the goals of religious community. But these tasks did not always fill the ship to capacity, leaving space for more profitable commerce. Van Vleck leased space on the *Irene* to both Moravian and non-Moravian merchants for profit when the church did not need her in her official capacity. The side business brought always welcome cash into Moravian accounts. Between 1750 and 1752, and then again from 1755 to 1757, the ship made a total of six round trips, never with more than sixteen Moravian passengers, and sometimes with none of the group on board other than the crew. Yet she was never empty. Captain Nicholas Garrison imported bricks from Holland on her, for example, which he sold upon arrival in New York. Non-Moravian merchants contracted to carry a wide range of goods in the ship. In 1752, the *New York Mercury* carried ads from Dirck Brinkerhoff, Gerard W. Beekman, William Cockroft, and Garrat Noel for goods "Just imported in the *Irene*." While the former two reported only "A neat assortment of European and Indian Goods," Noel, a bookseller, included a lengthy list of his wares, primarily classics. Five years later, in October 1757, five different merchants sold goods imported on the *Irene*: Bernard Lintot, John Smith, David Clarkson, Andrew Barclay, and Francis Lewis. Through Van Vleck's business contacts, the Moravian's ship participated in New York's regular commerce, turning a profit for the church all the while.[18]

The *Irene* earned a profit and transported Moravian travelers. When these two roles came into conflict, church leaders prioritized the ship's community function, placing shared religious goals ahead of the bottom line. Those priorities became evident when imperial war heated up in the late 1750s and commerce became more difficult. Van Vleck tried to keep the ship in the commercial role that he considered most important. In March 1757, he wrote to Timothy Horsfield in Bethlehem, expressing concern over rumors that church leaders wanted to sell the *Irene* to a Dutch Moravian merchant, removing her from the transatlantic routes altogether, because "it was Warr and bad Times for the Brothers & Sisters to Come over &c. and in Europe the Brethren seemd to want to get rid of her." Van Vleck was relieved to find that the "Brethren [in Bethlehem] think Otherwise." From his perspective, the ship was still profitable, and he wanted to expand her business. "I have wrote to Sir Sameul Fladyer & Brother, John Strittell, &c. Merchants in London to favour us with their Freights and have to that End wrote to them for Goods on my own Account to Encourage them to ship in her." For the *Irene* to take on this added business, however, she had to be a reliable merchant ship, and sail on a schedule—a restriction that conflicted with her role as a Moravian transport vessel. "Some Gentlemen here having recommended me to said Houses," Van Vleck continued, "and if We woud keep her regular in the Trade and Endeavour to be an Earley Fall Vessel, and not detain her on account of passengers &c. as she Used to be, they woud also order their Goods to be shipt in her, and which some have Even now already done." The *Irene* was sunk before such plans could come to fruition, but Van Vleck's effort to shift the ship's role toward the more commercial suggests that combining functions was not always a simple matter.[19]

Van Vleck's agency for Bethlehem and for the *Irene* blended the goals of supporting missionary work and turning a profit until they were nearly identical. Moreover, concern for moral economic behavior in this system was almost absent from the discussions over these projects, which ran mainly to the mundane matters of currency, bills of exchange, and the details of international debts. This silence can be read in two equally important ways. First, and most obviously, the Moravian leaders were not concerned about the nature of the transactions Van Vleck engaged in. Taking out bonds, engaging in international commerce, leasing space on a ship, selling dry goods on the open market, and advertising: none of these activities in and of themselves raised an immediate moral problem. Second, leaders could assume that the business would conform to their expectations, because the transactions were carried out within a largely Moravian context. Moravian merchants administered the church-owned ship, which was captained by a Moravian. Bills of exchange were transmitted between church members on both sides of the Atlantic. While the discussion over the timing of voyages attests to the sometimes conflicting needs of the religious community and its commercial projects, the procedure of using agents to manage church-owned assets facilitated the blending of profit and religious work, while minimizing (though never eliminating) the potential for immoral trading practices.

After the loss of the *Irene* to a French privateer in 1757, a new commercial endeavor rose to the fore, and so plans to replace the ship never came to fruition. Instead, the Unity chose a different, more financially conservative way to profit from its unique configuration of merchants and missions around the Atlantic. As early as 1749, Jonas Paulus Weiss, a prominent member of the church leadership in Herrnhut, had wondered about the potential for profit from the Unity's dispersed networks. He posed the question "whether or not, for the maintenance of the affairs of the Savior, a permissible, honest, upright commerce, manufactures, etc. is to be regarded as a proper thing for the Gemeine of the Savior, particularly because, with our extensive establishments in all provinces, the nicest opportunities would be there."[20] Over the next decade, such opportunities only increased, and the *Irene*'s commercial expeditions went some distance toward proving it. By 1758, missionary outposts on the western side of the Atlantic, particularly in Suriname, were including goods for trade in their requests for supplies, a situation that Weiss thought could become problematic for missionary collections, since contributors might assume their donations went to further a business and not to save souls. In May of that year, just a few months after the *Irene* was lost, Weiss proposed that the Moravian church erect a Commercial Society dedicated to both profit and missionary work, which would centralize trade and yet also clearly separate it from the work of spreading the Gospel.[21]

The proposed organization combined personal and community profit through a society of merchants who would capitalize on the Moravian network to create new commercial opportunities. Weiss intended to "find Brethren who, at their own risk and solely for their account, [will] take care of the buying and conveying of wares, and who will freely dedicate half of the profits found therein to the [mission] establishments, and make do for themselves with the other half." With such an arrangement, "neither the Unity nor the establishments can or should ever be harmed" by the trade, but the church and missions would benefit greatly.[22] This semi-private project, however, raised new questions about ethical economic behavior—not because it differed fundamentally from the trade in which the *Irene* had been engaged, but because it would exist outside the church's tight control. Weiss felt it necessary to address the issue explicitly: "It is not my idea to erect a great company," he wrote, "from which one has to fear danger and disadvantage over time, or [my purpose to create a company] out of the intention of becoming rich or otherwise making great profit, where one could be seduced to serve oneself with unequal advantages, or to do someone harm; but rather that one should no longer hesitate to start a commerce, if it were also first very gently and small, that the Lord could sanctify and bless."

Weiss continued, addressing directly the issue of the ethical differences between commercial and traditional economic activities. He rejected the idea that the commerce he proposed was more dangerous than any other, more traditional business. "The objection," he wrote, "has no more ground than with cobbler's and tailor's work or with other Professions, or from beer and spirit making business, or by the sale of natural goods." In those trades too, he continued, "people can also suffer damage, but always, when it happens, are themselves responsible for it, not the commerce or the industry." To avoid such an outcome, "one will try to erect [the Society] in the best way possible so that all damage will be avoided."[23] Avoiding damage, in Moravian terms, meant insuring that those who participated in international trade kept their eyes on God. As long as this happened, commerce was no more dangerous than any other worldly pursuit. Count Zinzendorf said as much in 1754, addressing what had been perceived as his ambivalence toward those engaged in commerce, "It's all the same what one does. If the Savior has given one what is necessary, one takes the talent and uses it."[24] Commercial activity, carried out in an appropriate manner, was therefore seen as of no danger to the community, while the profits it engendered could offer great benefits.

In 1758, shortly after Weiss introduced the proposal for the Commercial Society, the Unity's Directorial College and Count Zinzendorf both gave their approval. Only one significant change was made to the initial plan. The Society's chartering articles stipulated that at the end of each year, "one third of the clear Profit [be] applied to the Use of the United Brethren according to the Order which is to be given by the general Directory," a notable decrease from the half Weiss had wanted.[25] Yet benefits still accrued to the Unity. The Society segregated Moravian commerce into a distinct structure, separate from mission finances but able to lend crucial support. Moreover, the level of remove between the Commercial Society and the church protected the Unity from the financial risks that inevitably accompanied such trade, and also may have resolved some of the feelings that led Van Vleck to worry that the *Irene* would be sold. Weiss believed that it would even help the church's credit, "Because when such things [trade] are handled orderly and right (I might almost say with grace), it will support the Brethren's reputation more than when they are only pursued half and half, as it has been going up to now."[26]

Unfortunately, Bethlehem's participation in the Commercial Society can only be described as less than what the Society's planners had hoped. The periodic protestations from Pennsylvania that the town was "not well situated" for transatlantic commerce suggest the limits of its international economic possibilities. Its artisans were better placed to serve the local community than the international market. In addition, the Gemeine's heavy reliance on Van

Vleck in New York, to the exclusion of building economic ties in Philadelphia, proved an economic detriment in this case. "Perhaps if we had someone appropriate in Philadelphia," one writer commented, "as there many streets, possibilities, and correspondence run together. The goods from Europe could arrive there, and there could be a warehouse, from which things would be sent out. None of that is in Bethlehem, however, for other than the Bethlehem Road, there is no convenient path or the least commerce cross the country." Leaders in Bethlehem tried to participate in a minimal way, nonetheless. One resident, Andreas Anton Lawatsch, became a member of the Society on the town's behalf, and the Diacony Conference resolved that "everything possible should be done to make the Commercial Society flourish," but it gave as a reason that "one Gemeine should help another," suggesting they saw no financial benefit for Bethlehem itself. Van Vleck's presence in New York was useful, but not enough to make up for Bethlehem's strategic choice to serve its local economy first.[27]

With the Commercial Society, the Unity outpaced Bethlehem's ability to participate in the international economy. Nonetheless, that sector played an important role in the town's economic life. Through Van Vleck's efforts, and the use of the *Irene*, the international Unity had used the commercial potential of the Atlantic world to serve the ends of supporting religious work. Because all the profits from the *Irene* and a portion of the profits from the Commercial Society went directly into church work, the desire to maximize return was uncomplicated by concerns over individual greed. In the Commercial Society, this engagement in the transatlantic economy reached its height, and it struck a middle path between furthering the community's religious work, earning a profit, and the concerns of moral economic behavior. It continued the pattern of Moravian merchants working with other Moravians, but it moved beyond simple agency over church-owned assets—such as the role Van Vleck played for Bethlehem and the *Irene*—into the realm of profitable partnership. The Society's private structure, which existed outside the church, allowed the merchants freedom to act, even as it protected the church from potential financial harm. As Weiss immediately recognized, this arrangement raised issues of ethical practice which had been obscured before, yet on balance the Moravians believed they successfully used international trade to support their shared religious goals. Missionary work, the saving of souls, and the spread of evangelicalism all flowed more smoothly when there were sufficient profits to grease the wheels.

Local Profits

In the international sector, the Moravians' projects neatly dovetailed profit with the furtherance of shared religious goals of missionary work. By striving for profit within the confines of agency over church property, Moravian merchants used their skills for church-sanctioned ends. Moreover, the church implicitly sanctioned those projects, such as international commerce, when carried out independently. Bethlehem, however, relied much more heavily on a second series of trading ties, this time to its neighbors in the Mid-Atlantic. In its regional trade, as in its international trade, Bethlehem sought primarily profit, but the personal ties inherent in face-to-face exchange in the backcountry brought with them a much more complicated set of moral issues, requiring that church leaders carefully balance profit with moral economic behavior, all for the furtherance of the community's shared religious goals.

The Moravians had chosen well when they located Bethlehem at the "Forks of the Delaware" in the Lehigh Valley. The spot situated them a short distance from the urban centers of the Mid-Atlantic and from the frontier. To the south, Philadelphia was easily accessible, and to the east it was just a slightly longer journey to Brunswick and then to New York. The Moravians had interests in both directions. New York, as mentioned above, was home to a thriving congregation, including merchant Henry Van Vleck, and its port linked Bethlehem to the West Indies. While the Moravians were thus tied to New York by coreligionists, pragmatic reasons also brought them to Philadelphia on a regular basis. The Quaker City was the economic hub of eastern Pennsylvania, and, even though the group's attempts to organize a congregation there largely failed during the Oeconomy period, its shops and merchants nonetheless drew the Moravians often. Additionally, Pennsylvania's German community found its center in the city, and provided many other reasons for the Moravians to travel there. Though Bethlehem was more than a day's journey from either of the Mid-Atlantic's major centers, it was in nearly constant contact with both.[28]

Local connections were equally important. En route to and from Philadelphia, travelers passed through Center Valley and Saucon Valley, just south of town. To Bethlehem's north lay the small farms of the "Irish Settlement," and to the southwest, the broad countryside of southeastern Pennsylvania. These areas were filling with European colonists in the 1740s and 1750s, many of them German-speaking. From the Moravians' perspective, the whole area offered economic possibilities to a community of artisans and evangelists. The colony's inhabitants grew grain and other agricultural produce for their own consumption and for market. This mixed economy—called by Richard Bushman "composite farming"—indicated the importance and prevalence of the expanding market on the one hand, and also the ability on the part of many farm families to maintain some degree of independence. In this way, the Mid-Atlantic economy differed substantially from the staple-driven agriculture of the Southern colonies and the West Indies, where a focus on sugar, rice, and tobacco limited capacity to produce (in the case of the West Indies) even enough food for survival and therefore demanded extensive trade links. The residents of Pennsylvania, often called the "Best Poor Man's Country," were not as wealthy as the planting aristocracy in the South, but neither were they as poor as the enslaved. Instead, these small producers typically grew enough to feed their families and sell surpluses to merchants. They were embedded in the chain of ever more distant markets, and yet they were not wholly beholden to it for survival. In this landscape, the Moravians chose well when they emphasized artisanal work, and they fit smoothly into the local economy.[29]

The largest and most important of the town's three economic systems from a financial perspective was its most immediate: Bethlehem's workshops and trading connections to its neighbors. Expediency and profit were the driving forces behind this sector of the economy. Individuals came to town to shop, and the Moravians were eager to sell their wares. A large portion of those goods were produced in town. The customers came from a variety of places, and, though limitations in the records from the Oeconomy period prevent the systematic identification of those non-Moravians who came through, later evidence suggests a clientele that stretched as much as thirty or forty miles in some directions. They traveled from "above Gnadenhütten" or "at the Blue Mountains," and from closer places, such as Easton. Quite a few shoppers came from the "Dry Land," a section to Bethlehem's north toward Nazareth. Many customers were known by their relations to others, such as Frederick Krazer, who was also "Benjamin's Brother," or George Reichard, noted to be "Brother of Leonhard in the Settlement." Most purchased little more than a few pounds of sugar or coffee, or a pair of gloves made by the Single Sisters. Certainly, the town benefited from the rapidly growing population of the adjacent countryside. Not insignificantly, new, noncommunal Moravian congregations were also being organized, particularly at Emmaus, to the southwest of Bethlehem, and Warwick, later Lititz, in Lancaster County. This base of sympathetic neighbors provided a ready community of customers for Bethlehem's workshops. The presence of Moravians in the area but not in the Oeconomy may have balanced the town's obvious commercial disadvantage: with nearly everyone living in Bethlehem a part of the communal household, the most logical group of shoppers had only occasional need to purchase anything there. On the other hand, the wide variety of goods available must have made shopping in Bethlehem efficient, providing enough of a draw to bring in those who had no connection to the Moravians.[30]

Customers began coming to Bethlehem to shop long before there was a formal store in town, though initially they had to go from shop to shop, or to the community's central warehouse, because the town lacked any dedicated retail operation. In his 1748 portrait of the town's economic life, Frederick Cammerhof noted that artisans had more business than they could handle and were forced to reject much "turning, carpentry, wagon, weaving, tailors, coopers, and other work, because all of our neighbors would so much like to have their work done in Bethlehem." The steady flow of people in and out of the shops created an ideal business opportunity. Customers who came to Bethlehem's tannery and smithies had other needs as well, and by 1751 the Gemeine was doing a regular retail business in cash. Linen, powder, shot, locks, snuff, tobacco, and Indian blankets (or strouds), were all popular purchase items. In these informal sales, the Moravians sold both their own produce and also goods they had purchased elsewhere; indeed, they made no practical distinction in their stores between those two categories during their early sales efforts. Chest locks and gun screws, items that the Gemeine could produce internally, were sold alongside allspice and whalebone purchased in Philadelphia or New York. This early business was enough to inspire interest in the financial potential that retail had to offer, as the total value of sales reached nearly £100 in some years, even though most transactions involved only a few shillings or less.[31]

By mid-century, the Moravians were ready to follow a growing economic trend by entering into the burgeoning retail trade. The second quarter of the eighteenth century witnessed a dramatic expansion of Americans' consumer choices. As colonists of the middling and upper sorts began to distinguish between various kinds of tea sets and to demand the latest fashions in furniture and clothing, merchants responded by specializing in particular sectors of the market. They gained expert knowledge of their customers and their suppliers. International merchants matched Pennsylvanians' taste in fabric with the produce of English textile mills. Retailers located in smaller towns, farther from the coast, repeated the process for their communities, importing huge quantities of dry goods into rural regions where colonists were hungry for new items. These stores, the forerunners of the "country store," often became the dominant financial institutions of their regions. Farmers sold their produce to the shopkeeper, who in turn sold it to another set of merchants in the seaports, who would then sell to those plying the Atlantic. Storekeepers thus provided the first link in the chain of commerce that led to the Atlantic, but they performed other tasks as well. They extended essential credit during seasons when there were few crops to be sold, and they stocked the shelves from which farmers would make their purchases. As the material options available to average colonists increased, storekeepers guided the choices that farmers could make. They reported on changes in styles and provided access to new products, and they mediated, both culturally and economically, between the Atlantic economy and the "composite" farmers of the countryside.[32]

The Moravians entered the retail trade eagerly, but the store they envisioned differed from its frontier competitors in important ways. First, because the church, rather than a single well-heeled individual, owned the business, its functions were more specialized than other stores. Whereas a single merchant might expand his range of services in search of new profits, Bethlehem's storekeepers operated within a narrower mandate, and it was not for them to decide otherwise. As the retail arm of the Moravian economic system, the store, founded in 1752, was limited to purchasing goods for the Gemeine and selling goods to people outside the Oeconomy. This latter role gave it the name "Strangers' Store." During the communal period, the store did not become a major source of credit for non-Moravians in the area. Those people (either Moravian or non-Moravian) who received large lines of credit in Bethlehem received them from the church directly, not from its retail branch. Furthermore, the store did not purchase large quantities of agricultural surplus for resale in Philadelphia. While the storekeepers occasionally recorded a purchase paid for in kind, transactions were overwhelmingly carried out in cash, or on credit to be paid in cash at a later date. Because of these restrictions, the Strangers' Store was a simpler retail business than many of its contemporaries. From the Moravian perspective, however, this narrow and carefully controlled organization permitted the group to pursue a profitable trade without compromising either its basic attention to missionary work or its moral principles with regard to economic activity.[33]

Responding to growing regional demand, Bethlehem's craftspeople met in 1752 to discuss what wares they could sell in a single, centrally located retail shop, thus taking advantage of the ready opportunity their small-scale sales had already indicated. The meeting marked the first move toward a formal central store, one that would have its own stock, accounts, employees, and building. At this early stage in the venture, the Moravians envisioned it primarily an outlet to sell their products and only secondarily as an opportunity to sell goods purchased for resale at a mark up. The group created two lists of items they could sell: "ideas of what we could deliver to a store from our farms and workshops" and a list of items that could be bought, most likely in New York or Philadelphia, specifically for resale. The first list ran to 178 items. Leather goods such as shoe uppers and lowers, saddles, bridles, and pocketbooks formed a prominent part of the list, as did ironware, wool, butter, cheese, various kinds of oil, tin and pewter ware, and distilled liquors. The thirty items the Moravians planned to sell at Bethlehem on a retail basis show the ready availability of commodities and import items in the Philadelphia and New York areas. Tea, coffee, chocolate, and two kinds of sugar top the list, and in subsequent years those staples made up a central part of the store's overall business. Wine and spices figured as well, as did various textiles, including silk and canvas. Although the second list is much shorter than that of goods the artisans could make at home, the items on it were already a part of their regular shopping trips, and the Moravians could count on plentiful customers for them. Moreover, stocking the store with goods that they used themselves allowed for the efficient combination of their own provisioning needs and those of the new store.[34]

Dominated by the Moravians' own wares, the new store was a way to centralize retail operations within the Gemeine, a step that required specialization in the Bethlehem economy and coordination between shops in town. Consolidating all the retail business in one place offered clear advantages. Artisans were not distracted from producing their wares by the need to deal with customers, while the new store's shopkeepers developed special expertise in the local market's demands and prices. In January 1753, the Strangers' Store was ready for business and appeared for the first time in Bethlehem's account books. Given the care with which the Moravians discussed and recorded daily events, it is somewhat surprising that there is no mention of the store in the community records in the months surrounding January of that year. Perhaps the new business caused no excitement because, like all Bethlehem's economic endeavors, it was simply another branch of the church's financial structure. Leaders had given close attention to the organization of the store, so they were not concerned that retail activity would promote greed, or unethical trading of any other kind, without their knowledge. The store moved from the virtual world of accounting to the bricks and mortar world in the spring of 1753, when the business took its place in the new extension of Timothy Horsfield's house on the edge of town.[35]

The variety of goods available for sale in the Strangers' Store over the next few decades was impressive, including decorative items as well as farm implements and tools. Textiles and the accessories needed for making clothes made up a substantial portion of the wares for sale, including calico, check, dimity, linen, muslin, and flannel, all in a variety of colors. Buttons came in dozens of shapes and sizes, including mohair vest buttons, silver and china sleeve buttons, and flowered metal buttons for coats. Handkerchiefs, combs, and looking glasses were frequently restocked, as were gunpowder, knives, and snuff. The store did a regular business in Indian blankets, German and English Bibles, primers, and almanacs. Saffron and violin strings also made an appearance, indicating the breadth of the consumer market on the frontier. Leaders recognized the demand for finer goods. In December 1757, one council resolved that "a pair of Sisters, who are learning to sew, make leather gloves, which sell out of our Store." Although not all of these things were in the store at any one time, annual inventories begun in 1761 show several hundred different items each year.[36]

The store's inception and development can be read as a profit-motivated story, and it undoubtedly was that. Indeed, the need to run profitable businesses was crucial to Bethlehem's regional trade, and the bottom line dominated that sector of the economy. That focus does not mean that storekeepers were turned loose without limitations, however. Under the Oeconomy system, the store fell under the jurisdiction of the Diacony Conference, an administrative body that dealt with all aspects of the Oeconomy. In addition, a Store Conference—with a membership strongly overlapping the Diacony Conference—met irregularly in 1756 and 1757 to deal with issues specifically related to the business. Through these two bodies, and others like them, community leaders coordinated the different branches of the Oeconomy. Moreover, the Moravian leadership not only controlled the Strangers' Store, the church also financed it and managed the store's debts as part of Bethlehem's general financial situation. In May 1759, for example, the Diacony Conference briefly considered, then rejected, a proposition to borrow £500 to pay off store debts in Philadelphia. The following year it resolved to spend between £500 and £1,000 for that purpose. Because of its position in the Oeconomy, the store had access to much deeper pockets (and more credit) through the church than it could have acquired through its own small operations, but church leaders also controlled every aspect of the store's business, from purchasing, to prices, to inventory. Through such oversight, the retail trade in Bethlehem was carried out in a way that was consistent with Moravian beliefs about the moral behavior in the economy[37] (Figure 5).

But what were those beliefs about moral economy? Defining and monitoring economic behavior for the town's artisans and shopkeepers fell to community leaders, who sought to maximize the profits even as they ensured that business was carried out in a manner they considered proper. This was not a highly philosophical process, but rather a pragmatic one, and leaders handled

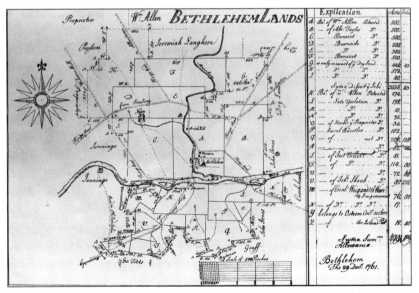

Figure 5. Bethlehem's lands, drawn by George Golkowsky in 1761, probably as part of the community's economic transition away from communalism. Courtesy Moravian Archives, Bethlehem.

issues as they arose. The need to make money required that the Moravians make use of the particular market advantages they had at hand, such as the ability to specialize and to use economies of scale. The store furthered these goals in two ways. It placed all the town's purchasing from outside merchants in the hands of experienced storekeepers, thus providing a service to the town's artisans. Second, as mentioned above, it centralized the retail business in one location, assisting outside shoppers while also freeing artisans from dealing with customers directly. Financially, the retail side of business was far more significant. A sampling of the Moravians' regular provisioning trips to Philadelphia indicates that on average only about 12 percent of the total number of items purchased and 5 percent of the total purchase value was comprised of items that were transferred to the Oeconomy; the remaining goods received a price markup and went for resale in the store. On the other hand, purchasing goods for the community was crucial to the Oeconomy's smooth operation. For this side of the business to work effectively, the store's activities had to be coordinated with the needs of the town's craftsmen. In March 1757, the Store Conference noted that it was important for supplies for the workshops be purchased at the correct time, as the alternative was a "great hardship" for the Oeconomy. The conference members also encouraged communication and cooperation among the various artisans. For example, they reminded Jacob Musch that when he "buys sole leather, it must not be only for him, but also divided among the other cobbler shops." One month later, Musch's leather business was again in the minutes, this time because Conference members felt it necessary to remind him that buying no leather was better than buying poor quality goods.[38]

By promoting profitable business practices, and keeping a watchful eye for transgressions, the community attempted to maintain a morally credible economic posture, but the two aims undeniably overlapped. In 1751, Spangenberg penned a plan for the community's businesses. Many of its points provided solid economic advice, such as keeping accurate accounts and not taking out loans at more than four percent interest if at all possible. In addition to financial tutoring, however, Spangenberg also discussed rules for purchasing and resale that would keep the Moravians from becoming embroiled in messy relationships with suppliers or customers. Regarding the purchase of foodstuffs locally, Spangenberg advised to "calculate according to the market price in Philadelphia," and then to subtract whatever costs the seller would have incurred in transporting his wares to the capital city, thus keeping their prices in line with what sellers could expect to get from other buyers.[39] Of particular concern was the issue of extending credit to customers, a common practice in the cash-starved region, because of the potentially unpleasant consequences of becoming a creditor—the store either might not get paid or might create a bad name for itself by going after a debt. The Store Conference for April 5, 1757, reiterated the idea: "It is necessary that we hold to our plan not to lend to anyone, because this makes our neighbors, who are our friends, into our enemies." Ultimately, however, this principle was honored mostly in the breach, and extant account books attest that many of the region's residents maintained long-term, though not large, accounts.[40]

For the Moravians, trading ethically meant not overcharging a customer or benefiting excessively from one's advantages, particularly in information, because, theoretically at least, trade should benefit all parties. Spangenberg advised that the store aid its neighbors by selling goods at reasonable prices, and not at the highest price storekeepers might possibly demand. Moreover, the store's employees were to ensure that Bethlehem's artisans "deliver good work and at the going rate; i.e., neither too much or too little, as both are damaging to someone." He provided a formula for mark-ups. Moravians were to buy goods some brothers and sisters deemed "indispensable," such as coffee, tea, and sugar, in large quantities. When these goods were sold in the store, however, they were to be offered at a price no higher than one could get at a "city shop." In this quick calculation, they could pass their own discount of scale on to outside customers by simply not including the cost of transportation to Bethlehem in their sale price. The shop would still benefit from having purchased bulk goods at a lower cost and reselling them at the market rate, but not as much as it would have benefited if transportation costs had also been included. In this way, customers reaped some, but not quite all, of the rewards of the Moravians' economy of scale. Most importantly, however, in this and all other matters, the Moravians were to comport themselves in their business transactions with the neighbors "so that they are glad to have dealings with us, and thank God for the presence of the Brethren."[41]

Pricing was an area of continual concern and one that raised particular moral issues. The concept of freely moving and market-determined prices had to be balanced against community values and religious principles about moral trade. Early Americans generally approached the issue with caution. While it was widely accepted that a "going rate" inevitably varied over time and from place to place, the idea that sellers might manipulate that system for their own gain was forcefully rejected by many Protestants. The moment of determining a price opened one to particular moral peril. Puritan John Winthrop had famously prosecuted Robert Keayne for "selling his wares at excessive rates" in 1639. Winthrop accused Keayne of the "false principle" that "a man might sell as dear as he can, and buy as cheap as he can." More than a century later, Jonathan Edwards preached, "'Tis certainly no good rule that men may buy as cheap and sell as dear as they can." Spangenberg also followed this line, acknowledging the role of the market and the need for ethical behavior within it. He instructed the group not to trade "in the way of the world" by haggling, but to name a price beforehand and stick to it. This distinction between "worldly" and "Moravian" economic practice is noteworthy. Trade was important, but it did not have to be sinful. Yet the group understood that prices could not remain static. When the Store Conference asked Christian Frederick Oerter, the Gemeine's accountant and a member of the conference, to draw up a general price schedule in 1757, the going rate in Philadelphia was used as a baseline, recognizing that prices were inherently dependent on the local market. On the other hand, leaders' constant monitoring of prices at the store reflected their wariness of profit for profit's sake.[42]

The Moravians recognized the potential for moral conflict involved in setting prices, but as business people they had to engage the question. It was not possible for the Unity, with its massive missionary projects, simply to issue warnings and injunctions against greed; it also had to act. Keayne had been prosecuted for taking a fifty percent (or more) profit, and on those grounds the Moravians would have been equally culpable. During the Oeconomy period, the overall mark-up for goods at the store, excluding those transferred to the Oeconomy itself, was fifty percent. A more detailed examination shows a wide variation in mark-ups across the sampling, however. At the high end, a few items had mark-ups over two hundred percent, most of them kinds of needles or chalk that customers probably bought only rarely. On the lower end, frequently purchased and widely available commodity items such as sugar and coffee had price mark-ups that tended to hover around twenty percent. The tendency to charge a lower mark-up on frequently purchased items points toward regional competition, high turnover, and ready availability. Actually, sale prices were far more consistent than mark-ups, indicating that the Moravians smoothed out some of the price fluctuations they found in purchasing, both taking a higher profit when possible and absorbing higher supply costs when necessary. On the whole, however, the store's pricing policies indicate the Moravians' understanding that prices reflected a variety of market pressures.[43]

The store reflected both the Moravians' desire for profits, and their belief that the business had to be carried out within a tightly controlled moral context. In an arrangement that resembled the corporate structures of later centuries more than typical eighteenth-century retailing, Moravian storekeepers were employees, while the larger Gemeine owned and was responsible for the shop. The Moravians as a community, and not the storekeepers who worked there, stood to gain or lose in reputation, moral authenticity, and influence, as well as profit, based on what happened there. Community leaders consciously pursued their business with that larger context in mind, and striking the balance between profit and religious principle was at the core of the group's regional economic life. These two priorities coexisted with the third mandate of furthering the community's shared religious work. The influence of this factor appears most clearly when the lens is widened from daily business practice within a single business and refocused on how the Moravians envisioned and distributed work in the community. When they chose where an individual would work, whether in a mission, in a workshop, or even in a distant community, church leaders had to balance the church's financial needs with their shared religious goals. The calculus was hardly simple. A good missionary was invaluable in the field, but that individual might also be the most skilled carpenter in town and the loss of his labor might seriously hinder Bethlehem's ability to pay for the missions. One answer was to minimize disruptions. The artisans were to "communicate their industry's needs" to town leaders, "so that when a Brother [goes] off on a [mission] Plan, or is called home by the Savior, his work does not come to a stop because of it." Such strategies were limited, however, and the problem posed for community leaders a seemingly unanswerable question: which was more valuable, an artisan earning enough money to pay for two missionaries or one talented missionary whose skill in preaching converted as many souls as two more ordinary pilgrims?[44]

Missionary skills were valued over business skills during the early years of the communal period. This is apparent from a brief examination of the store's workers. Joseph Powell, the first storekeeper, was born in England in 1711, and, like many others in England and the New World, he was first awakened by the preaching of George Whitefield. He apprenticed at a mercantile firm in London before encountering the Moravians. After joining the community and marrying within the church, he came to Bethlehem in 1742 as part of the First Sea Congregation. He and his wife Martha served as missionaries among the Germans in Danesbury (now Stroudsburg), Pennsylvania, and in the English-speaking congregation on Staten Island. In 1752, the pair went back to Bethlehem to work in the store, but soon left again to serve in Jamaica.[45] Powell was not alone among the storekeepers whose tenure in the business was cut short by a missionary call. William Smalling, who arrived in 1756 from Europe, left again just over a year later. He had trained as a merchant, but he kept religious matters uppermost in his mind. In his careful script, he inscribed a prayer in the first store ledger: "You God of Order, be and stay near to me in this business, and provide that all may be orderly and honest for You and for men, let no other goal come before You, and let nothing succeed which is not after Your heart. When I become tired and weary, remind me of Your toil." Smalling continued this entreaty using language that seems appropriate for a store ledger: "That You balanced my uncountable debts with Your Blood, and paid my obligations, let it ever be new to me that I am Your Debtor in body and soul."[46]

As Bethlehem's economy developed in the 1750s, expertise in commercial matters became more important and jobs more specialized. This turn toward professionalization also reflected the importance of profit in the regional economy. Skilled shopkeepers were essential to a well run and profitable store. Alongside its cadre of missionaries, the Gemeine needed professional businessmen, although the same geographic mobility that characterized the lives of the former marked those of the latter. After the tenures of Powell and Smalling, the store was put into the hands of William Edmonds and Johann Oberlin, men who ran Moravian retail businesses for decades, both before and after their tenures in Bethlehem. Edmonds began working in the Bethlehem store in the late 1750s, then moved north to Nazareth in 1762 to found a second Moravian shop. Oberlin used his experience as a storekeeper in three Moravian communities. He had worked in the congregation store (*Gemeinladen*) in Niesky, a Czech Moravian settlement in Germany, before coming to America in 1761. He remained in the Bethlehem store until 1781, at which time he returned to Herrnhut, where he again managed a store. Daniel Kunckler, who helped out in the store periodically, had a more varied career than either Edmonds's or Oberlin's, yet it too was marked by mobility as church leaders shifted him from position to position. He worked variously in Nazareth, in the Bethlehem store, for the ferry that transported people across the Lehigh River, in the nursery, and in the tavern. He also ran another, more independent, retail operation in town, after the Oeconomy's dissolution in

1762. Kunckler's occupational flexibility must have been of great value to the Gemeine during the communal period, when professional specialization never entirely compensated for disruptions caused by a steady movement of missionaries in and out of the community.[47]

Bethlehem's regional economy developed out of community leaders' intricate decisions about how to balance the requirement for moral behavior, the need for profit, and the demands of missionary work. The choices were not simple. While honest and responsible trade might eventually lead to greater profit, the need to bring in cash meant being flexible, whether in extending credit or in setting a price. Equally complicated was the problem of supplying the missions. Over time, however, the trend toward professionalization in the trades suggests that stable profits were a priority in this essential segment of the town's economy. On balance, the regional economy had one dominant goal: making money. But for the deeply committed missionaries that founded Bethlehem, this priority could not exist separate from the world of religion. Trade led to profit, and profit led to missionary work. Each was essential.

Mission Ties

Bethlehem's third economic system, exchange with Native Americans, differed fundamentally from the other two networks. In trade with Indians, profit always took a distant back seat to religious considerations, and Bethlehem never depended in any significant way on the missions for financial or material support. Yet because the Moravians used the same set of calculations to frame this trade as they did their more profit-driven ties, this network must be considered alongside the more traditional economic connections with neighbors and to Atlantic trade. When Indians engaged in exchange with Moravians, those transactions were recorded in economic terms. Goods were given monetary values and recorded. Debts were repaid, often in cash. The transactions shared directly by missionaries and missionized accounted for only a portion of the Moravians' economic relationship to the missions, however, as supporting the overall mission project figured significantly in Bethlehem's budget, and the town's leaders managed the costs of missionary work as they did all other aspects of their economy.

The differences between Bethlehem's economic ties to missions and to its other trading partners remain important, however. The Moravians' ties to Indians were initiated to promote Christianity, not to make money. Missionaries thus used financial exchange as a tool for furthering missionary work. As a result, the Moravians' economic relations with Indians contained a unique tension between the bottom line and the group's religious goals of spreading the Gospel. Good missionary work sometimes required losing money, or, more precisely, placing good relations gained through economic ties to Indians at a higher premium than the money that might be earned from such connections. Indeed, relationships built on trade or work were invaluable aids in the project of winning an audience among potential converts. The Moravians' willingness to be flexible in economic matters—born of their experience in the emerging market economy—stood them in good stead in the mission field. Different missionaries and missions came to different arrangements, and, as Indians faced ever harsher economic circumstances, mission economies continued to evolve. But the question of how much was too much to spend hung over these endeavors. In the realms of international and regional trade the group could pursue profit within the context of its religious efforts and moral standards. Failing businesses could be shut down. In the missionary field, however, the goals were different, and profits came in the currency of new converts. Financial losses, understood by the Moravians as the costs of missionary work, were acceptable, but only insofar as they did not imperil the financial stability of the larger project and the Moravian community.[48]

A further reason why Bethlehem's economic relations to Indians differed materially from its regional and international economic systems was the economic context in which they unfolded. As the Atlantic economy expanded, it created winners and losers. Because the Moravians were willing to take on new opportunities, act flexibly, and shoulder financial risks where necessary, they generally found themselves on the winning side of the equation. The retail and transatlantic trades each provided solid proof of this to the community: those endeavors were rewarded with stable returns. The Indians of the Mid-Atlantic region, the objects of Moravian evangelical labors, did not fare nearly as well. For more than a century they had traded with Europeans, specializing in the foodstuffs and furs that were valued by the newcomers. They had long since learned to be wary of European traders, who often misused alcohol and information to gain the upper hand. Notable too was the long history of land transactions in which Indians found themselves progressively isolated or displaced. In the recent past, the native residents of the Lehigh Valley had suffered the indignities of the Walking Purchase, through which Pennsylvania's authorities defrauded the Delaware of a broad swath of land on the northeastern end of the province—land on which the Moravians had, not coincidentally, built Bethlehem. Yet the Mid-Atlantic remained a multiethnic territory, and the region's Indians lived in close contact with whites. Constant trade in skins, brooms, baskets, and other small products connected the two groups, as did the growing practice of Indians working for whites as day laborers. But the Indian economy offered fewer, not more, possibilities as time went on, and this dismal fact created chronic poverty among the Indians and shaped all economic relationships in the missions.[49]

Economic relationships between the Moravians and the Indians among whom they worked began in the missions themselves. Missionaries subordinated economic choices to religious ones in the mission context, and they used the Moravians' customary economic flexibility to sustain good relationships. Indeed, the primary goal was to maintain positive contact with the Indians. Furthermore, financial losses were justified if they bore other fruit. For example, the Moravians responded positively to a request from Shamokin, an Indian town on the Susquehanna, for a smith. Bethlehem's leaders complied despite the fact that the effort never made a noticeable profit, because "something will come of it which can be counted to pay for some of the costs." In addition, the religious returns would, from Bethlehem's perspective, make the expenditure worthwhile; if they did not, the missionary would never have been sent. Responsiveness to the economic needs of the Indians facilitated religious work.[50]

Economic flexibility was equally important in Gnadenhütten, the mission that was the most nearly integrated into Bethlehem's Oeconomy, and it extended to questioning the very structure of the mission's economy and, ultimately, moving from a communal system to a privatized system at the behest of the Indian residents. Founded in 1746, Gnadenhütten grew dramatically in 1747, when a group of refugees from the mission in Shekomeko, New York, arrived. The newly enlarged mission struggled with both internal dissent and limited resources. Many Indians began to object to the community's practice of sharing goods, though the practice had roots both in Moravian economic habit in Bethlehem and also in native economic traditions. Initially, Moravian missionaries tried to discourage the trend of Indians "living for themselves," urging native converts to think through the consequences of severing the economic ties they shared with missionaries, consequences that would clearly be negative from the missionaries' perspective. Yet they also assured the converts "that we would care just as well for those who lived alone, for themselves, if they have a heart that is given over to the Savior." On the other hand, if such people did not "behave well, [and] brought disgrace to the Savior and His people, and we showed them much patience and they did not want to change, we would ask them to leave again." There were more direct costs to leaving the community as well: "And when we also had something to eat and to drink, so we would give it first to those who work with us and were obedient and satisfied."[51]

The complaints did not end, however, and missionaries soon had to confront the fact that most of Gnadenhütten's native residents wanted to change the town's economic organization. In addition, missionaries had found that "our table is too small," meaning that they too lacked enough food to support the enlarged mission community.[52] Residents gathered to consider their options in late August 1747, and the missionaries agreed to divide mission land among different Indian families, so that each family would support itself from its own plot. It bears mentioning, of course, that the Moravians here entertained only the prospect of a new living arrangement, not of a fundamental shift in land ownership: at no time did the missionaries discuss giving the Indians outright title to pieces of land, nor did the Indians seem to have sought such an arrangement explicitly. Yet, the Indians had requested that their communal household be dissolved because it made them too dependent on the missionaries. From the missionaries' perspective, this was another opportunity to demonstrate their willingness to serve the Indians. It was, Bishop Cammerhof reported to Zinzendorf in the spring of 1748, "very significant and important that we can give the Indians land, because otherwise all white people take their land." Indeed, the group quite consciously considered its relations to Indians to be generous. "For the Little Lamb no little herd is too small," Cammerhof continued, "and for us also not, and we are still also gladly generous among and toward the Indians, from whom we already, from other corners, have difficulties." Had the Moravians been dogmatically invested in an ideological communalism, or even too invested in dominating the nature of the economy in the missions, they might very well have limited their influence among the Indians. But just as the Oeconomy was pragmatic, so too was the Moravian approach to the missions' economic forms.[53]

But economic flexibility was not the same as indifference to the moral dimensions of trade. Missionaries viewed economic contacts as more than a way to bring in converts; they were also opportunities to teach Christian behavior and to distinguish the Moravians from less scrupulous Europeans. When unfamiliar Indians frequented the mill in Gnadenhütten, the missionaries inquired as to the reason, reporting, presumably with pride, their reply "that the other millers scoop so much that they received hardly any grain."[54] They also used their transactions with the Indians as occasions to model what they considered moral business practice. The same standards of transparency and fairness that Moravians required in their regional trade applied in the missions. Christian Indians, when trading with the brethren, were instructed to avoid haggling—trading in the worldly fashion—and to use as few words as possible when they struck a bargain. Those engaged in commerce, whether Indian or European, should if possible transact business in cash; outstanding debts could only cause problems. Above all, industriousness—the capital Protestant economic virtue—appeared as a guiding principle. Those guilty of laziness were chastised, while the industry of others received praise.[55]

The missionaries tried to teach Native Americans what they considered to be moral trading practices, but rather than demanding that Christian Indians trade only with Moravians, or conform to a European version of civilization, they seem to have provided a sort of safety net. Whether this passive approach to economic missionizing grew out of philosophy or learned experience that they could compel their converts to do very little is difficult to ascertain. Certainly, Indians regularly left on hunting journeys, and they sought out their own markets for the goods they produced. This was particularly true in the mission at Pachgatgoch, which was at a much greater distance from Bethlehem than Gnadenhütten was. There, missionaries tried to help Indians deal with their ties to the white economy by navigating debts, and they recorded the efforts of individuals to sell their wares on the open market.[56] Likewise, in Gnadenhütten, missionaries did not compel the Indians to trade at the mission store, but did provide what they considered good fallback options. On May 10, 1748, European Moravians Lischert and Lesley returned to Gnadenhütten from the nearby town of Allemängel with wheat. "Shortly after them," reported the community diarist, "also returned [Indians] Joshua, Nathanael and David. They could not get wheat in Allemängel for under 4 s 6 d, so they took our offer and picked up 3 s. from our wheat."[57] Through such daily interactions, missionaries integrated themselves into the lives of their congregations, economic and otherwise, and used those relationships to ingratiate themselves. Money could be used to further the shared religious goals of missionary work, but Indians retained a great deal of autonomy over the nature of their own economic lives.

The missions blended together multiple economic practices, some rooted in native practice, some deriving from Moravian influence, and some a part of the larger frontier economy. Most of the Indians' support in the missions came from their own labors. Men hunted for food and for furs to trade on the market, and labored for wages both in the missions and outside them. Women performed agricultural labor, gathered foodstuffs from the surrounding forests, and made items that could be sold in the marketplace, especially brooms and baskets. They also, like their husbands, worked for wages in the surrounding frontier communities. These activities recreated a traditional gendered division of labor among the Mahican and Delaware who lived in Gnadenhütten, in which women farmed and gathered food while men hunted, but they also reflected the growing presence of an interracial frontier economy. Native men and women alike engaged in the cash economy and came into regular contact, via trade, with Moravian and non-Moravian Europeans. In a further evolution, by the 1750s men also moved into agricultural production, traditionally the realm of female labor, under the influence of the Moravian missionaries, and the kinds of crops they produced also changed. Wheat and barley joined the corn in the fields around the missions; those harvests could either be sold for cash or consumed.[58]

Missionaries played complicated roles in the economic lives of the missions. They were simultaneously representatives of European society who had access to the capital, resources, and skills of the international Moravian church network, and also individuals on the frontier, struggling against the same difficult conditions their converts faced. Thus, during the hard times just before Gnadenhütten's communal economy was dissolved, Anna Mack worried about what she could cook for dinner one night, and the actions of one of the Indian converts solved her dilemma. "As she thought this," the community diarist wrote, "so a young deer came near to our house, and Phillipus shot it and so we had immediately something to cook." Missionaries had to collect wood and look to their material well-being in other ways as well.[59] And yet, these apostolic pilgrims also had undeniable advantages compared with the Indian residents of the missions. Regular letters tied them to Bethlehem, where they could retreat for respite and comfort. Their children were assured lives of relative comfort and safety in Bethlehem or Herrnhut.

Indeed, even the comings and going of the *Irene* were reported to missionaries, so that they too were connected to the church's international projects. Unlike so many Native Americans, their poverty and trials were essentially voluntary[60] (Figure 6).

Over time, the missionaries' distinct economic role in the missions only increased, as the missions, particularly Gnadenhütten, came to depend more

Figure 6. Anna Mack was a missionary in Gnadenhütten. Portrait by Johann Valentine Haidt. Courtesy Moravian Archives, Bethlehem.

directly on the Moravians. Simultaneously, those of the Moravians' economic relationships to Indians that were transactional—between two independent financial actors—declined, only to be replaced, from Bethlehem's perspective, by a more one-sided set of ties in which Moravians supported Indians. As Indians continued to suffer in poor conditions, missionaries guided them down a path that entailed greater dependence and greater assimilation to Moravian models. Increasingly, Gnadenhütten's economy focused on Bethlehem. Boards from the sawmill floated down the Lehigh, deerskins, baskets, and brooms made in the mission were sold there, and firewood collected from nearby also went down to the central town. The Indians found themselves with decreasing options. Missionaries addressed the situation as they could. At a conference in early December 1750, they reminded their flock that it was essential "to be very careful with respect to the buying and selling of goods with white people, and particularly to avoid making any debts." The Moravians also sought to correct what they viewed as a lack of proper planning and foresight. The Indians should "arrange their households so that they could live and survive not just during the hunting time and during the winter, but also in spring." That meant, the missionaries continued, that "the Brethren, who go hunting, think also of the poor and old and widowed in Gnadenhütten, and also bring them meat and the like and give it to them."[61]

Mission Indians inhabited a more stable place in the frontier economy than did their non-mission kin, but they still faced significant, and increasing, hardships. In January 1752, a group of Moravian leaders from Bethlehem visited the town and convened another conference. The meeting was composed of both "white and brown," and included the some of the most important leaders of each community, both male and female. The conference began with Joseph Spangenberg "remembering the brown [people] here and their poverty." While the Indians were objectively less economically stable than European Moravians, it should also be noted that the perception that the Indians were destitute also functioned to position the missionaries as their rescuers, and opened a space for the Moravians to take a more active role in guiding Gnadenhütten's economy. Spangenberg reported that he was sympathetic, but wanted to give good advice, if the peoples were to work as one. Nathanael, an Indian man, spoke up next, saying that he was no longer able to feed his family through hunting, as he had in the past. Another native convert, Abraham, added that he too could no longer hunt, then said that "when I was last in Bethlehem, I received shovels to make, which I now do, and when that is at an end, must find something else." As a group, the Indian men felt they were at their limits. "I often have had thoughts on these matters," added another Indian man, "I do not always trust such thoughts in my heart, however. I have thought often of the poor, I would gladly like to help them. I cannot do it though, but I have sympathy with them."[62]

Spangenberg responded to these statements of distress with suggestions of wage labor that only emphasized the superior economic position the Moravian missionaries had with respect to their flock. He defined the work, such as cutting wood for the sawmill, cleaning wheat, harvesting, making rails and cordwood, and cutting the branches from surrounding trees to burn for tar, as "very useful and for their best." Spangenberg thus directed the Indians into economic activities that would benefit Bethlehem: cordwood, wood from the sawmill, and tar were necessary resources. Yet for the Indian men in particular (whom the missionaries viewed as each family's primary breadwinner) this represented a significant departure from supporting their families through hunting, and a move toward working exclusively in a wage labor environment. Martin Mack, one of the missionaries who lived in Gnadenhütten full time, framed the transition for the Indians in terms that placed Protestant values of work at the fore. He "presented to them how necessary, useful, and becoming it is, when children of God work diligently, and comport themselves in an orderly fashion, and behave as an example to each other and to the other white Brethren in Gnadenhütten." The Indians, when asked at this point for their opinions, responded that the plan was a good one, though not because of the moral value of work. They based their assent, rather, on the problems that made hunting impossible, suggesting they had few other options[63] (Figure 7).

The 1752 conference was a pivotal moment in the nature of the economic ties connecting Bethlehem to its missions. From the Indian perspective, becoming more reliant on missionaries for daily life provided a route out of poverty, or at least the potential for its amelioration. For the missionaries, the new economic relationships represented a different sort of change. For most of the history of Moravian missions in North America, economic ties had been built to further missionary work, rather than directly to make money. Profit was less important than the potential benefits of building economic ties. Whether it was sending a smith to Shamokin or feasting on a felled deer in order to fend off hunger, missionaries had used economic tools to gain and retain access to Indians who might hear their message and become Christian.

Figure 7. Sketch of the Moravian Indian mission at Gnadenhütten, Ts.Mp.205.5. Courtesy Unity Archives, Herrnhut.

The Moravians had been, in other words, using financial transactions as a way to negotiate with Indians, a pattern that was quite different from efforts to "civilize" Indians by forcing them to conform to white agricultural or economic patterns. It is possible the strategy found success because it coincided with the Indians' understanding that trading goods carried meanings that could not be quantified, such as friendship or reciprocity.[64] By 1752, however, Christian Indians in eastern Pennsylvania were in difficult straits, and the Moravians, by virtue of their access to the European-American economy, could dictate rules of economic life in the missions in much broader ways than they had before, because their converts were that much more vulnerable. In the new environment, missionaries no longer simply suggested the value of moral economic behavior to their native converts (who could, after all, choose to trade in the mission or elsewhere), they instead defined the terms of Gnadenhütten's economic life and couched that relationship in the language of Protestant industriousness. The Indians moved from being transactional partners to being recipients of charity and ethical lessons.

The consequences of this shift in the economic relationship between

Bethlehem and the missions were reflected in Bethlehem's economic record as well, as Indians moved from being economic partners, even if not particularly profitable ones, to being the recipients of charity. Whereas before, Indians had appeared in Bethlehem's account books as individuals capable of purchasing goods and even receiving credit, afterwards Indians appeared only as members of groups at whom missionary efforts were directed. Many accounts representing economic relationships between the Bethlehem Gemeine and natives, particularly those accounts held by individual Indians, simply vanished. Where such ties had previously been used as opportunities to build missionary relationships, they were now largely disregarded, at least in Bethlehem. The Moravians stopped subjecting their trading relations with natives to the complex calculus that balanced shared religious goals, the bottom line, and moral economic behavior, and missionary work now became quite simply a cost of the community's shared religious life.

A brief examination of the account books kept in Gnadenhütten illustrates the change. During the years before 1752, Indians in Gnadenhütten could run accounts with the missionaries. On the debit side, they received small items such as strouds and nails. To balance their accounts they sold skins, brooms, and baskets to the missionaries, or worked in the sawmill. Nearly all Indians in the account books were in debt at the end of 1751, however, as the economic situation deteriorated. Only a few accounts contain any entries at all for the period between 1752 and 1755, when the mission was destroyed in an attack during the Seven Years' War, and a significant number of those records belonged to Indians not a part of the mission, but rather visiting from elsewhere. Gnadenhütten itself even dropped from the Bethlehem accounts in 1753, two years before the mission there ended, and in September 1756, after the destruction of Gnadenhütten, most of the remaining accounts—including the majority of those inactive since 1751—were forgiven. In Bethlehem's account books, where Indians had long been peripheral but present, individual missions and even many individual Indians disappeared from the record as the costs of missionary work were transferred to the Society for the Furtherance of the Gospel, a charity organization which was not expected to *earn* anything, only steer money to the Moravians' shared work of evangelizing. Indians ceased to be transactional partners and became, simply, costs.[65]

Other more distant missions, such as Pachgatgoch, in Connecticut, continued for a time to have an independent economic existence after this transition, but for the most part the Moravians' work among the Indians had turned a corner, the consequences of which would only become clear in the 1760s. In the meantime, from the perspective of Bethlehem's economic life, the importance of financial ties to Indians during the 1740s and 1750s should not be neglected. During that period, the Moravians applied the same economic logic in their relationships to Indians as they did in their ties to the regional and international economies. Bethlehem's leaders balanced the various needs of shared religious work, financial imperatives, and the requirement to maintain moral economic behavior, in order to shape a wide variety of market-based relationships. They responded to new economic opportunities in the missions, and, even though they subordinated profit to religious work in that context, their careful account-keeping indicates that they did not lose sight of the bottom line. Their economic lives, as they conceived them, thus extended from the mission sites of Shamokin, Pachgatgoch, and Gnadenhütten all the way to the port cities of New York, London, and Amsterdam. When missionaries rejoiced in the news of the *Irene*'s arrival, and reported Van Vleck's doings in the mission records, they indicated just that.

The Moravians built a complicated international economy, and they benefited from its opportunities even as they took care to act in a way that conformed with their beliefs. But no amount of prudent planning or scrupulous accounting could protect the Moravians from the consequences of engaging in the Atlantic, regional, and frontier economies, no more than it could from the reality that the Moravians' religious networks, which extended far beyond Bethlehem's confines, exposed the community to the same forces to which all early Americans were exposed. Unfortunately, during the century's middle decades, those consequences of those networks and connections were dire. Religious and military events far removed from Bethlehem's artisans, the *Irene*'s cargo manifests, or Gnadenhütten's sawmill changed the Moravians' economy forever, and forced Bethlehem's residents to find a new way to understand their labors. They had created a world in which their community, their missions, and their desire to unify the Atlantic's evangelicals all provided incentives for work and meaning for their lives. They had developed an intricate financial network to pay the costs of their responsibilities while doing so in manner they considered responsible. The outside world, however, would soon complicate their plans.

CHAPTER 5

Atlantic Currents: Global War and the Fate of Moravian Communalism

THE MEMBERS OF the Moravian community at Bethlehem pursued ordered lives centered on devotion to Christ and mission work. Internal dissent was rare; leaders exercised their prodigious authority over individuals' lives without much interference. Evangelists traveled in and out of town and to and from the West Indies. They married, had children, and brought those children to Bethlehem to be raised. New workers arrived from Herrnhut, and others returned to Europe for new assignments. The course of Moravian life that emerges from most of Bethlehem's records recounts daily matters marred only by minor inconveniences. This picture accurately describes Bethlehem during the Oeconomy, but only up to a point. Bethlehem's internal harmony existed within a far more clamorous world from which the little enclave was hardly immune. Quite the opposite: because the Moravians actively engaged the world around them, as evangelists and as businesspeople, Bethlehem's history became intertwined with the course of global events.

During the latter years of the Oeconomy, the world was torn apart by the Seven Years' War, an international conflagration that Winston Churchill would later call the first world war. In that conflict, the local and the international intertwined, clashed, and folded back on one another. It was the result of nearly three centuries of Atlantic exchange. The same sorts of ties that knit together Moravians in Bethlehem, London, Amsterdam, and Herrnhut bound together people of all walks of life and multiplied in countless ways to

create a single Atlantic world, at once extraordinarily diverse and deeply interconnected. Imperial conflicts that began in London and Paris started military campaigns in New England. Merchants kept one another apprised of
events and markets a world away. Ministers in the New World reported on
events in the Old, and vice versa. Shocks on one continent were thus quickly
felt in another, and the Moravians, who had settled communities in nearly
every corner of the Atlantic world, were insulated from very little. Pennsylvania, like the Moravians, was also in the thick of things during the middle
decades of the eighteenth century. The combustible combination of imperial
competition and native displacement in western Pennsylvania ignited the
spark that set off the Seven Years' War. In that conflict, Bethlehem was not
just on the frontier, it was on the front line. Those volatile years, superheated
by racial violence, changed Bethlehem in fundamental ways, and the experience forced the town's essential mission projects to adapt and readapt in a
changing religious and political landscape.

Bethlehem's residents engaged in an extended discussion about the fate
of their communal Oeconomy during the war years, even as they fended off
threats from outside. Though leaders drew no explicit connection between
increasing frustration with the communal structure and the war, the difficulties and dangers of those years certainly strained a system that had already
grown far larger than anyone had intended. Bethlehem still fulfilled its role
as a base for missionaries, a pilgrim congregation, but it had become more
than that as well. The people who lived there considered it home, and a generation of children knew no other place. The town's residents had an investment in what they had built, and they considered the Oeconomy of equal
importance to the missionary work it supported. Town leaders, particularly
"Joseph" Spangenberg, valued Bethlehem's unique status as a pilgrim congregation, but were also concerned about where it was headed. With good
cause they worried about whether it could be sustained, both financially and
spiritually. Moravian leaders in Germany also began to reconsider Bethlehem's economic form. The war exacerbated serious financial problems for
the Unity, and Herrnhut's governors suspected that the Oeconomy prevented Bethlehem's Moravians from shouldering as many burdens as they
otherwise might have done. During its last five years, the Oeconomy
reached its pinnacle, but it teetered there with its purpose under debate and
its future in doubt, as Bethlehem weathered its era of greatest and most
rapid transformation.

War on Many Fronts

Although missionary Christian Henry Rauch had once found the peace of mind to sleep among unknown Indians in the mission field, by the mid-1750s, true tranquility became elusive on the Mid-Atlantic frontier. The imperial forces that held the province's northern and western regions in their grip began to close in, causing the frontier to ignite in a bloody guerrilla war. The flash point was the Ohio Valley, a fertile area claimed by both the British and French empires despite being home to a substantial Indian population, including Delaware communities who were seeking to avoid both European encroachment and Iroquois domination. Once fighting in that region began in 1754, the British and Americans quickly proved their inability to handle either the complexities of Indian diplomacy or the difficulties of frontier warfare. By the summer of 1755, the Virginia and Pennsylvania borders collapsed in a wave of violence, bringing Bethlehem into the theater of conflict. The Delaware, among whom the Moravians had many mission contacts, faced the ire of all parties, and they were themselves divided between western groups striving to avoid the hegemonic imperial powers around them and eastern groups following a more accommodationist strategy. The fighting also made racial lines between whites and Indians, frequently blurred in the practical negotiations of daily life, stand out in increasingly sharp relief. For whites, all those with Indian ties became newly and deeply suspect. Bethlehem's neighbors had accused the Moravians of having dangerous pro-Indian and thus pro-French sympathies for years because of their close ties to the Indians, and their situation now became distinctly precarious.[1]

They did not know it, but Bethlehem's Moravians, the native people whom they had converted, and all the other residents of Pennsylvania and the Ohio Valley had just become embroiled in a war that would engulf the world before it was through. Though it is perhaps most convenient to call it the Seven Years' War, the conflict that stretched from the Ohio Valley to Calcutta has no good name, perhaps because its startlingly global character was as challenging for people of the eighteenth century to assimilate as it is for historians of the twenty-first. British colonists in North America fought against the French and the Indians, and so the North American portion has gone by "the French and Indian War," but that name obscures the global nature of the war, as well as the truth that native peoples were engaged on all sides of the struggle. In Europe, it was the Seven Years' War, referring to the period between

1756 and 1763, when peace treaties ended the European fights. But the formal declaration of war in 1756 came only after two years of fighting in North America, and peace did not return there until 1765, eleven (arguably twelve) years after it began. The "Great War for Empire" might best describe the Franco-British portion of the war. Those two powers had been vying over territories, islands, and continents for centuries, and this culminating conflict took place in the Caribbean, on the Indian subcontinent, and in North America. But that name too is insufficient, in light of the conflict in continental Europe, touched off when Prussia's Frederick II invaded Saxony and engaged Austria, Russia, France, and Britain in a struggle for control of Europe.[2]

In truth, the unmanageable complexity of the war reflected the nature of the eighteenth-century world. Global empires stretched out from European powers, knitting together the fates of peoples on distant continents. Yet those empires were, by the standards of later centuries, only vague gestures at centralized political entities. Leaders in European capitals had little practical control on the ground in places like the Pennsylvania frontier. Regional conflicts, such as the corrosive struggle over land between Euro-American settlers and Native Americans, prodded the empires into fighting, but they could not be solved by great-power negotiations. In the conflict that resulted, local fights and imperial struggles joined each other in a terrible synergy that fed off ties between continents that had been two hundred years in the making. The wars may have appeared separate to those on the ground—what did Frederick's lust for Silesia have to do with the Delaware's fight to maintain their homelands, for example—but they were in fact utterly interwoven.

The Moravians' experience illustrates the pervasiveness of the war. Bethlehem lay at the heart of much of Pennsylvania's fighting, and, in a different theater entirely, Herrnhut also found itself on the front lines. When Frederick invaded Saxony on his way to Silesia, his armies marched through Herrnhut. The Moravian central town had the misfortune to be situated just a few miles from the Saxon-Silesian border. The location was hardly coincidental; the town's original settlers had fled Catholic Austria and settled just inside Protestant territory. During the war years, armies, whether marching, camping, or fighting, became a regular fixture. In July of 1757, a Moravian leader wrote from Holland to update Bethlehem on events in the town so many members of the Unity considered home. "But what do you think of our wretched war in Saxony, and Herrnhut already almost a year between both armies?" he exclaimed. "What we have already endured in fear and worry over dear Herrnhut!" The winter had seen almost daily visits by Prussian princes and generals, and then the spring had brought the Austrians in equal measure. Though no Moravians had been hurt, the "whole countryside is completely ruined, it can well be imagined, by the constant foraging to the two armies. The people in this area have nothing left to live on, and this winter many hundreds will die or have to leave the region."[3]

More news arrived via Barby and London, reporting Herrnhut's place in the center of the action of the 1757 campaigns. "I can't help sending you the News just now received here;" wrote one British Moravian to another, "our Brethren sent it by a messenger to Dresden, the Post being now at an End in Lusatia for the present." He continued: "Zittau is certainly burnt entirely down, & the Prussians obliged to fly; the greatest part went thro Ruppersdorf, but so many thro our little City as to fill it; they begged Bread from House to House." One hungry army was problem enough, but in war they tended to come in pairs. "The next day the Austrians came," the report continued, "& their Van meeting the Prussian Rear, a Skirmish ensued before our Count Henry's Door. He [and two other Moravians] waited on [Austrian Marshal Leopold J. von] Daun & the Saxon Princes. 2 Prussian Princes were also there." The Moravians fortunately avoided any harm, but the welcoming party's members "were detained to Dinner, & whilst in the Tent, a Canon-Ball from the Prussian Side fell at the Tent-Door, so they had a narrow Escape." As the Prussians had done the season before, the Austrians provided the Moravians an order of protection. They also "employ the [brothers and sisters] with Work, & pay very orderly." The Moravians were deeply grateful that no one had been hurt in all the chaos, but times were difficult nonetheless, as "the Corn &c. is all trod down about Herrnhuth with the March of both Parties."[4]

Moravians throughout the world tried to carry on as usual despite the war. The naval conflict hit them particularly hard. Henry Van Vleck and his colleagues continued to send the *Irene* on regular trips across the ocean, and they even imported arms for New York City on one occasion. They knew of the dangers, but they valued their religious work and community more than they feared the consequences of political instability. Unfortunately their gamble failed. The ship sailed from New York for the last time on November 20, 1757. She was full of cargo, including a "Large parcell Indigo & Coffee." Van Vleck instructed Captain Jacobsen to "Ransom her as Cheap as he possibly Can but not to Exceed £2000 Sterling" if they were taken by privateers. Andreas Schoute, a Moravian sailor, "will goe as Hostage."[5] Nothing more was heard in Bethlehem for months. In April 1758, five months after the ship departed, Bethlehem still waited anxiously for information, thinking of "our *Irene* with the wish that an angel will soon bring us news of her." The first report came on May 19, announcing that a privateer from Louisbourg had taken the ship. On June 9, letters from Europe confirmed the story, adding that Captain Jacobsen was in prison in France. Finally, in September of 1758, Schoute arrived unexpectedly in Bethlehem to tell the whole story.[6]

On November 20, 1757, the *Irene* had sailed from New York harbor. Nine days out the crew spotted a ship flying British colors, but

> Mistrusting the stranger, we showed no colors, but crowded on all sail in the hope of effecting our escape. Hereupon the stranger ran up the French flag. It was now a trial of speed, in the course of which the *Irene* gave proof of her excellent sailing qualities, but at eleven o'clock at night our storm-sails parted. The privateer now gained rapidly upon us, and as she did so fired shot after shot. I counted thirty, not including the volleys from small arms. It being bright moonlight and no further hope of escape in our disabled condition, we backed our sails, and at midnight our ill-fated vessel was boarded—Lat. 36° Long. 62°.[7]

After the French took control of the ship, "Capt. Jacobsen and two of the crew were immediately transferred on board the privateer," and a French crew came aboard. The privateer captain ordered his sailors to head for Louisbourg, but instead they sailed around, seemingly without destination, for four weeks while "the supply of provisions ran short, so that our daily allowance was a quart of water and three biscuits." The Moravians on the *Irene* found comfort in their faith, and "in all this time of harassing uncertainty, we did not fail to meet in the evenings for singing, and on Saturday for praying the Litany," according to Schoute.

The ship finally sank on January 12, 1758, six weeks after her capture. She had wandered in among some breakers during a foggy morning, and she struck them shortly after the weather cleared. The ship filled with water, and, according to the ever-modest Schoute (whom the French had apparently not chosen to hold for ransom), only his quick thinking saved those on board. "The Frenchmen became so demoralized that I ordered the boat launched, into which we all got (twenty-two in number) and rowed for the shore, which we reached in safety but wet to the skin. On landing the French captain fell upon my neck, kissed and thanked me for saving the lives of us all. . . . The next morning only the masts of the *Irene* were to be seen above water." Despite the loss of the ship, Schoute's adventures were not over yet. French officials in Louisbourg imprisoned him until that town was captured by the British, at which time he slowly made his way back to Bethlehem to tell his story. Meanwhile, Captain Jacobsen and the other crew members who had been taken aboard the privateer had been transported to France, from where they eventually returned safely to their friends in Europe.[8]

The *Irene*'s loss struck the Moravians a severe blow. The community depended on transatlantic communication and travel. The monthly Congregation Days celebrated throughout the Moravian world relied on the regular transmission of news. Missionaries in distant places were even more dependent on communication than those in larger communities, not just for religious life, but also for crucial practical support. Church leaders immediately looked to repair the damage of the ship's loss. Brother Broderson, a British Moravian, wrote to Spangenberg in April 1758, "You see, my dear heart, from Br. Schmaling's letter, that all the Congregation Reports and letters that the *Irene* brought with her were thrown into the sea; to replace the loss, you could, as much as possible, try to help with duplicates." Some items were irreplaceable: "in the correspondence, there will be some lacunae and [they] must remain for a time." The war's "disturbances" upset the most basic parts of the Moravians' tightly coordinated community.[9]

For the Moravians in Pennsylvania, the missions and the mission project bore most of the brunt of the Seven Years' War. The imperial and racial violence of the conflict threatened their ability to proselytize among the Indians, exactly that facet of their religious work that had become central to Moravian mission work during the preceding decade. For residents of Bethlehem, connections to Pennsylvania's Indians had been a regular feature of daily life as well as the justification for their unique economic arrangements. The town itself had a small number of native residents who were integrated into the Choir system, and the community's schools in particular received the children of baptized Indians, though not always to the pleasure of the children themselves.[10] Beyond these individual contacts between European and native Moravians were the network of mission communities throughout the region. Gnadenhütten, to the northwest of Nazareth on the Lehigh River, stood out as the principal mission settlement. It was the most visible and proximate connection between the congregants in Bethlehem and their religious work, and, as a partially integrated part of the communal Oeconomy, it was also a branch of Bethlehem's household and family. "Ah our dear Gnadenhütten," wrote Bishop Cammerhof, "where the marks of [Christ's] wounds so dearly shine light on our dear brown people that [they make] one's heart flutter, when one thinks of them."[11] That mission's presence so nearby inspired Bethlehem as simple mission reports could not.

Disaster struck on the evening of November 24, 1755, when a group of Delaware Indians attacked. Neighbors had told the missionaries at Gnadenhütten that armed men would arrive during the night to protect them, so when a dog started barking outside during dinner, those seated around the table in the mission house assumed it was their guards and opened the door. According to the report later sent to Pennsylvania's governor, four barrels immediately emptied into the room, killing one person. A ball from this volley "grazed" the chin of Joseph Sturgis, and "set his Hair on Fire." Another round killed some of the diners "on the Spot," while "the rest [ran] into an Adjoining Room from whence [George] Partsch escaped through a Window." Sturgis and seven others, including a child, fled up the stairs and slammed a trap door, hoping to keep their attackers at bay, but their assailants shot through the ceiling. Sturgis and Partsch's wife escaped through a window, but the rest perished when fire engulfed the house. The attackers also burned the barns and stables, killing "40 head of Cattle therein besides 5 Horses & 3 Colts, & also to the rest of the Houses & Buildings." When Partsch and Sturgis returned the next day, they found an eerie signature: "a Blanket & a Hat with a Knife stuck thro' them upon the Stump of a Tree which I have heard is a signal among the Indians 'This much we have done & are able to do more.'" Before it was over, eleven members of the Bethlehem community—all of them European Moravians—were dead, the mission was destroyed, and refugees, both white and Indian, were straggling into Bethlehem.[12]

The Gnadenhütten attack provided the Moravians with new opportunities and new challenges vis-à-vis their Euro-American neighbors. The fact that they too had become targets seemingly justified their protestations of loyalty to Pennsylvania and the British. Many in the Mid-Atlantic region had long suspected that the Moravians—with their strange economic system and their many ties to Indians—might be in league with the French, were certainly unreliable neighbors, and could even be papists. These suspicions had only increased as the war broke out. In the days leading up to the attack, Bethlehem's situation had been tense, to say the least. A story representative of general sentiment toward the Moravians had been printed in the *New York Mercury* the preceding week. It recounted that when a group of militia had tried to buy gunpowder in Bethlehem, someone there (presumably a Moravian, and thus also presumably a French sympathizer) "laughed at the Man for a Fool" and refused to sell the supplies. In response, the company's officers "sent the *Moravians* Word, by three honest and sober Men, that if they did not send them Powder, they would actually come and burn their Buildings to Ashes." Apparently, according to the newspaper, the threat did the trick, because "upon this they sent it."[13] The Moravians responded to these accusations by printing their side of the story, but only to limited effect. "I don't so much as suppose 'tis in my Power," wrote Timothy Horsfield, a leading member of the community and one of Northampton County's justices of the peace, "to convince the World of [the Moravians'] Innocency, either in this Aspersion, of refusing the People Powder, or of their having joined the *French* and Indians and supplying them with Powder, Guns, &c. or in many others, that in a most wicked and base Manner, are laid to their Charge." Nonetheless, Horsfield insisted, the Moravians were loyal to the Crown: "But for my own Part, I am satisfied, and fully assured, of their being good and faithful Subjects to our most gracious Sovereign, King GEORGE the Second; and have not the least scruple, will be found so by every impartial Enquirer."[14]

The attack on Gnadenhütten changed this tense equation. It offered vivid proof that the Moravians were on the side of their Pennsylvanian neighbors, or at least not in league with the Indians, and Spangenberg admitted as much even as he gave the news to his congregation at dawn the next morning. "As it seems that some of our Brothers and Sisters became victims, certainly out of the wise intentions of the Savior that are quite unknown to us," he explained, "but yet our neighbors can now see that we do not hold with the French." This was cause for relief, "since we have been in danger for some days of being attacked by a mob, that freely said [']before we campaign against the enemy, no stone in Bethlehem can remain on top another.[']"[15]

Over the next several years, the Moravians negotiated a complex strategy of protecting their remaining missions and converts, working with Pennsylvania's government and élites in furtherance of the war effort, and trying to fend off continued hostility from neighbors. The town served as a hub for military planning, a haven for both white and Indian refugees, and a base for Indians attending the treaties in Easton. Benjamin Franklin, in his capacity as a provincial commissioner of the new militia, visited Bethlehem on December

19, 1756, and stayed in the area through January. He was favorably impressed with the Moravians' preparations for their defense, and he described them positively in his *Autobiography*. The commissioners organized the building of a series of forts along the Blue Mountains, including Fort Allen near what remained of Gnadenhütten, a plan that Spangenberg had been suggesting to the governor and other provincial officials for some time. Horsfield, the community's principal liaison with Pennsylvania officialdom, maintained a periodic correspondence with the governor, managing both details of defense and the financial problems created by war. The Moravians shouldered substantial burdens of the latter type, hosting both refugees and also visiting Indians (some Christian but many not) on behalf of the colony, because of the war's dislocations and also because of the nearby treaty talks at Easton.[16]

The treaty talks held at Easton, first in 1756 and then again in 1758, kept Bethlehem in the middle of the action of Pennsylvania's Indian diplomacy, even as they also required substantial attention from the town's leaders. Because their ties to the Indians had become useful to the provincial government, however, the Moravians were able to preserve a narrow zone of safety between hostile neighbors and their own religious commitments. Briefly, Bethlehem became the center of a form of interracial community as refugees from the missions and also Indians participating in treaty talks stayed in town, and thus the group's connections to missionary work were more visible than ever before.[17] The new situation also carried with it steep costs. In October 1756, Spangenberg wrote neighboring Moravian congregations, asking for help supporting converted Indians for whom the Oeconomy could not adequately care: "We have given them what work we can, and they have been diligent," he explained. "They have dug, chopped wood, mown grass, and done what they could, and for their earnings, they have acquired clothing and other necessities. We have given them land, corn to plant, and they reaped a considerable harvest. It's not enough, however, because there are many widows and orphans among them that still need help."[18] These expenses came on top of the damage done to Gnadenhütten. This was a very difficult time for the community financially, and the Moravians turned to outside sources for help, including both provincial authorities and private charity from Pennsylvania's Quaker community. Ultimately, however, Bethlehem's Oeconomy continued to bear the brunt of the costs, and opportunities for the Indians to support themselves remained limited. One chief means of procuring food, hunting, was impossible; the prospect of armed Indians searching through the forest for prey could only mean more danger. "Hunting they could not and may not do," the Elders' Conference wrote, "as long as the war flamed." Consequently, town leaders "had to think of work for them, at a time when it was hard for us to find money to give them something to earn so that they could at least acquire the necessary clothing."[19]

The Moravians eventually began to put the chaotic mission situation back into order with the establishment of a new Indian town, Nain, in 1758. It lay directly opposite Bethlehem across the Monocacy Creek, a few hundred yards from the buildings of the industrial quarter. Placing a mission near, but not in, Bethlehem followed Moravian precedent. During the 1740s the presence of a large Indian community in town had led to the creation of a short-lived mission called Friedenshütten adjoining Bethlehem on the banks of the Lehigh. In addition to Nain, Wechquetank, north of Nazareth across the Blue Mountains, followed in 1760, and these congregations, along with the persistent Pachgatgoch in New England, formed the remainder of Bethlehem's missionary work among Native Americans during the uneasy years between the end of fighting in Pennsylvania and the Paxton Boys crisis in the mid-1760s.

The new era of missionary work was quite different from the years that preceded it. Faithful Indians, particularly those in Nain, were now quite nearby, and yet new outreach to unconverted Indians living separate from Europeans virtually ended, as (in the words of a report made to Herrnhut) the community's missionaries "may not live among the Savages [*Wilden*], as we would then go body and soul to ground for it." This shift represented a geographic and spiritual contraction of Moravian outreach work in response to the changing nature of the racial environment around Bethlehem. The Moravians ceased to seek new mission fields, because such activities angered their neighbors and consequently endangered their existing settlements. At the same time, the Christian Indians, who had chosen to follow a path of greater accommodation with their white neighbors, found that they had few remaining options for refuge, and even Nain was hardly a bastion of interracial harmony. It adjoined Bethlehem, but its residents were part of a mission, not part of the town's congregation. The distinction between the two was important to European Moravians: though individual Indian converts had occasionally been incorporated into the Bethlehem Choirs over the past decades, the European Moravian congregation resisted the wholesale integration that would follow if all the refugees became part of Bethlehem proper, and it is likely that native leaders would have opposed such a move as well. The Moravians provided their Indian converts with shelter, yet a clear distinction between the two communities remained.[20]

The Moravians' compromise strategy of the late 1750s and early 1760s, maintaining a small number of missions and avoiding major efforts that would incite more anti-Moravian sentiment among frontier Pennsylvanians, worked for a short while, but was doomed to failure as interracial conflict in that region continued and accelerated. Between 1758 and 1763, Pennsylvania's diverse peoples enjoyed an uneasy truce, but the recent struggles for land and power, as well as the sharp memories of the violence those struggles had caused, had destroyed many of the informal strategies and relationships that had allowed the region to function peacefully before 1755. The word "enemy" took on new meaning: residents used newly sharpened racial categories of "white" and "Indian" to interpret their increasingly hostile environment. Economic relationships slowly developed again, though, as Jane Merritt has argued, the impetus behind trade was more about politics than profit in the unsteady postwar environment. New leaders emerged among the Indians, including religious innovators propounding a philosophy of separate creations for the two "races." Similarly, new waves of Europeans moved into the region and created further reasons for whites and Indians to distrust and even attack each other. When the Peace of Paris formally ended the imperial conflict in 1763, Pennsylvania's two major ethnic populations had come to see each other as racialized and hostile "others."[21]

Whither the Oeconomy?

By the time of the attack on Gnadenhütten in 1755, Bethlehem had entered its second decade. The town that weathered the crises of the Seven Years' War had grown into something quite different from the pilgrim congregation planted by travelers from the ill-fated Georgia project fourteen years before. The two parts of the larger Bethlehem pilgrim congregation, the missionary pilgrims and the house congregation (those at home in Bethlehem), remained intimately connected, but the Oeconomy developed a weight and permanence of its own. It supported more than twelve hundred people in 1758, and it demanded a great deal of attention from its leaders for matters from ever-changing work assignments to concerns that a cobbler might be pilfering from the till. Zinzendorf had admonished the residents of Bethlehem to maintain their "Pilgersinn," or sense of being pilgrims. But pilgrims were supposed to be a mobile group of evangelists able to travel wherever their mission took them, and the Oeconomy had taken on a decidedly settled feel, despite its ongoing and significant ties to missionary work. Indeed, the fortified town of the war years was prized for its stability and solidity. Bethlehem's residents had succeeded in their efforts to build a stable home, capable of supporting the work they hoped to carry out in the region, but the other side of the coin appeared to be the creation of something Moravian leaders had never intended: a substantial town with a communitarian economic structure. As this reality became inescapable, the extended Moravian community, leaders and lay people, councils in Herrnhut and in Bethlehem, struggled with the question of what to make of the Oeconomy.

Bethlehem's leaders had never planned for the Oeconomy to be a permanent economic system, and this colored their approach to the structure throughout its history. It had been founded as a matter of expediency, another of the Moravians' flexible economic accommodations, and leaders in town remained true to that interpretation. This outlook made the system itself eminently expendable, in their view. In May 1756, for example, the Jünger Conferenz, one of the many periodic governing bodies in Bethlehem during the 1750s, briefly considered ending the Oeconomy in an offhand manner that would appear shocking to most outsiders and probably those within town as well. The meeting's initial discussions that day were mundane, the ordinary governance of the community: "Francis Jons's daughter obtained permission to come to Bethlehem," and "Culver's son, who is still with his father, comes to Br. Hanke in Friedensthal." The Conference settled both of these issues through the Lot. Buried near the end of the day's discussions, the participants put the question of the Oeconomy before the Lot. In the meeting's minutes, the group recorded the four options it laid before the Savior:

> Regarding a change in—or ending of our communal housekeeping [*gemeinschaftliche Haushaltung*], it was asked with 4 Lots:
> 1) It is time that the change with our communal housekeeping is begun and is carried forward until it is completed.
> 2) It is the Savior's will that the communal housekeeping will continue as before.
> 3) The plan for the change is good, and has the Savior's approbation, but should first be communicated with [Zinzendorf].
> 4) Empty.

The final slip offered the option to reject all of the options laid before him, but the group drew the second Lot, indicating that Christ desired the Oeconomy to continue. This answer must have seemed incomplete to the town's leaders—containing some but not all of what they thought the Savior had to say to them—because they cast a further Lot asking whether a change in the Oeconomy must wait until either Zinzendorf or Johannes de Watteville arrived in Bethlehem. The Oeconomy's indefinite continuation could not, they believed, be God's plan, as it was neither part of wider Moravian economic practice, nor part of the congregation town ideal as defined by noncommunal Moravian towns, such as Herrnhut. But the Lot had nothing more to add, and the second query received a blank response. The members of the Jünger Conferenz may have been disappointed, but their question reveals the assumption on the part of those in charge of Bethlehem that the communal system would not endure forever. Quite the contrary, they merely waited for the right moment, and God's approval, to begin dismantling it.[22]

In early 1758, only two years later, discussion about ending the Oeconomy took place on a much wider scale and included a greater portion of the community. This was the only broad-based discussion of what the Oeconomy meant to its members during its existence, a fact that reflects the town's initial commitment to supporting missionary work through whatever economic system seemed expedient, rather than to communalism per se. In 1758, leaders still desired a change, and additionally some residents were dissatisfied with the arrangement as it was. On January 18, Spangenberg addressed the congregation, asking each member individually to express his or her feelings on the Oeconomy. He and the other "Conference" Brethren then discussed the responses with the individual Brothers and Sisters over the next few weeks. Four hundred thirty-nine written responses still exist, records that provide important insight into how ordinary Moravians viewed their Oeconomy. They represent the opinions of 36 percent of the 1,192 people associated with the communal household at that time. If one assumes that children and Indians were not polled, a likely scenario, the proportion is much higher.[23] The declarations' most striking characteristic is their universally positive tone of devotion and piety, a fact which strongly suggests that the compiled responses were edited, either by removing negative answers altogether or by excising disparaging passages.[24]

A few people confronted the possibility of ending the Oeconomy outright by stating that the system was both good and needed, and by asserting that it continued to support the church's religious work. These responses came from leaders and from those who merely followed obediently. Christian Frederick Oerter, the community bookkeeper and the person who best understood the financial intricacies of the communal structure, wrote, "The Oeconomy and communal housekeeping [*gemeinschaftliche Haushaltung*] is for us an important and respectable thing." He intended to stay within it "as long as the Oeconomy continues for the purpose and in the way it was at the beginning, and still is."[25] Other leaders also supported the system. Johannes Ettwein, who later guided Bethlehem through the Revolutionary War, understood that his position "regarding the Oeconomy is already well known, but I will do as my Brethren and also offer it in writing." For him, the Oeconomy was a "particularly wise and Godly system, which the dear Savior started here for us, for the support of His goals with the Brethren in America." In what was likely a reference to the war and the financial challenges it brought, he added that the system was well suited to the challenges the Moravians faced in their work, and thus Christ had chosen it "out of prudence for the times and circumstances that we have in part already seen and of which perhaps much is still concealed from us."[26]

Though neither Ettwein nor Oerter could be considered an average member of the Oeconomy because of their leadership positions, other less distinguished residents shared their sentiments. Johann Brandmüller, a Married Brother, "found in my heart nothing against the conditions of the Oeconomy" and felt content within it. David Tanneberger, a well-known organ maker, "had nothing to say about the Oeconomy," but "[believed] that it is good and needful for the affairs of the Savior."[27] Daniel Kunckler and his wife found the discussion unnecessary. They reported that they felt the same way about the Oeconomy as they had when they resolved to come to Pennsylvania in 1743. Likewise, Anna Maria Kraus had "in 14 years never asked herself how it would be" to live outside the Oeconomy; similarly, Johann Matthias Otto wrote that "it never occurred to me to want to be outside the Oeconomy."[28]

Indeed, for some, like Kraus and Otto, the Oeconomy may have come to be Bethlehem's central feature, more important even than its connection to religious outreach or its position as part of the larger Unity. Bethlehem's leaders had long expected to transform Bethlehem into a congregation town (*Ortsgemeine*) like Herrnhut. Some respondents specifically rejected this idea. Christian Werner, a Married Brother, wrote: "I do not require for myself to live in something like an Orts-Gemeine, rather, I am thankful from my heart that I can be in a communal housekeeping." Daniel Kliest agreed with him. "I want with my whole heart to be in the Oeconomy." No sacrifice was too great for Kliest. If it was required by so great a purpose, he was willing to "suffer hunger with God's people," and "go naked" if he had to.[29] Kliest and other like-minded residents of Bethlehem imbued the Oeconomy with religious meaning beyond its pragmatic origins, as such statements separated the Oeconomy from its role supporting missionary work and assumed that the communal household had value in and of itself. In effect, these respondents believed Bethlehem was preferable to other Moravian congregation towns on the basis of its economic system, rather than because of its ties to the pilgrim congregation ideal. The statements represent a significant departure from the economic outlook demonstrated by most of the Oeconomy's history: efficiency and flexibility for the sake of spreading the Gospel, coupled with a healthy respect for private property and for the self-reliance of earning one's own bread, to use the Moravians' phrase. They also indicate a divide between the town's leaders and its residents. Leaders remained committed to the Oeconomy only insofar as it was expeditious, yet some residents now seemed to argue for its permanence.

A further set of respondents suggest what residents had come to value about the Oeconomy, and how it fitted into Moravian religious beliefs. If members of the Oeconomy were willing to suffer without food or clothes for their Savior and for the community, it was because the overriding sentiment when it came to material affairs in Bethlehem was gratitude. Though the unsettled nature of the Pennsylvania frontier during the Seven Years' War may have contributed to this emotion, the terms residents used to describe their economic system reflected roots in Moravian beliefs. Childlike devotion to Christ was one of the highest spiritual attributes a Moravian could possess and a central tenet of Zinzendorf's theology. Bethlehem's residents connected this idea to living in the communal household. The pleasure of living in the Oeconomy and having all their physical needs provided for meant feeling cared for *wie ein Kind*—like a child. Johann Christian Peterson, a Single Brother, felt that "Everything I received in the Oeconomy, I have taken as from the dear Savior, and when I can be as a child in the Oeconomy, I am satisfied." This sentiment echoed throughout the community. Single Sister Anna Schaefer stated that with regards to the Oeconomy, "I am satisfied and believe that the dear Savior brought me himself into this family, where I can be like a child and have nothing to care for." Maria Barbara Erick thanked Christ that "I have the blessing to be as a child in the house." In the face of her spiritual joys, her material well being was unimportant. "I am satisfied from my whole heart with everything, I ask for no life for myself, the dear Savior and his wounds are my everything, if He is only ever near me, then I have enough."[30]

Being cared for by the Oeconomy like a child, essentially an economic relationship, enhanced these respondents' feeling of closeness to Christ. For some the link was clear and direct: "I would like to be a child in the Gemeine and want with my whole heart to be and to stay in the Oeconomy, and to do what I can," wrote Elizabeth Holder, "I mean this with my whole heart."[31] In this conception, the Gemeine and Jesus stood hand in hand, providing religious meaning to the Oeconomy. George Partsch, a survivor of the Gnadenhütten attack, shared Holder's view that the Oeconomy promoted the pious life he sought. He was "already 14 years here in the Oeconomy, and the time has not become long for me. It has also not occurred to me to be for myself and to organize a household [*wirtschaften*]; I gave myself once to the dear Savior and the Gemeine, and it is a blessing to me willingly to lend my heart and body to please Jesus, as little and slight as it is, what I can do. When he alone stands before my eyes in the bloody martyr-picture, then everything goes right."[32] Bethlehem's pilgrim congregation meant, to these individuals, something very different from what it had to its founders and leaders. What had once been a means to accomplishing missionary work, and thus serving God, now became itself a way of expressing devotion to God, a fundamental change from the Oeconomy's pragmatic origins (Figure 8).

On February 11, 1758, nearly a month after the discussions about terminating the Oeconomy had begun, the congregation gathered to hear the results. On the whole, the community supported the Oeconomy, and supported as well its leaders, temporarily setting aside plans to end it in favor of measures to make it better. Whether Spangenberg was relieved or disappointed with the decision is unclear. Instead, he reported that he and the other leaders thought "it would be nice for the Gemeine to know the substance of what the Brothers and Sisters had written," since "it had been a pleasure for him to see and to hear the heart of his Brothers and Sisters." He read those responses that were "positively <u>in favor</u>" of the Oeconomy, which, according to the Bethlehem Diary, "were most pleasing and shaming to hear." The town diarist was overcome by his pride and affection for the Gemeine:

Figure 8. August Gottlieb Spangenberg, known within Moravian circles as Joseph, guided Bethlehem between 1745 and 1762, when he returned to Herrnhut to take up leadership of the Unity. Portrait by Johann Georg Ziesenis, GS.210. Courtesy Unity Archives, Herrnhut.

"While listening, one thought: Where is such a God like our God? As well as: Where is such a people as our people?"[33]

Yet practical difficulties remained, according to Spangenberg, and in their recital the difference between the streamlined pilgrim congregation and the mature Oeconomy becomes evident. Spangenberg discussed the problems aired during the month, admonishing and instructing his congregants as to how to solve the "trivialities" and "misunderstandings" that had been brought to light. The thrust of his message was simple: everyone wished that the "grumbling" and "ingratitude" would end and that each person would pull his or her own weight. To this, Spangenberg added only, "We wish the same." To the problem of insufficient resources, including shortages of food and clothing, all of which were now exacerbated by war, and the fact that "we live so closely together and particularly that the Married People do not have their own rooms," he replied by reiterating the financial demands placed on the Oeconomy. "We are still a young colony," he said, and "have had to build much, take care of the work of the Savior, clear the land, and maintain the schools." Organization and the rationing of resources remained paramount: "Keeping the household randomly and just giving each what he demands— that wouldn't do." He also reminded the group of the principle of the pilgrim congregation. They had not come together because they "wanted to enjoy good days, but rather to do the work of the Savior. If now the Savior should put us to the test and leave us hungry for several days, like the children of Is- rael, or we should lack for clothing, or we must live closer together, should we on that account run from it and leave lay His affairs? Far be it!"[34]

Spangenberg's references to complaints and worries that not everyone was receiving equal treatment suggest some of what must have been edited out of the responses—frustrations with the community's strictures and Spartan lifestyle. Yet, in the most telling indicator of community support for the Oeconomy, its leaders did not undertake to end the Oeconomy in Bethlehem in 1758, even though they had entertained the idea for years. In effect, they permitted the survival of two distinct and increasingly intermingled ideas of Bethlehem's religious purpose, the missionary-focused pilgrim congregation and the spiritually charged communitarian settlement. Over the nearly two decades it had existed, residents had ideologically linked the Oeconomy to the Gemeine and to the Savior, bonds that bolstered their commitment to the un- orthodox communal economy and lifestyle.

Herrnhut Intervenes

While those in Bethlehem debated the meaning of communalism, those in Herrnhut were concerned with a different problem. The Brüdergemeine faced an ever-growing mountain of debt, significantly exacerbated by the war, and Unity leaders believed that Bethlehem, one of the church's largest settlements, should carry a greater portion of the load than those in Bethlehem felt able to shoulder. The resulting financial disputes between the Unity and its daughter church after 1758 laid the groundwork for the end of communalism that ultimately came in 1762, but these unfolded against the backdrop of Bethlehem's internal ambivalence over the Oeconomy, and the pressures of the war. Each set of leaders felt that the other failed to appreciate the financial burdens under discussion. Unsuccessful requests for Bethlehem to contribute a greater share to the Unity created in Herrnhut the sense that Bethlehem was recalcitrant, generally out of order, and, worst of all, increasing the financial burden the church faced by straining an already stretched system. In Bethlehem, Spangenberg and his fellows sought to preserve the pilgrim congregation, even as they continued to doubt that its missionary ideal, precious to them, could be served by the continuance of the Oeconomy.

The Unity's financial situation had developed over a long period. During the three decades after 1727, Count Zinzendorf's church grew at an enormous rate. Just in terms of membership, the Unity had increased from a few dozen refugees in Saxony to many thousands of people across the globe. Moravian missionaries spread everywhere, and industrious communities built whole towns from the ground up in Germany, Britain, the Netherlands, Pennsylvania, and North Carolina. The church assumed control of massive tracts of land in the process, including those in America. Such development gave concrete form to the success and appeal of the Renewed Unitas Fratrum, but it also cost a great deal. Particularly expensive was the settlement in Herrnhaag, south of Frankfurt. The Moravians built a substantial town there, only to abandon it abruptly when the period of spiritual and material exuberance known as the "Sifting Time" ended with the Moravians' eviction from the place in 1753.[35] More important still was Zinzendorf's policy of funding the Unity himself and through his network of aristocratic friends rather than suffering the limitation of his church's expansion by the mundane realities of finance. When he left Pennsylvania in 1743, he instructed his followers there to depend on him for whatever funds they needed. The cost for "all purchases of goods, all required support of the Brothers and Sisters, necessarily falls on me."[36] In effect, he allowed the church to live beyond its means.

Such a policy might have worked if Zinzendorf led a successful business empire, but unfortunately he was not known for financial acumen. Even Spangenberg doubted the count's capacity to handle money matters. "I cannot deny that to me [Zinzendorf's] addresses often appeared paradoxical and his methods of business extraordinary," mused even that most trusted advisor. Moravian businessmen scrambled to generate enough income to support the Unity's labyrinthine financial system, but particularly during the church's first two decades, expansion outpaced real economic capabilities. When Saxon authorities sent Zinzendorf into exile in 1732, the count transferred all his property into his wife's name, which she then managed for him and for the church. Her leadership, coupled with a steady stream of gifts, bequests, and loans from wealthy friends of the Moravian movement, kept the network afloat into the 1750s, but only barely. It was vulnerable should any in a long chain of notes be called in.[37]

In 1753, in yet another part of the community's engagement in the Atlantic economy, the Unity faced its most serious financial crisis when a Portuguese banker holding substantial church deposits failed. Zinzendorf responded by assuming those debts personally, solving the immediate problem and signaling a new era in Moravian finance. Members of the church dedicated themselves to paying regular installments of interest to the count's creditors and eventually eliminating the large debt. Austerity and organization gradually replaced rapid expansion, as church leaders faced the need to make substantial payments of both interest and principal. In 1755, they created a new governing body (first known as the College of Administrators and later replaced by the Directorial College) to handle outward affairs, curtailing Zinzendorf's charismatic and autocratic leadership of financial matters in the Unity. Operating from Europe, the new governors worked to safeguard the security of the entire system, but they naturally had the most detailed understanding of the European situation. They were also fighting an uphill battle. The Seven Years' War spread to Saxony in 1756, devastating harvests and ruining commerce. The church's financial situation became only more dire as warring troops crisscrossed its homeland.[38]

The Directors sought to control and diffuse the church's debts (as Zinzendorf's debts were viewed) by distributing them throughout the Unity. In 1757, they established the "Mitleidenheit," a fund collected annually from each community, depending on its ability to pay, as determined by Herrnhut. The Directors reminded members throughout the world that these funds were essential, and that they were different from the general collections that already supported missionary work. Specifically, they wanted every member to believe that each shared the church's debts equally and that their payment was obligatory. This was quite a shift from the era when the Unity (and the Zinzendorf family) had heavily and regularly subsidized many of its members' expenses, from travel to clothes. In 1759, Zinzendorf explained how the new fund should be understood, in attempt to rally support for this potentially unpopular plan. "Mitleidenheit means" he wrote in a circular letter, "when one has and puts oneself with a common body in all ways and helps to support it." This new fund differed fundamentally from collections to support the church's work. He continued, reiterating a common theme, "It can also be that for you the word Mitleidenheit also has the meaning: 'I give 1, 10, 50, 100 or more Thaler so that I help the Children's Schools, and the heathen, and the [Zinzendorf household] that has become poor for us, and the building fund, and the colonies, and so forth.' I wish that it was so, dear hearts!" Unfortunately, the Mitleidenheit could not go to such worthy goals, but rather had to maintain the community itself by paying down the debt. In short, the new fund supported only the church, not its work.[39] These pleas arrived in Bethlehem, but Spangenberg felt helpless to respond with the funds the count desired. "But oh! We are so poor in housing and must handle everything like Pilgrims [auf Pilgerfuß]," he complained in a letter to Zinzendorf. He explained that he did not intend "to make [the count's] heart heavy, but rather to give the reasons why neither Bethlehem nor Nazareth [was] in a position to help the Administrative College with the interest." Quite the contrary, Bethlehem needed help itself. "It would not be too much if each year we received a thousand pounds Sterling to help."[40]

For the next two years, Bethlehem and Herrnhut moved into a new kind of financial relationship marked by acrimony, as leaders in the two largest Moravian towns each pled poverty and pushed debts onto one another. Spangenberg laid out his case in a long letter to the Directorial College in January 1759, complete with nine appendices listing all of the Oeconomy's assets and liabilities down to seven piglets in Bethlehem, valued at twelve shillings apiece. In Pennsylvania, he argued, they had only one fund, which they had "started with nothing and with debts and have continued with His blessing and help." Their income derived only from the "sweat and work" of the

Brothers and Sisters in the Oeconomy, and "from the blessings connected to them." Expenditures all went to "what was to be done for the Savior and His people and affairs in America." No one in the community had been growing rich off a communal system dedicated to missionary work and shared religious experience. His letter went on to describe all the land they had purchased, cleared, and planted; the different artisanal shops in the Oeconomy (numbering 41) as well as the mills, inns, and the store; the buildings built; the schools, "which are quite numerous"; the missions among the Indians; the Indians whom the Oeconomy supported; the other missionary trips "both over water and over land," that had been charged to Bethlehem; and the payments that had gone to interest on money borrowed to finance these extensive operations. Spangenberg again turned the tables on Herrnhut by not only declining to send funds to Herrnhut in this difficult time, but going so far as to ask for relief from the international church, particularly with refinancing some of their debt from six percent down to three or four percent.[41]

As the two sides sniped at each other across the ocean over who needed money more, the problem of Bethlehem's unusual economic organization smoldered under the surface, irritating Spangenberg. In July 1758, four months after the community had reaffirmed the system through the lengthy process of discussion described above, Spangenberg wrote a pleading letter to Zinzendorf: "There are yet some people among us who are not suited to our communal Oeconomy. There is, at times, dissatisfaction."[42] Six months later, in his extensive report on the state of the Oeconomy, he repeated his feeling that Bethlehem had grown too large and suggested that it was time for a change. His lengthy ruminations made clear that, in his view, the Oeconomy was no longer suited to Bethlehem's needs as a pilgrim congregation, but hinted at the challenges that would confront whoever tried to end it:

When [Zinzendorf] was in America, then everyone who was called Brother and Sister lived together, . . . in commune oramus, in commune laboramus, in commune patimur [we pray together, we work together, we endure together]. When Nazareth was settled, which occurred in the beginning of the year [17]44, it was established so that everyone lived in common. When I came to America at the end of [that year], I thus found everything in that course, and it has continued so. What is now to be done? . . . Nonetheless, it would be good to continue an Oeconomy, in my humble estimation, because who shall pay the interest? Who should take care of the schools? Who will offer help to the missionaries? If all of that had to be paid for in cash, how could we manage it?

"The thing should get a new form and new people," Spangenberg wrote, referring to Bethlehem. His exasperated utterance avoided any of the available Moravian terms for the town—Oeconomy, pilgrim congregation, congregation town—leaving vague what exactly would be changed. The Oeconomy perhaps should end, but not the pilgrim congregation it supported. The pilgrim congregation was, however, inhibited by the existence of the bloated Oeconomy, whose residents did not want to move into a European-style congregation town. Perhaps understandably, Spangenberg did not want to attempt such a change alone. "Above all," he concluded, "we wish that the Savior could turn [Zinzendorf's] path to us, so that the Plans here could be looked at anew, corrected, and newly ordered." To drive home his point, Spangenberg noted that Wachovia in North Carolina must soon receive a leader for its economy, "or else there they will become, before you know it, an Oeconomy like Bethlehem."[43]

Spangenberg's sentiments were not well received in Herrnhut, though he had made sure to note that all the other leaders in Bethlehem shared his point of view. In December 1759, Johannes de Watteville, Zinzendorf's son-in-law and a member of the Moravian inner circle, sent back from Europe a scathing letter, which could only have been intended to invoke the deepest regret and guilt in the Pennsylvania community. "I see from all circumstance," he wrote, "that with respect to the Mitleidenheit, you have either not rightly understood, or have not wanted to understand rightly, this whole blessed institution. I could only wish that the contributions of the [international] Gemeine to the Mitleidenheit went so far that other most necessary general expenditures of the Unity could come out of it." Watteville pointed out that "some 1000" pounds of expenditures for Pennsylvania were included in the Unity debts, and yet the American divisions of the church had been assessed less than some other areas. "All the more painful it is to us that you hardly act as if you had received the writings of the General Directorate," he continued, "and until now have not yet thought about how to remit your apportioned quantum." For those in Herrnhut, the Unity's debts were the issue at hand. In his most cutting line (one might say his most manipulative), Johannes (as Watteville was familiarly known in Moravian circles) added that Zinzendorf was so upset that "they could hardly write a letter to America, so long as you do not conform with the other parts of the Gemeine in the area of the Mitleidenheit."[44]

Johannes also disagreed with his coreligionists in Bethlehem on the issue of ending the Oeconomy, because he connected it to Bethlehem's essential role as a pilgrim congregation. "I notice that for some time there have been quite a few movements to make a change in the previous communal house-keeping," he wrote. "I am honestly shocked at this and wish that such un-timely projects would not come up again. Nothing but damage can come of it, and I am assured that the communal Oeconomy is a basic tenet" of Beth-lehem's organization. If Zinzendorf came to America, there might be some al-ternations, "but no total change could be made." This rebuke cloaked another underlying issue, however, that of obedience. "Above all, dear Brothers and Sisters! I wish that no change would be made in the Plan of major impor-tance, without working in concert with" Zinzendorf and those in Herrnhut.[45]

By 1760, Bethlehem's Oeconomy was caught in an impasse, trapped by disagreements over its future within the town and between Pennsylvania and Germany. The war forced the issue, putting pressure on the Unity from Herrnhut to Bethlehem and even on the high seas. In every way, that conflict was expensive, exacerbating the church's financial woes and exposing the dif-ferences of opinion that had developed about Bethlehem's distinctive system. Both Bethlehem and the international Unity needed financial help, and nei-ther could provide it to the other under existing circumstances. The Oecon-omy stuck out in the Moravian economic picture like a sore thumb. It included more than 1,000 members at the end of the 1750s, not least the Moravian Indian refugees from Gnadenhütten who needed continual aid and protection, and Spangenberg reported in June 1760 that it "begins to go very hard." Two years after the majority of Bethlehem's residents voted to retain the Oeconomy, leaders in Bethlehem remained convinced that it had to end, but they had no clear direction about what the town should become.[46]

This precarious situation changed utterly on May 9, 1760, when Zinzen-dorf died. He had been the Brüdergemeine's guiding spirit for more than thirty years, and his distinctive theology and energy had shaped everything the group had accomplished. Amid the grief, however, his death cleared the way for a needed reorganization in the international church. Bethlehem received the news on August 19, 1760, and with it the information that Anna Nitschmann, Zinzendorf's second wife and the most important female leader in the Unity, had also passed away.[47] It is impossible to say how long the

Oeconomy would have survived if Zinzendorf had lived, and it is not clear whether Zinzendorf was personally committed to the communitarian aspects of Bethlehem.[48] His comments on the matter, all indirect, conflict, though they suggest that the issue of Bethlehem's relationship to missionary work was, for him, paramount. Johannes de Watteville had scolded Bethlehem's leadership on the count's behalf for the rumors that the Oeconomy might be abrogated just six months before his death. A few weeks after Zinzendorf died, however, Watteville reported a very different sentiment to the group that now undertook to lead the international church. According to Johannes, the count had (presumably in his final weeks) begun to worry about Bethlehem, wondering if it was truly "according to Jesus's heart and, according to circumstances the best and most blessed [development] that Bethlehem has grown so and was no longer a simple Pilgerhaus as in the beginning." Perhaps it would be better, Zinzendorf thought, if Bethlehem were set "on the footing of a Congregation Town, like Herrnhut," i.e., noncommunitarian.[49] With such conflicting accounts (reported by the same person), the count's position is blurred at best. Regardless of Zinzendorf's opinion on the matter, however, the Unity's new leadership believed the Oeconomy had outlived its usefulness and set about ending it.

CHAPTER 6

Two Revolutions: Ending the Oeconomy and Losing the Missions

ZINZENDORF'S DEATH IN 1760 was a watershed event for the Unity. It opened the way for a serious evaluation of the Brüdergemeine from top to bottom, and those who took up the helm in Herrnhut seized the opportunity. Over the next four years, through and after the time of the General Synod held in 1764, every aspect of Moravian life came under the keen scrutiny of men focused on restoring financial stability and ensuring denominational security. They systematized and regularized, and along the way they significantly increased Herrnhut's power in the international Unity. For Bethlehem, the changes resulted in two separate revolutions. Both originated in Herrnhut, but in each case the way those developments took shape depended on local circumstances in Pennsylvania. First, almost immediately after Zinzendorf's death, the Oeconomy was dissolved. This complex process required the insertion of market relationships within a community that had never known them, but the trauma of that transition was minimized by the fact that the Moravians had never opposed a market economy in principle. Just as Bethlehem's economic situation stabilized, however, renewed racial violence threw the missions into disarray. At that unfortunate moment, Herrnhut undertook a second transition with enormous consequences for Bethlehem's religious life by seeking to centralize the missions in Germany. The combination of events proved powerful, and by 1765 Bethlehem's pilgrim congregation had been eliminated, the house congregation dissolved, and the town stripped of almost all its ties to missionary work. These events transformed the Bethlehem pilgrim congregation into what it had never been, a Moravian congregational town (*Ortsgemeine*) on the model of Herrnhut. Yet the Pennsylvania town was not infinitely malleable, and its location in the Mid-Atlantic limited its ability to conform to directions from above. The renewed conflict between whites and Indians, the final episode of the war begun a decade before, forced Bethlehem's leaders to make uncomfortable choices between their missions and their neighbors, and equally difficult choices about whether to follow Herrnhut's increasingly ill-suited dictates. What Herrnhut viewed as Bethlehem's eventual rebellion challenged the nature of the Moravians' Atlantic community.

Herrnhut Redesigns Bethlehem

After Zinzendorf's death, the fact that something had to be done about Bethlehem no longer required explanation or justification among the Unity's leaders, who cared little about whether Bethlehem should be a pilgrim congregation or a congregation town. They wanted, above all, for the Pennsylvanians to do their part to erase the Unity's crippling debt. The questions about whether the communal system was a pragmatic way to facilitate missionary work or an entity that promoted a distinct kind of spirituality were moot from their perspective, as neither missionary work nor the church as a whole would continue if it went bankrupt. Moreover, the congregation town model had shown itself highly successful in the European context, and leaders in Herrnhut did not consider that system spiritually inferior to Bethlehem's because of the latter's communalism. Just two months after the count's death, therefore, the interim leadership council in Europe turned to the problem of Bethlehem's economic organization. On July 7, 1760, before Bethlehem had even received the news of Zinzendorf's passing, the council members agreed that Spangenberg, who was heir apparent as spiritual and administrative head of the international Unity, must return to Herrnhut, where he "would be a necessary and useful ingredient in the whole of our church." Two weeks later, "much was discussed about the outward affairs of Bethlehem, and the necessity of bringing it in order, and finally deciding it through [the Lot]." Though they did not state it outright, the "it" was the dissolution of the Oeconomy.[1] That was the way the Oeconomy ended, with an oblique reference in place of either a bang or a whimper, and thousands of miles from Pennsylvania. For Herrnhut, it was merely a bureaucratic detail.[2]

Many questions about the upcoming transition remained, however, and the effort to settle these indicated that Spangenberg, like his fellow townspeople, believed there was something special in Bethlehem to preserve, though for him it was the pilgrim congregation rather than the Oeconomy. Unity leaders took a pragmatic approach. Johannes de Watteville, writing from Europe in July 1760, sketched the basic shape of the new community structure, an outline that, in time, was largely realized. Under the new organization, the church in Bethlehem would continue to earn substantial sums from town industries, but would place many of its former duties, such as procuring food and clothing, into the hands of individual members. Key profitable businesses, including the mills and the store, would remain in the church's hands in order to support missionary work, church workers, and the schools. The workers in those industries would receive an annual wage, but businesses that were less profitable or less capital-intensive could be privatized by turning them over to the craftsmen. Living arrangements also needed reorganization. Single and multiple-family houses would be built to provide private space for the Married People's Choir. Finally, the Single Brothers' and Single Sisters' Choirs would be transformed into economic organizations where individuals paid for their own room and board.[3]

Spangenberg's initial response to this plan was mixed. Whereas Unity leaders worried about the inefficiencies concealed by the Oeconomy's massive figures (its members consumed 34,925 pounds of butter in 1758, for example), Spangenberg understood that the Oeconomy had become part of Bethlehem's spiritual life. He couched his concerns over the transition within his acceptance of the larger situation, however. He and the other leaders in Bethlehem "all truly [believed] that a change is necessary, because [the Oeconomy] is no longer what it was in the beginning." He saw a plethora of causes (which he unfortunately did not enumerate) for a change that defied simple explanation. "One could well give ten reasons, which could all be responsible, and still not hit on the main cause," he offered. Regardless of how they got there, however, the time for alteration had arrived. "The question is only, how does one change the Oeconomy so that no spiritual damage comes of it."[4] Spangenberg rejected Watteville's initial plan for two reasons. First, Bethlehem needed all the income it could get to survive, and he believed that shedding even a few businesses would ensure the town's failure. Second, he worried that creating a mixed economy, where some residents worked for themselves and others for the church, would harm the community's spiritual tenor. Among some of their congregants, the Moravians might face the same problem that "the Quakers, Mennonites, Separatists, Schwenkfelders, etc. now have." That is, some members might "become rich and complacent, and stray from the Plan [i.e., Moravian religious projects]."[5]

Spangenberg saw such an outcome as more likely in Pennsylvania than in Europe, because the American economy differed from the European economy, where the Moravians had planted their other towns. A congregation town on the European model would not work in the generally prosperous New World, he worried. "Anyone who knows the land here will understand [this worry] well," he explained. In Europe, "a townsman must work quite hard just to survive with his family, but here one ordinarily becomes rich, and as soon as one sees that one is becoming rich, the desire to help and to give where it is needed ordinarily stops." Although almost all other Moravian towns had a traditional, noncommunal organization, Spangenberg feared that the proposed transformation threatened Bethlehem's special existence as a pilgrim congregation because workers who left the Oeconomy ("worked for themselves," in Moravian parlance) would not maintain the level of devotion they had inside the Oeconomy. As a result, the two categories of workers, those who still worked for the church and those who did not, should not stay together in one place.[6]

Spangenberg suggested his own solution as a counter to the Herrnhut plan, and in it he fought to protect the concept of the pilgrim congregation. Rather than changing Bethlehem, he proposed that anyone who wanted to leave the Oeconomy could move to an expanded Nazareth, thereby shrinking Bethlehem back down to a manageable size for a missionary town. There would thus be two similar Moravian towns ten miles apart: a congregation town, or noncommunal Moravian town, in Nazareth; and a pilgrim congregation, a communal town dedicated to missionary work, in Bethlehem. This would preserve a missionary-based religious experience for those who desired it. He proposed other alterations to the existing system as well. The simple impracticality of having church leaders decide the daily minutiae of their congregants' lives ranked high on the list of problems in the Oeconomy. To remedy it, he proposed giving each member of the diminished Bethlehem Oeconomy an annual sum for acquiring clothes and other necessities "according to their taste." Importantly, however, such payments were not to be regarded as salaries, since trying to pay competitive wages in Pennsylvania would bankrupt the church quickly.[7]

Spangenberg's concerns were ignored across the Atlantic. The silence of his European correspondents on the matter suggests that the majority of Moravian leaders in Europe either did not think that abrogating the Oeconomy would damage Bethlehem's religious life or did not care about such matters in the face of the Unity's debt, which was by far their more pressing concern. Probably both sentiments came into play. They hoped, after all, to transform Bethlehem into a town much like their own Herrnhut, a community whose spiritual health they hardly doubted. The Pennsylvania town's residents had produced an innovative Moravian spirituality, but the Unity as a whole had not adopted such a course and so had no problem with marginalizing or eliminating Bethlehem's peculiar commitment to communalism. Furthermore, the Unity could not go forward with its missionary projects in America or anywhere else if it could not keep its creditors at bay. From the vantage point of Herrnhut, changing Bethlehem's internal economic organization was merely one aspect of the larger job of putting the church's finances in order. Spangenberg's fears about the different economic opportunities available to Moravians in America did not change their minds, or even prod them to discussion.

Time worked against Spangenberg's plan as well. His objections, written in November 1760, did not reach Herrnhut until the end of February 1761, by which time the Directorial College felt the matter was all but closed. After a flurry of discussion in the fall of 1760, the Directors had appointed a committee to investigate all financial matters in America, assessing both risk and potential. The committee reported in January 1761, with an extensive examination of the American situation, and over the next month the Directors hashed out the economic details of the church's holdings, rationalizing what had, in many cases, developed organically. The land purchased years before in Easton, Pennsylvania, the details of future settlement in North Carolina, and what to do with the site where Gnadenhütten had stood, all fell under their prerogative. In a conservative move that foreshadowed the years to come, they decided that Bethlehem should cease any further land purchases, as the Unity already held more acreage than it could settle or cultivate in the conceivable future. For Bethlehem, even as Spangenberg's missive traveled across the ocean, the Herrnhut committee started by accepting the basic outlines of Watteville's plan, a structure that fit its overarching aims of privatizing as much as possible and making financial transactions quantifiable. As they went through the American accounts, the Directors lamented more than once that Bethlehem had not been designed initially as a congregation town. At the very least, they concluded, the "communal Oeconomy had lasted ten years too long and should have been changed a long time ago."[8]

While the Directorate neglected Spangenberg's concerns about Bethlehem's spiritual life and mission, Johannes de Watteville surprisingly responded with more empathy. In a long letter that once again sketched the central points of Bethlehem's transition, Johannes reached out to his friend, reassuring him that the Unity's plans were indeed for the best. He had a "deep-lying thought that the Savior himself was the author and cause" of Bethlehem's development, wrote Watteville. Christ had "let Bethlehem grow so large, because he intended it to be the American Herrnhut." Moreover, the divine plan was for Bethlehem to have an economy that should become a "mixture of a general Oeconomy and a Congregation Town," as Johannes felt Herrnhut was. The suggestion of a congregation town at Nazareth had been around for a long time, he reminded Spangenberg, but had always been rejected in favor of Bethlehem as the primary community. Building a competing town in Nazareth after so many years could only cause problems. Yet, although the transformation of Bethlehem was the best course, it was still a daunting task. Speaking to all the members of Bethlehem's leadership, Johannes wrote: "You have a heavy burden on you, this I know. So many missions, schools, etc. are to be cared for that only the blessing of the Lord can sustain such a burden, and so I pray that He bestows it on you in sufficient order"[9] (Figure 9).

Watteville also sought to calm Spangenberg's worry that ending the communal economy would admit a spirit in Bethlehem that undermined devotion to the Lord. For him, Bethlehem's new structure had a religious component, just one that was different from the old Oeconomy. After all, Bethlehem's new organization would resemble other Moravian communities. "Bethlehem and Nazareth remain dedicated to Him," he wrote. "All establishments must have that goal and all Brothers and Sisters who live there must have that intention, and thus, as in all our Congregation Towns, work not for themselves but for the Savior." He outlined the shape of the new system once again—which businesses should remain in the hands of the church and which should be made independent, the new organization of the Choirs—and then returned to the central point. "If perhaps you are thinking: how then will our Oeconomy be able to survive with this new organization?" he asked, then answered: "There

Figure 9. Johannes de Watteville, born Johann Michael Langguth, was Count Zinzendorf's son-in-law and close associate. Portrait by Johann Georg Ziesenis, GS.060. Courtesy Unity Archives, Herrnhut.

will come over your people a new spirit of industriousness, the Savior's diligence at work will make them diligent." Watteville believed that the costs of the transition would be balanced by a new spirit of productivity and a new pleasure in giving. "Your people will learn to work hard so that they can contribute much to the collections for your schools, missions, and other needs of the Gemeine," he wrote optimistically, "it will be a joy to them, to give what they have, which they have given before without noticing."[10] Whatever Spangenberg's fears, privatization of the communal economy did not distress Watteville, nor was it linked to worries of incursions by a corrosive market economy. On the contrary, he thought the new system, so badly needed for so many reasons, would spiritually rejuvenate Bethlehem's residents by making their financial contributions more apparent, rather than causing a cycle of secularization and decline.

Bethlehem's Oeconomy captivated the attention of Herrnhut's administrators because of their driving need to stabilize the Unity financially, but the entirety of the Brüdergemeine came under scrutiny in these years. Spangenberg, Bethlehem's long-time leader and Zinzendorf's successor in the church hierarchy, returned to Herrnhut to oversee the task. It was a daunting job. Spangenberg reported as much to his former congregants in Bethlehem upon his arrival in Herrnhut in December 1762: "There are so many things that are not yet completely after the spirit of Christ and that through his mercy should come into order, and O some Plans should still be set right, and be carried out according to his presence!"[11] Over the next few years, Spangenberg and his fellows led what Moravian historians have viewed as a conservative charge away from Zinzendorf's most exuberant creations and toward a more conventional denominational structure. Bethlehem's Oeconomy exemplified the sort of creative endeavor those in favor of retrenchment wanted to avoid. Likewise, women's leadership roles in the community were reevaluated and largely eliminated. Bethlehem's unique position in the international Unity as a pilgrim congregation with special responsibilities for missions, the arrangement that had been responsible for the Oeconomy in the first place, was also now superfluous and problematic.[12]

Missionary work, a central part of the Moravians' religious life since the early 1730s, received considerable attention during these years of reorganization. In 1762, Unity leaders created the Mission Diacony (also known as the Heathen Diacony) in Herrnhut. Consisting of three councilors and small number of corresponding agents, the new body had responsibility over the material needs of the missions worldwide. It was to supervise the dispersal of funds collected from Unity members throughout Europe, transport new missionaries to and from their posts, outfit them with the necessary goods to sustain them and their missions, and generally supervise the financial end of missionary work. In this task, the councilors answered to the Unity's central administrators, who reserved for themselves the right to select (via the Lot) which missionary they would place in each needed position. The North American missions played only a peripheral role in this new system; the years of dramatic success in the West Indies and in South America, coupled with almost a decade of war and strife in the British mainland colonies, made work in the latter seem minor and unstable. Likewise, Bethlehem, which had been key in the church's broad missionary project since its founding, was struggling in the early 1760s to handle the financial and logistical upheavals of a reorganized economy and chronic warfare. Promises of an optimistic future for the Unity's missions thus had little to do with Bethlehem or Pennsylvania, and the community turned its attentions elsewhere. Indeed, the Mission Diacony's first set of instructions specifically discussed missions in Greenland, St. Thomas, St. Croix, St. Jan, Antigua, Jamaica, and Suriname, yet made no mention of any projects among North Americans. As the international mission project was reinvigorated, the role of the Pennsylvania-based missions within that project flagged.[13]

Herrnhut's Small Conference (the principal governing body of the Unity in these years) formalized Bethlehem's marginalization in the mission effort in April 1764. The conference had been struggling for some time with the cumbersome communication system that required letters and decisions about the major mission in the Caribbean to go through Bethlehem, though it saw those outposts as part of Herrnhut's territory. Vacancies in Jamaica prompted the comment that "it is most necessary finally to set the matter of the direction of the heathen posts in the American Islands on a certain and firm footing." The mixed governance of Herrnhut and Bethlehem, the conference continued, "had made several difficulties" and created a situation where the true circumstances in those places were very difficult to ascertain. Even more problematic, the members worried that "jealousy" could arise among the missionaries if some reported directly to Herrnhut and others to Bethlehem. To resolve the situation the group resorted to the Lot—a mechanism members had reminded themselves just a few days before to use in moments of doubt—and asked if "the Savior would prefer that the direction of the Caribbean and English islands occurred immediately from here" or whether he would prefer the administration to be mediated by Bethlehem. Although the blank Lot, which would indicate that the Savior found neither alternative appealing, was also included, the option of clarifying the situation by devolving all authority to Bethlehem was not considered, because such an arrangement was simply unthinkable. The Lot indicated the first choice of directing the Caribbean missions from Herrnhut, and Spangenberg was detailed to send the information along to Bethlehem.[14]

This rapid decision made by a small group of leaders represented a further move toward the realization of a deep and radical shift in Bethlehem's place within the Unity. The town's origins as a pilgrim congregation, as a settlement made up of mobile individuals dedicated to missionary work, had dictated its location and ultimately even its organization as a communal economy. In the years leading up to the economic transition of 1762 leaders—especially Spangenberg while he was still in Pennsylvania—had fought to preserve the special character of the pilgrim congregation, even as authorities in Herrnhut had championed the vision of Bethlehem as one of many Moravian congregation towns. Surprisingly, however, Spangenberg, now serving in Europe in the role of Unity administrator, did not concern himself with the spiritual implications of ending missionary responsibilities for the pilgrim congregation he had governed for so long. When he wrote to inform Bethlehem of the decision, he framed the news in terms of practicalities. Having learned of the death of a missionary in Jamaica, he wrote, the Small Conference had wondered if "they now have someone in North America whom they can send in Christ. Heinrich's place?" Further, if such a person could not be found in Bethlehem, "will we learn in time to locate someone in Europe?" He detailed the pros and cons of the current situation as they had been discussed in the meeting and finally reported the results of the Lot. Although he reassured Bethlehem's leaders that the new arrangement would not sever all ties between Bethlehem and the West Indian missions, that the change went only to the "direction" of the missions, ultimately the distinction was hard to maintain. "It will henceforth be, therefore, [that] both the diaries and the reports from all brothers and sisters in the West Indian Islands will only be sent to Europe," he wrote, and furthermore, "the resolutions will also be sent directly from here, without first being communicated to Pennsylvania, to the West Indian islands." Financial support would follow the new lines as well. Spangenberg repeated the same news more sympathetically two months later when he acknowledged that Bethlehem had been shouldering such responsibility in the past and suggested that those duties helped explain the difficult financial times the town found itself in. In his view, the recent decision would ease much of that burden.[15]

Moravian habits of obedience make it difficult to discern how leaders in Bethlehem felt about the change in their town's status, whether they experienced relief at the lifting of a troublesome responsibility or felt slighted by the decrease in their authority. The news reached Bethlehem four months after the Lot was drawn, in August 1764, when tensions on the Pennsylvania frontier over Bethlehem's ties to Indians were again very high. Town leaders recorded the information in their records simply, including that the decision had been submitted to the Lot in Herrnhut, a factor that made the result uncontestable. "We submit ourselves happily to this establishment," they continued, "but we would gladly have seen that the decision of this matter had been saved until the Gen[eral] Synod that was held shortly after."[16] In truth, the administrative adjustments may have paled against the second piece of news they received: that the synod had already commenced without any new representatives from North American being sent. The first and most important Unity-wide gathering since Zinzendorf's death, the General Synod of 1764 was seen as the basis for the church's future. Nathanael Seidel, one of Bethlehem's leaders, sent a resigned letter back to Herrnhut a few days later acknowledging both the synod and the change in the "twenty-and-some-year plan" of mission organization and explaining the ongoing difficulties with the Indian missions. These two comments—pointing out the premature timing of the Lot and the age of the system that had been so rapidly overturned— can be viewed as subtle protests against the new policy, and suggest that Bethlehem knew its future as a center of mission activity was deeply threatened. Yet Bethlehem's leaders chose accommodation to their Herrnhut brethren. They prioritized the stability of the settlement itself and its relationships to other whites over missionary work. Faced with pressures from outside, Bethlehem began to turn inward.[17]

Effecting the Economic Transition

The decisions to end the Oeconomy and sideline Bethlehem in mission administration had been made in Europe, but the details of those complex transitions unfolded in Pennsylvania. The implications of the change in mission administration were subtle and took longer to develop. The economic shift, on the other hand, was the easier and faster of the two, and Bethlehem's leaders effected the change with remarkable rapidity. Nonetheless, transforming Bethlehem's communal system into a market-based town was an intricate process, and one that required the Moravians to create or acknowledge financial relationships between people in places they had never been before. Even after the debates over the town's meaning had been put to rest by Herrnhut's decisions, residents still had to confront a series of deeply charged practical questions. But just as Moravian economic ideas about private property and financial innovation had differed little from the economic mainstream of the day, the details of the transition reveal that the Moravians possessed a vision of society that resembled their neighbors' in terms of racial, gendered, and social hierarchies. As leaders systematically worked through each aspect of the transition, the new economy that emerged was more marked for its similarities to Pennsylvania's society than for its differences.

Initially the links to the past, and to the pilgrim congregation ideal, remained strong. Indeed, Bethlehem's mission responsibilities did not change at all until two years later, when Herrnhut issued its surprising ruling about mission administration. The church's ongoing commitment to missionary work therefore provided the context within which Bethlehem's new economy developed. As a result, missionary work and the powerful role of the church in town continued to differentiate Bethlehem from its Pennsylvania neighbors. For the church to continue to fund mission projects, it still needed an income, and most of the town's major businesses stayed in its hands. Likewise, the Oeconomy's debts, over £20,000, remained the property of the church; no one considered dividing them among the various individual members. The sheer scale of the Bethlehem congregation's economic needs therefore preserved its position as the biggest financial player in the town and continued to channel much of the town's productive labor toward mission work, if now more indirectly than before. The church also retained ownership of all the land in town. Those who worked for themselves and lived in private homes still paid rent for the land on which their homes stood. This system ensured that no one could move into Bethlehem without the permission of the church, a situation that maintained the religious uniformity of the town until the mid-nineteenth century, eighty years after the transition and a full century after Bethlehem's founding.[18]

After the economic transition, Bethlehem's Moravians still supported missionary work with their labor, but they did so in a different way. In general outlines, following the plans laid out in Herrnhut, the transition accomplished one gargantuan administrative shift: whereas before, all of Bethlehem's residents had donated their labor to the Oeconomy (effectively synonymous with the Moravian church in Bethlehem), afterward individuals worked for cash—whether for a salary from the church or as independent artisans. Church businesses, the majority of the large industries in town, still put their profits toward the Unity's work. The transition process can be divided into two different areas: first, reorganizing the trades and providing the newly in-dependent family households with an income, and, second, establishing the Single Brothers' and Single Sisters' Choirs (whose members did not fit into a nuclear family structure) as self-sustaining economic units. Each aspect en-tailed a complex series of decisions about whose labors deserved—or would have—what kind of financial recognition or independence.

The trades, Bethlehem's economic backbone since its earliest days, re-ceived attention first. Because the church needed regular income to support its substantial burdens of debt and ongoing missionary work, leaders in both Herrnhut and Bethlehem recognized the necessity of maintaining ownership of key businesses. The result was a divided economy, in which half the arti-sans in town worked for the church and earned a salary, while the other half worked independently. The Directors in Herrnhut suggested keeping the "the farms with the mills, taverns, and the processing of their products, be that mowing, brewing, baking, slaughtering, candle making, tanning and tawry work, distilling, and brickmaking, also linen weaving, the store, the apothe-cary, the bookstore, the pottery house, the dye house, and the farrier and blacksmith, also builders and carpenters." On the other hand, there were many artisans who could be set up to work for themselves, including the "glove maker, cooper, hat maker, furniture maker, tinsmith, nail smith, lock-smith, gun stocker, stocking weaver, cobbler, tailor, turner, wagoner, saddle maker, haberdasher, watchmaker, silversmith."[19] Account books indicate that these lists reflect much of what eventually came to pass. In 1763, the first com-plete fiscal year after the transition, the store, apothecary, mills, tannery, bak-ery, dye house, and taverns all remained in the church's hands, while the cooper, hatter, joiner, pewterer, and saddler disappeared from the community ledgers. The categories of ownership were flexible, however. The pottery shop and breeches maker dropped and then reappeared in the mid-1760s in the church's annual accounts. Blacksmiths maintained a steady presence, but the quantity they brought into church coffers declined precipitously—from £174 in 1761 to £60 in 1763, suggesting that some but not all of the town's smiths stayed in the church's employ.[20]

Independence was a relative concept for those artisans who worked for themselves, for as individuals they now shouldered financial burdens for their new shops. Much of the risk and all of the financial management was priva-tized. Residents immediately lost, therefore, the feeling of being protected as children by a benevolent Oeconomy—that sentiment prized by so many in the late 1750s. Because the capital invested in the businesses had originated with the church, each artisan paid interest on his "Stock in Trade," the value of his business's tools and supplies. This charge was set at the local going rate of 6 percent, because leaders had their own debts to pay and did not foresee themselves being able to borrow at a lower rate. Artisans faced other costs in addition to the interest. For example, the locksmith paid the "salaries of [his] journeymen, house rent, interest on his inventory [his Stock in Trade], and for his child." As the last fee indicates, children who were already in the community schools did not necessarily leave them, so when the Oeconomy ended parents had to pay for their children's upkeep. Gottlieb Lange, the saddler, set up business on a similar footing to that of the locksmith, as did the cooper. Formal contracts and annual inventories assessing the value of each business's stock supported these arrangements, limiting the church's obligations and clarifying the artisan's responsibilities. The church could potentially lose the funds already invested, but in the meantime it earned a steady income with no worries as to how the artisan would pay his bills. From the artisan's perspective, the situation was not quite so rosy. Leaving the church and working independently meant, for many, becoming at least for a time financially beholden to, rather than dependent on, the church, and, unlike the situation under the Oeconomy, these new relationships were a matter of balance sheets, not shared religious goals.[21]

Those who continued to work directly for the church also entered a system defined by wage labor and the profit motive. This aspect of the transition revealed, in vivid terms, church leaders' willingness to work with one of the market economy's most basic tools: individual reward for individual labor. Furthermore, leaders chose to reward some labor more highly than others, just as the larger Atlantic economy valued the work of skilled adult white males more than it did any other category of workers. The sequence of events was smooth, and, because it was consistent with a heritage of market-oriented behavior, unsurprising. The artisans who managed Bethlehem's major workshops and stores needed financial support in the form of cash, since they no longer received all their food and clothing directly from the Oeconomy. Consequently, town leaders had to decide what each man—or his work—was worth. Master craftsmen, they suggested, particularly of the larger businesses like the mills or the tannery, should earn a percentage of their annual profits. Johann George Geitner, the head of the tannery, for example, was offered a minimum of £60 a year, but if one-third of the "clear profits" of that business ran to more than his salary, he would be entitled to keep the greater amount. From his earnings, he would support himself and his family, including paying for his two children.[22] Geitner's workers were offered significantly less than he was and had no share in the profits. Journeymen tanners and their peers in other trades received a regular wage. Two of the tanners received £40 per year, while the remaining three got £35. Among the latter was Andreas the Mohr, a member of Bethlehem's small slave population. The transition's planners explicitly acknowledged that they did not need to pay Andreas at all—the community owned him, after all—but decided to do so anyway because "he is an industrious person." They agreed, therefore, "as long as he works hard, one should give him that much payment out of love."[23]

The tanners could readily take responsibility for their equipment, but the mills raised more complicated issues. In addition to the machinery of each mill, the millrace, the stream used to turn the millwheels, had to be maintained. Yet it was a resource that was shared by several mills, a fact that posed significant problems. Bethlehem's physical infrastructure reflected the integrated nature of its economy before the transition; pulling apart financial responsibility was hardly simple. In 1761, the industrial quarter included a gristmill, a sawmill, an oil mill, and a fulling mill. Hans Christensen, a wheelwright who built twenty mills in America during his career, took care of the various buildings. After the transition, he continued his craft, earning £40 per year for himself while the church paid his assistant £35. Church leaders did not want his time monopolized by maintenance, however. "Above all, in the future system it will be useful if the mills were established so that each miller keeps his apparatus in order himself," they wrote, "as is the custom in every place."[24]

The millers were the most independent of the businessmen who worked for the church. The grist miller paid, out of the mill's revenue, 6 percent interest on £800 for his building and equipment, the cost of two-thirds of the repairs for the milldam and the race, and for all repairs to his mill. After these expenses had been paid, he kept half the mill's profit, while the other half went to the church. From his share, he had to support himself, his workers, and his children. Presumably, his wife also fell under this category, although women were not discussed specifically when setting terms for the trades. The fulling miller and oil miller received similar deals. Only the saw miller worked on a different basis. The community required all of the mill's output, so he could not have a share of the profit because he could not sell to outsiders.

Instead, the church paid him by the hundred-foot produced. Because the sawmill remained dedicated to Bethlehem's internal economy, the saw miller did not pay interest on his building, although he was required to keep the mill operating and set his own saws. To fill out his schedule, "when the mill is not operating, he can earn enough with [miscellaneous work] in town, particularly for the Single Sisters' house."[25]

Labor took on a new symbolic role after the transition, and town leaders embraced this. Before, hard work had received its positive value from its relation to missionary endeavors. Afterward, artisans, whether they worked independently or for a salary, entered an economic system where what they earned reflected—in principle at least—how hard they worked. This was perhaps the most fundamental change for Bethlehem's labor force after the transition, but, as the arrangements set up for the master tanner and millers suggest, it was not limited to independent artisans. Leaders made regular use of the profit motive even in businesses owned by the church, by instituting systems where artisans and shopkeepers shared in the profits of the businesses they ran, rather than having all money come into the church and the workers receive a salary. The church both implicitly—with those whom it moved into independent status—and explicitly—with those who earned a salary—embraced the principle that individuals worked better when they saw direct return from their efforts. Leaders felt that attitude led to greater industriousness. In fact, the very first observation made by the committee designing the transformation was a statement of this principle. "Because it will serve as an encouragement for industry in work," the planners wrote, "we hold it to be advisable [to arrange] everything to work by the piece rather than by the day, where applicable." When discussing the proposed position of forester, someone to manage the wood resources in Bethlehem, they agreed "it would be best if he receives a portion of his industry [*Fleißes*] as payment."[26]

The new system also made pragmatic sense from the church's perspective, and it resonated with the wider trend in the international church, most evident with the change from direct ownership of ships to the Commercial Society discussed previously, to minimize the church's exposure to risk. In addition to encouraging hard work, giving artisans a share of their profits placed the incentive to produce a profit onto the artisan (at least in theory), and also decreased the church's responsibilities in the management of the business. It thus partially privatized what could not, for financial reasons, be made wholly independent. Although as owner the church remained the deep pockets behind the scenes, taking a loss in bad years and paying the minimum salary of the artisan even if no profits came in, the profit-sharing system distanced the business from the church by creating at least the appearance of joint ownership. It also increased private responsibility for business practice on the part of the artisan. Each master had to keep clear accounts of his transactions and stock-in-trade so his business could be regularly evaluated. Christian Frederick Oerter, the town's bookkeeper, was delegated to teach the masters how to do this. Incorporating the profit motive into church businesses presented an interesting dilemma as well: cutthroat business practice could, in theory, bring more money into church coffers and enrich both the artisan and the church. Ensuring that profit would be pursued in a Godly manner became a primary occupation of the new system's governors in the years after the transition, but leaders readily endorsed the profit motive as a business tool at the time of the transition, and they never disavowed it.[27]

The new wage structure also reflected another important aspect of a market economy: inequality of wealth. Under the Oeconomy, everyone in Bethlehem had enjoyed roughly equal access to resources, unless funds owned before one joined permitted the softening of austere frontier communalism. (Notable exceptions, like Timothy Horsfield, had remained outside the Oeconomy entirely.) Under the new system, people earned different amounts. The grist miller was offered half of his business's annual profits, the tanner only a third. The various artisans had an opportunity to negotiate over the details of their contracts—the tanner, Geitner, seems to have declined the offer of a share of the profits for a steady salary—but there was no suggestion that all were equal. They bargained, instead, based on their individual situations. Moreover, their businesses fared differently based on any number of economic factors, only one of which was the artisan's skill. Inequalities were not limited to master craftsmen, either. Some journeymen made £40 a year, while others made less. Master millwright Christensen earned only £40 a year, but he was a Single Brother until his death in 1776. Andreas the Mohr, a slave, received £35 a year (on good behavior), but he was married and supporting a wife. Moreover, the presence of craftsmen in town who did not work for the church made it impossible to ensure any sort of equality in wealth in Bethlehem after 1762, nor does there seem to have been any effort to do so. In short, although wages clustered around a rate of about £40 a year, Bethlehem's leaders accepted disparity of wealth between people as a natural part of their new economic system.[28]

The inequalities and hierarchies of labor joined the inequalities of gender. The single household of the Oeconomy became many separate households after the transition, and these new units were generally built around nuclear families. Hundreds of people in Bethlehem did not have such an option, however. In December 1761, the Single Brothers' and Single Sisters' Choirs contained 323 individuals. Under the Oeconomy system, the Choirs served as the centerpiece of the spiritual life for their members and daily life revolved around them, but they were not economic units, merely branches of the larger Oeconomy. In the transition, however, the Unity leadership in Herrnhut instructed that the Choir houses be set up "on a German footing," where each Choir existed as its own economic entity, owning businesses, charging its members for room and board, and, when necessary, borrowing funds on its own behalf.[29]

As a consequence, the new Choirs became, much like Bethlehem as a whole, more transparent and rational from a financial perspective. Each Choir had to have businesses to support itself, but it also earned money from the fees paid by those members who worked outside of the Choir. In the case of the Single Brothers, many of the town's journeymen lived in the Choir House. They paid a portion of their annual wages to the Choir for room and board. The Brothers continued to eat and pray together, but the "Table Book" beginning in 1762 indicates that the men began to pay for every meal consumed. Each Choir also took responsibility for its own workers, paying its ministers and *Vorsteher* (financial overseer) directly. In addition, the Choirs were financially separate from the church itself in Bethlehem—the unit that owned the land, the main businesses, and ran the missions. Each Choir paid an annual house rent for its building, 8 percent of the value, to the church.[30]

The Single Brothers faced the easiest transition. Full of able-bodied men, the Choir had the greatest opportunity to earn money. Perhaps on account of that potential, John Arbo, their new *Vorsteher* and the former leader of the Single Brothers in England, felt compelled to assert the Choir's devotion to the Gemeine as a whole, reassuring the rest of the community that it would not look only to its own interest. The Choir would naturally become more autonomous after the transition, but this did not mean that "the Single Brothers want to be independent and seek to make it so." Quite the opposite, in fact, he went on to insist: "No! That is far from [our intention], rather [the Brothers] want to be <u>free servants</u> of their Lord and the Gemeine." Indeed, the "Choirs should never, must never, and will never gather any treasure, rather their first desire will be when they can give where it is needed. Thus their entire economy and industry must be so established that they can well manage their necessary building, repairs, interest, and other payments whatever they may be, and above all take good care of their brethren." The Single Brothers, who naturally possessed the great resource of abundant labor, thus felt compelled to reiterate that they would remain committed to Bethlehem's general welfare.[31]

The Single Sisters faced as many challenges as the Brothers faced opportunities. While the majority of Single Brothers supported themselves by working either for the church or for independent artisans, the Single Sisters lived in a much more confined economic realm, limited to household work and traditionally female tasks, such as spinning and cooking.[32] Indicative of the economic problems the Single Sisters had to confront during the transition was a line written by Arbo during a session brainstorming what to do with the women's Choir: "There are two chief difficulties, which will be dealt with in time. The first is that a Choir House cannot well survive if it does not have a master's or merchant's profit from several industries. The other is that [the Single Sisters' House] has neither a cellar nor business accommodations." In other words, the Single Sisters had neither an obvious means of support, since there were no female masters, nor the architectural infrastructure to begin such an endeavor. To cobble together enough income to survive, Arbo's committee expected the Sisters to find whatever domestic work they could throughout the community, mending clothes or doing laundry. The transition committee remarked that some of the English women had experience as weavers and suggested that a linen weaving operation might be undertaken. Moreover, "maybe one could allow them a small piece of field in order to sow flax or hemp, which they could prepare and spin, and in time more could come to weave." The Sisters "could also buy wool, spin it in the House, and give it to the boys to be woven, for sale in the House."[33]

The Single Sisters responded to these plans with a detailed list of questions and requests. They pointed out that their house's kitchen was "not usable" as it was. They required more space, more dishes, and more cooking equipment. They were content with the suggestion that they take on the old Married People's dining room for a storeroom, but they required a garden for the future, and it had to be fenced in. It was early spring, and they could plant soon, but "Until something grows in the garden, . . . the Brothers and Sisters will be so good as to supply us with vegetables from the Gemein garden, or

else it will not look good for us." In addition, they needed space for their livestock, and eventually a bread oven, so they would not be forced to buy their
bread at full price from the bakery, "because we certainly must come into debt
in a half year." They worried as well about the girls from the country, who
lived in the Single Sisters' House and attended the schools, and about the care
of "old and weak" Sisters, who could not contribute to their own upkeep. On
the positive side, to show the resources they did possess, they made a catalog
of all the Sisters who could earn a living, dividing them up into occupations.
The list included tailors; twine twisters; cotton, worsted, wool, flax, and shoe
yarn spinners; kitchen workers, both in the Sisters' House and elsewhere in
town; women to work in the stables; and last, Agnes Meyer, a maid at the
Horsfield house. Clearly, more than a few of the women knew how to spin,
and that work became the core of the Single Sisters' new economy.[34]

The new system needed more than an invisible hand to make it work.
The Oeconomy had had a constitution of sorts, the 1754 Brotherly Agreement, but it had been little more than a list of principles and hardly fit the reorganized Bethlehem. A new 1762 Brotherly Agreement, in comparison, set
up a much more detailed form of government and explained the new state of
affairs. The document's core economic statement established that each person
was responsible for him- or herself. In its phrasing, the document bore a distinct resemblance to Herrnhut's 1727 Manorial Injunctions and Brotherly
Agreement. In each town, a person had to "work and earn his own bread,"
though both documents assured residents that no one would be left destitute.
The Bethlehem document added two additional clauses to this statute, however, that reflected the town's history as a pilgrim congregation, one emphasizing the community's religious work and the other the trend toward
privatization. First, the new document qualified the severity of the edict to
"work and earn" one's own bread by mentioning those church workers who
remained within the now drastically reduced Oeconomy. "Whoever has official business in the Gemeine and thus cannot support himself," it stated, "for
him the Gemeine must provide the necessities." This change reflected the reality of Bethlehem's ongoing status as a mission center and preserved some of
the old system in the new regime. There were more than a few such individuals, as many missionary families, widows, and Unity administrators still
called Bethlehem home. Second, the new statute stated that an impoverished
person would be fed only "insofar as he has no relatives who are responsible
to do so according to God's law." There are several possibilities for why the

transition's architects added the new clause. Perhaps they were responding to lessons learned during the intervening thirty-five years of Moravian town governance, or perhaps twenty years under the Oeconomy system had so weakened familial ties that leaders felt the need to acknowledge them explicitly. Either way, the new Brotherly Agreement made clear that family duties came before community responsibilities, unless, of course, religious work was at stake. Bethlehem's dual nature as a private and a religious economy coexisted even in this most basic statement.[35]

Setting up a new wage structure, establishing and outfitting independent households, and putting the Choirs on an independent footing laid the groundwork for a new economy in Bethlehem, one that incorporated substantial elements of a market system by introducing market relationships between the church and its members and between Bethlehem's residents, and yet the new economy also continued to have close connections to the church and its work. Many of the town's artisans still worked for the church, and their labors supported the ongoing missions of the Unity and the essential project of paying Bethlehem's sizable debts. Individuals lived in nuclear families, but the new houses they built were on lands owned by the church. The "House Rents" they paid went into the community's coffers. As the congregation gathered to worship and to hear the Daily Texts and mission reports, as they had done before the transition, they prayed together with retired missionaries and their widows, whom they collectively supported. Following the 1762 transition, Bethlehem's Moravians lived and worked in a market-based system, but they also continued to live in a town dedicated to the project of spreading the Gospel.

Taking Sides in a Renewed War

Bethlehem's economic transition proceeded with remarkable peace and order. The same cannot be said for the development of its missions, where the town's leaders tried to navigate a course between the needs of the missions, the increasing anger of their neighbors at the presence of Indians near Bethlehem, and Herrnhut's new centralization of mission authority. The immediate need for change came from renewed violence. With the start of Pontiac's War in 1763, Pennsylvania's tense truce between Euro-American colonists and Native Americans fractured and fell into violence once again.[36] Both European and native Moravians had to find new strategies for survival, and the consequences of those new strategies permanently altered Bethlehem's relationship to the missionary work the town had carried out for more than two decades. Thenceforth, Bethlehem's residents worked with a far more limited range of options when it came to expressing the outreach work that was at the center of the town's religious purpose.

As with the start of the Seven Years' War the preceding decade, the events of the mid-1760s began to the west. When the imperial conflict between France and Britain drew to a close and France agreed to relinquish its North American territories, native leaders in the Great Lakes region sought ways to reestablish the delicate balance between European powers—or at least the political space to maneuver it represented—that they had maintained in the past. The resulting war set off a renewed wave of interracial violence in Pennsylvania. From the native perspective, the long years of war had solved little in terms of competition for land. In the relatively peaceful years between 1759 and 1763, for example, Europeans had begun moving into the Wyoming Valley, north of Bethlehem. Both colonial and imperial officials attempted to control the growing crisis by separating the settlers and Indians (most notably through the Royal Proclamation of 1763) and also by subduing native groups, who understandably looked with trepidation on their future within the expanding British Empire. The Indians' problem was tragically intractable, however. British colonists continued to move onto lands Indians did not want to cede, and the vision of a settled society that Europeans brought with them did not leave any room for Indian neighbors. There was no simple or peaceful solution as long as Indians remained in large numbers in the territories the British and Americans now considered their own.[37]

In 1763, Bethlehem found itself once more at the heart of the violence, as it had been eight years earlier at the time of the assault on Gnadenhütten. In April, the Delaware leader and erstwhile Moravian Teedyuscung was murdered at his home in the Wyoming Valley, and the village he lived in burned. In August, several Moravian Indians were killed, and more Indians were found murdered by Europeans near the Susquehanna and as far south as Virginia. The killings set off cycles of retaliation on both sides. A group of Susquehanna Delaware attacked a band of Pennsylvania militiamen at a tavern, and white residents of the Wyoming Valley were also murdered. Those Indians who lived most closely among Europeans bore the brunt of the anger, however. Moravian Indians at Nain and Wechquetank were accused of the killings at the tavern. Most tragically, a group of twenty Conestoga Indians in Lancaster County were murdered, six in their homes and then a further fourteen in the county jail where they had been taken for their "protection"; their guards did nothing to intervene for their safety. The renewed violence trapped the Indian Moravians and their European coreligionists in an impossible bind, as the interracial community that existed around Bethlehem became a political impossibility. Trying to quench the spreading fire, Pennsylvania's provincial authorities moved to eliminate the Moravian Indians as a potential source of conflict.[38]

Colonial leaders believed the close proximity maintained by European Moravians and their Indian converts simply could not be permitted in the colony's increasingly stark racial environment. Effectively, provincial authorities believed the Indians at Nain and Wechquetank had to be removed from the region. (The irony that the European and Indian Moravians had themselves already placed the Monocacy Creek between them likely went unnoticed.) On November 5, 1763, government officials contacted those in Bethlehem to inform them that "all of the Indians, those in Nain as well as those who already fled to Nazareth from Wechquetank, young and old, should come to Philadelphia, where they are to be directed to a residence where they will be more secure." The Moravians reacted with "prayers and entreaties that He blessedly prevent all feared of disadvantages for His affairs among the Indians in this land and not allow Himself to be robbed of any of those whom He chose and received as the wages of His pain." The next day, Moravian leader Nathanael Seidel informed the Indians in Nain that they were "to surrender themselves willingly as befits a people of God and afterwards deliver their guns to the specified persons, according to official order."[39] Shortly thereafter, the Indian communities gathered their belongings and prepared to move to Philadelphia. In the three days before the Indians left town, residents organized what material relief they could, and missionaries arranged to accompany the Indians, but no evidence suggests that the European Moravians fought to maintain the close ties to missionary work that they had built.

Indeed, though the European Moravians mourned the loss of the missions at Nain and Wechquetank, they did not view the Indians' removal as a tearing apart of "their" community. On November 8, the Indian congregations left for Philadelphia under sheriff's escort. Peter Boehler, another of Bethlehem's leading ministers, preached a sermon that indicated both the pain and the finality of this turning point for the Moravians and the Indians with whom they had worked. As the diarist recorded, Boehler drew on the surprisingly apt Daily Text, Psalm 5:8–9, which read, "Lead me, O LORD, in thy righteousness because of mine enemies; make thy way straight before my face. For there is no faithfulness in their mouth; their inward part is very wickedness; their throat is an open sepulchre, they flatter with their tongue."[40] He applied the text to the "extraordinary experiences of these two oft-mentioned Indian congregations, after which the Gemeine sent the heart-felt wish: Hold them tight—You have spilled Your blood for this heathen Gemeine." Bethlehem's European Moravians saw the Indians as a separate congregation, a separate Gemeine. They mourned for the Indians, and "on their knees, under a rich flow of tears, they commended them as the first fruit from the heathen here—whom He won through his bloody sweat and gathered with pure work—to the watch and protection of Israel," but they did not attempt to resist the provincial authorities.[41] Bethlehem's European Moravians found comfort for these events in their faith, but by accepting and grieving the loss of the Indian community, they tacitly accepted the governmental and popular decision that natives should not live among Euro-Americans, though that choice effectively ended the possibility of significant missionary work among Native Americans for the foreseeable future.

While those in Bethlehem quietly accepted a segregated racial environment, the Moravian Indians embarked on a long and difficult ordeal. Within a few days, Bethlehem received word from Bernhard Grube, one of the missionaries, that the Indians had been housed on Province Island, just outside the city of Philadelphia. The journey had not been easy, as "the fury of the people in Philadelphia was indescribable, and we had to stand in front of the barracks for fully three hours and take all kinds of disgrace and scorn." The Moravian Indians "like sheep, had many thousands accompanying us through the city, yet it came off without harm." Their trials had only just begun, however, and, for the next eighteen months the members of Bethlehem's principal mission in America remained imprisoned, endured violent threats, and suffered shortages of food and lethal epidemic disease.[42]

Meanwhile, Bethlehem's Moravians encountered mounting evidence that biracial communities would no longer be accepted in eastern Pennsylvania. As the months wore on, they pursued a path of accommodating this new environment, rather than searching for new ways to establish a permanent and local mission community. They had good reason to be concerned about hostility from their neighbors. Pennsylvania's wider European population continued to distrust those who had worked with the Indians for so long, and those in Bethlehem "could not look on the situation as anything but a persecution of the people of God here." In November 1763, just a few days after the Indians had left Nain, "our watchers caught sight of fire in the oil mill" in the middle of the night. Although rapid action saved the town's nearby industrial buildings from damage, residents were badly shaken nonetheless, not knowing if hostile Indians were lying in wait, or if the danger came from white neighbors bent on vigilantism. Either way, maintaining a good watch seemed essential. The situation made Pennsylvania a frightening place for the Moravians, as Bethlehem reported back to Herrnhut, and there was no doubt that the cause was the group's close relationship to the Indians. "We must say," Nathanael Seidel wrote a few months later, "that it is presently an evil and grievous time in Pennsylvania, almost through the whole land, and the unrest has not yet subsided." Threats were renewed, even after the Indians moved south to Philadelphia, "For we heard, first a couple days ago, that evil attacks against Bethlehem were in the works, and [the rumors] say the nest that so long had the Indians by it must be totally destroyed."[43]

Prosecution followed the threats and vandalism. Renatus, one of the Indian men who had been in Nain (and had since been moved to Philadelphia) was accused of having participated in the 1763 attack on the Irish Settlement, a few miles northwest of Bethlehem. This was not the first such encounter the Moravian Indians had had with the law. In October 1758, Moravian Indians "had come under suspicion for having killed people over the Blue Mountains, and robbed their houses." In that case, however, even though there had been individuals willing to swear to having witnessed the events, the accused had been in Philadelphia at the time of the attack and were consequently cleared. In Renatus's case, six years later, the Moravians doubted that he would receive a fair trial. Rumors had been circulating in the area about who the true perpetrators were, but "a misfortune in the English law" meant that witnesses had to be eyewitnesses, and Indians could not be witnesses in any case. In the emotional trial that ensued, "the grieving widow . . . knew to play her role so perfectly, that many tears were extorted from the listeners." The defense presented its case, not least of which was that the widow had spent four days in Bethlehem after the attack and had assured people that she recognized none of the murderers. But others argued, "it was impossible to recognize painted Indians." Renatus was ultimately found not guilty, but the verdict did not resolve the sticky situation either for Renatus or for the Moravians. "Regardless, most [people] remained by the opinion that they had had before," recorded one Moravian leader. The case drove one point home to Bethlehem's leaders: as long as the Moravians maintained close ties to their missions, the entire community remained in a difficult position in relation to its neighbors.[44]

The increasing tension in Pennsylvania's racial environment had a direct effect on the Moravians' missionary work. Bethlehem's leaders began making decisions about the missions and about Moravian Indians that reflected their willingness (if not their happiness) to work within the terms set out by the Euro-American colonists. At this point, the Moravians redefined their own racial communities in a move that resembled the return of European captives by Indians that British authorities were demanding at the same time.[45] In January 1764, two months after those from Nain and Wechquetank moved to Philadelphia, four Indian women who had been living as full members of Bethlehem's Single Sisters' Choir were relocated to Nazareth, where leaders thought they could be hidden more effectively. When that situation too turned out to be inadequate, the women were transported to Philadelphia to join the Indian community housed there. The episode was a complicated one: while town leaders accurately read that their neighbors perceived an ongoing Indian presence in Bethlehem as dangerous and even traitorous, the individuals involved had been living for years among European Moravians and were integrated into that community. One of the women, a Mahican from Shekomeko named Maria, for example, had been living with the Choir for over fifteen years and had been a communicant since January 1748. She had been working in the children's laundry and had received wages for her labor since the end of the communal Oeconomy. The transition to Philadelphia came as an affront to her. During the brief time the native women spent in Bethlehem on the way to the capital, Maria "was very angry." The Moravians emphasized, however, her subsequent reconciliation with her fate and what they viewed as her humble Christian behavior. They recorded that "she spoke with Anna Rosel," her Choir leader, "in a sinnerlike way and believed finally that it was the Savior's will to go to her nation." In this process of physical removal, Bethlehem's leaders literally and figuratively relocated the women to "nations" of which they had not effectively been a part for years, recreating an ethnic identity that had become quite blurred, despite the ubiquitous appellation of native converts by names such as "Marthel the Indian" or "Elias the Indian." After the women left, Bethlehem had little local evidence of their decades of missionary work.[46]

The Indian community imprisoned in Philadelphia endured far more than their coreligionists in Bethlehem, however, as Pennsylvania's countryside erupted in a continuation of Pontiac's War. The 1763–64 Paxton Boys riots, in which hundreds of Pennsylvania's angry Western colonists demanded that the provincial government act more aggressively to protect their settlements, turned their anger directly on the Moravian Indians in Philadelphia. Threats forced the whole group to flee under a military escort. An ill-formed plan to move the Indians to northern New York failed when the governor of that colony refused them passage, and they had to turn back toward Philadelphia at the last minute. There they moved into the vacant army barracks, where they weathered the trials of poverty, boredom, and confinement until the spring of 1765. The captives attracted much attention. Curious Pennsylvanians dropped by to ogle them and occasionally to buy a hunting bow or a basket. Provincial authorities attempted to make sure supplies were sufficient, but they often failed. Meanwhile, the missionaries struggled to maintain control over the community, but time made clear that they could do little to change the situation, and the Indians' patience wore thin.[47]

Over the course of the year, more Indians trickled into to the barracks, reflecting the increasing tendency of European Americans to lump all Indians into a single category. Meanwhile, death took a terrible toll. Both trends gradually decreased the mission's integrity as a Moravian community. In June, Joseph Fox, the group's primary liaison with Pennsylvania authorities, arrived with fourteen "Nanticokes and Delawares . . . who have been staying in the Jerseys for a while and were maintained by the Quakers, who have asked the Honorable Governor to take them into the barracks for better security." The Moravian missionaries remained in charge, however, at least as far as the government was concerned, as Fox "reminded [the newcomers] to be obedient and to follow our advice so that we would not make any complaints about them."[48] Meanwhile, disease decreased the community's ranks. Roughly 140 Indians had arrived in Philadelphia from Nain and Wechquetank. By the end of 1764, almost exactly a year after their arrival, fifty-six had died, twenty-one of them children. The missionaries watched the demise of their community with considerable dismay, seeing their years of energetic work among Pennsylvania's Indians expire around them. Two of the adult dead in 1764 were the "first fruits of the heathen Gemeine in North America, Jacob and Sara." Their deaths marked the end of an era for Moravian mission work, and a far more significant change for Bethlehem than the economic changes that preceded them.[49]

In January 1765, the situation moved toward resolution, after a cautious peace was declared between the British and the Western Indians. In Philadelphia, it was not the Moravians but the Indians who took the initiative, though they sought a solution that kept them within the Moravian fold. Representatives met with William Allen, Pennsylvania's chief justice, and suggested that the Indians return to Nain, just outside Bethlehem, at least for the winter, and "be cared for with necessary provisions" there. Allen passed the request along to the governor's secretary. The missionaries described themselves as "totally passive in this matter." Instead of taking a position, they "left it to our dear Father, who will direct everything according to his will." Leaders in Bethlehem were not as circumspect, however, and they had already decided that reviving Nain was not possible. A few days after the proposal was given to Allen, "Br. Nathanael's letter was read to the Indians, and their hope to live in Nain again therewith completely changed, because the white people were still hostile, etc. etc. This made a *stop* so that our Indians, who were ordered to go to Mr. Allen again this afternoon, did not go."[50]

At the end of March, fifteen months after leaving Bethlehem the first time, the party began its return journey northward. Before they left, representatives of the community made a formal declaration to the governor of their loyalty, their gratitude for his care and protection, and their intention to continue as Christians under the teachings of the Moravians. The travelers would pass through Bethlehem this time, but, from the perspective of the European Moravians, the possibility of their staying either in the central Moravian town or in the adjacent Nain was no longer under consideration, regardless of what the mission community hoped. By the time the Indians were freed from the Philadelphia barracks, Moravian decisions in Pennsylvania were operating in accordance with, rather than in opposition to, Pennsylvania's emerging racial divide.[51]

The Moravian Indians and their missionaries returned to a Lehigh Valley very different from the one they had left. The number of places available to them for settlement within easy distance of Bethlehem had sharply decreased. Concurring sentiments from Bethlehem's leaders, Pennsylvania's authorities, and the region's European population in general precluded the possibility of settling in the town or even on Moravian lands nearby. They journeyed, therefore, to Wyalusing (Wyoming) on the northern branch of the Susquehanna. The town they established, Friedenshütten, proved one of the most successful of this era of mission work, due in no small part to David Zeisberger, one of the Moravians' most prominent evangelists in the Revolutionary era. Unfortunately for the Indians, however, the towns established in the late 1760s were all short-lived, as both encroaching white settlement and continued Iroquois hegemony over the native peoples of the area forced the Christianized Delaware to move farther west. By the early 1770s, Friedenshütten and a series of small missions on the Allegheny River had all been abandoned in favor of new settlements in Ohio—ushering yet another phase in the Moravians' mission work. Those villages, including another doomed Gnadenhütten (this one the site of a massacre by American soldiers), lasted until the end of the Revolutionary War, when they too were abandoned, and missionaries again followed their congregations farther from American settlement[52] (Map 4).

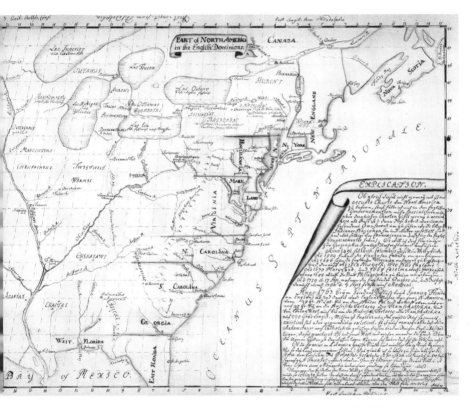

Map 4. This map of North America was drawn shortly after the French defeat in 1763. The text outlines the history of North America, beginning with Columbus's arrival. Moravians in Herrnhut were intrigued by the missionary possibilities of Great Britain's vastly expanded empire, but those in Bethlehem were wary of the tense racial climate in the Mid-Atlantic. Ts.Mp.212.2. Courtesy Unity Archives, Herrnhut.

Troubles in the Unity

By 1764, Bethlehem's status as a pilgrim congregation, left largely unchanged at the end of the Oeconomy, faced assault from two directions. Most obviously, the Mid-Atlantic's increasingly polarized racial environment no longer made close relationships to Indians in Bethlehem's vicinity a viable option. The centralizing process underway in Herrnhut had also deprived the town of its key role in the West Indian missions. Indeed, the news of that shift arrived just after Renatus's trial, while the Nain and Wechquetank Indians were still imprisoned in Philadelphia. The consequences of these changes for Bethlehem's religious life became evident only in the following years, but in the short term, one final trauma shook Bethlehem, forcing the town's residents to confront their future as a Moravian community and as a missionary community.

As Unity leaders took the helm of the missions, the prospect of Bethlehem's having Indian neighbors, much less Indian residents, became a source of conflict between American Moravians and their European directors. The roots of the conflict lay in the different experiences the two groups had during the long years of the war. In Herrnhut, the deepest wounds were financial. Unity leaders believed the crisis could be surmounted only through careful planning, which to them meant centralized management. They rightly worried that if the whole system were not brought under control, all the achievements of the Brüdergemeine would slip away. Bethlehem's experience was equally visceral, but the racialized frontier war in Pennsylvania taught the American Moravians that the key to survival was keeping peace with the neighbors. Bethlehem would be in danger, they believed, as long as Indians lived in or near town. The disagreement began when Herrnhut's desire for centralization ran headlong into Bethlehem's conviction that the days of new, local missions were over.

Maintaining an international network was difficult enough in the eighteenth century, and slow communications exacerbated all other issues. After the 1764 General Synod, a committee convened in Herrnhut to reexamine the future and needs of all the Unity missions, completing the process begun more informally (or, rather, more autocratically) in the years before the synod. The problem of encroaching white settlement dominated the conversation on North America, as Herrnhut's leaders recognized that the chief difficulty facing native Moravians was their vulnerability to whites who were unwilling to tolerate the Indians in their midst and sought to eliminate them from their borders. The Indians at Pachgatgoch, Connecticut, the sole remaining mission outside of the community then confined in the Philadelphia barracks, "live among the white people and are in everything subject to the English laws, even those who still are not Christians." Nonetheless, the conference determined to maintain Pachgatgoch for the sake of the converted Indians who lived there and because of the hard-fought legal battles of the 1740s in which the Moravians had struggled to win permission to proselytize in New York and Connecticut.[53]

Much more problematic was the future of the Indians then in Philadelphia. "What the Savior will do with this little Indian Gemeine in the future, we must wait [to discover]," they commented, though the parameters of what He might suggest seemed limited to them. In particular, they wrote, "They will probably never again come to live in Nain," a circumstance which perhaps was not so unexpected, since "it was nothing but dear need that caused the Indian brothers and sisters to have to live among the white people before, which in any case has its difficulties." Furthermore, they added, "on the borders of the white people they should probably also never be established, because in that case, if a war broke out, they are first and most exposed to danger from all sides." An abortive discussion of new mission fields in America followed, but some ideas were now impracticable because of war, others because of changed political circumstances. The conference found hope in the prospect of Britain's now greatly enlarged empire, but did not see a quick way to make use of it. It ultimately decided, via the Lot, to recommend merely that Bethlehem be "attentive" to the Indian missions.[54]

Herrnhut's awareness of the political challenges then facing the missions to the Indians seems to have faded from mind, however, when leaders there contemplated a second issue weighing on their hearts: that the missions already in existence were failing from within as formerly faithful Indians drifted away. Letters received in March 1765, a few months after the mission conference, raised this worry for German Moravian leaders. "The Indians are going out of the city and into the countryside again," reported the missionaries in Philadelphia, "which however has no good effect on their hearts." Furthermore, as those in Herrnhut observed, "most Indians are in a sad situation and do not follow their missionaries [*Arbeitern*], so that life for Brother and Sister Grube and Schmick becomes difficult." Nonetheless, the presence within the troubled congregation of a small number who continued to be faithful to the

Moravian way gave the Unity's governors hope, if only they could be protected from all the dangerous influences—white and Indian—around them.
After brief consideration, they submitted a new question to the Lot:
"Whether one should write to the Conference in Bethlehem as a good suggestion the idea to settle the faithful hearts among the Indians in Nain?" The Lot
indicated that the Savior concurred, and Peter Boehler, another leader who
had spent much time in Bethlehem (indeed, he had preached in Bethlehem
the day the Indians were removed to Philadelphia), quickly drew up the necessary letter to Bethlehem reflecting what amounted to a complete about-face
in Herrnhut's Indian policy in just a few short months.[55]

News took considerable time to traverse the Atlantic, however, and this
reality could damage transatlantic relations, even within the Unity. Bethlehem's leaders did not meet to discuss the suggestion, raised at the synodal conference, that they should be attentive to missionary opportunities, until July
1765, at which point they also had before them the contradictory instruction,
endorsed by the presumably infallible Lot, that they resurrect Nain. At that
time, shortly after the Indians in Philadelphia had traveled north to Wyalusing, leaders with particular interest or expertise in the area—including David
Zeisberger, and the Schmicks, who had been in Philadelphia—convened to
determine what could be done to preserve this essential aspect of Bethlehem's
religious life. For the most part, the assembled leaders avoided discussing
plans for new or major undertakings in missionary work, and Zeisberger
noted that "for this time no missions were to be thought of among the Indians, because they had not yet resettled since the war." Despite Britain's vastly
enlarged territory, which Herrnhuters had seen as a great opportunity, the
combined forces of Bethlehem's financial challenges and the tense racial atmosphere of the region made new projects unthinkable. References to future
plans were oblique and minimal; even attempting to teach Indian languages
to new missionaries appeared too complicated to be undertaken at that time.
Instead, Bethlehem's leaders focused their energies on how to handle the immediate futures of the two congregations they retained. The rumor that the
Six Nations were about to sell a large piece of land on the upper Susquehanna
to the English seemed to imperil the new mission at Wyalusing, while an in-
vitation from the Cayuga to move into Iroquoia was politically complicated.
In sum, though the nature of Bethlehem's relationships with its Indian missions had changed significantly as the Indians steadily moved farther from
town, the ongoing needs of those congregations provided church leaders in

eastern Pennsylvania with both plenty to do and reason to be cautious about attempting anything new.[56]

The Bethlehem conference addressed the specific issue of Nain with an eye toward skirting the imperative of the Lot sent from Herrnhut and yet also avoiding conflict within the Unity. Shaping their logic, however, was the desire to protect Bethlehem's peace vis-à-vis its white neighbors. "As concerns the move back to Nain of the Indians," they concluded, "there are great reservations there, because since the Indian attack on the Settlement, their lives were neither day nor night safe, and [they] were therefore brought to Philadelphia." Time had passed, but racial anger had not cooled. Even the Indians' brief passage through the Lehigh Valley on their way north had been enough to excite new problems, they said, and in just a couple of days "before they moved to Indian land, the opposition of our neighbors was raised into being again, so that the authorities themselves deemed it necessary to give them a safe escort to the border and to let them take another retreat than was first intended." The impossibility of a new mission at Nain was clear, "because this opposition has not yet lifted, so those Indians, who settled in Nain again, would always be in danger." Bethlehem's leaders hoped to convince Herrnhut that they had good cause for ignoring the Lot, but they also wanted to assuage the concerns that the Indians would be better served through bringing the faithful few into the fold. "Because now however the complete Gemeine of the Indians in Machilusing [Wyalusing] is again together, as they were in the barracks," they wrote, "and therefore the circumstance is not there, for which the direction of the Directorate was given us, thus we have found nothing to consider for <u>this</u> time regarding Nain."[57] These technical grounds for avoiding the Herrnhut Lot—that they could not identify a specific subset of the larger Indian Gemeine that should be given special spiritual care at Nain—may have been somewhat disingenuous, but the overarching sentiment was clear. From Bethlehem's perspective, intimate relations between Moravians in town and the Indian missions were a thing of the past and dangerous, even impossible.

For Bethlehem, all future mission projects were in doubt, and without this connection, so too was the town's central purpose. The Oeconomy, founded to support missionary work, had ended. Bethlehem's connections to the West Indies had been eliminated, and the volatile local situation precluded new missionary outreach in America. The Moravians' deep ties to their coreligionists across the Atlantic remained important, however, so handling the disagreement itself, rather than fighting over Nain, became the paramount issue. In the year surrounding the conference on the future of the Indian missions, a tense series of transatlantic exchanges made this point clear. In May 1765, Herrnhut received word that the Indians in the barracks at Philadelphia had requested but been denied permission to return to Nain for a short time. Early the next month, Unity leaders learned that Bethlehem had decided it was too dangerous to resettle Nain, though they assumed that "they had thus not yet received the Lot from here that they should keep the faithful Indians in Nain." By late July, when another detailed set of reports arrived from Bethlehem, the Unity leaders' frustration began to show through. "It was very difficult for us," they recorded, "that the direction [of the Lot] that we have regarding Nain was completely not reflected by the [leadership in Bethlehem], likewise that Pachgatgoch will be left and in the whole region the Indians shall not be taken on any longer."[58]

Finally, in late September, the report of Bethlehem's missionary conference arrived, reporting the Americans' view of Nain. Before this happened, however, the Unity moved to solve the issue, as well as others that had begun to divide the two settlements, by sending a representative from Herrnhut on an extended "visitation" to North America. The instructions accompanying David Nitschmann, a principal Moravian leader, on his journey demonstrate the difficult situation in which Bethlehem found itself. It could not follow Herrnhut's instructions to found new missions and survive in Pennsylvania; it could not violate the Lot and remain in good standing with Herrnhut. Nitschmann's instructions reiterated, verbatim, earlier comments that the Lot "regarding Nain was completely not reflected" by leaders in Bethlehem, and they further noted that the disassembling of Nain's physical structures that had followed cut them "very near." In this moment of anger over the daughter congregation's disobedience, Herrnhut's leaders took refuge in Bethlehem's history as a mission settlement: "The Chief purpose [*haupt Destination*] of Bethlehem is to be a faithful mother and wet nurse for the poor Indians." So fundamental was missionary work to Bethlehem and the larger Unity that "we would have sooner expected to see Bethlehem to spill a thousand tears at the real departure of the remaining faithful Indians, as that it would be reported to us as something minor." Furthermore, they continued, there was the not insignificant issue of having ignored the Lot, which was viewed as the word of God.[59]

Nitschmann's 1766 visitation, and the concurrent arrival of Bethlehem's

explanation for why it had not resettled Nain, soothed the tense waters separating the two Moravian settlements, but did nothing to change the marginal
position to which Bethlehem's missionary work had fallen in larger Moravian
plans. Intradenominational harmony could not reverse the twin streams shaping the future of religious work in Bethlehem. New Indian missions would
never again surround Bethlehem and tie a significant number of its residents
to the evangelical project they represented, and Herrnhut's emphasis on a
more centralized church and missionary organization would continue to con-
sign North America and particularly Pennsylvania to a peripheral position for
the foreseeable future. Indeed, in May 1766, even before Herrnhut heard of
Nitschmann's safe arrival in America, Unity leaders decided to reorganize further the mission bureaucracy so that "everything would be set on one footing
in America as in Europe." Agents appointed in Herrnhut, and reporting only
to Herrnhut, would thenceforth replace Bethlehem's governing council at the
head of day-to-day mission issues regarding America. Bethlehem no longer
had any formal role in the spread of the Gospel.[60]

The struggles between Bethlehem and Herrnhut indicate how difficult it
was to maintain a cohesive transatlantic community. Closer ties, and shorter
reins on decision-making in North America after Zinzendorf's death, exacerbated rather than lessening the problems. They also suggest something more
basic with regard to Bethlehem, however. Though leaders in Pennsylvania
fought to assert their knowledge and authority over the town's missions, ultimately they acquiesced to the larger need for harmony within the Unity. In
doing so they fully accepted the role Herrnhut had been guiding Bethlehem
into: that of a congregation town, a "baptized town," whose primary purpose
was to encourage the spiritual life of those within it. The Unity carried out
missions, Bethlehem, for the most part, did not. In the more peaceful years
that followed, between 1765 and the end of the era of the American Revolution, Bethlehem's residents worked out what it meant for them to live in this
new place, no longer communal and no longer closely tied to evangelical outreach. In the process, religion came to play a significantly different role in
their economic lives from the one it had had in the quarter century since the
town's founding.

CHAPTER 7

A Change in Mission

IN JANUARY 1777, Revolutionary leader John Adams traveled through Bethlehem on his way to Baltimore, where Congress had convened after fleeing from British troops in Philadelphia. In his account of what he termed "that curious and remarkable Town," he described (as many visitors did) the high quality of the accommodations at the Sun Inn and remarked that "it belongs it seems to the Society, is furnished, at their Expence, and is kept for their Profit, or at their Loss." He noted the impressive mechanical water works that delivered fresh water throughout the town, and remarked that "they have a fine Sett of Mills." This included "the best Grist Mills and bolting Mills, that are anywhere to be found," as well as "the best fulling Mills, an oil Mill, a Mill to grind Bark for the Tanyard, a Dying House where all Colours are died, Machines for shearing Cloth &c." Adams went on to discuss the Single Brothers', Sisters', and Widows' establishments, which were the most visible vestiges of the communal economy that had been abrogated fifteen years earlier. He was clearly impressed by the Moravians' industrious operations in Bethlehem, but that fact made him question whether a true Christian spirit animated the town. "Christian Love is their professed Object," he wrote, "but it is said they love Money and make their public Institutions subservient to the Gratification of that Passion."[1]

Adams's comments, no matter how cynical, indicate a changed role for religion in the economic life of Bethlehem during the twenty years after the end of the Seven Years' War. The social, political, and racial upheavals of the early 1760s changed the tenor of British America and initiated a new era in the region's history. The strains of more than a decade of fighting led to economic disruption throughout the Atlantic world, while the elimination of the French from North America remade the political relationships among all the continent's peoples. Euro-Americans soon found they resented the new impositions of empire that followed the triumphal successes of 1763, while Native Americans, including the Moravian Indians, faced the problems of encroaching settlement by ever more aggressive colonists. All of these factors changed the environment within which the Moravians made choices about how to govern their economic lives. For most people in town, the missions receded as a justification for their labors and as a dominant force in their life choices, and they were replaced by attention to individual behavior.

Bethlehem's newly individualized economy represented both the continuation of earlier trends and a significant departure from the town's older economy. Moravian economic practice had always resembled the mainstream, and this remained true. As they had in the heady and expansionistic days of the 1740s and 1750s, the Moravians responded flexibly to economic situations in the 1770s and 1780s, balancing profit with what they considered moral behavior. Economic change was, of course, a constant reality in an evolving marketplace, and thus the need to innovate provided a form of economic consistency. Despite these continuities, however, the Moravians' longstanding economic practices took on a new character, and a new kind of spiritual significance, with the end of the town's close connections to missions. Before the town's transitions, all who took part in the pilgrim congregation used their skills for the shared goal of spreading the Gospel. Without that common project, a laborer's efforts, his or her profit or loss, accrued only to that individual. In the new economy, workers built careers and protected their own and their families' interests, even as they also submitted themselves to church oversight. Profits, once a matter for leaders who balanced missionary work with collective economic labors, now became a concern that individuals addressed when they managed their personal financial lives. Labor, which before had received its meaning from its relationship to missionary endeavors, now had to provide spiritual sustenance of a different kind. Individuals who had found joy in their submission to the will of the Savior now had to assume control of their own moral and economic lives. The reconfiguration of economic choices required a new kind of religious lens for framing economic choices. Individual responsibility and individual conscience became the hallmarks of Moravian economic life, in the place of shared religious outreach. Residents now turned inward for religious meaning. After 1775, the crises of the Revolution only served to intensify that trend.

Creating Careers

Work, the labor of an individual person, provided the structure upon which Bethlehem's new moral economy grew. The ideas the Moravians drew on were rooted within the broader context of European and American Protestantism. In the sixteenth century, Martin Luther turned centuries of Catholic doctrine on its head when he argued that ordinary toil had the same value as the contemplative life of the monk. John Calvin and his Puritan followers also emphasized the belief that a disciplined life, including diligent labor, was a moral imperative for Christians, who were performing God's work on earth. Political economists like John Locke and Adam Smith performed a similar transformation in political thought, arguing that industriousness led to a better and more prosperous society. By the time Bethlehem was founded in the mid-eighteenth century, most of the Moravians' European neighbors shared the belief that hard work signified an admirable moral life and accepted productive labor's positive value as compared to that of both of its premodern opposites: religious contemplation and privileged leisure.[2]

During the Oeconomy, the Moravians' emphasis on communal effort to support shared religious goals minimized the relationship between an individual and his or her labor, even while the group continued to embrace a traditionally Protestant valuation of hard work as beneficial. What mattered was the shared outcome, not the individuals' effort. After the termination of the Oeconomy and the removal of the missions to greater distances from Bethlehem in the mid-1760s, two interrelated developments reshaped the nature of work in Bethlehem, opening ideological space for individual economic labors to become a more prominent part of life over the next decades. First, individuals could no longer move easily between mission posts and the Bethlehem workshops, because they had personal responsibilities for homes, families, and businesses. The likelihood plummeted that an individual Moravian after the 1760s might spend some time in the mission field furthering the church's shared goals of evangelizing. Though nearly a third of the adult men in town in 1752 performed religious work at some time during their careers, in just under two decades this total fell to 18 percent. An even more precipitous decline, from 53 percent to 23 percent, can be seen among married men. Those living in Bethlehem in 1770 were far less likely to be full-time religious workers than their peers a generation earlier. This trend points to the second change to come out of the transitions: the work lives of Bethlehem's men in the period between 1765 and 1780 centered primarily on the secular trades for which they were trained rather than on proselytizing, and they shouldered the burdens of those trades, as well as the significant costs of their newly disaggregated households, as individuals. Work in Bethlehem during these years entailed new financial responsibilities at the same moment as it was deprived of the connection to religious labors that had been so important for providing religious meaning in the past. The two factors reinforced each other in a powerful cycle: fewer people went on mission, and those in town undertook lives and responsibilities that made it more difficult to take up a mission post.[3]

For those Moravians who came of age after the end of the Oeconomy, their life stories told very different tales from those produced in their parents' generation. Rather than moving to follow mission calls or at the request of the community, they made decisions shaped by their professions, and they moved between established Moravian towns. Take, for example, Joseph Horsfield, the son of Timothy and Mary Horsfield. He was born a year after his parents moved to Bethlehem, into the town's first private house. He grew up within the community and learned the trade of a saddle-maker. His lebenslauf, written by his children rather than by Joseph himself, recorded the ebb and flow of his fortune. He built a side business as a lawyer and justice of the peace, gave up the saddler's trade, and tried his hand at land speculating. He rose to important positions within the town hierarchy, but he never served a mission post and, most strikingly, he lived his entire life in Bethlehem and Nazareth, a sharp change from the common experiences of the earlier, extremely mobile, generation. One of the young Horsfield's contemporaries, Christian Renatus Heckewelder, moved several times as an adult, but each time in search of professional fulfillment and always between established North American Moravian communities. He was born in York, England, in 1750, and he came to Bethlehem with his parents in 1754. In 1765, he traveled with a group of young men to North Carolina to help with the building of Salem, where he stayed and learned his chosen trade. Although he drifted a bit over the next decade, he did not leave the Moravian fold, and in 1781 he took over the job of storekeeper in Bethlehem. In 1794, "he took over the store in Emmaus, because he had occasionally mentioned his desire to run a store on his own account."

After six more years, Heckewelder desired to be back in a congregation town, and took the opportunity to work in the store in Hope, New Jersey, a new Moravian settlement. He died there he died two years later. His short life manifests one of the new opportunities of the post-Oeconomy era: the ability to reshape one's business environment at will, while still remaining within Moravian communities. Both Horsfield and Heckewelder lived lives defined by professional transitions, and missionary work was largely absent. (Heckewelder's older bother, John, followed a very different path and became a famous missionary.) Though their spiritual experiences loomed large in their biographies—Heckewelder's was punctuated with devotional poetry—the individual's labors, not the community's, determined career paths.[4]

Bethlehem's Moravians responded to the reconfiguring of labor as primarily an individual economic enterprise by defining the terms of their occupations and their ongoing relationships with the church, which was often their employer. The Strangers' Store, the most important single business in town, is indicative of larger trends. Leaders recognized its financial importance for the church during the 1762 transition and moved quickly to put it on a professional footing. In that year they asked Johann Francis Oberlin, a relative newcomer in town though not to the Moravian church, if he would consider taking complete charge of the store. Oberlin carefully negotiated the terms of his employment, as he recognized his personal interest was at stake too. He responded to the offer by saying that he would be uncomfortable taking on this duty with William Edmonds, the previous storekeeper, still working alongside him, because the latter had had charge of the store for so long that the reversal of the lines of authority might create personal difficulties: "what if there was something to clean in the cellar or the store, and I had something else to do at that time, how could I ask him to do it, when until now he has been accustomed to doing just the reverse with me?" Oberlin also laid down certain conditions under which he was willing to take on the store. He would receive the current inventory at a 15 percent discount and afterwards pay 6 percent interest to the church either yearly or half-yearly. He would also pay interest on the space that the store occupied, but he expected financial help for enlarging the store, which was "truly too small, and soon will be yet smaller."[5]

Oberlin also took initiative in defining what kinds of business the store would pursue, even though its ownership stayed in the hands of the church. Indeed, unlike many artisans in town who worked for a share of their shop's profits, Oberlin received a salary. Out of the store's receipts, he paid the salary of his assistant, August Franke, oversaw the apprenticeship of Abraham Van Vleck (son of the New York merchant), paid interest to the church on the store's stock, and cared for the building. Only after these and other costs of business had been deducted would the remaining profits go to the church. Yet Oberlin took personal responsibility for the business. He described a vision for the store's future as simultaneously expanded and more specialized. "It would be preferable to me if the purchase of deer skins went out of the store, particularly as there is no separate capital for it, and the future Dry Goods Store would suffer from it." Oberlin explained that he feared the loss of his primary business from continuing what he apparently viewed as an ancillary function. "Now . . . the Brethren work for themselves or for a salary, and would gladly buy summer and winter clothing, but [if the deer skin trade continued] there would be either little or nothing of such goods available." On the other hand, not all purchasing functions had to be moved away from the store. "The butter can still be bought, as before," Oberlin wrote, "and sold again where it is most profitable." It is also worth noting here that Oberlin paid no attention to the implications for Indians of shifting the deer skin away from Bethlehem. His interests were confined to the economic well-being of the store; the idea that business with Indians might be part of the church's missionary project, or that they might have been adversely affected by the change, was not a matter of his (or, most likely, his employers') concern.[6]

As anticipation of an expanded clothing market indicates, Oberlin contemplated focusing the store on those areas that would be most profitable, even if that left other parts of the store's former business behind. Oberlin wrote that the remaining Oeconomies (groups like the Single Sisters, Single Brothers, and Widows, which persisted in a reorganized form after the transition) could receive credit at the store, but "they must also pay punctually at the time determined at the time of purchase, otherwise [the store] would be hindered" in its own shopping. During the Oeconomy period, the store had been an outlet for goods from the various shops in town, but he made clear that this would not necessarily continue. Oberlin hoped that "soap and lights" would be removed completely from the store, though since the Oeconomy's transition was bound to be long and complicated, they could remain during the interim. Concluding his letter, Oberlin wrote, "Concerning my salary, I am accustomed to leaving it over to the care of my Brethren, as I now simply give it over to them."[7] Perhaps he left this crucial detail to church leaders so as not overstep the moral limits of self-interested behavior.

Oberlin's direct involvement in outlining his new business indicated a clear sense that he had something at stake in the undertaking. Other shopkeepers and artisans shared that outlook. A key issue for many was the arrangements made with apprentices who came to work with them. For masters to protect their professional standing in the wider world, they had to bring the local apprenticeship system in line with regional norms in order to protect themselves financially. The difficulty came from Bethlehem's continued status as a church town that maintained its own standards for who could live in town and how they could behave. Standard apprenticeship agreements, legally enforceable relationships requiring the master to train and support the boy for a designated period, did not provide for the intervention of church authorities, but Bethlehem's leaders were not willing to abdicate responsibility over the boys in town. The Moravians found "the English laws are so very difficult," so leaders had to move cautiously in this area, carefully balancing legal necessities and the customs of Pennsylvania with their own religious goals in what was fundamentally an economic system.[8]

Under the Oeconomy, the problem had been nicely finessed. Apprentices had been bound to Bethlehem's trustee, rather than directly to their masters. The practice enhanced that flexibility in the labor pool on which church leaders depended. If an artisan went into the mission field, his apprentices could be reassigned to whoever took the original master's place. In June 1762, the Committee of Arbitrators, the new body which oversaw economic matters, solidified a new, more privatized system. The impetus came from the masters themselves, who felt that "they could not prosper in their Professions with their apprentices when the same were not bound to them as their Masters." Some even went farther, stating they would not take on any more boys without such an arrangement.[9] In the Committee's opinion, if such a change were to be made, two conditions had to be placed in the indenture "for the security of the apprentice as well as for the protection of our Gemeine and Choir Plans." First, the indenture would be legally binding only as long as the master remained in Bethlehem, and, second, if the apprentice turned out to be a "seducer," someone who could not be tolerated in Bethlehem, the master had to find the boy a position somewhere else for the remainder of his term. Inserting the second condition in the legal document was necessary since, without such a provision, an apprentice could legally object to and prevent a reassignment. By codifying religious concerns into a new contractual system, church leaders allowed apprenticeships in Bethlehem to operate with minimal supervision from congregational authorities.[10]

The arrangements worked out by individual parents, boys, and masters could not violate the basic ground rules set up by the Committee, but otherwise they became essentially private concerns, and, in this way, labor performed under these contracts moved a step farther from church oversight and from immediate connection with the church's religious work. The conditions laid down in the indentures were sometimes invoked, however, indicating that communal intervention did not disappear. Several apprentices left because they objected to remaining within the religious community. In October 1762, for example, one apprentice at the wagoner's shop and another in a cobbler's shop decided that they did not want to stay in Bethlehem because they had "no heart and mind for the Savior." The boys' fathers arrived from Warwick, a Moravian community in Lancaster County, to pick them up. One of them made ready to steal away with his son in the middle of the night. After he was caught, he, along with the other father and son, was called before the Committee. Because neither boy wanted to stay in the Gemeine, everyone agreed to tear up the indentures. The second father was more contrite than the first and wanted his son to stay in Bethlehem, but since the boy did not wish it, he too was released from his obligation. Six years later, Peter Volz, an apprentice in the smithy, was asked to leave Bethlehem because of his bad behavior. His master, George Huber, had to find the boy "another and good master from whom he can learn the trade." Other problems could be handled internally. Daniel Kliest, a locksmith and a member of the Committee, mentioned that the boy assigned him on a trial basis had no skill at his trade. The boy preferred to be a linen weaver, though his skill there was in doubt too. The matter was postponed until the hapless boy could be reassigned.[11]

The church benefited financially from separating out individuals' work lives from the church's concerns. It limited the church's responsibilities and minimized financial risk. No longer did the community retain any but the most rudimentary financial responsibility for the support of workers not directly in its employ. The strategy was reasonably successful. Returns from church businesses fluctuated significantly, though in most years more than £1,000 clear profit came in. 1765 was undoubtedly the hardest year for the Diacony, the church's financial arm, between the end of the Oeconomy in 1762 and the end of the Revolutionary War two decades later. In that year, the trades earned only £676 clear profit, with only 71 percent of the trades in the black. Those that did bring in some cash had to offset the £422 in losses rung up by less fortunate artisans. Excluding 1765, the Diacony saw returns of greater than £900 in every year between 1763 and 1771, including more than £1,900 in the opening and closing years of the period. The 1770s saw an improvement over the 1760s. Between 1773 and 1779, nearly every business remaining in church hands turned a profit. Moreover, the trades earned more than £1,000 each year, though those numbers must be viewed with caution, given the inflationary pressures caused by the Revolution at the end of the decade. Only nine businesses existed throughout the entire period from 1763 to 1779 and remained profitable in every year; two more, the bakery and the tannery, consistently appeared, but occasionally lost money for the Diacony. The Strangers' Store earned the most money of these eleven shops, bringing in fully one-fifth of the total amount earned by the trades across the period.[12]

Leaders pursued a strategy of eliminating businesses that were unprofitable or difficult and transferring income to structures that limited risk. The Diacony reported results for 24 different trades in 1763 and only 16 in 1773. (The peak during the late Oeconomy period was 34.) In most cases, it is impossible to say exactly what happened to trades that disappeared from the church ledgers, whether the artisan in charge of that business chose to operate it on his own or the business closed down entirely. During the mid-1760s, for example, the cost of leather climbed steeply, causing both the shoemakers and the breeches maker to complain to church leaders about their ailing businesses. Between 1762 and 1763, the number of shoemaking operations was sharply curtailed, and the breeches maker disappears from the ledger in 1765. Between 1771 and 1773 (with a gap in the record for 1772), three more longstanding businesses were sold off, though they doubtless continued to exist in town: the blacksmith, the turner, and the Crown Inn, which lay across the Lehigh. Though the inn later reappeared after 1779, it rarely turned a profit. Most of the farms, long a problem investment, were converted to private lease arrangements in 1769, decreasing the risk to the community.[13] After 1773, two new lines appear in the accounts: house rents and interest on the stocks in the trades (i.e., the tools and stock on hand when the business was privatized). More properly understood as investments rather than as profits, the two items became dominant parts of the Diacony's revenue stream, comprising as much as 59 percent (1779) of the total "trade" income. In practical terms, the trend away from direct ownership of the trades in favor of interest income meant that Bethlehem's artisans enjoyed greater financial freedom and greater personal responsibility, even as they lost the insurance that had come from the church's deep pockets supporting their businesses through lean years.[14]

When Bethlehem lost its close ties to missionary work, its work force lost the justifications they had used for decades to understand their labors. In the void created by the missions' absence and the end of the Oeconomy, workers built new lives by turning to their families and the businesses they used to support them. They followed career paths of their own choosing, shouldered the risks that those careers brought, and defined the terms of their own labors. Though the church continued to employ many of the town's workers, and benefited greatly from their labors, a new level of remove existed between church and congregant, a private space where individuals pursued their own ends. Bethlehem's residents had always worked hard, but now, buttressed by centuries of Protestant doctrine, those labors had become an end in themselves.

New Parameters for Economic Behavior

Even as Bethlehem's work force moved a step away from the church, that institution continued to shape the town's religious life in powerful ways. Leaders oversaw the community as whole. In that fact, Bethlehem differed little from most early American towns, where governments regularly intervened to promote business and regulate marketplaces. Early Americans expected, even demanded, such interventions, including regulation of bread prices and standardization of weights and measures, as part of the idea that governments protected their citizens. When communities felt that essential goods were being withheld or sold at inflated prices, they acted in common to demand redress, in the form of mass protests or food riots.[15] Bethlehem addressed issues of market regulation from a different perspective, however, even as its leaders still conformed to the widespread expectation that governments managed markets. The principal distinction was one of approach, as leaders' interventions always had, explicitly or implicitly, religious character and meaning. The town's business and economic leadership remained, as it had been during the Oeconomy period, intimately intertwined with the Moravian church hierarchy in town, and all residents continued share deep ties to that church and its work.

Yet religious governance of Bethlehem's economy took on a new shape in the 1760s and 1770s, and Moravian beliefs about economic practice manifested themselves in new ways. Leaders still sought to uphold Moravian values about appropriate business practice, as well as to ensure that the church continued to earn as much money as it could to pay for its substantial and continuing expenses, but this oversight took on a different character after the loss of the missions. No longer focused on community goals, leaders turned a more careful eye to personal behavior. Individual workers—now, in the records, usually men—protected their own interests, though they also subordinated themselves to the governance of the church. Together, they created the economy that to John Adams evoked a love of money, but which, for the Moravians, continued to support in a new form the values they had long embraced.

Three separate governing bodies participated in creating the town' s new moral environment: the Elders' Conference, a group that existed in all Moravian communities, oversaw the town's spiritual life; the Diacony Conference cared for the church's property; and, most important from the perspective of moral economic behavior, the Committee of Arbitrators governed individuals and adjudicated disputes. The Committee's jurisdiction covered matters of personal economic choice, an arena that had barely existed during the communal period. But new choices opened up new opportunities for transgressions. The 1762 Brotherly Agreement spelled out rules covering marriage, overnight visitors, and the discharging of debts. Even relatively minor details received attention in the forty-one enumerated articles. No one, for example, "should allow swine or other livestock, except for turkeys, chickens, geese, or other feathered animals, to run free," and public paths had to remain clear and open. Paradoxically, then, greater freedom from the autocratic rule of church councils meant more attention to rules. A new category of behavior emerged, hardly "civil" in nature, but certainly far more individual than communal. Bethlehem's residents now had the freedom to choose to live up to, or not to live up to, community religious standards in a variety of ways every day. The new Committee oversaw such choices, enforcing moral behavior for its own sake, and not—as had been the case during the Oeconomy—for the sake of the members' shared religious work.[16]

The new governing structure also separated the conduct of the church's employees from the administration of the church's property, thus largely removing artisans and storekeepers from decisions over how the profits they garnered for the church would be spent. Unlike the Diacony Conference of the communal period, which blended the two, the new Committee had no direct responsibilities for the church's missions, and the Diacony Conference had little jurisdiction over individual economic behavior. Even though much of the town's resources continued to go to the church in support of ministers, missionary families and widows, and collective debt, average individuals were unlikely to encounter this fact. When a position opened in the gristmill, one of the church's most valuable assets, in March 1763, the Diacony Conference placed Christian Giers in the position of miller and determined the terms of his contract. But Giers's subsequent behavior while operating the mill fell under the watch of the Committee, as did the behavior of those in town who did not work for the church directly at all. Thomas Fischer, the hatter, for example, received regular reminders to hold his conduct to a higher standard (this despite his membership in the influential Committee), yet the hatter's business left the Diacony books with the first wave of privatization in 1762 and never returned. The coexistence of the Committee and the Diacony Conference defined two separate economic spheres in Bethlehem: one directly involved with church affairs and one concerned with individuals' economic choices viewed in a moral context. The Committee managed the second, balancing community religious expectations against individual choices.[17]

The experiences of Giers, the grist miller, exemplify the way the Committee wielded its moral authority, and also indicate the way it yielded jurisdiction in the creation of an individual moral space. In 1775, a customer at the mill, non-Moravian Andreas Schweitzer, accused Giers of returning too little flour after he had been given twelve bushels of grain. Giers maintained that such an oversight could only be an accident. If it were done intentionally, he claimed, it would have been too easily found out. Such protests aside, the Committee reprimanded Giers for the incident and strongly urged him to discuss the matter with Schweitzer in order to make amends. But mutual accusations and counteraccusations kept the issue from being resolved, and the passage of several months meant there was no way to discover the truth. Making matters worse, Schweitzer seemed to take pleasure in placing the miller in a difficult spot, bragging that he had forced a previous miller in Bethlehem to be removed. In the end, the problem was submitted to arbitration, and Giers had to pay for the three bushels as well as the costs, bringing great "blame before the world" on him, in the Committee's eyes. The whole matter clearly distasteful to its members, the Committee nonetheless decided to leave Giers in the mill for the time being, particularly since he had written a seemingly heartfelt letter to the Elders' Conference asking for forgiveness. They suggested that the religious penalties that body could inflict would bring about the desired effect, hoping "that the punishment, that he must remain away from Communion until one becomes aware of a complete change of heart in him, will have the desired effect on his heart and conduct." In their deferral to strictly religious punishment, the Committee reinforced that Giers's business habits, even in a church-owned business, grew out of his personal moral character. They appealed to his conscience, not to his sense of community.[18]

In another equally telling example, leaders again turned to arbitration, a solution that implied not only that the church was less directly involved, but also that some disputes might not have a simple resolution because the "moral" outcome was not obvious. On June 6, 1774, Brother Boeckel and Abraham Andreas came before the Committee. Andreas, a silversmith, wanted Boeckel to reimburse him for the loss of a barrel of coffee, which he had asked Boeckel's apprentice to fetch in Philadelphia. Apparently the boy had let the cask come open along the road and it had spilled before he noticed. "It was wished," the Committee recorded, that the matter might come before the "Arbitration of Brethren as soon as possible," so that no bad feeling might arise between the two men. They suggested that the parties might share the expense, keeping the total cost for any one person from being too high; "otherwise, according to the opinions of the majority of the brothers in the conference, [Andreas] would have to carry the full loss himself," since the carter could hardly be blamed. The Committee's position is interesting. The members deferred rendering a final judgment, perhaps because what they considered just differed from what they thought legally tenable. At the same time, however, they continued to rely on internal—that is, Moravian—solutions, as they wanted the issue to come before the "Arbitration of Brethren" for the sake of community harmony. The incident illustrates a noticeable but subtle withdrawal of community religious authority in favor of individual action.[19]

Incidents such as these arose only infrequently. The majority of the Committee's efforts addressed the more mundane details of life. Leaders monitored the town's work force by providing for the treatment of the poor and managing the apprenticeship system so that economic needs did not override communal goals. Balancing communal and individual needs required the Committee to care for the community's most vulnerable. As might be expected from Zinzendorf's wholehearted endorsement of work's spiritual value, the Committee considered labor essential for a moral life, and its members tried to ensure that everyone who could work, did. Nowhere can this be seen more clearly than among those for whom work presented real challenges. The problem of indigence was inevitable as soon as the Oeconomy ended; every community of any size includes people who cannot or do not want to support themselves. Moravian leaders had long acknowledged that the Unity's settlements would bear the burden of those who were enfeebled through no fault of their own. Herrnhut's 1727 statutes stated, "Every resident in Herrnhut shall work and eat his own bread. If, however, he is old, sick or impoverished, the Gemeine shall support him."[20] Although the problem of infirmity was obscured in Bethlehem when all labor was pooled, it came up immediately after the 1762 transition. The most pressing case was David Digeon, a Swiss shoemaker who spent the last two decades of his life "demented." According to the Committee, he had to receive relief "because he does not work like a man and therefore cannot earn his own bread." The solution was to establish an Arme Casse (poor fund), from which such individuals could be given periodic disbursements.[21]

Although the Committee wanted the Arme Casse to protect the Gemeine's most vulnerable members, they did not want to create a permanent class of charity cases. On September 13, 1762, Mary Digeon's request for more relief prompted the Committee to give her a few shillings, but also to note that she should "not count on receiving it in the future or weekly." She was then to "urge her husband to work as much as possible" for their support.[22] In order to avert such problems in the future, one member of the Committee was assigned to "inquire about those brothers and sisters who are already poor, or in whom one can see the likelihood that they will fall into poverty, either through their own fault by poor economy or from other reasons." In general, individuals received relief when the need arose because of injury or sickness. One person chose a loan over outright relief, presumably because he too believed that supporting oneself through one's own labor had moral worth that superseded the financial value involved. The Committee encouraged even the benighted Digeon to work—and not simply to preserve the Arme Casse from the expense of maintaining him: "Regarding Digeon, who does not like to work because of laziness, which is most damaging to him, it was found to be good to bring him to work forcibly, otherwise one can fear that he will finally become completely foolish."[23]

Through systems like the Arme Casse, Moravian leaders supported a concept of work where the primary value was attached to individual conduct, building upon the personal space for individual action created by Bethlehem's residents. Across the 1760s and 1770s, they consistently strove to ensure that all members of the community's work force were diligent, honest, and moral in their approach to work. Some people were reminded to work harder. In 1772, town leaders took up the subject of Jost Jansen's employee in the tavern, "Black Joh. Samuel," because the man had not had "a good upbringing" and was not diligent enough in his work. A year later, "all possible faithfulness and punctuality" was recommended to another worker, the town's chimneysweep, with regard to his business.[24] Of course, community concerns about safety and concerns about personal morality overlapped. Richard Poppelwell excited attention when he came to work at the fulling mill while drunk. The Committee told him that "if he did not change himself, he will be removed from his profession, not only because he is in danger of sometime doing damage to his own person, but also because the trade suffers loss through [his behavior], because no one likes to trust anything to him." Eight months later, the Committee made good on their threat, removing Poppelwell and replacing him with another artisan.[25] Although productivity in the trades was undoubtedly important to Bethlehem's overall economic health, such advice is strikingly similar to the admonitions given to the enfeebled Digeon. The consistency with which leaders encouraged diligence indicates a strong faith in the value of work as its own reward.

As artisans worked to improve their business environment, church leaders enforced a religiously informed moral framework for the new market system. This meant welcoming commerce with outsiders, as the group always had, and also defining the parameters of moral trade. Specifically, leaders encouraged orderly transactions, facilitated the town's reputation, and promoted fair competition and pricing. On August 30, 1762, the Committee ordered that the "marketplace be brought into order." In this context, order meant that the town's private spaces would not become places of business, as they were hard to monitor. Trade, leaders believed, should be conducted out in the open. The explicit purpose of the new market, the Committee wrote, was so that "strangers may not go up into the houses and on the third floors, and so that the prices will not be set so high."[26] On the other hand, the fact that town leaders neither banned this activity in favor of the authorized Moravian stores, nor attempted to control prices rigidly, demonstrates an acceptance of the open market's other dynamics, including competition and market pricing within Bethlehem, and these two areas required constant attention from the town's councils. Yet leaders also encouraged order. The following spring, after a market shelter had been built, the Committee assigned Andreas Schoute, the former sailor who survived the wreck of the *Irene*, to be the town's Market Meister. His job was to keep traveling vendors from wandering into the houses, and also to guide potential sellers to the new market and organize the trade that took place there. "Brothers and Sisters can place orders with Br. Schoute for the things they would like," town leaders noted, "and when afterwards something like it is brought [here], Br. Schoute can let them know." To ease transactions, the marketplace was provided with a set of weights and measures, so that buyers and sellers could agree on the proffered wares. Close observation mediated against the vagaries of a truly open marketplace, yet for the most part buyers and sellers still managed their own transactions, and church leaders encouraged trade as much as they controlled it. Indeed, the Committee was quite concerned when Schoute's successor, Christian Werner, became a hindrance to business through his "wonderful" and "absurd" behavior," threatening to give Bethlehem's market a "bad name."[27]

Moravian leaders sought to support, even promote, the town's new market economy, while continuing to protect community values. In this project, the town's governors joined their non-Moravian peers in local and provincial governments throughout the colonies, yet for Moravian leaders the project had an inherently religious character, because of the town's identity as a Moravian town. Creating and preserving a good reputation as a market town in the surrounding countryside was a key part of the process. As early as June 1762, the Diacony Conference noted that someone should be appointed to inspect and monitor the quality of the town's produce, particularly butter and grain, to ensure high quality products, "because through the opposite our credit will be ruined." In 1767, a conflict arose when Adam Von Erd, a leather worker, complained that Br. Kornman, the tanner, was selling leather breeches. After an investigation, the newly formed Commercial Council (which uncharacteristically kept its records in English) told Kornman not to continue in this business, but it also warned Von Erd to "see that he makes his Breeches good, that the people do not Complain with Justice, otherwise we cannot let the Business be lost, & when he do's not so, we must take other measures." Supporting Bethlehem's market reputation also meant producing recognizable products, thus creating a Moravian brand name. The Committee urged the hatter, Thomas Fischer, to purchase a stamp for his hats, "so that other people can not, as has been occurring, sell other and poor hats as Bethlehem hats." Of course, this would backfire if Fischer were not a reliable artisan.

Nine months later the hatter appeared again in the Committee records, this time because he had been selling hats that he had bought in Philadelphia as "Bethlehem made," and using the new stamp to do so. Moreover, he had been found working on Sunday, which was strictly forbidden in Bethlehem. The Committee put him on notice that such behavior "could not be tolerated."[28]

The church's regulation of economic behavior became more visible as artisans and storekeepers had more opportunities to make decisions and therefore more occasions to choose a path that conflicted with Moravian understandings of moral and Godly business practice. Potential conflicts between artisans and shopkeepers arose as individuals sought to pursue their own livelihoods. Oberlin, in the Strangers' Store, faced a new challenge in 1764 when the Committee allowed Daniel Kunckler, who had previously worked in the main store, to open a "Schmier Store," primarily for fats and oils. Before he could open his shop, Kunckler received and signed formal instructions enumerating exactly what he could sell, specifically molasses, cheese, butter, ham and bacon, oats, candles, various oils, and soap. None of these items were part of the Strangers' Store's core business, and indeed, in the case of candles and soap, Oberlin had specifically requested that he be relieved of selling them. Nevertheless, Kunckler's store introduced for the first time a second retail operation into town, changing the business atmosphere for Oberlin. The following year, the Committee became concerned that Kunckler was exceeding his instructions, and members felt they should make sure that "he keeps no unnecessary wares for sale, such as baked sugar." In a veiled comment it was also noted that Kunckler had "harmful pictures," which leaders thought inappropriate for their youth. The Committee determined to "speak firmly" with Kunckler about the issue.[29]

As artisans came into competition with each other, leaders stepped into guide the nature of the competition. From the perspective of church leaders, competition ought to depend on the quality of an artisan's produce, not on who could afford to charge the least. This trend too focused attention on individual moral choices, further defining the economic space inhabited by Bethlehem's residents. When Kunckler's business began to sag in 1767, he complained about competition from other businesses in town whose territory overlapped his. Community leaders addressed his concerns, sometimes protecting a piece of his market as it had been determined in his 1764 instructions, other times encouraging him to make his wares more competitive. When Kunckler complained that too many people were selling snuff, he was reminded "to make his Snuff so good that it may recommend itself." When the smiths complained that Oberlin was selling wares that they considered their territory, the leaders responded that "the many & different Tools which was wanted at one Time, [could] not be always had at any of the Smiths," and that they were not being sold so cheaply in the store as to "Hinder Trade." They reassured the smiths that if customers "found our Smiths Tools to be preferable they would soon find them out & buy of them." The smiths had an additional advantage as well, in that customers would know that the crafts-men would "make good what failed in" the wares they sold. In this case, the Moravians did not see any dangerous conflict between the smiths and the store, despite their competing for almost identical markets, because the goods and services they offered were essentially different.[30]

In a community new to the process of buying and selling one's daily bread, it is hardly surprising that prices became a contentious issue. Both Bethlehem and the international Unity recognized prices as a central issue in moral business practice. Merchants, upon whom it was always incumbent (as it was for all Moravians) to be in a close connection with the Savior, had to ensure that trade proceeded fairly. The central Commercial Council in Herrn-hut, a body formed in the aftermath of the 1764 General Synod, addressed the issue: "It is always a great departure when someone takes an exorbitant profit, be it out of a lack to the true merchant's principles, out of unfamiliarity with the wares, from mistaken calculation, misunderstanding, or because the wares were bought too expensively and not from the first hand." To avoid these harmful consequences, the Council aimed high: a good merchant should "try to please everyone, and set the price for wares as cheaply as possible," al-though he had also to remember his own costs. The Council reiterated Span-genberg's sentiments from the store's founding, fifteen years earlier, that bargaining, where "one suggests to offer goods [at a price] higher than one thinks to sell them at," and then negotiates until a price has been agreed on, was to be utterly avoided in Moravian commerce, despite its wide prevalence in worldly markets. Following these principles benefited all participants in the end, including the Moravian merchant's bottom line. "It makes sense for everyone to follow our method," the Council mused, "and it increases [our] credit when the people see from experience that they are handled fairly by us and are provided with good wares." Good business practice and Godly busi-ness practice were closely intertwined.[31]

Perhaps intentionally, these principles gave little practical guidance on the subject of prices. Instead, the Unity Commercial Council instructed that a dedicated committee of the same name be erected in each congregation town, where issues could be handled locally as they arose. The new Bethlehem Commercial Council and the already existing Committee of Arbitrators fielded many complaints on the topic of pricing, and their members tried to determine what appropriate prices really were for both buying and selling. In one of its first meetings, the Bethlehem Commercial Council asked, "if People will not rather go to such places where they can buy best & Cheapest, therefore when goods are Bought they ought to be sold according to the Market Price Whether dear or cheap [because] nobody would like to pay more than they can buy them for in other places." The Moravians understood that if they set a fixed price or mark-up, and then at some future point charged a price over the going rate because they had bought at a poor time, they would simply lose out—a consequence that was justifiably unappealing. What was not discussed in their deliberations was the truism that the fluctuations in market prices might just as easily go in their favor, leading to unexpectedly high profit margins.[32]

Because practical realities prevented Moravian leaders from monitoring prices in the store on a daily basis as they had during the Oeconomy, they struggled to keep Bethlehem's retail pricing in line with their stated principles. When conflicts arose, the councils first gathered information about prices in the surrounding areas, giving them a base line from which to judge. In July 1762, the Committee sought out prices for shoemaking in "Philadelphia, Lititz, Eastown, and other places," so that they could regulate Bethlehem's prices accordingly. In April 1767, the price and mode of payment for house painting became a topic of discussion, this time necessitating research in Lancaster and New York. A specific complaint did not always need to be lodged in order for there to be concern, however. Committee members worried when it appeared that "Commerce has been falling off for some time" in Bethlehem. "Our neighbors are said to complain," they continued, because "everything here, especially in the store, is very expensive."[33]

Even though Oberlin had no personal financial stake in the shop's success or failure, Moravian economic leaders heard many complaints about the storekeeper's conduct, placing them in an awkward position. While Oberlin did not profit personally from his business, the community did, and higher prices increased the profits that could be steered into religious endeavors. Upon receiving the statements for fiscal year 1766–67, the Commercial Council reported "how much pleased they were in hearing the Accounts Read from the Directorial and Unitäts Conference," and yet "all of them wished that perticularly in the Store another spirit than at Presant might direct & govern them therein." It was not only high prices that could be a problem; Oberlin's management techniques were also questioned. On one occasion, "it was mentioned that Strangers came to the Store very often early in the Morning as often late at Night & When Br. Oberlin was not up, they were not served because Br. Frank is not trusted with the Key." The consequences of this poor treatment were clear: "the Credit of the Store suffers," not to mention the loss of that sale. Indeed, "Strangers [were] saying that that Storekeeper doth not care whether he sells or not." The Moravians found themselves caught in another market-oriented dilemma. Oberlin had no personal incentive for the store's success; if he had ceased to care about the goals of the Gemeine, he had little reason to work hard. In other words, the Gemeine now had to rely on individuals' personal choices for its support, a far more precarious position than it had been in earlier.[34]

During the 1760s and 1770s, individual artisans in Bethlehem gained greater freedom from church leaders to make economic choices, and church leaders intervened in the town's businesses in more limited ways. Bethlehem's economic oversight shifted from the micromanagement characteristic of the communal period to the enforcement of principles through adjudication of transgressions and disputes. The principle can be overstated. Bethlehem remained a church town, and leaders did not hesitate to evict an unsavory character or to prevent an ill-conceived work placement that would have put single men and women in contact with one another. But the creation of a new individual moral space reflected a new role for religion in Bethlehem's economic life.[35] The distinctively Moravian balance among shared religious goals, the need to pursue profit, and attention to moral economic behavior that had characterized the communal period persisted, but did so in a recombined form. The religious work of missionary outreach had become the purview of a few individuals, and church financing of religious work now occurred within an environment that prioritized minimizing risk over maximum flexibility. The search for profits too reflected increased privatization. The church's increasingly bureaucratic structure separated individual workers from the church's needs, while artisans found themselves in a position where overseeing their own and their families' financial welfare had to take precedence. The church partially withdrew from the economic lives of the town's residents, and town residents returned the favor, all in the name of financial stability. Moral economic behavior—now primarily a question of individual choice and character—came to take center stage in the Moravian town's economic life, so that the way religious values infused economic life became a matter of one's personal character, not missionary calling. Protestant ideas about work, which the Moravians had always embraced, filled in the spiritual space which missionary work had vacated.

A Matter of Conscience: Pacifism and the Revolutionary War

The transformation of Bethlehem's economic life between 1762 and 1775 had the result of turning leaders' attention away from regional and international events and toward the life of the community, or, at most, the international Unity. But the quiet that settled over Bethlehem in the wake of Pontiac's War and the removal of the Indians in 1765 was supremely deceptive, as Britain's North American colonies began their episodic yet consistent progress toward a break with imperial authority. When Bethlehem's residents had sided with their fellow colonists in the racial warfare of the early 1760s, they had, intentionally or not, become part of a larger polity whose interests they only imperfectly shared. They argued for their loyalty to Pennsylvania and Britain, but generally felt only an indifferent affection for their neighbors who had been so ready, over so many years, to distrust the members of the Brüdergemeine for their ties to Indians. Moreover, the process of assimilation (buttressed by legal naturalization and land ownership) which had gradually integrated many German speakers into Pennsylvania's political community had largely passed by Bethlehem, whose residents remained distinct from their neighbors, despite deep and lasting economic ties. The political battles that marked Pennsylvania during these years, the struggle between the Proprietary and the Quaker parties in particular, meant little to the Moravians, who generally sought to stay out of controversial issues. The group was simultaneously within and separated from Pennsylvania society by virtue of its history and religious choices. The consequences of this uneasy membership in the colonial world for the Moravians' economic culture emerged during the Revolutionary War, when Bethlehem's Moravians chose to take a pacifist stance. That choice had the effect of reinforcing the individualizing trend already well underway in the Moravian community.[36]

If the Moravians were out of step with their neighbors in Pennsylvania in the early 1770s, they were even farther from the events driving the political events of the day. The central issues of the brewing imperial crisis—taxation, the potential of an Anglican bishop, the quartering of soldiers, the nature of the Parliament's sovereignty over the colonies—mattered little in Bethlehem. While the Stamp Act Congress was meeting in New York during the fall of 1765, for example, the Moravians were more concerned about David Nitschmann's upcoming visitation from Herrnhut than they were with imperial policy. References to the conflict with Britain were limited to those items that directly touched the community. In December, they briefly noted that the *Hope*, the ship the Moravians relied on after the loss of the *Irene* in the Seven Years' War, would not sail that winter due to problems with the Stamp Act, but, tellingly, they worried more about the loss of communications the delay would bring than about the philosophical implications of the tax. Eight years later, in 1774, the Elders' Conference noted that it had put a stop to a petition being circulated for "the Poor in Boston," and its principal concern was to keep there from being further conversation in the matter. Although the Elders left it unstated on that occasion, Bethlehem had embarked on a clear strategy of avoiding controversy with its neighbors over the tense politics of the day.[37]

The Moravians had good reason to be cautious of their fellow Americans' dissatisfaction with the British Empire, as neither the local situation in Pennsylvania nor their own position as residents of a British territory suggested clearly which side they should take. For many Americans, the two decades after the outbreak of the Seven Years' War in 1754 had been a process of questioning and redefinition. Just as surely as the triumphs of victory over France had inspired a deep sense of British patriotism, the war had also fostered an increasing awareness of a shared colonial cause. That common interest created in turn a foundation from which to challenge allegiance to a distant political system that seemed not to have the colonists' best interests at heart. In short, the process of the imperial conflict forced many residents of the British Atlantic world to question the basis of their collective political identity. Yet this shared process had very different meanings in the complex mosaic of the empire's diverse colonies. All politics is local, the saying goes, and the adage was as true in the eighteenth century as ever. While many in the colonies felt a sense of outrage at Parliament's increasingly insistent declarations of authority, significant portions of the population approached the conflict differently. In Pennsylvania, the new tensions were read against the long history of disagreement between local colonial interests and the Penn family proprietors, which blunted and redirected the wider struggle with Parliament in ways that slowed the rise of a clear political movement for independence in the province. Though Philadelphia provided some of the conflict's most radical voices, its political system remained internally hamstrung. Until nearly the last moment, strong forces, including Benjamin Franklin, pushed the Crown to take control of the colony, in a move to increase rather than eliminate royal influence, and the Pennsylvania Assembly remained mute on controversial issues. Many Pennsylvanians outside Philadelphia refrained from active participation in national events, out of either disinterest or prudence.[38]

Meanwhile, the Moravians—wary of their neighbors because of years of racial and religious tensions and unsure of the political direction of Pennsylvania and of the region—faced a further set of considerations. A 1749 Act of Parliament had granted the international Unity formal recognition throughout the British Empire, and the act had been a significant move toward stability for the church. Moravian communities around the British world benefited from the Crown's legal protection, and the Unity as a whole had no desire to alienate London. Though the Royal Proclamation of 1763, which theoretically limited the colonies' westward expansion, failed to reflect demographic realities in precisely the same way as Unity authorities had misread the local situation when they insisted on the resettlement of Nain by Indians, this shared failure of transatlantic governance did not goad Bethlehem's Moravians into throwing off either imperial or church authority. Quite the contrary, because they were primarily concerned with bringing souls to Christ, they willingly submitted to all legitimate governments, though exactly which government that would be was a question of some difficulty during the Revolution. Exacerbating the situation, the principal North American communities at Bethlehem, and at Salem, North Carolina, lay in regions distant from urban centers of revolutionary unrest, in areas where loyalists were numerous and recent conflicts between frontier colonists and seaboard authorities made the outcome of revolutionary tensions dubious at best. Discretion appeared to be the better part of valor. "When questioned concerning our sentiments in view of these sad controversies," Bethlehem's leaders reported in 1775, "we should answer that we look upon them as chastisement meted out to the Colonies and England alike and that, as for anything more, we consider ourselves too shortsighted and ignorant to apportion right and wrong to one side or the other." The group thus did its best to avoid taking either side in the conflict.[39]

Bethlehem's situation changed from uneasy to unsafe with striking rapidity. Beginning in 1774 and then with increasing speed after 1776, political authority in Pennsylvania collapsed and reformed in the hands of radical revolutionaries. Local county committees, organized by individuals hostile to the province's traditional government and sympathetic to the patriots in Philadelphia, sought to unify the new state behind the cause of independence through whatever means were necessary. The transition was extremely difficult from the perspective of the Moravians. The colony's traditional concentration of power in the hands of wealthy Philadelphia Quakers had protected Bethlehem, both because colonial authorities had relied on the Moravians' relations with the Indians for diplomatic reasons and because those leaders' investment in protecting religious freedom for their own sake also protected the Moravians. In the remade environment, however, circumstances changed. During the war years, Northampton County's majority German population, who had been largely excluded from formal political life before the war, seized power as part of the patriot forces. Furthermore, the region's residents worried about the alliance between loyalists and Indians, which made Pennsylvania's frontier vulnerable. The Moravians, seen as allies of both the Quakers and the Indians, were viewed with skepticism twice over. Neighbors who disliked the missionaries now had authority over them, making life increasingly difficult for a community that wanted more than anything to avoid trouble, at least until it was abundantly clear which way the wind was blowing[40] (Figure 10).

Bethlehem's principal leader during these years was Johannes Ettwein, a descendant of Protestant refugees who had settled in the Black Forest. Because his personal choices had a strong impact on Bethlehem's course during the Revolutionary War, a few words about him are warranted. He joined a Pietist community as a young teen in his home town, and there heard about the Moravians from his ministers. In 1738, while still an adolescent, he joined the Brüdergemeine at Marienborn. Ettwein's forceful personality and drive brought him quickly into positions of leadership, first in Europe and then later in America, where he guided Bethlehem for more than three decades and eventually was made a bishop. In many ways his life mirrored that of the eighteenth-century Moravian church more generally: he was born within months of Herrnhut's founding; he felt himself intensely drawn to Zinzendorf; became enveloped in the exuberant religiosity of the "Sifting Time"; worked in both North Carolina

Figure 10. Johannes Ettwein led Bethlehem during the American Revolution. His personal pacifism influenced the Moravians' stance during this difficult period. Portrait by Johann Valentine Haidt. Courtesy Moravian Historical Society.

and Pennsylvania; and in the years after Zinzendorf's death and the end of the Oeconomy, found himself in his middle age defending what had been built rather than continuing to reach for new goals. His quick temper likely exacerbated the tenuous situation in which Bethlehem found itself during the war years, giving a sharpness to correspondence at a time when patience would have been a particular virtue. Indeed, in the record of his life prepared for his funeral, a sympathetic voice opined, "His loving, tender, friendly, and sympathetic heart seemed to contrast with his peculiar style of tending to judge people and things quickly, and [this style] gave his short and general explanations and remarks the stamp of hardness and severity, so that they often hurt."[41]

Ettwein's leadership turned out to be pivotal in the stance that Bethlehem took on the issue of military service, because the church as a whole had an ambivalent record on this contentious issue. The 1749 Act of Parliament which granted the Moravians legal standing in the British Empire had made particular mention of bearing arms and swearing oaths, but in reality the community had never been unified on the subject. Unlike the neighboring Quakers and Mennonites, who made pacifism a central teaching, for the Moravians nonviolence was peripheral. The ancient Unitas Fratrum had split in the fifteenth century over participation in civil affairs, but the Bethlehem community was descended from those who were willing to accommodate governments, anticipating some engagement with the world. On the other hand, some members of the community at Herrnhut attributed the Hapsburg persecution of Protestants to that group's willingness to bear arms, thus making a practical, not theological, argument for abstaining from the use of force. The more recent American legacy was equally complicated. Some Moravians had scruples against swearing oaths and bearing arms, an issue that came to prominence as early as the settlement in Georgia in the late 1730s, but it had never been a defining issue for the larger Unity. In Pennsylvania, Moravians had more than a few times been forced by circumstances to arm and defend themselves, sometimes from Indians and sometimes from neighbors. During the Seven Years' War, for example, they had built a stockade around the town, purchased ammunition, imported weapons, and generally worked with provincial authorities on defending the frontier.[42]

During the Revolution, Ettwein responded to this legacy by emphasizing the importance of individual conscience in determining one's actions. Yet he also believed that if anyone stood against the conflict, the community as a whole should support that decision. The stance reflected his own personal pacifism, but it also pushed Bethlehem into an oppositional posture toward the conflict when many in town quite probably would have taken a more moderate tack. From a different perspective, however, Ettwein's emphasis on individual moral action matched and built upon the individual moral responsibility that characterized the town's religious and economic culture during these years. It also set Bethlehem at odds with the developing political situation in Pennsylvania for the duration of the war.

The town's course through the conflict was one of carefully navigating the rocky terrain between civil disobedience, popular anger, and forced support for the patriot cause. Bethlehem had been in difficult political positions before, of course, and nearly everyone would have been able to recall the problems of the racial conflicts in the early 1760s, but the Revolution presented a new challenge. Whereas the earlier fights had been over issues central to shared Moravian identity—particularly over the relationships to Indians that had grown out of missionary work—pacifism did not command the sort of loyalty from the Brüdergemeine that missionary work did, because it was not a fundamental part of the church's teachings. As a result, the challenges of the late 1770s did not have the effect of unifying Bethlehem behind a cause, but instead had the potential to undermine community sentiment already flagging from the loss of the missions.[43]

As the war intensified, the governments of Pennsylvania and Northampton County required progressively more expensive proofs of Moravian sympathy to the cause, and they also made avoiding a formal denunciation of the king difficult. The Moravians felt continually harassed, and Bethlehem's residents certainly did not overlook the fact that one of the key figures in the county leading the fight against them, John Wetzel, had been born a member and raised within the fold, only to reject the Unity as an adult. Bethlehem's leaders first pursued their long-trusted strategy of seeking support from high places, but had only minimal success. In May 1775, Nathanael Seidel, one of Ettwein's fellow leaders, wrote Benjamin Franklin on the latter's return to the colonies. Seidel reported that "Our good Neighbours . . . seem to be quite out of Humour with the Br[ethre]n." He implored Franklin "to be their Advocat in the present Congress and to use your undoubted influence with the Honorable Members," and gave the assurance that "none can or will withdraw themselves from the common Burden and Expence of the Province wherein they live." Franklin promptly responded that he would do his best, but also offered "a little Hint in point of Prudence." He reminded Seidel that during the

Seven Years' War he had learned "from my much respected Friend [Joseph] Spangenberg, that there were among the Brethren many who did not hold it unlawful to arm in a defensive War." After pointing out this undisputed fact, he continued on to say that, "If there still [are] any such among your young Men, perhaps it would not be amiss to permit them to learn the military Discipline among their Neighbours, as this might conciliate those who at present express some Resentment." Ettwein received a similarly unhelpful response in 1778 from his friend Henry Laurens, then president of Congress. Laurens kindly advised that the community make a formal petition to the Pennsylvania Assembly for relief, rather than seek to use back channel influence.[44]

These efforts had little effect, and the situation for the Moravians in the Delaware Valley became quite dire, particularly for the Single Brothers. Repeated taxes and fines emptied the Choir of cash. Officials frequently passed through town to report new developments, demand money, and requisition supplies.[45] Furthermore, individuals were fined separately, though the Choir did "ask [members] to help pay £3.10.– for poor Brethren unable to pay it." In more than a few cases, men chose to make a dramatic break with the community, and a steady stream of defections to the patriot cause depleted the Single Brothers' ranks. On July 3, the Choir diary recorded "Independence about to be declared. Decided we did not understand the matter, would not discuss it with strangers nor among ourselves." On July 6 and again August 26, in the aftermath of the Declaration of Independence, several men left to enlist. One of them, John Rasmus, passed through town again with a "battalion of 450 men with waving banners and music." At the end of the year, the diary poignantly recorded "we still number 122 in the Choir House."[46]

Defections were not the only reason the Single Brothers worried about their numbers. Disease took a toll too, as twice the Continental army located its hospital, filled with ailing and often contagious patients, in Bethlehem. The town's infrastructure was perfect from a medical perspective, because the large buildings remaining from the Oeconomy were well suited for caring for large numbers of wounded men. The first installation of the hospital began in early December 1776, after George Washington's evacuation of New York. Wounded soldiers moved first into New Jersey, then west across the Delaware to Bethlehem.[47] The hospital remained in place until March, lasting through the successful attack on Trenton and the subsequent winter standoff with Washington in New Jersey and the British holding New York. In the fall of 1777, the story repeated itself, this time from the south. The Continental defeat at the Battle of the Brandywine was followed by further routs, and the British occupied Philadelphia in September. As Washington moved into his winter encampment in Valley Forge, the Continental Hospital returned to Bethlehem in the early fall. The suffering witnessed and endured in Bethlehem during the second hospital stay was far worse than the first. The entire Single Brothers' House was dedicated to the cause, demanding major resources and disrupting all normal business. The moving day was "a day of confusion, feeling on the one side the power of darkness very much, on the other side could in childish manner trust the Savior, that He would look after us in these troubling times." The hospital's second stay lasted until the end of June 1778, nine months later.[48]

Hosting the patriots' hospital did not free the Moravians from harassment, which reached a peak in 1778. Rather than bringing the community together, however, leaders' management of the situation emphasized individual conscience, and thus the fact that the Brüdergemeine was ultimately made up of separate people. In April of that year, a number of Moravian men (not all of them single) from the town of Emmaus were jailed until enough money could be raised to pay their fines and bail. The response from Bethlehem to these events was conflicted. Bethlehem was the principal Moravian town in the region, and its leaders had the option, if they wished, to speak for the whole. Yet in this instance they chose to view the imprisoned as individuals to whom they owed religious allegiance, rather than as representatives of the larger community whose persecution required direct intervention. The Elders' Conference in Bethlehem discussed the matter, and they were certainly both outraged and deeply concerned about their coreligionists, but no one found any easy answers. Instead, they said that it "must fairly be left to the hearts and inner convictions of each brother, how far he had courage and strength to endure the bondage and the need and difficulties connected to it." Concluding their discussion, they reiterated the point that individuals, not the community, must decide their own right courses: "How far each one may have misgivings of conscience in this matter, that must appropriately remain left to him," as "only God can see in the heart, and we are not authorized in this matter to sharply judge one another."[49]

Though the Pennsylvanians' harassment of Moravian men was likely seen as persecution by all, the emphasis in Bethlehem's moral life had clearly shifted to the individual, making the leaders' response logical. And yet the prioritization of conscience also meant that the consequences of the Revolution were felt unevenly in Bethlehem. The Unity's commitment to pacifism was weak enough to make the teaching an individual matter, and thus its prominence in this era coincided with the trend, already underway, of prioritizing individual moral behavior as a key part of the religious experience in Bethlehem. The Single Brothers endured more than any other segment of the population, but even within that group different individuals responded based on their own perspectives and resources. Some left the community to fight in the war, others suffered through moves in and out of the Choir house, years of having armies march through, and the ignominy of having neighbors accuse them of treason. Even for the faithful it was a trying time. One Single Brother's lebenslauf recorded a judgment that damned many. "At the time of the American Revolution," it stated, "when .. the Choir House of the Single Brothers here was transformed into a military hospital and holding place for British prisoners, he fell, as did many of his peers, into a degenerate and licentious course." Whatever the individual experience, however, one common outcome of the conflict was to teach young Moravians that their neighbors resented them, thus excluding them from full participation in the defining moment of their generation, as even the Brüdergemeine's turn toward individual rather than group religious identity deprived Bethlehem's residents of a means of handling their shared persecution.[50]

Nonetheless, despite serious disruptions, expenses, and traumas during the period between 1775 and 1780, by the time the majority of the fighting had moved away from the Mid-Atlantic, its residents could return to the lives they had been building before the conflict broke out. When Ettwein wrote his history of the era in 1781, a document full of acid comments about the impositions of the illegitimate American and Pennsylvanian governments, he concluded simply by chronicling Cornwallis's defeat in the south, and he neglected to give any assessment of Bethlehem. In essence, the Revolutionary War was a far less significant event for the Moravians than the Seven Years' War that preceded it had been, because their much reduced missionary work no longer placed Bethlehem at risk. That earlier conflict had struck at the heart of Moravian religious life by transforming the way that the Unity could carry out its religious work. It had forced a substantial shift in the way religious beliefs influenced daily economic choices in the ensuing years. The struggle for independence from Britain, on the other hand, exacerbated already extant problems, particularly financial ones, for Bethlehem, but had only limited consequences for Moravian religious life. During the Revolution, Bethlehem continued on the path established in the 1760s, building a new religious community on the principles of hard work and individual conscience.[51]

CHAPTER 8

Unraveled Strands

THE 1780S SAW the beginning of a new era for Bethlehem, for the Moravians, for citizens of the new United States, and for the Atlantic world. The American Revolution transformed thirteen of Britain's mainland colonies into a new nation. The war brought economic challenges in its wake, and the struggling country, cut out of the protective fold of the British Empire, had to reestablish trading networks and rebuild its damaged infrastructure. The churches of the colonial period faced a changed environment as well. The departure was most marked in the South, where the established Anglican Church yielded to a rising tide of evangelical Baptist, Methodist, and Presbyterian congregations, but religious transformation, speeded by the freedom of religion guaranteed by the new Federal Constitution, touched all regions. The upstart, anti-establishment, international evangelicalism fostered by the mid-century Awakenings, which the Moravians and their many fellow travelers had helped to spread, moved into the mainstream and began to settle into institutional structures. In their religious lives and their economic lives, early Americans embarked on the engrossing process of building.[1]

Bethlehem's story, which by the end of the century was one of decline, sits uneasily in this energetic era of development. By the 1790s, young people were discontented and more likely to leave town to seek their fortunes elsewhere, either in other Moravian towns or outside the fold entirely, than previous generations had been likely to do. Those who remained pursued quiet, uncontroversial, and bureaucratic solutions to the challenges of life in the early republic. They declined to participate in the democratic and emotional religious movements of the "Second Great Awakening," and, though this is less surprising given their historic links to aristocratic establishment, they did not provide a religious critique of economic oppression when many of their neighbors rose up against taxation in the events known Fries's Rebellion. Bethlehem's residents—and the town remained exclusively Moravian throughout the eighteenth century—continued to support missionary outreach to native peoples, and they continued to find new economic strategies to do it, but the Moravians' moment of high energy had passed.[2]

That energy had tied together the religious and economic strands of Moravian life, and in its absence those strands unraveled. Everywhere, Moravians were more wary of risk, financial or otherwise. They turned away from shared economic projects in favor of privatization. Most mission direction was now centered in Europe. The debts of the Zinzendorf era still dogged the Unity, and as leaders attempted to eliminate the problem they turned to new, more cautious techniques to support ongoing missionary endeavors. The growing world of philanthropic fundraising, with its complicated dynamics of appealing to the wealthy, caught European leaders' attention and anticipated similar developments in North America later in the century. Meanwhile, Bethlehem's missions were far from the town itself, and their management lay largely in the hands of a few church officials. Those leaders used new mechanisms to support the missions—the Moravians never shied away from economic innovation—but these efforts had the result of further separating the congregation from what was theoretically its principal religious work. Bethlehem, divided from both the international and the regional missions, limped along. The culture of individual religious morality that had developed during the preceding decades continued to provide the town with a way to navigate its religious concerns about moral economic behavior, but that culture could not accomplish alone what the missions had done by galvanizing the community around a single, shared, religious purpose. The international Unity's mission, the Moravians' mission to the Indians in America, and the little town of Bethlehem followed separate courses into the nineteenth century.

Privatizing the International Mission

In the late eighteenth century, the international Unity was simultaneously a unified organization run by a single church hierarchy, and a collection of communities whose local histories each dictated a particular perspective. For Bethlehem, the years after 1760, when Count Zinzendorf died, were dominated, as we have seen, by the Moravians' efforts to cope with the changing racial climate around them, and the implications of those changes for their religious lives. For those in Herrnhut, the effort to pay off the Unity's debts from the Zinzendorf era overshadowed all else. The problem, as everyone was aware, dated from Zinzendorf's lifetime and from the expansionistic projects he undertook, and thus the Unity leadership developed a conservatism in financial matters that matched (and, of course, contributed to) Bethlehem's inward turn. The process of handling the debts was long and difficult. Efforts begun immediately after the count's death (including the abrogation of the Oeconomy in Bethlehem), and then again in the 1764 General Synod, to bring the debt under control, all failed. In 1769, leaders convened a second major synod, this time with the intent of solving the problem more effectively, and worry over financial matters preoccupied Unity leadership through the end of the eighteenth century.[3]

As the financial crisis developed—or rather failed to resolve itself—in the 1760s, Unity leaders turned increasingly toward a vision of the Brüdergemeine as a set of separate individuals with wealth, rather than a community that managed its shared assets and made its own investments. Private responsibility became the watchword, and members were reminded to believe that each person was individually accountable for the church's debt. In a parallel shift, Unity leaders believed that the best way to stabilize the international church's financial situation was to limit its risks. To do this, they limited the number of economic functions the centralized body would perform, likewise reducing the conception of the church's economic role. Ministers and missionaries were strongly urged to find independent funding, and church businesses were to be privatized. The goal was clearly to prevent the church from incurring more debts until old ones could be paid off, but in effect these new priorities represented a significant departure (albeit one that had been strongly foreshadowed in the years since Zinzendorf's death) from the financial strategies of the Brüdergemeine's early days, when massive and creative financial projects like the Oeconomy in Bethlehem had been undertaken to raise large quantities of money. The Unity of the late eighteenth century indulged in no such extravagances.[4]

"Joseph" Spangenberg, president of the 1769 Synod and the dominant figure in the international Unity until his death in 1792, culled Zinzendorf's writings to articulate the new philosophy within the context of the Moravians' customarily flexible approach to market engagement. It reflected both the new conservatism and also the continued need to balance economic values with material needs. In his own day, the count had hardly provided consistent financial leadership, but through Spangenberg's ever orderly selection of quotations, a new and coherent theme emerged: "All trade and commerce should have [private owners], and not be pursued under the name of the Gemeine and for her profit." Communally owned businesses had, at least on one occasion, raised a worrisome specter for the count, because "[they had] the appearance of a community of goods, which one should avoid on all counts, to avoid other inconveniences." When Zinzendorf had made the statement in 1749, at the height of the Oeconomy, it may have seemed incongruous to those who worked in such ventures and continued to do so for a long time. In 1769, however, it seemed prescient.[5] On the other hand, though Unity leaders in the 1760s emphasized privatization, they also continued to remind Moravians that trade was a positive thing when carried out in a Godly manner. Alongside Zinzendorf's mention of cautious practice, Spangenberg also listed quotations from the count that pointed to the complex negotiation between the material and the spiritual. "We must not think that nourishment and commerce are not convenient for the Savior, and a dishonor for his disciples and warriors [Streiter]," the count had said. On the other hand, this was, for him, a matter that called for caution, because "when commerce depends on a person, they can not all of the time extract themselves," so that "a warrior should not always enter into it." In this new era, as before, business projects were necessary, but had to be handled with care.[6]

The turn toward privatization in the 1760s and 1770s also had a significant impact on the way the international Unity financed its missions in subsequent decades. Mission directors in the newly centralized bureaucratic structure had three sources of income at their disposal. First, and most important, was a semiannual collection from all members of the international Unity. This system put the responsibility for supporting missions on individuals, and yet simultaneously, as would also occur in Bethlehem, channeled it through an indirect mechanism. Individual Moravians would therefore have little idea how their contributions directly served missionary work. Second, particular missions could rely on the businesses available to them, under the oversight of the mission directors. This complicated source of income required care in the managing, of course. There were dangers if missionaries mixed the Gospel and business. Leaders at the 1764 synod used a vivid example taken from the West Indies, where the Moravians had several missions as well as plantations: "it is like a sugar mill, which, when once it grabs the tip of a finger, pulls ever farther and after rips the whole arm away." Last, the Commercial Society, which had been erected in the late 1750s to maximize on the market information gleaned from missionaries (and which the 1769 Synod acknowledged as in keeping with the spirit of the new privatization), provided an additional source of income.[7]

Private financial appeals could also extend beyond the Unity, and when church leaders looked for likely territory, their eyes were drawn to Britain's wealthy and charitable souls. The Moravians had a substantial establishment on the island on which to base their efforts, and Britons were accustomed to such projects through the work of the Anglican Society for the Propagation of the Gospel and Society for the Promotion of Christian Knowledge. In 1769, Unity leaders drew attention to this source of income when they reminded mission directors to stay in "constant connection" with the Moravian-run Society for the Furtherance of the Gospel in England, a charitable organization designed to raise money for missions. Providing members of that Society with "detailed reports of the heathen" was also important. Key fundraising devices, these reports needed to strike just the right tone. "The rule [for] these short—but carefully and judiciously organized excerpts" from the larger mission reports, admonished the synod's members, "is above all this: that they may be edifying to every man, and to the praise of God, appeal to faithful participation in prayer and support, and so chosen and assembled that one could give one into the hands of the public itself," regardless of how such a thing might happen. Publications could certainly drum up support, but the physical presence of missionaries would help too. Missionaries should, consequently, according to Unity leaders, pass through England whenever possible, and be sure to share their stories. Moreover, a new society could also be erected in Holland, indicating that the Moravians hoped to gain monetary support in that financial center too[8] (Figure 11).

When they turned to publications and missionary societies as mechanisms for supporting their efforts, the Moravians fell into step with larger trends of Christian missionary circles of the day. Following the model of the seventeenth-century Jesuit *Relations,* the Halle Pietists had been publishing mission reports since 1710, and British societies, such as the SPG and the SPCK, had been doing so as well. In 1765, the Unity published David Cranz's *Historie von Grönland,* detailing the history of the Labrador mission. The

Figure 11. "The Power of the Gospel," by C. Schüssele. This depiction of missionary David Zeisberger suggests the lone missionary in the wilderness. Zeisberger's long career as a professional missionary was indicative of the distance between Bethlehem and its missions at the end of the eighteenth century. Courtesy Moravian Archives, Bethlehem.

Mission Deputation spent much time considering its distribution, including sending 6 unbound and 200 bound copies to Bethlehem for sale. Its success led to interest in further projects, and in 1767 leaders asked Christian Olden-dorp to write a history of the West Indian missions. Shortly thereafter, they started to publish in English as well. In 1769, John Heckewelder's *A Letter to a Friend* was the first such effort. In 1788 Spangenberg published in London *An Account of the manner in which the Protestant Church of the Unitas Fratrum, or United Brethren, preached the Gospel*, and he redoubled the Unity's former efforts by including in the volume Heckewelder's earlier effort, as well as the "Stated Rules of the Society for the Gospel Among the Heathen" and, rein-forcing the importance of publishing, a list of books available about the Moravians in English. By turning to publications to drum up support for their missions, the Moravians were using a method others had tested and found effective, and yet the strategy also tied the group to an external con-stituency beyond the Brüdergemeine's control.[9]

The twin trends of privatizing church finances and seeking outside support for missionary work indicate that in the later decades of the eighteenth century the international Unity strove for stability and harmony with the larger Protestant community. Even as they used Zinzendorf's words to smooth the way, leaders rejected ambitious communal projects, of both a religious and an economic nature, and eschewed the controversies those projects had frequently caused in the past. Moreover, they came to rely on mechanisms first developed by others, such as missionary societies, and thus became followers in the Atlantic world missionary scene. There is continuity here too, however: ever willing to innovate and renegotiate financial issues, the Moravians sought in this new climate, as they had before, a careful balance between moral economic behavior, financial necessities, and religious goals.

The Era of Professional Missionaries

Across the ocean, Bethlehem's Moravians faced a different set of challenges brought on by the American Revolution and its aftermath, but the same conservative trends seen in Herrnhut are evident in the town's ongoing relationship to its missions. Though Bethlehem enjoyed relative peace during the 1780s as compared with the violent period of frontier warfare two decades earlier, the Moravian Indians who had been forced west by those conflicts were not so fortunate. Under the care of the group's most famous career missionary, David Zeisberger, the community of Christian Indians who had left the Delaware Valley in 1765 had, after several additional moves, settled in central Ohio along the Muskingum Creek. The Revolutionary War years were a particularly challenging time for Indians in the Ohio Valley, who were caught in the middle of a political nightmare. The British and the Americans vied for control of the region, and, as the tribes living there took and sometimes changed sides, the Delaware's preferred strategy of neutrality failed them. Unlike Moravians in Bethlehem, whose resources were co-opted by the war effort but whose homes were safely removed from battle, the Moravian Indians were again (and not coincidentally, as Indian lands continued to define the boundaries between European empires and the new American state) caught between warring factions and armies, just as they had been in the Seven Years' War. The Moravian Indians attempted to maintain a neutral stance, but this was rendered problematic, both by the Delaware—most of whom, despite deep internal divisions, eventually allied with the Wyandot and their British allies in 1781 and wanted the mission Indians to follow suit—and by the British authorities in Detroit, who believed accurately that the missionaries were siding with the Americans.[10]

In the fall of 1781, under intense pressure from the pro-British Indians, particularly the Wyandot, the Moravian Indians, with Zeisberger and the other missionaries, left the three settlements they had built along the Muskingum in Ohio and moved to nearby Sandusky. According to the narrative written by missionary John Heckewelder, "Never did the Christian Indians, leave a Country, with more regret." On the other hand, since the Moravian Indians had been through the process so many times over the preceding two decades, one wonders if exhaustion took over as the primary sentiment. The missionaries were then ordered on to Detroit, where they were briefly interrogated, and then released. The winter of 1781–82 was difficult for the mission, and many people faced starvation. In February, late in the season when supplies were in a dire state, British authorities commanded the missionaries to return to Detroit, to answer again for charges that they were conspiring with the Americans. While they were gone, the Christian Indians decided to return to their mission settlements in Gnadenhütten in order to harvest their corps and stave off the hunger that was plaguing them.[11]

What followed was one of the most brutal events of the American Revolution, though the victims fought for neither the United States nor Great Britain. While the Indians were back in the mission at Gnadenhütten, a group of American militia captured them. The soldiers initially acknowledged the Indians as Christian, and therefore not at war with the Americans, but they soon changed course and accused the captives of being warriors engaged in the conflict. According to Heckewelder's later account, the evidence of the Moravian Indians' distinction from non-Christian Indians was obvious but ignored. "The Christian Indians were well known by their dress, which was plain and decent," he wrote, "no sign of paint to be seen on their skin or Cloaths—no Feathers about their heads, nor these shaved and trimmed, as every Indian Warrior does." But these facts mattered little in the ethnically charged border war. From the perspective of the American settlers, Christian Indians who strove for neutrality in the conflict with the British were simply an impossibility, or perhaps just easy targets. The soldiers imprisoned the Indians overnight, allowing them to pray and sing together, then systematically executed them in the morning with a heavy mallet. More than ninety Indians, including thirty-four children, were massacred. Two adolescent boys managed to escape (one of them after having been scalped), and they reported the story.[12]

This second Gnadenhütten attack contained disturbing parallels and also significant differences from the one in Pennsylvania. Most notably, both were illustrations of racial warfare; in Pennsylvania, Indians had killed white missionaries, and in Ohio white soldiers massacred Christian Indians. Yet the terms of the conflicts between Indians and whites had changed dramatically in the intervening twenty-seven years, becoming more racialized and more imbalanced as white American settlers and their governments came to control more and more of the territory. Additionally, between 1755 and 1782, Indians and whites in western Pennsylvania and Ohio had been in conflict more often then they had been at peace, and thus violence had become a key aspect of interracial relations.[13]

These changes in the continent's political and social climate had a direct effect on Bethlehem's religious life. This is evident from the town's differing responses to the two bloody events, and comparing them highlights the transition the town had undergone. In 1755, a young Zeisberger had rushed back to Bethlehem in the middle of the night to sound the alarm after he had approached Gnadenhütten only to meet terrified coreligionists fleeing the scene. He had wakened Spangenberg to warn him of what had happened at Gnadenhütten, and Bethlehem's residents were overwhelmed by the news of their losses at the mission and its implications for the whole community. The town diarist recorded that "November 24 is a day that will not easily be forgotten by us."[14] In 1782, nearly a month passed before the news even reached Bethlehem, and then it came not from Moravian lines of communication, but from a rumor heard by a Moravian in a New Jersey congregation. On April 5, 1782, the Elders' Conference convened because "Brother Leinbach . . . heard in his neighborhood from a man who, with his brother and another, returned home last Sunday from Pittsburg." The rumor held that "in February, 160 men, white people on horseback, from the area around the Monogehela had come together to destroy the towns on the Muskingum."[15] Although Bethlehem's leaders and residents felt the loss deeply, the sense of immediate connection to the mission, and the sense of their own imminent danger, that had prevailed in 1755 was gone. Distance provides the most obvious explanation for the difference, yet the distance was itself indicative of the Moravians' changed relationship to their missions.

Immediately after receiving the news of the second massacre, Bethlehem's leaders looked to Pennsylvania's government, not to their own agents, to prevent further tragedy, yet another sign that the support networks between the base at Bethlehem and the missions in Ohio had been stretched beyond reasonable utility. Over the next weeks, the Elders' Conference heard reports of efforts to get news to and from the Ohio Valley, but they also followed more mundane matters, such as the placement of apprentices and other church workers. On April 11, it was reported that a representative from Bethlehem would travel west at least to Pittsburgh—perhaps the farthest he could safely travel—in order to procure more information. The strongest remnant of the community's earlier, deep connections to the missions came through prayer. At the end of the day's minutes, the conference reported "Also one thought with a particularly special feeling about our dear Br[other] Dav. Zeisberger among the Indians, who today has his birthday."[16]

Zeisberger, too, represents the change in the Moravians' missions. In this new era, individuals—professionals—rather than the whole community, tied Bethlehem to its missions. David Zeisberger is arguably the most famous of all eighteenth-century North American Moravians, but his fame grows out of the decades he spent with the Indians, not out of his connection to the group itself. Zeisberger had been born in Zauchenthal, in Moravia, and had gone with his parents to Herrnhut when he was a child. In the 1730s the family moved to Georgia with the first Moravian settlement there, and they were also among the first in Pennsylvania. In his early twenties, he began working among the Indians, after first learning the Iroquois language. From that point on, his importance to the community was always coupled with a marked distance from it. He was an outstanding missionary, and his expertise was widely respected by the Brüdergemeine (in 1764 his views had been taken as definitive in the conference held to determine the future of Pennsylvania missions), but at the same time he did not truly participate in the Euro-American Moravian community, particularly after he took charge of the Ohio missions. He, along with his colleague John Heckewelder, was part of a new generation of pilgrims. Whereas most missionaries during the Oeconomy period had served for a relatively short time, returned to Bethlehem frequently, and almost universally were married, Zeisberger spent nearly his entire life working with Indians and did not marry until he was sixty. His lengthy career enabled the Moravian community at Bethlehem to remain connected to religious work among native peoples long after the missions had moved days' or weeks' journey from Bethlehem, but the missionaries themselves were no longer representative of the Moravian religious experience.[17]

The transition to professional missionaries of which Zeisberger was a part reflected the larger transition in Bethlehem from a pilgrim congregation intertwined with its missionary work to a congregation town that emphasized individual moral action within an increasingly complicated economy. This same transition is also evident in the structures used to finance missionary work in the post-Revolutionary era. Before the transitions of the 1760s, the Oeconomy had enabled every Moravian to participate in the group's religious work, whether by actually laboring in the field or by doing something as mundane as washing the clothes of those living in town. Mission finance had been Bethlehem's raison d'être. After 1764, mission finance had become the purview of a few community leaders, most notably Johannes Ettwein. The techniques they employed became sophisticated, bureaucratic, and abstract, as people in eastern Pennsylvania managed missions that were hundreds of miles away. The distance only increased after the 1782 massacre, when the remaining Christian Indians in Ohio fled north of Detroit, and settled on lands given to them by the British government (Figure 12).

During the next fifteen years, through the end of the century, Ettwein developed a two-pronged strategy to support the missions that was well suited to Bethlehem's and the Moravians' privatized sense of religious work. First, he secured from the federal government a piece of land within the United States where the Indians could live in peace under the oversight of the missionaries. Certainly, such efforts represented a recognition of the Indians' basic need for safety and security, but they would not bring the Moravians in Bethlehem closer to the work they supported, and they required the regular efforts of only a few people in town. Second, to provide funding for the missions, Ettwein resuscitated the defunct Society for the Furtherance of the Gospel (now under the name Society for Propagating the Gospel) in 1787, undoubtedly following the model that European leaders were also then embracing. Ettwein also had an American precedent, because Spangenberg had initially founded such an organization in the 1740s as a way to funnel money donated to the Moravians to the missions. Over time, however, the original SFG had deteriorated into an almost exclusively Moravian body, and since the vast majority of the missions' funding had come directly from the Oeconomy or from the international Unity, it had served little purpose other than to demarcate mission expenses in the accounts. By the 1760s, it fell from the books entirely. In

Figure 12. Johannes Ettwein is often remembered for the youthful vigor he brought to decades of service to the Unity as an administrator and bishop, but in his latter years he was cantankerous and wary of change. Artist unknown, GS.277. Courtesy Unity Archives, Herrnhut.

the 1780s, however, Ettwein saw that charitable donations would be an ideal way to sponsor mission work, which continued to be quite expensive. This was a logical step in Bethlehem's new economy, since now both Moravians and non-Moravians could be implored to donate to this particular cause, thus increasing the church's ability to keep missionaries in the field. In 1787, he chartered the new Society for Propagating the Gospel, and he had the body incorporated in both Pennsylvania and New Jersey.[18]

Ettwein envisioned a structure that would recreate the best practices of the Brüdergemeine over the preceding decades, while using the new business techniques of the early republic. He also recognized, as his predecessors had, the need to monitor economic activity continually, in order to ensure it proceeded in line with the community's beliefs about fair economic action. The society included all bishops and other officers of the Moravian Church in Pennsylvania, and any other members of the Brüdergemeine who wished to join. In addition, the society welcomed as "honorary" members people of other denominations who were interested in their projects, but the society as a whole remained a support body for the mission projects of the Moravian Church. Ettwein had wanted to go farther to ensure good behavior than simply requiring members be Moravian, however, as the final printed rules omitted a few additional points that Ettwein had proposed in his initial draft. Since they had more to do with the missions than with mission finance, they were presumably seen as interfering with the church's authority over its religious work. For example, Ettwein had suggested that "None of the Missionaries shall in public or private speak in derogation of any Christian sect or Religion or treat of their different tenets & Ceremonies," a proscription that was likely designed to ensure the widest possible support for the Moravian projects. In addition, Ettwein reinforced the notion that missionaries were professionals, and missionary work was a charitable endeavor segregated from the Moravians' own economy. "None of the Missionaries or Assistants who receives the Gifts of the Society, shall have a Hand in trading with the Indians," he wrote, "The assistants shall be Tradesmen & be chiefly employed to instruct the Indians in farming & other useful knowledge."[19]

Ettwein used the Moravian Society for Propagating the Gospel in his effort to secure land for the Moravian Indian community. The state of Pennsylvania granted the society 5,000 acres of land near Lake Erie in 1790, which Ettwein hoped would become a permanent mission site. This was just a precursor, however, to the federal grant of twelve thousand acres in Ohio that the Society received in 1798. Securing these land patents required enormous skill and diplomatic acumen on Ettwein's part, as the negotiations spanned the unstable period between 1785 and the end of the century. Congress linked the land grants to the 1782 massacre, which had been carried out by undisciplined members of the Pennsylvania militia, and the association had important symbolic implications: in the new republic the federal government would manage Indian relations and claim responsibility for its own shortcomings. The Moravians implicitly endorsed that position with their own policy of preferring governmental negotiation to on-the-ground politicking. But the Western land projects ultimately came to naught. Most of the Christian Indians preferred to stay in Canada, farther from white settlement, and the Ohio congregations never returned to their earlier strength. In the 1820s, the Moravians returned the land to Congress, acknowledging that the Ohio project had been a failure.[20]

Despite these difficulties, Ettwein was financially innovative with his efforts. The society used a corporate structure, which enabled the group to minimize risk. In addition, Ettwein even toyed with the idea of placing all the church's assets, including Bethlehem itself, in the formal ownership of the society, under the assumption that this would best facilitate the church's financial situation. These projects are perhaps striking for a religious community in any time, but taking a larger perspective, they also point to key continuities vis-à-vis the Moravians' engagement with the market economy before the transitions. The Oeconomy had been, in its day, a financially sophisticated means of supporting missionary work. It enabled the Moravians to make the best use of the capital they had in hand, and yet to devote a significant portion of their labor to religious outreach. That underlying economic creativity and flexibility continued into the early republic, and it represents an important and lasting aspect of the way the Moravians supported their religious goals using the economic opportunities around them. Ettwein's use of the charitable society and government land grants can thus be seen as bringing the economic ideology of the Oeconomy period, if not the specific form, into the early republic.

Concern over moral economic behavior remained an ever present issue, however, and an ongoing negotiation continued between preserving the community's moral standards, achieving its religious goals, and profits. The bishop's efforts to gain land in the West—in an era of widespread land speculation—drew attention, and he responded by repeating a formulation that echoed that of Moravian business people throughout the decades. "I heartily hate land speculation for the sake of acquiring wealth," he wrote, "nor have I sought for one foot of it for myself or my children. But I would rejoice, could I gain much of it for the Society's future use or profit, since I anticipate an active future for it."[21] Throughout the eighteenth century, the Moravians used the market around them as a way to facilitate missionary work, and Ettwein's labors fit firmly in that history. Yet contrasts are as significant as continuities. Many layers of remove now existed between Bethlehem's Moravians and the mission work the town supported. The individual artisan in Bethlehem who joined the society during the 1780s and eagerly awaited news of Zeisberger's activities did not engage in missionary work nearly as intimately as his predecessors had two generations before. Few Indians came through town, and the far-off lands they occupied seemed as foreign and remote as the West Indies. Authority over the missions now lay primarily in Herrnhut, and efforts to support the projects required negotiations with the likes of George Washington and John Adams. In that effort, Bethlehem's storekeepers, saddlemakers, and smiths were largely peripheral.

"An Industrious, inofensive people"

Visitors to Bethlehem at the end of the eighteenth century found a town that was quiet and orderly. Even as they enjoyed the tranquility, however, residents struggled to maintain a town that had lost its sense of purpose. The individualized religion that developed during the era of the Revolution continued, but it proved a shaky basis on which to build community cohesion. The result was a congregation at odds with itself. A successful new school; ongoing, though distant, connections to missionary work in the West; and an energetic spirit of enterprise shared space with a sense of frustration about the town's future, in general, and deep worry about its young men, in particular. Bethlehem had most certainly declined and the missions that had animated the pilgrim congregation were far away, but it was not at all clear what should be done about it.

Bethlehem's distance from its missionary past was ironic. After decades of persecution for theoretically dangerous and treacherous ties to Indians, the Moravians had, by the end of the eighteenth century, achieved a positive reputation for successful work among the Indians. In the public imagination, the Moravians were known as Indian experts, people with credibility when it came to the complicated problems of understanding and dealing with the peoples whom Americans were in the process of dispossessing with remarkable speed. Newspaper articles appealed to the authority of John Heckewelder and David Zeisberger when questions related to Indians arose, and the Moravians were heralded as "more successful than any others in propagating religious knowledge among savage nations, and reducing them to a settled and peaceable mode of life." If people thought of the Moravians at all, therefore, they probably thought of missionaries, but the association, no matter how positive it now seemed, was hardly current. In reality, the Moravian residents of the Lehigh Valley had almost no personal experience with missionary work or with "real live" Indians, and the international Unity treated its North American missions as an afterthought.[22]

This fact became vividly apparent in early March 1792, when a group of fifty Iroquois warriors and chiefs traveled from New York to Philadelphia to meet with President George Washington. The United States army had suffered a humiliating defeat in its effort to secure the Ohio Valley in November 1791, and Washington was in a mood to end the violence that plagued the nation's western border with, he hoped, the help of the Six Nations. The Iroquois delegation, accompanied by Presbyterian missionary Samuel Kirkland, traveled in a slow and deliberate procession south to the capital, and it stopped numerous times along the way.[23] With one day's notice, the party arrived in Nazareth, and its coming garnered particular attention from "those among us who have never seen an Indian, and hardly believed that any would ever again come here." The Moravians were entranced. The Indians' every move was recorded and analyzed, as were their clothes, decorative face paints, and jewelry. "Only a few carried flints with them," Nazareth's residents reported back to the Unity in Herrnhut, "and in general their appearance and clothing was not warlike, but peaceful, . . . their whole conduct was also lively and cheerful, though also very modest and humble." The Moravians revealed no confidence in their knowledge of "Indian" ways, and in their observations they used whites as their frame of reference, rather than even the Delaware Indians who still had Moravian missionaries living among them. They wondered at the Indians' demeanor, for example, and noted that "for such a large number, [they were] very still, such as no similar number of white people would ever be." When the visitors gathered for breakfast, their white hosts "were pleased by their order and calm, and how they so peacefully arranged themselves around a large table," and later noted with evident pride during a concert that their music came as a "great pleasure to the Indians, some of whom rose from their seats and gathered around the organ to see everything exactly." The Indians, they assumed, "could not understand how so many instruments could be played so harmoniously and agreeably." The visit provoked a sense of almost ethnographic fascination with Indian "others" in these Moravians, who, unlike their predecessors, had so few personal relationships with Indians.[24]

From Nazareth, the procession moved on to Bethlehem, transported through the late winter snow on sleds gathered from around the Moravian communities. Bethlehem's historic place as a center of missionary work did little to prepare the town's residents for the visit, and they were just as awestruck as their coreligionists in Nazareth had been. The sense of unfamiliarity was shared: though the Indians were rumored to have said that they would not rest on their hard journey until they reached Bethlehem, suggesting some knowledge of the place, in the proceedings that dominated the next two days references to the Moravians' missionary work seemed to conjure not a present reality but rather a forgotten history. In Bethlehem, as in Nazareth before, the visit entailed a series of speeches, assertions of friendship, and wishes for future peace. Ettwein welcomed the visitors, and reminded them of the bond once established between the Iroquois and the Moravians. "Our chiefs and your chiefs established sincere friendship fifty years ago, to love one another and to show each other good service," he said, and yet the scene was hardly one of familiarity. "We, the United Brethren, (for that is our real name)," Ettwein continued, "are lovers and friends of all peoples, because we have one father in heaven." The stilted formality of the moment could not have been more different from the busy days of the Easton treaty talks, in the late 1750s, when large numbers of treaty participants and their families had stayed in the area around Bethlehem, Moravian leaders had searched for ways to support them, and everything the Moravians did had been suspect in their neighbors' eyes because of their extensive ties with Indians.[25]

Though most of Bethlehem's Moravians no longer had personal ties to mission work, they did continue to find new ways to express their piety and share the Gospel. But these innovative strategies marked Bethlehem as a place to which others could come in search of spirituality, knowledge, or solace, if they so chose, rather than a place pulsing with the outward-pushing energy of itinerants and missionaries. After years of occasional discussion, Bethlehem decided to build a new church building to replace the long outgrown 1754 chapel. Central Church, completed in 1806, was a magnificent structure, built in the same style as other Moravian churches around the world and capable of housing more than twice Bethlehem's population. For those who wanted to enjoy the serenity of worship with the Moravians, there would be plenty of space.[26] Far more significant, however, was the new Bethlehem Female Seminary, opened to non-Moravians in 1785. It soon became a popular finishing school for the élite of the seaboard cities. The Unitas Fratrum had a deep history of promoting education—the most famous Moravian in the early modern period was probably education reformer and bishop Jan Amos Comenius—and thus the school built on a long tradition. Likewise, the early missions to Europeans in Pennsylvania had included numerous schools. But there was something passive and quiescent about opening schools and hoping for enrollees that differed from the town's earlier days of exuberant and often contentious organizing[27] (Figure 13).

The school flourished, and it quickly became the public face of Bethlehem in the new nation. In the process, Bethlehem finally shed its reputation as a cloistered, and perhaps dangerous, religious enclave, and replaced it with an image of girlish studiousness. Long discussions of the seminary circulated in the newspapers, emphasizing the regularity, beauty, and piety of the community and the school it sheltered. "We were drawn thither by the fame of that seminary, and high as our expectations were raised, we found them greatly exceeded," recounted "Constantina," whose praise appeared in the Massachusetts *Magazine* in 1790 and bordered on the extreme. She dubbed Bethlehem a "terrestrial paradise," where "nature hath shaped for us the most enchanting walks"; and "rivers pursue their glassy course, the margins of which are planted by the flourishing and highly perfumed locust, cedars,

Figure 13. View of Bethlehem from the north, drawn by Nicholas Garrison, c. 1780. In stark contrast to Pownall's 1754 image, Garrison's Bethlehem seems to be peacefully swallowed by the countryside. Courtesy Moravian Archives, Bethlehem.

chestnut, and a variety of trees bearing in their season, the most delicious fruit." Constantina found the Moravians no less enchanting, and she assured her readers that "All that was wrong in their system they seem to have rectified," by which she meant the community's practices of arranging marriages and housing married couples in gender-segregated housing. Of course, according to this observer, the girls received the highest education, preparing them for the upper echelons of American society. Another report, this one credited to a young girl studying at Bethlehem, highlighted the importance of music and worship, as well as instruction in "reading and grammar, both English and German, for those who choose; writing, arithmetic, history, geography, composition, &c." The near total absence of male figures or activities in these accounts was striking, and its readers might easily have assumed it was a town principally occupied by women.[28]

The Moravians embraced the role the school played in Bethlehem's public image. They highlighted their pupils' accomplishments, and also the girls' status as daughters and future wives of the nation's élite. When the Iroquois delegation passed through town in 1792, a representative of the girls presented one of the main addresses. She welcomed the visitors, and announced that the girls were "pleased to see you, and we look on you without fear or trepidation." She wished them well on their journey to see President Washington, and said that those studying at the school were there "to learn what is good." This, she continued, the chiefs should also teach their children, including that the girls and the Iroquois children were one, made by the same God. Good Peter, one of the Indian leaders, replied to the girls, confessing that it was an unusual sight to see such a group of young women, but still apparently taking their words as seriously as a previous speaker had treated Ettwein's official welcome. Because the pupils were not necessarily Moravians, their role in welcoming the official visitors is telling. When Bethlehem's leaders placed the school and its students at the center of the ceremony, they elevated the school above all other potential versions of the town's identity, including as home to a congregation that still supported missionary work among the Delaware. Samuel Kirkland, the Presbyterian minister accompanying the delegation, at least, was impressed; he enrolled his daughters in the school shortly thereafter.[29]

Bethlehem's religious work had changed significantly since its heyday decades before, but the town's economic life continued apace. Indeed, the transformation of Bethlehem as a place from which ministers went out into a place to which seekers traveled demanded new and better connections to the surrounding countryside. In 1794, town businessmen built the first bridge over the Lehigh River. Ettwein, whose cantankerous nature may have become more pronounced in his old age, resisted the bridge project, but the town's shopkeepers reasonably argued that a bridge was going to cross the Lehigh at some point, and that Bethlehem's shops would benefit significantly from having it there as opposed to Easton or some other location. Furthermore, a bridge would make it easier for area residents to reach Bethlehem's church. Some of the town's wealthier men created a Bridge Society, using much the same model as Ettwein's Society for Propagating the Gospel. Indeed, more than a few of the members overlapped. The new society continued the church's trend of providing the Diacony with a regular income from shares, and yet also transferring the risks for maintaining the bridge to the society. When the bridge came down a few years later in a spring freshet, this latter provision turned out to be a good one from the perspective of the Diacony, but nonetheless, the town's merchants had shown, as Ettwein had in the area of mission finance, that they were continuing to adapt to the changing market around them.[30]

Bethlehem's businessmen worked to improve other aspects of the town's infrastructure as well. Building decisions reflected these concerns. The Strangers' Store, which for decades had been located on the town's northern outskirts, was enlarged and relocated to a more central spot to encourage commerce. A stagecoach, which had run periodically since the 1760s, was established on a regular weekly schedule in 1790, and then quickly had to be replaced with a biweekly service. New roads made it easier to travel around the region. Even the new United States mail system acknowledged Bethlehem's central position in the region, and the Moravian town anchored two new mail routes. Residents bid for the postal contracts, as they continued to seek their town's economic advancement. These efforts, and the many years of trade carried by Moravians artisans and shopkeepers over the preceding decades, had earned Bethlehem a reputation as a place of business, little different from other nearby places. A storekeeper in Philadelphia advertised that his cotton goods were "equal to any manufactured in Bethlehem," and a regional booster listed Bethlehem as one of the places moving into the profitable business of manufacturing potash.[31]

Town leaders encouraged such activities, both by private businesses and by those still owned by the church, so long as they did no harm to the community as a whole. They oversaw the store's move, approved of new projects, and generally gave individuals a great deal of latitude in their business dealings. This became evident in 1794, when the increased "spirit" of land speculation came under consideration. Bethlehem itself was wholly owned by the church and those lands were not up for sale, so there was no danger of risky behavior resulting in the loss of key properties. But individual reputations could be damaged, and there was worry that "creditors might believe that the [congregation] represents in the end" those members who had been ruined in their private business dealings. Residents were thus advised explicitly that the church did not stand behind them in their business dealings, and that they should make that fact clear to those with whom they did frequent business. New enterprises undertaken by individuals in town departed from Bethlehem's economic tradition in that they were purely private, yet they also built on the Moravians' long history of economic flexibility and innovation. The church, however, followed a careful course to minimize financial risk.[32]

Leaders continued to deal with transgressions in the business arena, as they maintained oversight over the town's economy. Few such incidents arose, but when they did the situation was examined carefully. Christian Ebert, for example, ran afoul of the Board of Overseers on numerous occasions. He and his apprentice had a bad habit of shooting for fun in places that were dangerous and disruptive. More serious, however, were the events that unfolded in May 1793, when Ebert "grossly prostituted himself and the Gemeine [in Philadelphia] where he was variously drunk and was a public nuisance." This embarrassment led to a deeper examination of Ebert's "behavior in his business." The concern was that he "maintained and openly sold many wares that according to his contract with the Gemeine he should not." More serious yet were the rumors that he "kept wine and other strong drinks and sold them in town." Last, he seemed to be interfering with the stagecoach to Bethlehem, by trying to arrange its schedule so that visitors would overflow the inn and have to stay with him, for a fee. Despite these serious problems, leaders were sympathetic. Ebert had been for years one of the town's innkeepers, and now that he no longer held that post, he had no other way to make a livelihood. His sales of alcohol and his desire to shelter guests were both extensions of his former employment. He was permitted to keep a smaller scale version of his illicit trade, as long as he did it all publicly and avoided the sale of liquor altogether. The Overseers even acknowledged that his private inn might appeal to some female visitors who found the inn too raucous. Ultimately, Ebert's transgressions were read as symptoms of an economic problem to be solved, rather than as indications of sin or pernicious individualism.[33]

But if Bethlehem's leaders continued to govern the town's economy in much the same ways they had for decades, morale was quite low nonetheless. The Moravians believed their community to be on hard times spiritually in the 1790s, and they were quite clear about whom to blame. In a timeless jeremiad, they decried the behavior of the youth. Repeated laments about growing disobedience testified to concerns that Bethlehem's moral future was imperiled. The crimes generally fell under the category of pranks and indiscretions, often involving alcohol, and they rarely had any sort of economic component. Bethlehem's young men apparently bristled at the prospect of staying sober, shooting only where permitted, and being polite all the time. The boys gathered in the inn or in private homes to drink. They fought, and sometimes worse: during a song service one December someone attempted to put a "large block" into the water system, which, "if it could have been accomplished, could have killed people." Similar "horseplay" near the oil mill was equally troubling. A few youths showed an "increasing impudence" that would have "miserable consequences." Some of the problems arose from the behavior of boys who were apprenticed in Bethlehem but were not members of the community, but not all incidents could be blamed on outsiders. One master "complained how hard it often was for him to keep his outsider [*fremde*] apprentices in appropriately strict order, because he had brethren under him whose behavior was no better than that of the *Fremden*." He continued that "it would almost be easier" to have no Moravian apprentices at all.[34]

Rectifying the situation was hardly easy, and leaders vacillated between stern punishment and mercy. In March 1791, a neighbor complained that as he and several other people had walked by the Single Brothers' House, some boys in an upper window "treated him as he had never heard in the worst places." He named names and demanded action. After "painful reflection," the Elders' Conference had decided that corporal punishment was called for, and the Board of Overseers concurred. In other cases, leaders were more lenient. Several boys who caused recurrent problems were ordered to leave, then, upon their pleadings, were ultimately allowed to stay on a trial basis. Johann Barndt, for example, was labeled as a bad seed. He came to Bethlehem in 1785, and by 1787 he was admitted to Communion, suggesting that his behavior to that point was not a cause for concern. In April 1791, however, he

was called one of the "most impudent and damaging" of the men, and leaders said that he "should have been sent away several years ago." His master
tried to defend him, only making matters worse. "The sorry consequence that
can be seen," the Board of Overseers recorded, "is that with longer leniency
more of our children will be corrupted and maybe could be ruined forever."
Even after such dire language, however, the Board relented a few weeks later
"because while there is still any hope for the saving of this young man," mercy
was called for. Barndt disappointed the community, however. Within a year
he was in trouble again, this time for fighting while drunk, and he disappeared from the records after that.[35]

Bethlehem's young men bristled under a level of discipline that would
have been impossible outside a religious community, but the town's women
had a radically different experience. They probably enjoyed at least as much
freedom if not more than they would have had in their birth families, and
they were spared pressure to marry. They rarely entered the official records as
objects of community ire. Occasionally couples were chastised or expelled for
forming romantic attachments that the community had not approved, but
such events were infrequent. Quite the opposite; young women regularly pe-
titioned to move to Bethlehem. Some, like Hannah Langdon of Philadelphia,
had been students at the school. Some had grown up in other Moravian congregations around the region. With these influxes, and a low rate of attrition,
the size of the Single Sisters' Choir remained robust, even as the Single Brothers' Choir fell on very hard times. In 1794, there were 118 Single Sisters as compared with only 42 Single Brothers. The Brothers grappled with their decline
and tried to take comfort in the idea that those who remained were truly dedicated to the Savior, but the numbers were hardly encouraging. The quiet
town inhabited by the Female Seminary had little to offer young men, particularly those who, in an earlier generation, might have learned Mahican or
Dutch Creole and embarked on a life of adventure on the frontier or in the
Caribbean.[36]

Bethlehem's decline at the end of the eighteenth century was gentle. It encouraged nostalgia and poetic tributes to the town's history. The jubilee celebrating the fiftieth anniversary of the congregation looked backward rather
than toward the future. Residents recalled milestones achieved. 614 children
had been born; 150 white adults had been baptized, as well as 215 Indians and
Africans. A staggering 134 men had been ordained to perform religious work
throughout the region and the Atlantic world. But Bethlehem had changed

much. "Fifty years ago," recalled Ettwein, "the whole region around us, particularly to the north, was a pure wilderness and thick woods, where only here and there was an Indian village; and now for two hundred English miles beyond us to the north [there is] nothing but cultivated land."[37] In that "wilderness" had been opportunity. There were countless souls to be saved, Indians and Europeans. Across the ocean, a dynamic community propelled by revivals and sheer enthusiasm created an international stir. Much had been accomplished, and thousands of people had turned to Christ because of the Moravians' labor.

But the path had not been easy, and eventually the pilgrim congregation had unraveled, even if the individual strands did not fail. The international Unity's religious projects, Bethlehem's work among North American Indians, and Bethlehem itself all survived, though each now pursued its own path. In the 1740s, the Brüdergemeine had made use of every economic tool available to advance its religious mission, and in the 1790s the same was true. The pragmatism that marked Moravian economic endeavor also continued, and though the group approached economic activities with an eye toward moral pitfalls, no special worry was expended over innovative economic strategies. Yet the exhausting fervor of evangelicalism's birth, of which the Moravians were such an important part, had faded, and the Moravians, unlike their Methodist fellow travelers, neither sought nor achieved denominational growth. The violent spasms of the Seven Years' War, which stretched from the Ohio Valley to Silesia, depleted financial reserves and taught Bethlehem's Moravians to be wary of too close ties to their mission subjects. The decades-long search for denominational stability that followed Zinzendorf's death sapped the Unitas Fratrum of its initial energy and deprived Bethlehem of its larger place in the Unity's labors. As the century turned, the Unity relied heavily on private initiative to support its religious work, and left individual congregations to build their own ties to those projects through charitable donations. Bethlehem's mission ties were similarly indirect and left in the hands of professional missionaries. Those in town celebrated—and continue to commemorate—their distinctive past, but in place of the "pilgrim spirit" so prized by Zinzendorf, they were known among their neighbors for having, as one visitor put it, "progressed farthest toward the establishment of order and prosperity."[38]

Conclusion

BETHLEHEM'S EIGHTEENTH-CENTURY HISTORY started on a high note, but did not sustain the tune. The Moravians founded the town in a burst of evangelical energy felt from Suriname to St. Petersburg, and only a decade later Bethlehem's massive stone buildings and armies of pilgrims had made it a permanent part of the North American landscape. During the warfare of the 1750s, it was the most solid place on the northeastern Pennsylvania frontier, and the town's leaders were likely people from whom the provincial government could ask for regional information. But its population peaked in the 1750s and stagnated after the end of the Oeconomy. By the 1790s residents had good reason to worry that their home would be eclipsed if a road bypassed the town, or that local businesses would lose out if they lacked a bridge across the Lehigh to attract customers. This narrative, with its natural climax at the dissolution of the communal Oeconomy, would superficially seem to offer evidence that a corrosive spirit of individualism and acquisitiveness undermined a unified religious settlement, the epitome of Perry Miller's famed declension model. But close examination reveals a much more nuanced story of the way the Moravians' religion shaped their economic lives, one in which historical contingency and not corrosive acquisitiveness played the dominant role, and where the ties that connected Bethlehem to its wider communities, Moravian and non-Moravian, propelled the drama.

Religion shaped Bethlehem's economic life at every turn, from the creation of the Oeconomy to the recreation of a new economic ethos after the loss of the missions to distance and administrative fiat. Through it all, the record of daily transactions, conference minutes, and letters to and from Herrnhut left by the Moravians reveal a decades-long and widely varied negotiation between the spiritual and the material. Concerns over the pitfalls of economic sins were ever present, but those concerns never prevented the group from engaging in new and innovative projects. Protestant Christian belief about moral economic behavior provided the frame upon which the Moravians molded their actions. It was not a brake on that action. Something further also emerges from these ongoing attentions to moral economic behavior: when the Moravians evaluated their choices, they did not concern themselves with a grand clash between Christianity and capitalism. Indeed, they would probably have been surprised to hear that historians thought they were in the midst of such a fight. The tragic failure of religion at the heart of the declension model had little meaning in their lives, and at no point did the Moravians express such dire fears. There is an explanation for this silence: religious failure for the Moravians was defined in individual, spiritual terms. It was the failure of a person to maintain the sense of Jesus in his heart. In the 1740s and 1750s, it might manifest itself as a failure completely to support the mission effort; in the 1790s, the same sin might manifest itself by too frequent absences from worship. In neither case were such personal choices tied to the structure of the international economy. The idea that religious decline had its roots in the rise of capitalism, as opposed to the ubiquitous sin of greed, was not a meaningful one for the Moravians.

But the Moravians' economic choices were meaningful to them nonetheless, and the history of those choices describes a persistent and inevitable tension within the religious conversations and economic lives of early Americans that continued throughout the development of the market economy. The search by modern scholars for tragic moments of declension only obscures what Bethlehem's Moravians knew by virtue of their own very expensive religious work, itself a manifestation of their deep faith: each new economic situation, be it the arrival of a new buyer in a long established shop, the incorporation of a missionary project, or a new international market, required the same sort of careful moral calculus. The Moravians' economic choices were often minute and passing, inherently part of a specific transaction, but the larger world that framed those economic choices included some of history's most powerful forces: Christian thought about "right" or "moral" behavior, international economic structures, and the violent conflicts between empires and peoples that characterized the early modern era.

Recognizing the myriad ways that the Moravians navigated their economic lives suggests three conclusions. First, it challenges two competing notions: the idea that the religious and the economic are two separate worlds, forever engaged in a deadly standoff, ready to annihilate one another at the faintest sign of weakness, as well as the direct opposite, that evangelical Protestantism speeded the rise of a secular economy. The imagined conflict fails to explain the many and complicated ways that religious people have acted, and continue to act, in the economy. And yet the religious and the economic were not in harmony either, at least not in the powerful Christian tradition that shaped early America. Christian thought taught its adherents to be wary of sin at every turn, and thus it penetrated economic activity precisely at that intimate level where the individual made his or her most basic and mundane decisions. This tension need not have a historical trajectory of decline or triumph, however. Its varied manifestations, evident sometimes in practice, sometimes in sermons, sometimes in labor relations, sometimes in law, were part of an ongoing story.

Second, and closely related, daily economic calculations constituted a key aspect of this history. They represent the contested terrain where religious and economic priorities competed for space. Examining the small adjustments and minor choices made by Bethlehem's leaders, missionaries, and residents reveals that the Moravians neither embraced nor rejected market innovation, but rather employed their practical configuration of goals and values to guide them through the practical economic choices available to them. The artisans, missionaries, and leaders who lived in Bethlehem saw their town as one place in a long chain of Moravian settlements and missions around the Atlantic. Because they had access to the capital and know-how necessary to engage the economy at several levels, and because the expenses of missionary work demanded a constant flow of cash, the Brüdergemeine prized economic innovation and valued profit. Yet the Moravians were ever mindful of the need to keep their shared religious goals, and their sense of right and wrong, present in their decisions. When an artisan earned a profit to be put toward "the affairs of the Savior," or when Henry Van Vleck filled a ship with cargo to sail for London, what mattered most was the sense—enforced by the community—that the transaction had been carried out in a Godly manner.

Last, and most significant for the study of early American history, the Moravians' experience points to the fundamental problem created by examining the question of religion and economic life in isolation from the rest of life, be it politics, immigration, race, gender, war, or (literally) the price of tea in China. When mundane transactions are the terrain under examination, the scholars' lens is focused in very tightly. Yet such an approach also places the story on a much wider stage, for those transactions were part of an economy and political system that circled the Atlantic, encompassing four continents and many peoples. Bethlehem declined, but the insidious rise of acquisitiveness within the hearts of its residents was not to blame. For the Moravians, the pivot point came from another quarter entirely. The community's ties to a church hierarchy in Germany connected it to events and developments in far distant quarters. The Unity's circum-Atlantic presence created opportunities for it, such as the Commercial Society, that drew on the Caribbean and South American plantation economies. Likewise, the multiple pressures of the Seven Years' War, financial and, closer to Bethlehem, racial, sharply curtailed the Moravians' religious choices. The result was ineluctable: a renegotiation of the role of religion in Bethlehem's economy. The individualized economic ethic that characterized Bethlehem's religious life in the last quarter of the eighteenth century was fully Moravian, but it was fundamentally different from what came before.

Connecting Bethlehem's economic ethos to the larger narratives of the Atlantic world suggests the need to reframe studies of the interplay between religion and economic life, by recognizing that the dynamics between the spiritual and the material are both historically contingent and part of a wider story. The historiography spawned by Max Weber and Perry Miller has tested its theories in a variety of times and places in early America. In much of this literature, economic forces—particularly international commerce—are seen as invaders, external to an otherwise closed systems. Yet early American systems—communities—were never closed, and thus the various accommodations between religious and economic motivations made by early Americans were part of much larger histories, not the stuff of isolated Protestant failure.

A brief survey suggests the ways that religious and economic situations were dependent on larger narratives. The oft-termed irreligious and essentially acquisitive Virginians included many devout Puritans, who participated in the same currents of transatlantic Puritanism as their New English counterparts. Yet their choices about economic matters, while fully "Puritan," unfolded in a very different context from those of their fellows in either London or Boston. Paul Boyer and Stephen Nissenbaum's close analysis of religious breakdown caused by commercial growth and social stress in 1692 Salem is neatly modified by the acknowledgment of Salem's proximity to a violent frontier war. The New England Puritans' surrender to the forces of the market in the late seventeenth and early eighteenth centuries unfolded against a backdrop of dramatic imperial and political shifts brought about by the Glorious Revolution and the imperial reforms that came with the reign of William and Mary. Those evangelicals who provided a route for individuals to accommodate impersonal markets even as they revitalized their faith also developed new ways to communicate concern over economic relationships. Indeed, in the nineteenth century a wave of communal experiments rejected some aspects of the "market" even as they also accommodated others. Just as those with a Christian heritage evaluated their economic exchanges through a particular religious lens, so too the trade with Native Americans that sustained many European settlements was viewed, by the Indian participants, as more meaningful than could be summed up on a balance sheet. It should be no surprise that examples of these moments proliferate in the eighteenth century, particularly in the diverse eighteenth-century Mid-Atlantic, because of increased immigration, communication, and trade between the Old World and the New complicated the economic choices available to individuals, and because the rise of evangelical religion, which raised the general level of religious conversation in the Atlantic world. The Moravians rode the crest of this wave. They made use of the international economy to support their missionary work, and they became a part of local economies everywhere they went.

Only the Moravians possessed their particular configuration of skills, connections, and interests. They occupied a particular moment in time: the rise of an expansive evangelical revivalism within Protestantism; the growth of an Atlantic community of religiously minded individuals who sought to spread and create a sense of spiritual rebirth; the presence of an Atlantic economy capable of supporting the nearly constant crossings of migrants, missionaries, ministers, publications, and letters; and, last but not least, the Pennsylvania religious environment that, nearly uniquely in the Atlantic world at that time, endorsed the free practice of religion. Yet, although their specific combinations of enterprise and religious oversight were unique, the ever present negotiation between religious priorities and economic realities revealed in their history is not. Quite the contrary, it represents a sliver of the mighty effort by early America's religiously minded peoples to reconcile visions of right economic action with the material realities of a changing world.

ABBREVIATIONS

Archival Sources

MAB—Moravian Archives, Bethlehem. *All primary sources, unless otherwise noted, are held at the Moravian Archives in Bethlehem, Pennsylvania. The following abbreviations refer to specific collections there.*

  ACM—Aufseher Collegium Minutes, BethCong 131 & 132
  BD—Bethlehem Diary, Manuscript
  CAMM—Cammerhof Letters to Zinzendorf, 1747–1748
  CCM—Commercial Council Minutes
  CM—Conferenz Protocoll der Committee in Bethlehem, BethCong 130
  DCM—Diacony Conference Minutes, BethCong 238
  ECM—Elders Conference Minutes, BethCong, organized by date.
  JotC—Journal of the Commission of the Brethren in Bethlehem, BethCong 239
  MCT—Minutes of the committee overseeing the transition of the Economy, not paginated or dated, contained in "Trans." below.
  PHC—Provincial Helfers' Conference Records
  RMM—Records of the Moravian Mission, Box/Folder
  SBD—Single Brothers' Diary, Manuscript, BethSB 1–2
  SCM—Store Conference Minutes, BethCong 243
  SPBG—Spangenberg Papers, 4 Boxes.
  Trans.—Transition Period (From Economy to Committee System) 1761–1772

APS—American Philosophical Society, Philadelphia
HSP—Historical Society of Pennsylvania, Philadelphia

NYHS—New York Historical Society, New York
UAH—Unity Archives, Herrnhut, Germany

Published and Printed Sources

AHR—American Historical Review
CH—Church History
GdP—Martin Brecht, et al., eds. *Geschichte des Pietismus*, 4 vols. (Göttingen: Vandenhoeck & Ruprecht, 1993–2004).
JAH—Journal of American History
Levering—Joseph Mortimer Levering, *A History of Bethlehem, Pennsylvania, 1741–1892, with Some Account of Its Founders and Their Early Activity in America* (Bethlehem, Pa.: Times Publishing Company, 1903).
PMHB—Pennsylvania Magazine of History and Biography
PT—"Pennsylvanische Testament," in *Büdingische Sammlung: Einiger In die Kirchen-Historie Einschlagender Sonderlich neuerer Schrifften* (Büdingen: Johann Christian Stöhr, 1742–1745), vol. 2, 189–252.
S&G—Georg Neisser, *A History of the Beginnings of Moravian Work in America*, ed. William N. Schwarze, and Samuel H. Gapp (Bethlehem, Pa.: Archives of the Moravian Church, 1955).
SBDT—typescript translation of Single Brethrens Diary, by Historic Bethlehem Partnership, Reeves Library, Moravian College, Bethlehem, Pennsylvania. Original manuscript held at Moravian Archives, Bethlehem.
TMHS—Transactions of the Moravian Historical Society
UF—*Unitas Fratrum*
WMQ—William and Mary Quarterly 3rd series

NOTES

INTRODUCTION

1. RMM 117/2, 9/29/1757; *New York Gazette*, 10/2/1751.

2. Studies of Moravian economics have been divided into American and European historiographies, with the European side emphasizing their entrepreneurial character and American work depicting an (in my opinion inaccurate) anti-market communalism. Studies that emphasize the European side include Gisela Mettele, "Kommerz und Fromme Demut: Wirtschaftsethik und Wirtschaftspraxis im 'Gefühlspietismus'," *Vierteljahrschift für Sozial- und Wirtschaftsgeschichte* 92 (2005): 301–21; Peter Vogt, "Des Heilands Ökonomie: Wirtschaftsethik bei Zinzendorf," *UF* 49–50 (2002): 157–72; Otto Uttendörfer's two books *Alt-Herrnhut: Wirtschaftsgeschichte und Religionssoziologie Herrnhuts während seiner ersten zwanzig Jahre, 1722–1742* (Herrnhut: Missionsbuchhandlung, 1925) and *Wirtschaftsgeist und Wirtschaftsorganisation Herrnhuts und der Brüdergemeine von 1743 bis zum Ende des Jahrhunderts* (Herrnhut: Missionsbuchhandlung, 1926). See also Gutram Phillipp, "Wirtschaftsethik und Wirtschaftspraxis in der Geschichte der Herrnhuter Brüderemeine," in Mari P. Buijtenen, Cornelis Dekker, and Huib Leeuwenberg, eds., *Unitas Fratrum: Herrnhuter Studien/Moravian Studies* (Utrecht: Rijksarchief, 1975); Ilse Tönnies, "Die Arbeitswelt von Pietismus: Erweckungsbewegung und Brüdergemeine; Ideen und Institutionen: Zur religiös-sozialen Vorgeschichte des Industriealisierungszeitalters in Berlin und Mitteldeutschland," *Jahrbuch für die Geschichte Mittel und Ostdeutschland* 20 (1971): 89–133, 21 (1972): 140–83. W. R. Ward, "Zinzendorf and Money," in Ward, *Faith and Faction* (London: Epworth Press, 1993), 130–52; Hans Wagner, *Abraham Dürninger & Co. 1747–1939: Ein Buch von Herrnhutichem Kaufmanns- und Unternehmentun* (Herrnhut, 1940); Gillian Lindt Gollin, *Moravians in Two Worlds: A Study of Changing Communities* (New York: Columbia University Press, 1967), deals with both Europe and America. For the larger context of Pietist economic thought of which the Moravians were a part, see Peter Kriedte, "Wirtschaft," GdP, 584–616; and A. G. Roeber, *Palatines, Liberty, and Property: German Lutherans in Colonial British America*, 2nd ed. (Baltimore: Johns Hopkins University Press, 1998).

Bethlehem's religious and economic history has been the subject of four monographs.

Beverly Smaby, *The Transformation of Moravian Bethlehem: From Communal Mission to Family Economy* (Philadelphia: University of Pennsylvania Press, 1988) argued that the demise of the communal system led to secularization in the town, and Gillian Lindt Gollin, *Moravians in Two Worlds*, compared Bethlehem to the central European Moravian town of Herrnhut. See also Jacob John Sessler, *Communal Pietism Among Early American Moravians* (New York: Henry Holt, 1933); and Hellmuth Erbe, *Bethlehem, Pa.: Eine kommunistische Herrnhuter kolonie der 18 jahrhundert* (Stuttgart: Ausland und Heimat Verlags, 1929). For an anti-market version of the history of Salem, North Carolina, see Michael Shirley, *From Congregation Town to Industrial City: Culture and Social Change in a Southern Community* (New York: New York University Press, 1994). The image of Bethlehem as unusual to a degree that removed it from comparison has appeared in several prominent places. See James T. Lemon, *The Best Poor Man's Country: Early Southeastern Pennsylvania* (Baltimore: Johns Hopkins University Press, 1972, 2002), esp. 19, 105, 109; and James A. Henretta, "Families and Farms: Mentalité in Pre-Industrial America," *WMQ* 35 (1978): 5. The tendency of Moravian historians to look at Moravian communities in near isolation has exacerbated this phenomenon.

3. The literature on the Atlantic world has grown dramatically in the past decade. An important theoretical appraisal of the concept of the Atlantic world can be found in David Armitage "Three Concepts of Atlantic History," in Armitage and Michael J. Braddick, *The British Atlantic World, 1500–1800* (New York: Palgrave, 2002), 11–27. In Armitage's terms, Bethlehem's story would be "cis-Atlantic" history, which "studies particular places as unique locations within an Atlantic world and seeks to define that uniqueness as the result of interaction between local particularity and a wider web of connections (and comparisons)" (Quotation, 21). See also Bernard Bailyn, *Atlantic History: Concept and Contours* (Cambridge, Mass.: Harvard University Press, 2005). Too few studies of the Atlantic world economy consider religion. For exceptions, see April Lee Hatfield, *Atlantic Virginia: Intercolonial Relations in the Seventeenth Century* (Philadelphia: University of Pennsylvania Press, 2004), 110–36; Karen Ordahl Kupperman, *Providence Island, 1630–1641: The Other Puritan Colony, 1630–1640* (Cambridge: Cambridge University Press, 1993); Virginia De-John Anderson, "Migrants and Motives: Religion and the Settlement of New England," *New England Quarterly* 58 (1985): 339–83; and Boyd Stanley Schlenther, "Religious Faith and Commercial Empire," in P. J. Marshall, ed., *The Eighteenth Century*, vol. 2 of *The Oxford History of the British Empire* (Oxford: Oxford University Press, 1998), 128–50.

4. The literatures on the rise of evangelicalism and the Great Awakening are substantial. Good places to begin are W. R. Ward, *The Protestant Evangelical Awakening* (Cambridge: Cambridge University Press, 1992); Frank Lambert, *Inventing the "Great Awakening"* (Princeton, N.J.: Princeton University Press, 1999), Mark A. Noll, *The Rise of Evangelicalism: The Age of Edwards, Whitefield, and the Wesleys* (Downers Grove, Ill.: Inter-Varsity, 2003); Thomas Kidd, *The Great Awakening: The Roots of Evangelical Christianity in Colonial America* (New Haven, Conn.: Yale University Press, 2007); and Kidd, *The Protestant Interest: New England After Puritanism* (New Haven, Conn.: Yale University

Press, 2004). In addition to those listed above, works stressing the international nature of the movement are Susan O'Brien, "A Transatlantic Community of Saints: The Great Awakening and the First Evangelical Network, 1735–1755," *AHR* 91 (1986): 811–32; Leigh Eric Schmidt, *Holy Fairs: Scotland and the Making of American Revivalism*, 2nd ed. (Grand Rapids, Mich.: Eerdmans, 2001); Michael J. Crawford, *Seasons of Grace: Colonial New England's Revival Tradition in its British Context* (New York: Oxford University Press, 1991). Jon Butler, "Enthusiasm Described and Decried: The Great Awakening as Interpretive Fiction," *JAH* 69 (1982): 305–25, provides an important historiographical counterpoint.

5. The contest for the eighteenth-century Mid-Atlantic, and the importance of Indian history to understanding the development of European-American society, has been demonstrated by Jane T. Merritt, *At the Crossroads: Indians & Empires on a Mid-Atlantic Frontier, 1700–1763* (Chapel Hill: University of North Carolina Press, 2003); William A. Pencak and Daniel K. Richter, eds., *Friends & Enemies in Penn's Woods: Indians, Colonists, and the Racial Construction of Pennsylvania* (University Park: Pennsylvania State University Press, 2004); Peter Rhoads Silver, "Indian-Hating and the Rise of Whiteness in Provincial Pennsylvania" (Ph.D. dissertation, Yale University, 2001); Alan Taylor, *The Divided Ground: Indians, Settlers, and the Northern Borderland of the American Revolution* (New York: Knopf, 2006); Daniel K. Richter, *Facing East from Indian Country: A Native History of Early America* (Cambridge, Mass.: Harvard University Press, 2001), James H. Merrell, *Into the American Woods: Negotiators on the Pennsylvania Frontier* (New York: W.W. Norton, 1999); See also James Axtell, "Colonial America Without the Indians: Counterfactual Reflections," *JAH* 73 (1987): 981–96; and Alan Taylor, *American Colonies* (New York: Viking, 2001).

6. Prominent studies dealing substantially with the religion of German-Americans during the early American period include Roeber, *Palatines, Liberty, and Property*; Renate Wilson, *Pious Traders in Medicine: A German Pharmaceutical Network in Eighteenth-Century North America* (University Park: Pennsylvania State University Press, 2000); Hartmut Lehmann, Hermann Wellenreuther, and Renate Wilson, eds., *In Search of Peace and Prosperity: New German Settlements in Eighteenth-Century Europe and America* (University Park: Pennsylvania State University Press, 2000); John B. Frantz, "The Awakening of Religion Among the German Settlers in the Middle Colonies," *WMQ* 33 (1976): 266–88; Stephen Longenecker, *Piety and Tolerance: Pennsylvania German Religion, 1700–1850* (Metuchen, N.J.: Scarecrow Press, 1994); Steven M. Nolt, *Foreigners in Their Own Land: Pennsylvania Germans in the Early Republic* (University Park: Pennsylvania State University Press, 2002); Renate Wilson, "Halle and Ebenezer: Pietism, Agriculture, and Commerce in Colonial Georgia" (Ph.D. dissertation, University of Maryland, 1988).

7. Aaron Spencer Fogleman has argued that the Moravians were radical in their religious challenges. Certainly they were controversial. *Jesus Is Female: Moravians and the Challenge of Radical Religion in Early America* (Philadelphia: University of Pennsylvania Press, 2007), 2–9.

8. The Moravians' engagement in the market economy was overlooked by two of the leading figures of the study of how religion influenced economic development, Max Weber

and Ernst Troeltsch. Their misreadings have been quite influential, however. Weber, working from a theological typology, suggested that the Moravians were too pietistic and not sufficiently rational in their economic practice to embrace the rational asceticism that the proper spirit of capitalism required, though he acknowledged their practical business engagements for the sake of missions. He also noted that the theology of the "dilettante" Zinzendorf "is scarcely capable of clear formulation in the points of importance for [the study of religion and economics]." While it is certainly true that the group embraced an intensely emotional brand of religion, the idea that they resisted or impeded economic development is impossible to sustain. Ernst Troeltsch, another dominant figure of twentieth-century German sociology and Weber's colleague, came to the conclusion that the "Moravians felt a closer affinity with Calvinism than with Lutheranism," and that their economic lives exhibited "an excellent and increasingly successful business life, characterized by integrity and frugality." While Troeltsch's depiction was more accurate, he also consigned the Moravians (though he acknowledged some difficulty in doing so) to his category of "sect" (a position with which Weber agreed), suggesting that they were divided from mainstream religious and cultural values, or at the very least could be excluded from larger analyses. That interpretation undervalues the importance of the Moravians' and particularly Zinzendorf's deep ecumenism and expansive evangelicalism. Moreover, the effort at categorization which characterizes both of these projects minimizes the complexity of the lived past. Many scholars have followed Troeltsch's lead and discussed the Moravians' economic lives in isolation from the mainstream. Max Weber, *The Protestant Ethic and the Spirit of Capitalism*, trans. Talcott Parsons (1930; London: Routledge, 1992), 96, 134–36; Ernst Troeltsch, *The Social Teaching of the Christian Churches*, trans. Olive Wyon (1931; Chicago: University of Chicago Press, 1981), 719–21, 788–90.

9. Mark Valeri, "Religion, Discipline, and the Economy in Calvin's Geneva," *Sixteenth Century Journal* 28 (1997): 123–42; Mark Valeri, "Religious Discipline and the Market: Puritans and the Issue of Usury," *WMQ* 54 (1997): 747–68; Jesper Rosenmeier, "John Cotton on Usury," *WMQ* 47 (1990): 548–65; Paul S. Seaver, *Wallington's World: A Puritan Artisan in Seventeenth-Century London* (Stanford, Calif.: Stanford University Press, 1985); Roeber, *Palatines, Liberty, and Property*, 71–74; Margaret C. Jacob and Matthew W. Kadane, "Missing, Now Found in the Eighteenth Century: Weber's Protestant Capitalist," *AHR* 108 (2003): 20–49.

10. Edward Winslow, *Good news from New-England* (London, 1624), 64; Cotton Mather, *Magnalia Christi Americana*, ed. Kenneth B. Murdock (Cambridge, Mass.: Belknap Press of Harvard University Press, 1977), 143–44. Wesley is cited by Max Weber, *The Protestant Ethic*, 175. Mark Valeri, "The Economic Thought of Jonathan Edwards," *CH* 60 (1991): 37–54.

11. Perry Miller's *New England Mind: From Colony to Province* (Cambridge, Mass.: Belknap Press of Harvard University Press, 1953) is the starting point for the idea of declension in early America. The concept, though still influential, has had many detractors. For a recent historiographical appraisal of declension in the context of religious history, see

Charles L. Cohen, "The Post-Puritan Paradigm of Early American Religious History," *WMQ* 54 (1997): 695–722. See also Katherine Carté Engel, "Bridging the Gap: Religious Community and Declension in Eighteenth-Century Bethlehem, Pennsylvania," *1650–1850: Ideas, Aesthetics and Inquiries in the Early Modern Era* 11 (2005): 407–42.

12. Michael Zuckerman finds fault with the chronological fluidity with which the declension model has been applied when he comments that studies suggesting "a passage from a self-subordinating to a self-seeking orientation place that passage in every generation from the founding of the colonies to the middle of the twentieth century." See "The Fabrication of Identity in Early America," *WMQ* 34 (1977): 183–214. Weber's thesis was originally published in essay form in 1904–5. See also James A. Henretta, "The Protestant Ethic and the Reality of Capitalism in Colonial America," in Hartmut Lehmann and Guenther Roth, eds., *Weber's Protestant Ethic: Origins, Evidence, Contexts* (Cambridge: Cambridge University Press, 1993), 327–47. Key works in the body of scholarship positing a conflict between religion and economic life include Miller, *The New England Mind*; Bernard Bailyn, *New England Merchants in the Seventeenth Century* (Cambridge, Mass.: Harvard University Press, 1955); Richard L. Bushman, *From Puritan to Yankee: Character and the Social Order in Connecticut, 1690–1765* (Cambridge, Mass.: Harvard University Press, 1967); Frederick B. Tolles, *Meeting House and Counting House: The Quaker Merchants of Colonial Philadelphia, 1682–1763* (Chapel Hill: University of North Carolina Press, 1948); Paul Johnson, *A Shopkeeper's Millennium: Society and Revivals in Rochester, New York, 1815–1837* (New York: Hill and Wang, 1978); Charles Sellers, *The Market Revolution; Jacksonian America, 1815–1846* (New York: Oxford University Press, 1991). Although much recent work has emphasized the compatibility of particularly Puritanism and economic growth, the conflictual model is still present. See Mark Y. Hanley, *Beyond a Christian Commonwealth: The Protestant Quarrel with the American Republic, 1830–1860* (Chapel Hill: University of North Carolina Press, 1994); Louise A. Breen, *Transgressing the Bounds: Subversive Enterprises Among the Puritan Elite in Massachusetts, 1630–1692* (New York: Oxford University Press, 2001); Kenneth Moore Startup, *The Root of All Evil: The Protestant Clergy and the Economic Mind of the Old South* (Athens: University of Georgia Press, 1997).

Debates over the corrosion of a cohesive communal society, which often neglected the direct discussion of religion, played a major role in the scholarship on early America in the second half of the twentieth century. In the 1960s, this included the gesellschaft-gemeinschaft discussion, and in the 1980s and 1990s, the "transition debate." For an assessment of (and perhaps even the last word in) the transition debate, see Naomi R. Lamoreaux, "Rethinking the Transition to Capitalism in the Early American Northeast," *JAH* 90 (2003): 437–61. T. H. Breen and Timothy Hall argued for the parallel impact of revivalism and commercial change on a previously cohesive New England society in: "Structuring Provincial Imagination: The Rhetoric and Experience of Social Change in Eighteenth-Century New England," *AHR* 103 (1998): 1411–39. The concepts of gemeinschaft and gesellschaft, in the context of early American history, are most closely associated with Thomas Bender, *Community and Social Change in America* (New Brunswick, N.J.:

Rutgers University Press, 1978). See also Joyce O. Appleby, "Value and Society," in Jack P. Greene and J. R. Pole, eds., *Colonial British America: Essays in the New History of the Early Modern Era* (Baltimore: Johns Hopkins University Press, 1984), 290–316.

13. Certainly, many scholars of early America have disputed persuasively the idea of a fundamental conflict between religion—particularly evangelical Protestantism—and market economies. Stephen Innes and Mark Peterson working on the seventeenth century, Christine Heyrman on the eighteenth, and a host of scholars examining the nineteenth, have argued for a powerful congruence of values between the religions that dominated North America and the economy that developed there. In making their case for Protestant-capitalists, however, those who have sought to learn how religious actors engaged the economy have often substituted one metanarrative for another. Instead of religious sentiments preventing economic engagement, they served instead to enhance economic development. The two groups of scholars tend to talk past one another, however. Thus, while this literature has done a great deal to elaborate Protestants' varied responses to the economy, it remains, as Mark A. Noll recently pointed out, primarily focused on the question of religion's "role in either retarding or accelerating the turn to markets." Mark A. Noll, ed., *God and Mammon: Protestants, Money, and the Market, 1790–1860* (New York: Oxford University Press, 2002), 16. Noll's introduction to this volume provides an excellent historiographical background to the topic. For further historiographic treatments, see Robert Wuthnow and Tracy L. Scott, "Protestants and Economic Behavior," in Harry S. Stout and D. G. Hart, eds., *New Directions in American Religious History* (New York: Oxford University Press, 1997); and Michael Zuckerman, "Holy Wars, Civil Wars: Religion and Economics in Nineteenth-Century America," *Prospects* 16 (1991): 205–40. Works that argue for religion's role in the creation of a modern economy include Stephen Innes, *Creating the Commonwealth: The Economic Culture of Puritan New England* (New York: W.W. Norton, 1995); Mark A. Peterson, *The Price of Redemption: The Spiritual Economy of Puritan New England* (Stanford, Calif.: Stanford University Press, 1997); John Frederick Martin, *Profits in the Wilderness: Entrepreneurship and the Founding of New England Towns in the Seventeenth Century* (Chapel Hill: University of North Carolina Press), 1991; Christine Heyrman, *Commerce and Culture: The Maritime Communities of Colonial Massachusetts, 1690–1750* (New York: W.W. Norton, 1984); and Barry Levy, *Quakers and the American Family: British Settlement in the Delaware Valley* (New York: Oxford University Press, 1988). For the nineteenth century, see the collected essays in Noll, ed., *God and Mammon*, as well as William R. Sutton, *Journeymen for Jesus: Evangelical Artisans Confront Capitalism in Jacksonian Baltimore* (University Park: Pennsylvania State University Press, 1998); Boyd Hilton, *The Age of Atonement: The Influence of Evangelicalism on Social and Economic Thought, 1795–1865* (Oxford: Clarendon Press, 1988); Stewart Davenport, "Moral Man, Immoral Economy: Protestant Reflections on Market Capitalism, 1820–1860" (Ph.D. dissertation, Yale University, 2001). Ultimately, both arguments—that religion encouraged the growth of capitalism and that it stood as a hindrance—coexist, and the question of the role religion played in creating the American economy remains unresolved.

14. The vast majority of the Moravians' sources were kept in German, the shared language of an ethnically diverse community. Unless otherwise noted, all translations that appear within these pages are mine. In a few places, a German word has been included in brackets adjacent to the translation, where the original might prove informative to readers familiar with German. On occasion, the Moravians wrote letters or community minutes in English, or corresponded with others in that language. When these are reproduced, they have been reprinted exactly, with the exception of expanding standard abbreviations for the ease of the reader.

15. Frank Lambert, *"Pedlar in Divinity": George Whitefield and the Transatlantic Revivals, 1737–1770* (Princeton, N.J.: Princeton University Press, 1994); Renate Wilson, *Pious Traders in Medicine*; Renate Wilson, "Halle and Ebenezer"; Susan Garfinkle, "Quakers and High Chests: The Plainness Problem Reconsidered," in Emma Jones Lapsansky and Anne A. Verplanck, eds., *Quaker Aesthetics, Reflections on a Quaker Ethic in American Design and Consumption* (Philadelphia: University of Pennsylvania Press, 2003), 550–89; Boyd Stanley Schlenther, "Religious Faith and Commercial Empire"; Cynthia J. Van Zandt, "The Dutch Connection: Isaac Allerton and the Dynamics of English Cultural Anxiety in the *Gouden Eeuw*," in Rosemarijn Hoefte, and Johanna Kardux, eds., *Connecting Cultures: The Netherlands in Five Centuries of Transatlantic Exchange* (Amsterdam: VU University Press, 1994), 515–76; Michael McGiffert, "Religion and Profit Jump Together," *Early American Literature* 40 (2005): 145–61. See James H. Merrell, "Indian History During the English Colonial Era," in Daniel Vickers, ed., *A Companion to Colonial America* (Oxford: Blackwell, 2003), 118–37, for the historiographical debate about reciprocity and native economics. Kathryn Burns, *Colonial Habits: Convents and the Spiritual Economy of Cuzco, Peru* (Durham, N.C.: Duke University Press, 1999). See also Michael Everton, "'The Would-Be-Author and the Real Bookseller': Thomas Paine and Eighteenth-Century Printing Ethics," *Early American Literature* 40 (2005): 79–110.

16. CCM, opening document, MAB.

CHAPTER I. THE PILGRIMS' MISSION

1. "Grundsteinlegung u. Einweyhung des ersten Ledigen Brüder-Hauses in Bethlehem ao. 1744," Single Brothers' Diary, BethSB 1, p 5.

2. W. R. Ward, *The Protestant Evangelical Awakening* (Cambridge: Cambridge University Press, 1992), 15–63; W. R. Ward, *Early Evangelicalism: A Global Intellectual History, 1670–1789* (Cambridge: Cambridge University Press, 2006), 6–39. Scholars of Pietism debate the definitions and origins of the movement. See Jonathan Strom, "The Problems and Promises of Pietism Research," *CH* 71 (2002): 536–54; Ward, *Early Evangelicalism*, 1–5.

3. The best biography of Zinzendorf in English is John R. Weinlick, *Count Zinzendorf: The Story of His Life and Leadership in the Renewed Moravian Church* (New York: Abingdon Press, 1956). See also Dietrich Meyer, "Zinzendorf und Herrnhut," GdP, vol. 2,

1–106, esp. 30–34. For Pietist beliefs about the *Bußkampf*, see Markus Matthias, "Bekehrung und Wiedergeburt," GdP, vol. 4, 49–79. For women's roles in German Pietism, see Lucinda Martin, "Women's Religious Speech and Activism in German Pietism" (Ph.D. dissertation, University of Texas, 2002); and Renate Wilson, *Pious Traders in Medicine: A German Pharmaceutical Network in Eighteenth-Century North America* (University Park: Pennsylvania State University Press, 2000), 31–41.

4. Weinlick, *Count Zinzendorf*, 45–47; Colin Podmore, *The Moravian Church in England, 1728–1760* (Oxford: Clarendon Press, 1998), 160–67; Ward, *Protestant Evangelical Awakening*, 116–28.

5. Ward, *Protestant Evangelical Awakening*, 57–83; Mark A. Noll, *The Rise of Evangelicalism: The Age of Edwards, Whitefield, and the Wesleys* (Downers Grove, Ill.: InterVarsity Press, 2003), 62–64; Craig D. Atwood, *Community of the Cross: Moravian Piety in Colonial Bethlehem* (University Park: Pennsylvania State University Press, 2004), 21–42. The question of how closely the "Renewed" Unitas Fratrum can be linked to the ancient Unitas Fratrum is a complex one that continues to have meaning for modern Moravians. Most scholars, however, place the movement within the German Pietist movement. See Atwood, *Community of the Cross*, 21–25, and W. R. Ward, "The Renewed Unity of the Brethren: Ancient Church, New Sect, or Interconfessional Movement?" in Ward, *Faith and Faction* (London: Epworth Press, 1993), 112–29.

6. Dietrich Meyer, *Zinzendorf und die Herrnhuter Brüdergemeine, 1700–2000* (Göttingen: Vandenhoeck and Ruprecht, 2000), 19–24.

7. Meyer, *Zinzendorf und die Herrnhuter*, 24–29. For discussion of the official name of the Brüdergemeine, see Peter Vogt, "Brüdergemeine—das theologische Programm eines Namens," *UF* 48 (2001): 81–105.

8. Atwood, *Community of the Cross*, 43–114, 233–37; Ward, *Early Evangelicalism*, 99–118.

9. Ward, *Protestant Evangelical Awakening*, 130–53; John Wesley, *The Works of John Wesley*, ed. W. Regniald Ward, vol. 18, *Journal and Diaries 1* (Nashville, Tenn.: Abingdon Press, 1988), 260. For a working definition of evangelicalism, see D. W. Bebbington, *Evangelicalism in Modern Britain: A History from the 1730s to the 1980s* (London: Unwin Hyman, 1989), 1–19.

10. Ward, *Protestant Evangelical Awakening*, 1–10, 103–7. See also Thomas S. Kidd, *The Protestant Interest: New England After Puritanism* (New Haven, Conn.: Yale University Press, 2004).

11. *Works of John Wesley*, vol. 18, 136–42, quotations 142–43. For the Moravians in Georgia see Aaron Spencer Fogleman, "The Decline and Fall of the Moravian Community in Colonial Georgia: Revising the Traditional View," *UF* 48 (2001): 1–22; and Adelaide L. Fries, *The Moravians in Georgia, 1735–1740* (1905; Baltimore: Genealogical Publishing Company, 1967). For the development of the Halle-Salzburger community in Georgia, see Renate Wilson, "Halle and Ebenezer: Pietism, Agriculture, and Commerce in Colonial Georgia" (Ph.D. dissertation, University of Maryland, 1988).

12. Podmore, *Moravian Church in England*, 29–96; Frank Lambert, *Inventing the "Great Awakening"* (Princeton, N.J.: Princeton University Press, 1989), 87–124; Susan O'Brien, "A Transatlantic Community of Saints: The Great Awakening and the First Evangelical Network, 1735–1755," *AHR* 91 (1986): 811–32; Wilson, *Pious Traders in Medicine*, 25–31.

13. Hermann Wellenreuther, "Pietismus und Mission: Vom 17. bis zum Beginn des 20. Jahrhunderts," GdP, vol., 4, 166–93; Ernst Benz, "Pietist and Puritan Sources of Early Protestant World Missions," *CH* 20 (1951): 28–55. Richard W. Pointer, "'Poor Indians' and the 'Poor in Spirit': The Indian Impact on David Brainerd," *New England Quarterly* 67 (1994): 403–26.

14. Rachel M. Wheeler, *To Live upon Hope: Mohicans and Missionaries in the Eighteenth-Century Northeast* (Ithaca, N.Y.: Cornell University Press, 2008), ch. 5; David Schattschneider, "'Souls for the Lamb': A Theology for the Christian Mission According to Count Nicolaus Ludwig von Zinzendorf and Augustus Gottlieb Spangenberg" (Ph.D. dissertation, University of Chicago, 1975), 63–108; R. Pierce Beaver, "American Missionary Motivation Before the Revolution," *CH* 31(1962): 216–26.

15. Weinlick, *Count Zinzendorf*, 93–101; J. Taylor Hamilton and Kenneth G. Hamilton, *History of the Moravian Church: The Renewed Unitas Fratrum, 1722–1957* (Bethlehem, Pa.: Moravian Church of America, 1967), 34–59; Hans-Christoph Hahn and Hellmut Reichel, *Zinzendorf und die Herrnhuter Brüder: Quellen zur Geschichte der Brüder-Unität von 1722 bis 1760* (Hamburg: Wittig, 1977), 350–58. Early Moravian missionary work in the Caribbean is described by Jon Sensbach, *Rebecca's Revival: Creating Black Christianity in the Atlantic World* (Cambridge, Mass.: Harvard University Press, 2005).

16. Computer file AUSZ1313, Gotha Synod, 1740, R.2.A.3.A1, p. 171–2, UAH. Bebbington, *Evangelicalism in Modern Britain*, 10–12.

17. Aaron Spencer Fogleman, *Hopeful Journeys: German Immigration, Settlement, and Political Culture, 1717–1775* (Philadelphia: University of Pennsylvania Press, 1996), and *Jesus Is Female: Moravians and the Challenge of Radical Religion in Early America* (Philadelphia: University of Pennsylvania Press, 2007), 25–33; Atwood, *Community of the Cross*, 35–40; Sally Schwartz, *"A Mixed Multitude": The Struggle for Toleration in Colonial Pennsylvania* (New York: New York University Press, 1987), 81–119.

18. S&G, 68–69. For Moravian work in Georgia, see Aaron Spencer Fogleman, "Shadow Boxing in Georgia: The Beginnings of the Moravian-Lutheran Conflict in British North America," *Georgia Historical Quarterly* 83 (1999): 629–59; and Adelaide L. Fries, *The Moravians in Georgia, 1735–1740* (Raleigh, N.C.: Edwards & Broughton, 1905).

19. Quoted in Joh. Plitt, *Denkwürdigkeiten aus der Geschichte der Brüderunität*, 1828–1841, Volume II, § 205, Manuscript, MAB.

20. Computer file AUSZ1210, Ebersdorf Conferenz, 1739, R.2.A.2, p. 59–60, UAH.

21. The founding of Bethlehem is discussed in Levering, 31–58. See also Vernon Nelson, "Peter Boehler's Reminiscences of the Beginnings of Nazareth and Bethlehem," *TMHS* 27 (1992): 1–25; and "Kurze Historische Nachricht Vom ersten Anfange des

Gemein-Orts Bethlehem und ersten Einrichtung der Brüder-Gemeine daselbst," BD, 1787, Beylage zum Monat Junius 1787.

22. Amy C. Schutt, *Peoples of the River Valleys: The Odyssey of the Delaware Indians* (Philadelphia: University of Pennsylvania Press, 2007), 86–87, 89–90, 98. Levering, 50–51, 155.

23. S&G, 32. For the context and fallout of the Walking Purchase, see Steven Craig Harper, *Promised Land: Penn's Holy Experiment, the Walking Purchase, and the Dispossession of Delawares, 1600–1763* (Bethlehem, Pa.: Lehigh University Press, 2006).

24. The Moravians used the word "Gemeine" to mean both community and congregation. It is ubiquitous jargon in the Moravian records, and it can mean, at various times, any single congregation or the whole Unity. S&G, 34. "Kurze Historische Nachricht."

25. Although Bethlehem has been compared more deeply to Herrnhut (Gillian Gollin, *Moravians in Two Worlds: A Study of Changing Communities* [New York: Columbia University Press, 1967]), because of Bethlehem's connection to missionary work, Heerendyk is a more apt comparison. See Paul Martin Peucker, "Heerendyk: Gründung und Auflösung einer Herrnhuter Kolonie in den Niederlanden," *UF* 26 (1989): 7–36.

26. Computer file AUSZ1210, Ebersdorf Conferenz, 1739, R.2.A.2, p. 65, UAH. Although plans for Pennsylvania were already underway at this time, the 1739 conference did not use the word "Pilgergemeine" to refer to work in that colony specifically. The first instance of the connection I have found was made by Zinzendorf in 1742, discussed below. Already in 1740, however, there is evidence that Zinzendorf intended the term to refer to a category of people that reached beyond his own household. At the Gotha Synod he referred to two *Pilgergemeinen*, "a large one in Marienborn, and the small one of Conrad Lange and his brethren and sisters." Computer file AUSZ1313, Gotha Synod, 1740, R.2.A.3.A1, p. 197, UAH.

27. Computer file AUSZ1314, Gotha Synod, 1740, R.2.A.3.A1, p. 197, UAH; PT, 235–236.

28. Kenneth G. Hamilton, ed., *The Bethlehem Diary*, vol. 1, *1742–1744* (Bethlehem, Pa.: Moravian Archives, 1971), 17–20, 112. Beverly Smaby gives a schematic depiction of the *Pilgergemeine* and its place in the Moravian typology of communities in *The Transformation of Moravian Bethlehem: From Communal Mission to Family Economy* (Philadelphia: University of Pennsylvania Press, 1988), 25.

29. PT 230.

30. "General-Plane mit welchen ich an 1744. von Europa nach America abgereiset," SPBG II. *The Dansbury Diaries: Moravian Travel Diaries, 1748–1755*, trans. William N. Schwarze and Ralf Ridgway Hillman (Camden, Maine: Picton Press, 1994), 31, 96. James H. Merrell also noted this phenomenon, though he cites it as an example of the ongoing cultural divisions that separated missionaries and the Indians they wished to convert. James H. Merrell, "Shamokin, 'the very seat of the Prince of darkness': Unsettling the Early American Frontier," in Andrew R. L. Cayton and Fredrika J. Teute, eds., *Contact Points: American Frontiers from the Mohawk Valley to the Mississippi, 1750–1830* (Chapel Hill: University of North Carolina Press, 1998), 46–47.

31. For descriptions of early Bethlehem and the communal economy, see also Atwood, *Community of the Cross*, 115–39; Smaby, *The Transformation of Moravian Bethlehem*, 9–32; and Gollin, *Moravians in Two Worlds*, passim; Hellmuth Erbe, *Bethlehem, Pa.: Eine kommunistische Herrnhuter Kolonie des 18. Jahrhunderts* (Stuttgart: Ausland und Heimats Verlag, 1929), 25–83; and John Jacob Sessler, *Communal Pietism Among Early American Moravians* (New York: Henry Holt, 1933), 72–92. Although these tellings differ little from each other in essentials, each frames Moravian communalism in terms of a unique larger research question. None places missionary work at the center of analysis of Bethlehem's internal organization, though most acknowledge its importance.

32. Peter Vogt, "Zinzendorf und die Pennsylvanischen Synoden 1742," *UF* 36 (1994): 5–62. Fogleman, "Jesus Is Female: The Moravian Challenge in the German Communities of British North America," *WMQ* 60 (2003): 295–332; Weinlick, *Count Zinzendorf*, 151–78.

33. The word "Oeconomy" was used in wider Moravian circles to refer to any particular economic unit. In Bethlehem, it was also used to refer specifically to farms. The predominant meaning, however, and the only one used in the present work, is as the name of Bethlehem's communal household, between 1741 and 1762. "Economy," *Oxford English Dictionary*, 2nd ed., 1989. Donald D. Eddy, "Dodsley's *Oeconomy of Human Life*, 1750–1751," *Modern Philology* 85 (1988): 60–79. For another discussion of the word *Oeconomy*, see Jeanne Boydston, *Home and Work: Housework, Wages, and the Ideology of Labor in the Early Republic* (New York: Oxford University Press, 1990), 18–20.

34. Gillian Lindt Gollin provides a sociological comparison of Herrnhut and Bethlehem in *Moravians in Two Worlds*. John R. Weinlick, *Count Zinzendorf*, 65–82; Hamilton and Hamilton, *History of the Moravian Church*, 23–33; Otto Uttendörfer, *Alt-Herrnhut: Wirtschaftsgeschichte und Religionssoziologie Herrnhuts während seiner ersten zwanzig Jahre, 1722–1742* (Herrnhut: Verlag Missionsbuchhandlung, 1925), 9.

35. Uttendörfer, *Alt-Herrnhut*, 9–13; Weinlick, *Count Zinzendorf*, 60–62; Gollin, *Moravians in Two Worlds*, 148–51; Directorial College to Spangenberg et al., 3/31/1761, PHC Misc. Corr., mostly from Europe, 1760–1847, Box 2, Folder 10.

36. Hahn und Reichel, *Zinzendorf und die Herrnhuter Brüder*, 71–72, quotations, 71, 72. Herrnhut's early economic organization is discussed in Uttendörfer, *Alt-Herrnhut*, passim; Gollin, *Moravians in Two Worlds*, 131–38; Gutram Phillipp, "Wirtschaftsethik und Wirtschaftspraxis in der Geschichte der Herrnhuter Brüdergemeine," in Mari P. Buijtenen, Cornelis Dekker, and Huib Leeuwenberg, eds., *Unitas Fratrum: Herrnhuter Studien/Moravian Studies* (Utrecht: Rijksarchief, 1975), 402–8.

37. Elisabeth W. Sommer, *Serving Two Masters: Moravian Brethren in Germany and North Carolina, 1727–1801* (Lexington: University Press of Kentucky, 2000), 7–32; Gollin, *Moravians in Two Worlds*, 25–30; Uttendörfer, *Alt-Herrnhut*, 14–24. The Brotherly Agreement and Manorial Injunctions appear in Hahn and Reichel, *Zinzendorf und die Herrnhuter Brüder*, 68–80.

38. Hellmuth Erbe, *Bethlehem, Pa.*, 188. "General-Catalogus," 1753, BethCong 360. For discussion of Moravian immigration to America from Europe, see Aaron Fogleman,

Hopeful Journeys, 100–126; and John W. Jordan, "Moravian Immigration to Pennsylvania, 1734–1765," *TMHS* 5 (1899): 49–90.

39. Smaby, *Transformation of Moravian Bethlehem*, 86–105; Levering, 195–96. See also William John Murtagh, *Moravian Architecture and Town Planning: Bethlehem Pennsylvania and Other Eighteenth-Century American Settlements* (1967; Philadelphia: University of Pennsylvania Press, 1998). For a comparative perspective on other Pennsylvania towns, see James T. Lemon, "Urbanization and the Development of Eighteenth-Century Southeastern Pennsylvania and Adjacent Delaware," *WMQ* 24 (1967): 501–42.

40. "General-Catalogus," 1753, BethCong 360.

41. "Spangenbergs Gedanken," SP A. II, SPBG 1.

42. "Spangenbergs Gedanken," SP A. II, SPBG 1.

43. "Spangenbergs Gedanken," SP A. II, SPBG 1.

44. "Spangenbergs Gedanken," SP A. II, SPBG 1.

45. Helfer Conferenz Minutes, May 6, 1746, BethCong 84. I am grateful to Vernon Nelson, retired archivist of the Moravian Archives, for bringing this quotation to my attention.

CHAPTER 2. INTERCONNECTED WORLDS

1. For the development of the Choir system, see Craig D. Atwood, *Community of the Cross: Moravian Piety in Colonial Bethlehem* (University Park: Pennsylvania State University Press, 2004), 173–78; Gillian Lindt Gollin, *Moravians in Two Worlds: A Study of Changing Communities* (New York: Columbia University Press, 1967), 67–89; Beverly Prior Smaby, *The Transformation of Moravian Bethlehem: From Communal Mission to Family Economy* (Philadelphia: University of Pennsylvania Press, 1988), 10–11. For the segregation of the sexes in Bethlehem, see Smaby, *Transformation*, 100–105; Atwood, *Community of the Cross*, 186–88.

2. Gollin, *Moravians in Two Worlds*, 38–40, and Hellmuth Erbe, *Bethlehem, Pa.: Eine kommunistische Herrnhuter Kolonie des 18.Jahrhunderts* (Stuttgart: Ausland und Heimats Verlag, 1929), 30–31, describe static committee government for Bethlehem. Although such committee structures may have existed in theory, in practice a small group of individuals, led by Spangenberg and the various Choir leaders, dominated a changing set of conferences and committees. Conference minutes, held in the Archive at Bethlehem, provide the best means of determining which committee met at which point. Extant minutes for the Elders' Conference begin in 1753. The "Committee for Outward Affairs" began its sessions in 1752 and lasted until 1760. Curiously, this committee maintained its minutes in English, probably so that the legal issues with which they dealt would be transparent to outsiders. The Helpers' Conference met as early as 1744, although extant minutes for this group are sparser. The Diacony Conference met regularly from 1757 forward, reorganizing itself several times during the eighteenth century but maintaining a consistent jurisdiction. The

records of this group form a substantial part of the research for this study. Many other small councils, including the Council of Attenders of the Sick, the Building Conference, the Handworkers' Conference, the Store Conference, and various others, met briefly to deal with specific issues, but there is no evidence that they consistently played a role in governing the town. All the minutes discussed here are held in the Moravian Archives at Bethlehem, most in the BethCong collection.

3. For discussion of the process by which the Moravians came to see Jesus as their chief elder, see J. Taylor Hamilton and Kenneth G. Hamilton, *History of the Moravian Church: The Renewed Unitas Fratrum, 1722–1957* (Bethlehem, Pa.: Moravian Church in America, 1967), 71–75.

4. Elisabeth W. Sommer, *Serving Two Masters: Moravian Brethren in Germany and North Carolina, 1727–1801* (Lexington: University Press of Kentucky, 2000), has done the most comprehensive study of authority in the Moravian church and of the lot in particular. Although her work focuses on the Wachovia tract in North Carolina, the same principles applied to authority and governance in Bethlehem. See also her "Gambling with God: The Use of the Lot by the Moravian Brethren in the Eighteenth Century," *Journal of the History of Ideas* 59 (1998): 267–86.

5. DCM, 1/4/1760; 3/20/1760.

6. Lebenslauf of Benigna Zahm, translated and reprinted in Katherine M. Faull, *Moravian Women's Memoirs: Their Related Lives, 1750–1820* (Syracuse, N.Y.: Syracuse University Press, 1997), 19–26. For an extended discussion of Moravian ritual, see Atwood, *Community of the Cross*, 141–70.

7. Faull, *Moravian Women's Memoirs*, 21. Smaby, *Transformation*, 17–18. Atwood, *Community of the Cross*, 158–70; Arthur J. Freeman, *An Ecumenical Theology of the Heart: The Theology of Count Nicholas Ludwig von Zinzendorf* (Bethlehem, Pa.: Moravian Church in America, 1998).

8. Smaby, *Transformation*, 159–65; Faull, *Moravian Women's Memoirs*, 29–30.

9. For "sterbensleben," see the lebenslauf of Michael the Indian, BD 7/24/1758. The spiritual significance of death in Bethlehem is discussed in Atwood, *Community of the Cross*, 194–99.

10. Johann Böhner, Lebenslauf, NazMem 3.

11. Hamilton and Hamilton, *History of the Moravian Church*, 38–39; Smaby, *Transformation*, 14–15.

12. "Theure und Zartlich" 3/20/1742, SP A III, SPBG 1 (Hosea 14:7). Biblical translations are from the King James Version unless noted otherwise.

13. R.14.A.41 a, UAH., Jeremiah 14:13.

14. Smaby, *Transformation*, 14–17.

15. Atwood, *Community of the Cross*, 161–64; Hamilton and Hamilton, *History of the Moravian Church*, 36; Gollin, *Moravians in Two Worlds*, 20.

16. Kenneth G. Hamilton, *The Bethlehem Diary*, vol. 1, *1742–1744* (Bethlehem, Pa.: Moravian Archives, 1971), 207–8. Susan O'Brien credits the Moravian *Gemeintage* for in-

fluencing the mechanism by which evangelical revival spread throughout the Atlantic world in the mid-eighteenth century. Susan O'Brien, "A Transatlantic Community of Saints," *AHR* 91(1986): 811–32.

17. CAMM XI, 15.

18. This view mirrors the Puritan perspective, which emphasized Christian love. See Charles L. Cohen, "The Saints Zealous in Love and Labor: The Puritan Psychology of Work," *Harvard Theological Review* 76 (1983): 455–80.

19. Hellmut Reichel, "Zinzendorfs Auffassung von Arbeit und Dienst," in *Zinzendorf-Gedenkjahr, 1960* (Hamburg: Ludwig Appel Verlag, 1960), 41–58. Quotations from Zinzendorf cited 43, 46–47, 43–44. See also Peter Vogt, "Des Heilands Ökonomie: Wirtschaftsethik bei Zinzendorf," *UF* 49–50 (2002): 157–72; and Gutram Phillipp, "Wirtschaftsethik und Wirtschaftspraxis in der Geschichte der Herrnhuter Brüdergemeine," in Mari P. Buijtenen, Cornelis Dekker, and Huib Leeuwenberg, eds., *Unitas Fratrum: Herrnhuter Studien/Moravian Studies* (Utrecht: Rijksarchief, 1975). Hellmuth Erbe discussed Moravian attitudes toward work in Bethlehem during the Oeconomy in Erbe, *Bethlehem, Pa.*, 84–96.

20. Quoted in Hellmut Reichel, "Zinzendorfs Auffassung von Arbeit und Dienst," 45.

21. Spangenberg to Zinzendorf, quoted in Erbe, *Bethlehem, Pa.*, 89.

22. CAMM XI, 42; also quoted in Erbe, *Bethlehem, Pa.*, 90.

23. S&G, 173; Augustus Schultze, "The Old Moravian Cemetery of Bethlehem, Pa., 1742–1897," *TMHS* 5 (189): 112; "Journal of a Visit to the Moravian Settlements in the Forks of the Delaware," *Jerseyman* 1 (1895): 8–9.

24. Edmund de Schweinitz, "Clergy of the American Province of the Unitas Fratrum," Unpublished manuscript, 65, MAB; Schultze, "The Old Moravian Cemetery of Bethlehem, Pa., 1742–1897," 125; "General Table" 1752, BethCong 424. The Moravian Archives in Bethlehem holds many catalogs for the Oeconomy period that list postings of individuals at particular times.

25. For the methodology behind these figures, see Katherine Carté Engel, "Of Heaven and Earth: Religion and Economic Activity Among Bethlehem's Moravians, 1741–1800" (Ph.D. dissertation, University of Wisconsin, 2003), appendix.

26. Single Sisters Instructions, 1785, BethSS 19.

27. For Margarethe Jungman, see Faull, *Moravian Women's Memoirs*, 48–57. For discussion of Moravian "Streiter-Ehe," see Smaby, *Transformation of Moravian Bethlehem*, 159–65.

28. The Moravians employed outside wage labor on a limited basis, but did not make it a core part of their economy. "Specification," found in CAMM III.

29. CAMM XI, 12, 23, 32, 45.

30. Thomas Pownall and Lois Mulkearn, eds., *A Topographical Description of the Dominions of the United States of America, being a Revised and Enlarged Edition* (Pittsburgh: University of Pittsburgh Press, 1949), 107.

31. CAMM XI, 67–68.

32. "Spangenbergs Gedanken," SP A. II, SPBG 1.

33. "Einige Observation," Trans.

34. "Einige Observation," Trans.; Letter to the Directorial Collegium, 1/13/1759, Beilage, BethCong 425.

35. Bethlehem Account Extracts, 1752, 1753–55. For 1753–55, see also http://bdhp. moravian.edu/community_records/business/ledgers/17531755/17531755h.html, accessed May 29, 2007, originals held at MAB.

36. "Specification Aller unsrer Gebäude und Landereyen am 31. May 1758," http://bdhp.moravian.edu/community_records/business/specs/bldgspecscover.html, accessed May 29, 2007, original held at MAB.

37. "Specification Aller unsrer Gebäude und Landereyen am 31. May 1758," Farm Extracts.

38. CAMM XI, 38.

39. Stephen Innes, *Creating the Commonwealth: The Economic Culture of Puritan New England* (New York: W.W. Norton, 1995), quotations 7, 214. Mark Peterson posits that wealth was essential to Puritan religion in *The Price of Redemption: The Spiritual Economy of Puritan New England* (Stanford, Calif.: Stanford University Press, 1997). Scholars since Perry Miller have debated the Puritan attitude toward the economy. In addition to the works listed above, see Mark Valeri, "Religious Discipline and the Market: Puritans and the Issue of Usury," *WMQ* 54 (1997): 747–68, which argues against a simple endorsement of market capitalism by early Puritan leaders, but also discusses the transitional nature of ideas regarding economic development during the early seventeenth century.

40. Although both Innes and Levy base their arguments on property in form of land, rather than the movable assets maintained by Moravians within the Oeconomy, the essential argument about private property holds true. Frederick B. Tolles, *Meeting House and Counting House* (Chapel Hill: University of North Carolina Press, 1948), quotations from 57, 65; Barry Levy, *Quakers and the American Family: British Settlement in the Delaware Valley* (New York: Oxford University Press, 1988), esp. 123–52; Gary B. Nash, *Quakers and Politics: Pennsylvania, 1681–1726*, 2nd ed. (1968; Boston: Northeastern University Press, 1993), 11–18. Teachings on wealth differed from teachings on property. While the Quakers did not challenge private property, wealth came under fire from the community in the second half of the eighteenth century. See Jack D. Marietta, *The Reformation of American Quakerism, 1748–1783* (Philadelphia: University of Pennsylvania Press, 1984, 2007), esp. 98–105. A. G. Roeber, *Palatines, Liberty, and Property: German Lutherans in Colonial British America*, 2nd ed. (Baltimore: Johns Hopkins University Press, 1998), 65–80. Renate Wilson addresses the social works of the Halle Pietists in "Halle and Ebenezer: Pietism, Agriculture, and Commerce in Colonial America" (Ph.D. dissertation, University of Maryland, 1988).

41. Edwards quoted in Gordon Wood, *The Radicalism of the American Revolution* (New York: Vintage, 1993), 19. Tolles, *Meeting House and Counting House*, 109–43, Barclay quotation, 110–11. See also Philip Greven, *The Protestant Temperament: Patterns of Child-*

Rearing, Religious Experience, and the Self in Early America (Chicago: University of Chicago Press, 1988), 194–98. Richard L. Bushman, *From Puritan to Yankee: Character and the Social Order in Connecticut, 1690–1765* (Cambridge, Mass.: Harvard University Press, 1967), 3–21. For Luther, see Thomas A. Brady, Jr., "Luther's Social Teaching and the Social Order of his Age," *Michigan Germanic Studies* 10 (1984): 270–90.

42. There are also important counterexamples of Moravian leaders with very humble backgrounds, including Anna Nitschmann, who was a descendant of an important Moravian family but not wealthy, and Johannes Ettwein, an important figure in Bethlehem during the 1770s and 1780s. Sommer, *Serving Two Masters*, 21–22, 82–83; Gollin, *Moravians in Two Worlds*, 32–36; Otto Uttendörfer, *Alt-Herrnhut* (Herrnhut: Missionsbuchhandlung, 1925), 40–43. There is no evidence of socially based clothing distinctions in Bethlehem, although Moravians there did wear a uniform costume during the Oeconomy period. For discussion of Moravian clothing, see Elisabeth Sommer, "Fashion Passion: The Battle over Dress Within the Moravian Brethren," paper presented at Wake Forest University, German Moravians in the Atlantic World Conference, 2002, manuscript in author's possession.

43. Timothy Horsfield, Lebenslauf, Box 3 MS.

44. CAMM IX, 93–94; Timothy Horsfield Lebenslauf, Box 3 MS; Diacony Ledgers B & C, MAB. For more on the problems in Connecticut, see Rachel Wheeler, "Living upon Hope: Mahicans and Missionaries, 1730–1760" (Ph.D. dissertation, Yale University, 1999), 256–271; and Aaron Spencer Fogleman, *Jesus Is Female: Moravians and the Challenge of Radical Religion in Early America* (Philadelphia: University of Pennsylvania Press, 2007), 159–60.

45. Diacony Ledgers C & D, Horsfield Account; "Specification Aller unsrer Gebäude und Landereyen am 21 May, 1758." Levering, 237. Harry Emilius Stocker, *A History of the Moravian Church in New York City* (New York: n.p., 1922), 81.

46. In a 1761 tax assessment, Horsfield ranked tenth of 82 individuals in Bethlehem township, an area which extended significantly beyond Bethlehem itself and included much land not owned by the Moravians. Horsfield was assessed £14, while the wealthiest individual in the township was charged £40. The median assessment was £6. The Oeconomy, including Bethlehem, Nazareth, Christiansbrunn, and Gnadenthal, were assessed £1500, indicating the relative size of the Oeconomy's assets in the county. Northampton County Records, vols. 58–67, Miscellaneous Manuscripts, HSP. See also "Proprietary, Supply, and State Tax Lists of the Counties of Northampton and Northumberland, for the Years 1772 to 1787," *Pennsylvania Archives* 3rd ser. 19 (Harrisburg, Pa.: William Stanley Ray, 1897), 24.

47. Although Josua was a member of the Moravian community, racial identity continued to matter to him, at least according to those who wrote his lebenslauf: "He was much attached to his nation, and often wished for the occasion to be able to show them something of the mercy and the holy peace that he had found in the Savior's wounds. Therefore, he also loved Brother Andreas the Mohr dearly, and lived with him in a beautiful harmony." Andreas had been Thomas Noble's slave. He came to Bethlehem in 1746

when his master died and left him to Bishop Spangenberg. Josua, Lebenslauf, Box 2 MS. For Moravian beliefs and practices regarding slavery, see Jon F. Sensbach, *A Separate Canaan: The Making of an Afro-Moravian World in North Carolina, 1763–1840* (Chapel Hill: University of North Carolina Press, 1998). Although Moravian sources make no mention of the matter, Timothy Horsfield and his brother Israel each owned a slave who was deported as part of the New York slave conspiracy of 1741. See Jill Lepore, *New York Burning: Liberty, Slavery, and Conspiracy in Eighteenth-Century Manhattan* (New York: Vintage, 2006), 266–67.

48. Diacony Ledgers B, C, & D, manuscript index, at MAB. Levering, 146, 208. Eloise Bassett Miller, *James Burnside: Moravian Missionary and Pennsylvania Assemblyman* (Bethlehem, Pa.: Historic Bethlehem Partnership, 1998, 1999), 53–56. Another individual who deserves mention here is Henry Antes, a prominent member of Bethlehem's circle during its early days and the first of the community's representatives in Pennsylvania. When Zinzendorf took leave of his followers and returned to Europe in 1743, he suggested that they rely on Antes when it was necessary to conduct official business in Pennsylvania, essentially naming him to the same position that Horsfield, Burnside, and the others would eventually occupy. Antes moved away from Bethlehem in 1750, however, and played a smaller role until his death in 1755. PT 228; S&G 121–26.

49. Aaron Spencer Fogleman, *Hopeful Journeys: German Immigration, Settlement, and Political Culture in Colonial America, 1717–1775* (Philadelphia: University of Pennsylvania Press, 1996), 127, 210 n2.

50. Because it happened more often that a poor person joined the community than a rich person, those seeking admission to the Oeconomy were asked a series of questions to ensure that the person knew what he was doing, and the community would not be exposed to any financial or legal risk. Thus, only "safe" individuals were permitted to enter the community. These questions included: "Is it with the Knowledge of your Parents, Relations or Guardians that you are come and think to continue here with us in the Congregation?" "What Profession or Trade have you? Or what manual Labour can you do?" "Do you know that we here live together in Common, and that no One receives any Wages for his Work, but are like Children in one House, contented with necessary Food & Rayment?" "Is there any Person in the World that has a lawful Demand upon you?" "Are you indebted to Anyone?" After the interview, the individual signed a brief statement attesting to the fact that he or she was coming to Bethlehem of their own free will, knowing what that entailed. Questionnaire and statements, Box: Economy Papers: 1743–1761, Declarations of Brn. entering the "Economy"; also JotC, passim.

51. Diacony Ledger C, folio 193.

52. JotC, 8/23/1753, 5/27/1754.

53. CAMM XI, 65; William Cornelius Reichel, *The Crown Inn, near Bethlehem, Penna.* (Philadelphia: E.P. Wilbur, 1872).

54. George Vaux, ed., "Extracts from the Diary of Hannah Callender," *PMHB* 12 (1888): 449. Charles P. Keith, *The Provincial Councilors of Pennsylvania, 1733–1776* (1887;

Baltimore: Genealogical Publishing Company, 1997), 188–90; Diacony Ledgers, C-F, Benezet accounts; Levering, 63–75, 140.

55. Elizabeth Horsfield Lebenslauf, http://bdhp.moravian.edu/personal_papers/memoirs/horsfield/horsfield.html, accessed May 8, 2007; Hamilton, *Bethlehem Diary*, vol. 1, 35. Benezet Letters, SPBG IV. Levering, 75. Marriage records at http://bdhp.moravian.edu/community_records/register/marriages/marriages1742.html, accessed May 29, 2007.

56. George Vaux, ed., "Extracts from the Diary of Hannah Callender;" CAMM XI, 10, 25, 53; Andreas Schoute, Lebenslauf, BD 11/7/1763; MCT. RMM 115/6, 8/8/1756. See also Daniel B. Thorp, *The Moravian Community in Colonial North Carolina: Pluralism on the Southern Frontier* (Knoxville: University of Tennessee Press, 1989), 178–98.

57. PT, 225–226; JotC, 3/4/1752.

58. JotC, 12/5/1752, 5/27/1754, 7/3/1755, 12/5/1755, 11/21/1754, 12/10/1754.

59. JotC 2/17/1755, 2/28/1755, 6/19/1754, 2/10/1757.

60. JotC 6/19/1754, 6/24/1754, 5/12/1755, 5/16/1755.

CHAPTER 3. MORAVIAN EXPANSION IN THE MID-ATLANTIC

1. The literature on the Great Awakening in North America is enormous. A good starting point is Frank Lambert, *Inventing the "Great Awakening"* (Princeton, N.J.: Princeton University Press, 1999); and Thomas S. Kidd, *The Great Awakening: The Roots of Evangelical Christianity in Colonial America* (New Haven, Conn.: Yale University Press, 2007). For the role of itinerants, see Timothy D. Hall, *Contested Boundaries: Itinerancy and the Reshaping of the Colonial American Religious World* (Durham, N.C.: Duke University Press, 1994). For George Whitefield, see Frank Lambert, *"Pedlar in Divinity": George Whitefield and the Transatlantic Revivals, 1737–1770* (Princeton, N.J.: Princeton University Press, 1994); and Harry S. Stout, *The Divine Dramatist: George Whitefield and the Rise of Modern Evangelicalism* (Grand Rapids, Mich.: Eerdmans, 1991).

2. Gilbert Tennent's sermon "The Danger of an Unconverted Ministry" is reprinted in Alan Heimert and Perry Miller, eds., *The Great Awakening: Documents Illustrating the Crisis and its Consequences* (Indianapolis: Bobbs-Merrill, 1967), 71–99. See also Milton J. Coalter, Jr., *Gilbert Tennent, Son of Thunder: A Case Study of Continental Pietism's Impact on the First Great Awakening in the Middle Colonies* (New York: Greenwood Press, 1986), 64–67 and passim; Marilyn J. Westerkamp, *Triumph of the Laity: Scots-Irish Piety and the Great Awakening, 1625–1760* (New York: Oxford University Press, 1988), 165–94; Patricia U. Bonomi, *Under the Cope of Heaven: Religion, Society, and Politics in Colonial America* (New York: Oxford University Press, 1986), 133–49.

3. Nicolaus Ludwig Zinzendorf, *A Collection of Sermons from Zinzendorf's Pennsylvania Journey, 1741–42*, ed. Craig D. Atwood, trans. Julie Tomberlin Weber (Bethlehem, Pa.: Moravian Church of America, n.d.), 55.

4. Zinzendorf, *A Collection of Sermons*, 21–22.

5. Aaron Spencer Fogleman argues that the Moravians' challenge to the "gender order," as well as their ecumenical challenge, led to the religious conflicts of which they were a part in *Jesus Is Female: Moravians and the Challenge of Radical Religion in Early America* (Philadelphia: University of Pennsylvania Press, 2007), 156–215. Looking at both the German and English-speaking communities, Peter Silver also places the Moravians at the core of the conflicts, which he accounts for in ethnoreligious terms. Peter Rhodes Silver, "Indian-Hating and the Rise of Whiteness in Provincial Pennsylvania" (Ph.D. dissertation, Yale University, 2001), 66–133.

6. Studies that emphasize the Great Awakening in the Middle Colonies using an ethnoreligious lens include Sally Schwartz, *"A Mixed Multitude": The Struggle for Toleration in Colonial Pennsylvania* (New York: New York University Press, 1987), 120–58; John B. Frantz, "The Awakening of Religion Among the German Settlers in the Middle Colonies," *WMQ*, 33 (1976): 266–88; John Fea, "Ethnicity and Congregational Life in the Eighteenth-Century Delaware Valley: The Swedish Lutherans of New Jersey," *Explorations in Early American Culture* 5 (2001): 45–78; Stephen L Longenecker, *Piety and Tolerance: Pennsylvania German Religion, 1700–1850* (Metuchen, N.J.: Scarecrow Press, 1994). For works on Presbyterians and revivalism, see Leigh Eric Schmidt, *Holy Fairs: Scotland and the Making of American Revivalism*, 2nd ed. (Grand Rapids, Mich.: Eerdmans, 2001); Westerkamp, *Triumph of the Laity*. A. G. Roeber, *Palatines, Liberty, and Property: German Lutherans in Colonial British America*, 2nd ed. (Baltimore: Johns Hopkins University Press, 1998), argues for the significance of German Lutheran and particularly Pietist influence on the development of German culture in early America, 63–65 and passim. For the ministerial dearth among European immigrants to the region, see Fogleman, *Jesus Is Female*, 19–33.

7. PT 189–252, quotations, 200, 208. See also Fogleman, *Jesus Is Female*, 104–13.

8. Fogleman, *Jesus Is Female*, statistics 117; traveling preachers 113–30.

9. August Gottlieb Spangenberg, *Das Leben des Herrn Nicolaus Ludwig Grafen und Herrn von Zinzendorf und Pottendorf*, Barby, 1773–75, reprinted in Erich Beyreuther and Gerhard Meyer, eds., *Nikolaus Ludwig von Zinzendorf, Materialien und Dokumente*, vol. 2 (Hildesheim: Olms Verlag, 1971), 1389.

10. John R. Weinlick, *Count Zinzendorf: The Story of His Life and Leadership in the Renewed Moravian Church* (New York: Abingdon Press, 1956), 114–27.

11. Spangenberg, *Das Leben*, 1393.

12. Fogleman, *Jesus Is Female*, 192–95; J. Taylor Hamilton and Kenneth G. Hamilton, *History of the Moravian Church: The Renewed Unitas Fratrum, 1722–1957* (Bethlehem, Pa.: Moravian Church of America, 1967), 90–91.

13. Henry Melchior Muhlenberg, *The Journals of Henry Melchior Muhlenberg in Three Volumes*, trans. Theodore G. Tappert and John W. Doberstein (Philadelphia: Muhlenberg Press, 1942), 1: 75.

14. Fogleman, *Jesus Is Female*, 185–216. Fogleman emphasizes the often violent schisms that divided the congregations in question. Equally important, however, was the persistence of a Moravian community after the initial controversies died down. For a listing of

Moravian congregations with their (sanitized) short histories, see "A Register of the Moravian Church and of Persons Attached to said Church, in this country and abroad, between 1727 and 1754," *Transactions* 1 (1868–1876), 289–426. Muhlenberg's journals are explicit on his feelings about the Moravians. Cf. esp. Muhlenberg, *Journals*, 1: 104–5, 108–9.

15. Antes later became a prominent Moravian and citizen of Bethlehem, before eventually leaving the community over religious differences. A particularly laudatory biography of him is Edwin McMinn, *A German Hero of the Colonial Times of Pennsylvania: or, The Life and Times of Henry Antes* (Moorestown, N.J.: W.J. Lovell, 1886). Antes used the connections he had formed as a member of the short-lived ecumenical group, the Associated Brethren of Skippack, an important predecessor to the Moravian efforts. Longenecker, *Piety and Tolerance*, 71–77. See also Schwartz, *A Mixed Multitude*, 135.

16. Peter Vogt, "Zinzendorf und die Pennsylvanischen Synoden 1742," *UF* 36 (1994): 5–62, esp. 29–29. Vogt has done the most in-depth treatment of the synods, and my interpretation draws heavily on his. See also Fogleman, *Jesus Is Female*, 108–9. For more about Gruber, see Donald Durnbaugh, "Johann Adam Gruber: Pennsylvania-German Prophet and Poet," *Pennsylvania Magazine of History and Biography* 83 (1959): 382–408.

17. Vogt, "Zinzendorf und die Pennsylvanischen Synoden 1742," 49–57. Zinzendorf discusses Gruber's plan in the Pennsylvania Testament. PT 201–202. The anti-Zinzendorfian material was published in Europe by Fresenius in the *Bewährte Nachrichten von Herrnhutischen Sachen* (Frankfurt am Main: Johann Leonard Buchner and Heinrich Ludwig Broenner, 1746–1751).

18. Moravian controversies in England are detailed in Colin Podmore, *The Moravian Church in England, 1728–1760* (Oxford: Clarendon Press, 1998), esp. 72–80, 80–86, 266–89. For the continental conflicts, see Fogleman, *Jesus Is Female*, 135–55. For Tennent: Coalter, *Gilbert Tennent*, 91–112.

19. *Journals of Henry Melchior Muhlenberg*, 1:63; W. R. Ward, *The Protestant Evangelical Awakening* (Cambridge: Cambridge University Press), 255–64; Elizabeth Lewis Pardoe, "Poor Children and Enlightened Citizens: Lutheran Education in America, 1748–1800," *Pennsylvania History* 68 (2001): 162–201; Roeber, *Palatines, Liberty, and Property*, 243–310. Jon Butler argues for the mid-eighteenth century as a period of increased denominational coherence. Jon Butler, *Awash in a Sea of Faith: Christianizing the American People* (Cambridge, Mass.: Harvard University Press, 1990), 162–93. See also Mark Häberlein, "Reform, Authority, and Conflict in the Churches of the Middle Colonies, 1700–1770," in David K. Adams and Cornelis A. van Minnen, eds., *Religious and Secular Reform in America: Ideas, Beliefs, and Social Change* (New York: New York University Press, 1999), 1–28.

20. Fogleman, *Jesus Is Female*, 206–12; "A Register of Members of the Moravian Church," 383–87.

21. "A Register of Members of the Moravian Church," 388–89.

22. "A Register of Members of the Moravian Church," 395–99; Fogleman, *Jesus Is Female*, 123–24.

23. Harry Emilius Stocker, *A History of the Moravian Church in New York City* (New

York: n.p., 1922), 39–70. For New York City's religious climate, see Randall Balmer, *A Perfect Babel of Confusion: Dutch Religion and English Culture in the Middle Colonies* (New York: Oxford University Press, 1989), 121–27. See also "Papers Relating to Quakers and Moravians," in E. B. O'Callaghan, ed., *The Documentary History of the State of New York*, vol. 3 (Albany, N.Y.: Weed, Parsons, 1850–51), 1012–30.

24. The literature on Moravians in North Carolina is vast and, unfortunately, quite separated from the literature on Pennsylvania. Significant recent monographs include S. Scott Rohrer, *Hope's Promise: Religion and Acculturation in the Southern Backcountry* (Tuscaloosa,: University of Alabama Press, 2005); Elisabeth W. Sommer, *Serving Two Masters: Moravian Brethren in Germany and North Carolina, 1727–1801* (Lexington: University Press of Kentucky, 2000); Jon J. Sensbach, *A Separate Canaan: The Making of an Afro-Moravian World in North Carolina, 1763–1840* (Chapel Hill: University of North Carolina Press, 1998); and Daniel B. Thorp, *The Moravian Community in Colonial North Carolina: Pluralism on the Southern Frontier* (Knoxville: University of Tennessee Press, 1989). Wachovia Bank, which was founded in Winston-Salem in the nineteenth century, is named after the Moravians' Wachovia Tract.

25. William C. Reichel, ed., *Memorials of the Moravian Church* (Philadelphia: J.B. Lippincott, 1870), 23–114; John R. Weinlick, *Count Zinzendorf* (New York: Abingdon Press, 1956), 175–76. Jane T. Merritt, *At the Crossroads: Indians & Empires on a Mid-Atlantic Frontier, 1700–1763* (Chapel Hill: University of North Carolina Press, 2003), 70–76; James H. Merrell, "Shamokin, 'the Very Seat of the Prince of Darkness': Unsettling the Early American Frontier," in Andrew R. L. Cayton, and Fredrika J. Teute, eds., *Contact Points: American Frontiers From the Mohawk Valley to the Mississippi, 1750–1830* (Chapel Hill: University of North Carolina Press, 1998), 16–59.

26. For a brief summary of Moravian missionary work in this period, see Hermann Wellenreuther and Carola Wessel, eds., *The Moravian Mission Diaries of David Zeisberger, 1771–1781*, trans. Julie Tomberlin Weber (University Park: Pennsylvania State University Press, 2005), 41–51. A still useful survey of Moravian mission work during this period is George H. Loskiel, *History of the Mission of the United Brethren Among the Indians of North America*, trans. Christian Ignatius Latrobe (London: The Brethren's Society for the Furtherance of the Gospel, 1794).

27. Amy C. Schutt, *Peoples of the River Valleys: The Odyssey of the Delaware Indians* (Philadelphia: University of Pennsylvania Press, 2007) argues that the Delaware were made up of a flexible series of interwoven communities. See also Rachel M. Wheeler, "To Live Upon Hope: Mahicans and Missionaries, 1730–1760" (Ph.D. dissertation, Yale University, 1999), 18–22.

28. Schutt, *Peoples of the River Valleys*, 62–93.

29. This interpretation relies on the work of Jane T. Merritt, in *At the Crossroads*.

30. Merritt, *At the Crossroads*, 129–66; Rachel M. Wheeler, *To Live upon Hope: Mohicans and Missionaries in the Eighteenth-Century Northeast* (Ithaca, N.Y.: Cornell University Press, 2008), chapter 5; James H. Merrell, *Into the American Woods: Negotiators on the Penn-*

sylvania Frontier (New York: W.W. Norton, 1999), 84–87; Amy C. Schutt, "Female Relationships and Intercultural Bonds in Moravian Indian Missions," in William A. Pencak and Daniel K. Richter, eds., *Friends and Enemies in Penn's Woods: Indians, Colonists, and the Racial Construction of Pennsylvania* (University Park: Pennsylvania State University Press, 2004).

31. Schutt, *Peoples of the River Valleys*, 96–100; Merritt, *At the Crossroads*, 121–28.

32. Rachel Wheeler, "Women and Christian Practice in a Mahican Village," *Religion and American Culture* 13 (2003): 27–67; Merritt, *At the Crossroads*, 95–121.

33. Merritt, *At the Crossroads*, 99–101, 134–39; Amy C. Schutt, "Tribal Identity in the Moravian Missions on the Susquehanna," *Pennsylvania History* 66 (1999): 378–98.

34. For Shamokin, see James H. Merrell, "Shamokin, 'the very seat of the Prince of darkness,'" passim; and Merritt, *At the Crossroads*, 72–74. For a brief portrait of the role of Moravian missionary activities in the Indian communities of the Mid-Atlantic, see Merritt, *At the Crossroads*, 129–66.

35. Loskiel, *A History of the Mission of the United Brethren*, part 2, 111–16, 151–52.

36. For the missions in New York and Connecticut, see Wheeler, *To Live upon Hope*; Corinna Dally-Starna and William A. Starna, "American Indians and Moravians in Southern New England," in Colin G. Calloway, Gerd Gemünden, and Susanne Zantop eds., *Germans and Indians: Fantasies, Encounters, Projections* (Lincoln: University of Nebraska Press, 2002), 83–96. The end of the Shekomeko mission is detailed by Karl Westmeier in *The Evacuation of Shekomeko and the Early Moravian Missions to Native North Americans* (Lewiston, N.Y.: Edwin Mellen Press, 1994).

37. The relationship between Bethlehem and Gnadenhütten will be discussed in greater detail in subsequent chapters. Gnadenhütten's founding is discussed in Loskiel, *A History of the Mission of the United Brethren*, 82–85. For population statistics, as well as connections between Bethlehem and Gnadenhütten, see 1747 Catalog, BethCong 348; "General Catalog," 1753, BethCong 360; "Extract of the Oeconomy Book, 1753–1762," esp. 115–16, Box: "Economy Books 1753–62 [ext.] 1756–62 Daybook"; CAMM XI, 54–55, 58. Levering, 193.

38. American Provincial Synod, January 1749, Bethlehem, Synod Result, English Version (hereafter, 1749 Synod Result), Numbers 1 and 8; Atwood, *Community of the Cross*, 73, 123–25.

39. For the Moravians' "blood and wounds" theology, see Atwood, *Community of the Cross*, 95–112.

40. Number 9 (Silent omission of the insertion and then deletion of the phrase "in the name of our" after "Mind."), Number 12, and Number 37, 1749 Synod Result, MAB.

41. "General Catalog," 1753, BethCong 360; Minutes of the Jüngercollegium, 10/29/50, 11/1/1750, BethCong 88.

42. "General Catalog," 1753, BethCong 360; BD Memorabilia for 1757. Moravian missions in the West Indies are discussed in Jon F. Sensbach, *Rebecca's Revival: Creating Black Christianity in the Atlantic World* (Cambridge, Mass.: Harvard University Press, 2005).

43. Johannes to Mattheus, 6/29/1753, BethCong 340; BD 1/18/1758; MAB. Spangenberg to Johannes, 10/2/1758, R.14.A.20.7.19, UAH.

CHAPTER 4. THE MORAL PARAMETERS OF ECONOMIC ENDEAVOR

1. John W. Jordan, "Moravian Immigration to Pennsylvania, 1734–1765," *TMHS* 5 (1899): 49–90.

2. The quotations in this paragraph and the next come from the *Pennsylvania Gazette*, June 10, 1742. For life in Philadelphia in the eighteenth century, see Aaron Spencer Fogleman, *Hopeful Journeys: German Immigration, Settlement, and Political Culture in Colonial America, 1717–1775* (Philadelphia: University of Pennsylvania Press, 1996); Peter Thompson, *Rum Punch & Revolution: Taverngoing and Public Life in Eighteenth-Century Philadelphia* (Philadelphia: University of Pennsylvania Press, 1999); Marianne Sophia Wokeck, *Trade in Strangers: The Beginnings of Mass Migration to North America* (University Park: Pennsylvania State University Press, 1999); Marcus Rediker, *Between the Devil and the Deep Blue Sea: Merchant Seamen, Pirates, and the Anglo-American Maritime World, 1700–1750* (Cambridge: Cambridge University Press, 1987); Gary B. Nash, *The Urban Crucible: The Northern Seaports and the Origins of the American Revolution* (Cambridge, Mass.: Harvard University Press, 1986).

3. For overviews of eighteenth-century economic development, see Marc Egnal, *New World Economies: The Growth of the Thirteen Colonies and Early Canada* (New York: Oxford University Press, 1998); John J. McCusker and Russell R. Menard, *The Economy of British America, 1607–1789* (Chapel Hill: University of North Carolina Press, 1985, 1991). For Pennsylvania, see Thomas M. Doerflinger, *A Vigorous Spirit of Enterprise: Merchants and Economic Development in Revolutionary Philadelphia* (Chapel Hill: University of North Carolina Press, 1986); for New York, Cathy Matson, *Merchants & Empire: Trading in Colonial New York* (Baltimore: Johns Hopkins University Press, 1998). See also Cary Carson, Ronald Hoffman, and Peter J. Albert, eds., *Of Consuming Interests: The Style of Life in the Eighteenth Century* (Charlottesville: University Press of Virginia, 1994); and Catherine Anna Haulman, "The Empire's New Clothes: The Politics of Fashion in Eighteenth-Century British North America" (Ph.D. dissertation, Cornell University, 2002).

4. For the Benezet-Zinzendorf connection, see John R. Weinlick, *Count Zinzendorf: The Story of His Life and Leadership in the Renewed Moravian Church* (New York: Abingdon Press, 1956), 155, 177. The working relationship between Benjamin Franklin and George Whitefield is explored in Frank Lambert, "Subscribing for Profits and Piety: The Friendship of Benjamin Franklin and George Whitefield," *WMQ* 50 (1993): 529–54.

5. Sally Schwartz, *"A Mixed Multitude": The Struggle for Toleration in Colonial Pennsylvania* (New York: New York University Press, 1987); Gary B. Nash, *Quakers and Politics: Pennsylvania, 1681–1726*, 2nd ed. (1968; Boston: Northeastern University Press, 1993); Fogleman, *Hopeful Journeys*; W. R. Ward, *The Protestant Evangelical Awakening* (Cam-

bridge: Cambridge University Press, 1992); Frank Lambert, *Inventing the "Great Awakening"* (Princeton, N.J.: Princeton University Press, 1999); Frank Lambert, *"Pedlar in Divinity": George Whitefield and the Transatlantic Revivals, 1737–1770* (Princeton, N.J.: Princeton University Press, 1994); Susan O'Brien, "A Transatlantic Community of Saints: The Great Awakening and the First Evangelical Network, 1735–1755," *AHR* 91 (1986): 811–32.

6. Many religious groups have used intragroup trading. See April Lee Hatfield, *Atlantic Virginia: Intercolonial Relations in the Seventeenth Century* (Philadelphia: University of Pennsylvania Press, 2004); Thomas Doerflinger, *A Vigorous Spirit of Enterprise*; Frederick B. Tolles, *Meeting House and Counting House: The Quaker Merchants of Colonial Philadelphia, 1682–1763* (Chapel Hill: University of North Carolina Press, 1948); Bernard Bailyn, *The New England Merchants in the Seventeenth Century* (Cambridge, Mass.: Harvard University Press, 1955); Nuala Zahedieh, "Making Mercantilism Work: London Merchants and Atlantic Trade in the Seventeenth Century," *Transactions of the Royal Historical Society* 9 (1999): 143–58; J. F. Bosher, "Huguenot Merchants and the Protestant International in the Seventeenth Century," *WMQ* 52 (1995): 77–101; and Jonathan Howes Webster, "The Merchants of Bordeaux in Trade to the French West Indies, 1664–1717" (Ph.D. dissertation, University of Minnesota, 1972).

7. Jacobsen to Lawatsch, 6/16/1756; General Diacony Receipts & Business Letters, 1744–1757, Box 1; DCM 6/29/1759. This entry can be found in the Diacony Conference Minutes volume beginning 1759, where it was inserted. Smalling, 10/7/1757, Box: Schriften das Oeconomicum Betreffend; Diacony Journal, 12/15/1749, 3/12/1748/9; Diacony Ledgers B, C & D, Accounts for the Strangers' Store, the Society for the Propagation of the Gospel, and Van Vleck's Account; Society for the Furtherance of the Gospel Catalogues, Early to 1753. *Irene*'s account printed in "A Register of Members of the Moravian Church and of Persons Attached to Said Church, in this Country and Abroad, Between 1727 and 1754," William C. Reichel, *TMHS* 1 (1876): 330.

8. Van Vleck, Lebenslauf, Gemein Nachrichten 1785, Beilage XII.

9. Matson, *Merchants and Empire*, 141. For Van Vleck's business, see, for example, advertisements and notices, *New York Gazette Revived in the Weekly Post Boy*, 9/11/1749, 9/18/1749, 6/18/1750, 12/5/1757, 12/19/1757; *New York Mercury*, 9/19/1757 (pp. 3, 4), 9/26/1757, 10/3/1757, 7/21/1760 (supplement).

10. The ships are the *Irene; Hope; Two Brothers* (*New York Gazette*, 1/17/1757); *Concord* (*New York Mercury*, Supplement, 7/21/1760); *Charming Rachel* (*New York Gazette*, 6/18/1750); *Prince of Wales*, and *Lamb* (*New York Gazette*, 12/5/1757). For business connections, see Henry Van Vleck Receipt Book, NYHS; Joseph A. Scoville, *The Old Merchants of New York City*, Third Series (New York: Carleton, 1865), 182–83; Virginia D. Harrington, *The New York Merchant on the Eve of the Revolution* (New York: Columbia University Press, 1935), 185.

11. The Commercial Society provides the best means of identifying those merchants who worked on behalf of the Moravians, particularly in London, Amsterdam, and Herrnhut. See R.4.A.41, UAH.

12. Jordan, "Moravian Immigration," 53–54; Fogleman, *Hopeful Journeys*, 113–26; Levering, 105–27, 166–69.

13. Peter Boehler Collection, Authorization for sale of the Catherine, Box 1, Folder 6. Jordan, "Moravian Immigration," 56–57.

14. Jordan, "Moravian Immigration," 58–62. Those on board the *Little Strength* survived and eventually reached their destinations, although Garrison was in prison in Cuba for quite a while. For his vivid descriptions of his captivity, and his spiritual development while there, Nicholas Garrison, Lebenslauf, BD September 1781.

15. Israel Acrelius, *A History of New Sweden or, the Settlements on the River Delaware*, William M. Reynolds, trans., Memoirs of the Historical Society of Pennsylvania, Vol. 11, (Philadelphia: Publication fund of the Historical Society of Pennsylvania, 1876), 415.

16. Jordan, "Moravian Immigration," 63–81. For Thomas Noble's will: "Abstracts of Wills on File in the Surrogate's Office, City of New York, Vol. IV, 1744–1753," in *Collections of the New-York Historical Society for the Year 1895*, 67–68.

17. Henry Van Vleck Receipt Book, NYHS. Jordan, "Moravian Immigration, 63–86. *New York Gazette*, January 17, 1757. See also newspaper advertisements listed above. *Irene* account printed in Reichel, "A Register of Members of the Moravian Church," 330.

18. *New York Gazette Revived in the Weekly Post Boy*, 6/18/1750; *New York Mercury*, 10/8/1752, 9/24/1752, 10/15/1753, 10/3/1757.

19. Van Vleck to Horsfield, 3/7/1757, Horsfield Collection.

20. Quoted in Otto Uttendörfer, *Wirtschaftsgeist und Wirtschaftsorganisation Herrnhuts und der Brüdergemeine, von 1743 bis zum Ende des Jahrhunderts* (Herrnhut: Verlag der Missionsbuchhandlung, 1926), 37. For discussion of Zinzendorf's attitude toward economic development, see Uttendörfer, 36 ff.

21. See also William J. Danker, *Profit for the Lord: Economic Activities in Moravian Missions and the Basel Mission Trading Company* (Grand Rapids, Mich.: Eerdmans, 1971).

22. Proposal presented to the Directorial College by Jonas Paulus Weiss, May 17 and 20, 1758, R.04.A.41.1, UAH.

23. Proposal by Jonas Paulus Weiss.

24. Quoted in Uttendörfer, *Wirtschaftsgeist*, 48.

25. Approval from the Directorial College, R.4.A.41.2; Approval from Zinzendorf, R.4.A.41.4; Artickel des Londonischen Brüder Commercien Collegii, UVC I 45, UAH.

26. Proposal by Jonas Paulus Weiss.

27. Marshall to JPW, June 26, 1762, R.14.A.41.c, UAH. DCM 6/7/1762.

28. Harry Emilius Stocker, *A History of the Moravian Church in New York City* (New York: n.p., 1922); Abraham Ritter, *History of the Moravian Church in Philadelphia from its foundation in 1749 to the present time* (Philadelphia: Hayes and Zell, 1857).

29. Richard Bushman, "Markets and Composite Farms in Early America," *WMQ* 55 (1998): 351–74; James T. Lemon, *The Best Poor Man's Country: Early Southeastern Pennsylvania* (Baltimore: Johns Hopkins University Press, 1972, 2002), 150–83; Allan Kulikoff,

From British Peasants to Colonial American Farmers (Chapel Hill: University of North Carolina Press, 2000), 211–12.

30. This portrait of the town's economy is based on the accounts in the Diacony Ledgers, particularly C-F, the ledgers that record the financial records of the entire Gemeine in Bethlehem, the community cash books, and on the Strangers' Store ledgers. For ledger detail, see Store Ledgers C & D.

31. CAMM XII, 46; Diacony Journal, "Account of Goods sold for Cash," 1750–1752.

32. Timothy Breen, *The Marketplace of Revolution: How Consumer Politics Shaped American Independence* (New York: Oxford University Press, 2004); Cary Carson et al., *Of Consuming Interests*; Richard L. Bushman, *The Refinement of America: Persons, Houses, Cities* (New York: Knopf, 1992); Daniel B. Thorp, "Doing Business in the Backcountry: Retail Trade in Colonial Rowan County, North Carolina," *WMQ* 48 (1991): 387–408; Thomas M. Doerflinger, "Farmers and Dry Goods in the Philadelphia Market Area, 1750–1800" in Ronald Hoffman et al., eds., *The Economy of Early America: The Revolutionary Period, 1763–1790* (Charlottesville: University Press of Virginia, 1988); Diane E. Wenger, "Creating Networks: the Country Storekeeper and the Mid-Atlantic Economy" (Ph.D. dissertation, University of Delaware, 2002).

33. Strangers' Store Ledgers B & C, MAB.

34. "Beylage zu dem Mem. wegen eines Stores," Box: Trade & Commerce, Various Records.

35. Diacony Journal, 1753; Diacony Ledger C, esp. folio 245.

36. SCM 12/21/1757; Strangers' Store Inventories, 1756 (in 1756–61 vellum ledger), 1761, 1762, 1763, MAB.

37. DCM 5/5/1759; 8/14/1760.

38. SCM 3/1/1757; 4/5/1757; 12/21/1757; Diacony Journals, 1753–1760. See, for example, April 8, 1754, folio 257, Ledger C and accompanying Journal entry.

39. Reprinted in Hellmuth Erbe, *Bethlehem, Pa.: Eine kommunistische Herrnhuter Kolonie des 18.Jahrhunderts* (Stuttgart: Ausland und Heimat, 1929), 164–65.

40. SCM 4/5/1757; 12/21/1757.

41. Erbe, *Bethlehem, Pa*, 164–65.

42. Quoted in Stephen Innes, *Creating the Commonwealth: The Economic Culture of Puritan New England* (New York: W.W. Norton, 1995), 168–70; Mark Valeri, "The Economic Thought of Jonathan Edwards," *CH* 60 (1991): 37–54, quotation, 50. Erbe, *Bethlehem, Pa*, 164–65. SCM 10/6/1757; 12/21/1757. See also Bernard Bailyn, "The Apologia of Robert Keayne," *WMQ* 7 (1950): 568–87; Raymond de Roover, "The Concept and Theory of Just Price: Theory and Economic Policy," *Journal of Economic History* 18 (1958): 418–38.

43. Diacony Journals, 1754–1759. For retail mark ups, see Carole Shammas, "How Sufficient was Early America?" *Journal of Interdisciplinary History* 13 (1982): 247–72, esp. 265.

44. SCM 3/1/1757.

45. Aaron Fogleman has found that as many as 20 percent of Moravian immigrants

to America were ministers or church leaders, a number drastically higher than in that in the broader German migration pattern. Fogleman, *Hopeful Journeys*, 111. For information on Powell, see S&G 177–78. There is no specific evidence that Martha Powell, or any other woman, worked in the store, although Moravian wives often shared the posts of their husbands.

46. Strangers' Store Ledgers, 1756–57, 1759–61, Single Brothers' Catalog, BethSB 47, 16. The Unity made use of Smalling's commercial skills again, however. In 1759, he became clerk of the church's Commercial Society based in London.

47. Oberlin: Johann Francis Oberlin Lebenslauf, UAH; Levering, 514. Edmonds: "Catalog of Men in their trades," BethCong 403.1; Katherine M. Faull, *Moravian Women's Memoirs: Their Related Lives, 1750–1820* (Syracuse, N.Y.: Syracuse University Press, 1997), 33–39; Daniel Kunckler, Lebenslauf, BD 1777, 201–6; Jordan, "Moravian Immigration," 49–90.

48. For early Moravian mission financing in an international context, see Danker, *Profit for the Lord*. The literature on Moravian missions to natives is vast. For works on the missions directed from Bethlehem, see Amy C. Schutt, "Female Relationships and Intercultural Bonds in Moravian Indian Missions," in William A. Pencak and Daniel K. Richter, eds., *Friends and Enemies in Penn's Woods: Indians, Colonists, and the Racial Construction of Pennsylvania* (University Park: Pennsylvania State University Press, 2004), 87–103; Rachel Wheeler, "Women and Christian Practice in a Mahican Village," *Religion and American Culture* 13 (2003): 27–67; Jane T. Merritt, "Dreaming of the Savior's Blood: Moravians and the Indian Great Awakening in Pennsylvania," *WMQ* 54 (1997): 723–46; Elma E. Gray, *Wilderness Christians: The Moravian Mission to the Delaware Indians* (Ithaca, N.Y.: Cornell University Press, 1956); Hermann Wellenreuther and Carola Wessel, eds., *The Moravian Mission Diaries of David Zeisberger, 1771–1781* (University Park: Pennsylvania State University Press, 2005).

49. Amy C. Schutt, *Peoples of the River Valleys: The Odyssey of the Delaware Indians* (Philadelphia: University of Pennsylvania Press, 2007), 62–93; Jane T. Merritt, *At the Crossroads: Indians and Empires on a Mid-Atlantic Frontier, 1700–1763* (Chapel Hill: University of North Carolina Press, 2003), 19–49; Pencak and Richter, eds., *Friends & Enemies in Penn's Woods*; James H. Merrell, *Into the American Woods: Negotiators on the Pennsylvania Frontier* (New York: W.W. Norton, 1999). For the economic climate in the region, see Peter C. Mancall, *Valley of Opportunity: Economic Culture along the Upper Susquehanna, 1700–1800* (Ithaca, N.Y.: Cornell University Press, 1991). See also James H. Merrell, *The Indians' New World: Catawbas and Their Neighbors from European Contact Through the Era of Removal* (Chapel Hill: University of North Carolina Press, 1989), esp. 134–91; Daniel H. Usner, Jr., *Indians, Settlers, and Slaves in a Frontier Exchange Economy: The Lower Mississippi Valley Before 1783* (Chapel Hill: University of North Carolina Press, 1992).

50. CAMM XI, 51. Merritt, *At the Crossroads*, 72.

51. RMM 116/1, 4/25/1747.

52. RMM 116/2, 8/21/1747.

53. CAMM XI, 33–34.

54. RMM 116/2, 7/27/1747. Other missionaries also tried to distinguish themselves as honest. See RMM 115/6, 8/18/1756.

55. RMM, 116/2, 8/21/1747, 9/2/1747; 119/1, 10/29/1747, 11/1/1747.

56. RMM 115/7, 5/4/1757; 115/9, 10/10/1759; 114/1, 3/21/1749; 114/3. 4/30/1751.

57. RMM 116/3, 5/10/1748.

58. Merritt, *At the Crossroads,* 148–55.

59. RMM 116/2, 8/21/1747. See also 114/4, 10/11/1751; 115/6, 8/18/1756; 115/9, 10/10/1759; 119/1, 11/1/1747.

60. RMM, 115/6, 8/18/1756; 116/4, 8/20/1748.

61. RMM 117/1 12/4/1750.

62. RMM 117/3, 1/12/1752. For the role of perceived poverty in structuring missionary ideologies, see Laura M. Stevens, *The Poor Indians: British Missionaries, Native Americans, and Colonial Sensibility* (Philadelphia: University of Pennsylvania Press, 2004), 17–22. Daniel K. Richter argues that European observers mistakenly perceived Indians as poor because they misread Indian agricultural and commercial activities. See his "'Believing That Many of the Red People Suffer Much for the Want of Food': Hunting, Agriculture, and a Quaker Construction of Indianness in the Early Republic," *Journal of the Early Republic* 19 (1999): 601–28.

63. RMM 117/3, 1/12/1752.

64. Schutt, *Peoples of the River Valleys,* 57. The literature on native trade is substantial. A good starting place is James H. Merrell, "Indian History During the English Colonial Era," in Daniel Vickers, ed., *A Companion to Colonial America* (Oxford: Blackwell, 2003), 124–25.

65. RMM, 119/4, Gnadenhütten stewards account book; 311/1, Rechnungs-buch mit denen Indianern; Diacony Ledgers, C, D & E, esp. C folio 251.

CHAPTER 5. ATLANTIC CURRENTS: GLOBAL WAR, AND THE FATE OF MORAVIAN COMMUNALISM

1. Jane T. Merritt, *At the Crossroads: Indians and Empires on a Mid-Atlantic Frontier, 1700–1763* (Chapel Hill: University of North Carolina Press, 2003), 169–97; Daniel K. Richter, *Facing East from Indian Country: A Native History of Early America* (Cambridge, Mass.: Harvard University Press, 2001), 151–88; Steven C. Harper, "Delawares and Pennsylvanians after the Walking Purchase," in William A. Pencak and Daniel K. Richter, eds., *Friends and Enemies in Penn's Woods: Indians, Colonists, and the Racial Construction of Pennsylvania* (University Park: Pennsylvania State University Press, 2004), 168–79; Matthew C. Ward, *Breaking the Backcountry: The Seven Years' War in Virginia and Pennsylvania, 1754–1765* (Pittsburgh: University of Pittsburgh Press, 2003), 36–90. There is a burgeoning literature on the increasingly racialized relations between whites and Indians in the second

half of the eighteenth century. See, in addition to the works cited above, Nancy Shoe-maker, *A Strange Likeness: Becoming Red and White in Eighteenth-Century North America* (New York: Oxford University Press, 2004); Peter Rhodes Silver, "Indian-Hating and the Rise of Whiteness in Provincial Pennsylvania" (Ph.D. dissertation, Yale University, 2000); and Gregory Evans Dowd, *A Spirited Resistance: The North American Indian Struggle for Unity, 1745–1815* (Baltimore: Johns Hopkins University Press, 1992).

2. David Armitage, "Global History of the Seven Years' War," *Commonplace* 1 (2000), http://www.common-place.org/vol-01/no-01/crucible/crucible-armitage.shtml. The best single volume on the conflict is Fred Anderson, *The Crucible of War: The Seven Years' War and the Fate of Empire in British North America, 1754–1766* (New York: Knopf, 2000).

3. De Watteville to Spangenberg, 9/20/1757, Folder 3, SPBG III.

4. Broderson to Spangenberg, 10/8/1757, Folder 3, SPBG III. The "Count Henry" re-ferred to is most likely Count Heinrich XXVIII von Reuss, whose family had many con-nections to the Moravians. The Prussian Lieutenant General, the Duke of Bevern, also passed through Herrnhut that week. For the 1757 Prussian and Austrian campaigns, see Daniel Marston, *The Seven Years' War* (Oxford: Osprey, 2001), 37–45.

5. I. N. Phelps Stokes, *The Iconography of Manhattan Island, 1498–1909* (1922; New York: Arno Press, 1967), 4: 672. Van Vleck to Horsfield, 11/17/1757, Horsfield Collection. On its previous journey, the captain of the *Irene* was instructed to ransom her for not more than £800 sterling. On that trip, she was underwritten by "R. Livingston and David Van Horne." Although the *Irene* was most likely insured on her final journey, no record of the terms remains. Van Vleck to Horsfield, 3/7/1757, Horsfield Collection; *Irene*'s Ransom, 3/1/1757, Box: Early Letters (*Oeconomy* Period). For marine insurance, see Cathy Matson, *Merchants and Empire: Trading in Colonial New York* (Baltimore: Johns Hopkins Univer-sity Press, 1998), 268, 419–20, n9.

6. BD 4/15/1758, 6/9/1758 and "Extract der Europaeischcen Briefe" following June diary; Broderson to Spangenberg, 4/8/1758, SPBG III. Levering, 363; John W. Jordan, "Moravian Immigration to Pennsylvania, 1734–1767, with Some Account of the Transport Vessels," *TMHS* 5 (1899): 51–90.

7. Schoute's account of the *Irene*'s end appears in Jordan, "Moravian Immigration," 82–86. Smalling and Jacobsen also wrote accounts, which were circulated with the *Gemein Nachrichten*.

8. Jordan, "Moravian Immigration," 84–85.

9. Broderson to Spangenberg, 4/8/1758, SPBG III.

10. Merritt, *At the Crossroads*, 161–64.

11. CAMM III, 39.

12. Horsfield to Governor Morris, undated, Horsfield Collection, 55–58, APS. This account is taken from a draft of Horsfield's letter to the governor, now housed at the Amer-ican Philosophical Society. Another record of the events appeared on December 8, 1755, in the *New York Mercury*. The account was "sent by a Gentleman, at Bethlehem, in a Letter of the Second Instant, to his Friend in New York." Although it is impossible to be certain,

it is likely, given Van Vleck's other correspondence with the paper, that this account was written by Horsfield and sent to Henry Van Vleck in New York. Slightly varying versions of the story appear in Levering, 311–19; and George Henry Loskiel, *The History of the Moravian Mission Among the Indians in North America, from its commencement to the present time* (London: T. Allman, 1838), 126–35. See also Merritt, *At the Crossroads,* 184–87; Ward, *Breaking the Backcountry,* 64–68.

13. New York *Mercury,* 11/17/1755, p. 3.

14. New York *Mercury,* 11/24/1755, supplement.

15. BD 11/25/1755.

16. Benjamin Franklin, *The Autobiography of Benjamin Franklin,* ed. Louis P. Masur (New York: Bedford Books, 1993), 139–40. For refugees, see Spangenberg, "Meine l. brüder u. Schwestern," 12/4/1755, SP A IV, SPBG. For treaty negotiations, see Francis Jennings, *Empire of Fortune: Crowns, Colonies, and Tribes in the Seven Years War in America* (New York: W.W. Norton, 1988), 323–48; Anderson, *Crucible of War,* 164–65; Merritt, *At the Crossroads,* 250–52. Horsfield to Governor, June 21, 1756, Horsfield Collection, 131–32, APS. Timothy Horsfield to Gov. Denny, November 6, 1756, Samuel Hazard, ed., *Pennsylvania Archives,* Series I, Vol. III (Philadelphia: Joseph Severns, 1853), 34–35.

17. Levering, 347–58.

18. "Lieben Brüder u. Schwestern," 10/14/1756, SP A V, SPBG I.

19. Beilage to Letter to the Directorial Collegium, 1/13/1759, BethCong 425; Benezet Letters, SPBG IV. "Account of the United Brethren at Bethlehem with the Commissioners of the Province of Pennsylvania During the Indian War of 1755, '56 and '57," in William C. Reichel, ed., *Memorials of the Moravian Church* (Philadelphia: J.B. Lippincott, 1870), 221–24.

20. BethCong 425. The short-lived settlement at Friedenshütten and the Moravians' physical proximity to natives are discussed in Beverly Smaby, *The Transformation of Moravian Bethlehem: From Communal Mission to Family Economy* (Philadelphia: University of Pennsylvania Press, 1988), 97–100. See also Levering, 192–93.

21. Merritt, *At the Crossroads,* 235–308; Krista Camenzind, "Violence, Race, and the Paxton Boys," in *Friends and Enemies,* 201–20; Paul Moyer, 'Real' Indians, 'White' Indians, and the Contest for the Wyoming Valley," in *Friends and Enemies,* 221–237; Dowd, *A Spirited Resistance,* 21–46; Richter, *Facing East,* 180–82.

22. Jünger Conferenz, 5–12 May 1756, MAB. The fact that communalism was seen as temporary is further highlighted by the fact that the communal projects in Wachovia were always intended to be replaced by a congregation town at Salem.

23. In December 1757, there were 1,192 people associated with the Oeconomy, including both Bethlehem and Nazareth. 172 Moravian Indians (many were the remnant of the Gnadenhütten mission, soon to be reorganized as Nain) then living outside Bethlehem are included in this total, as are 20 (presumably white) refugees living in Nazareth. There were 328 children. Bethlehem Diary, Memorabilia for 1757. For Spangenberg's address, see BD 1/18/1758, 2/11/1758, appendix to February, 1758. See also Single Brothers' Diary, BethSB 1, 1/18/1758, 2/12/1758 for a different assessment of the process, one critical of Spangenberg.

24. These short statements were compiled into a single document and sent to Herrn-hut, along with a copy of the Brotherly Agreement (R.14.A.41 a, UAH). A second copy is contained in the Moravian Archives in Bethlehem: Box: Termination of the Economy, 1758–1764. This compiled version, which is extant in both the Herrnhut and the Bethle-hem archives, was probably edited to emphasize devotion to community. Spangenberg's talk clearly indicates that there were significant and specific areas of frustration with the Oeconomy, none of which appear in the compiled document. It is likely, of course, that some of these more specific issues came up only orally in the interviews that Spangenberg and his fellow leaders conducted, rather than in the written format, but the almost univer-sally positive tone of the compiled statements is striking. The original letters apparently no longer exist.

25. Oerter, R.14.A.41.a,UAH.

26. Ettwein, R.14.A.41.a, UAH.

27. Tanneberger, R.14.A.41.a, UAH.

28. Krausin; Joh. Mat. Otto, R.14.A.41.a, UAH.

29. Kliest, R.14.A.41.a, UAH.

30. For Zinzendorf's concept of "childlikeness," see Craig Atwood, *Community of the Cross: Moravian Piety in Colonial Bethlehem* (University Park: Pennsylvania State Univer-sity Press, 2004), 66–70, 144–46, and passim. Peterson; Schaeferin; Erickin, R.14.A.41.a, UAH.

31. Elizabeth Holderin, R.14.A.41.a, UAH.

32. G. Partsch, R.14.A41.A, UAH.

33. BD 2/11/1758.

34. BD Appendix to February 1758. For more thorough discussion (and translation) of Spangenberg's speech, see Katherine Carté Engel, "Brother Joseph's Sermon on the Oeconomy," in Craig Atwood and Peter Vogt, eds., *The Distinctiveness of Moravian Cul-ture: Essays and Documents in Moravian History in Honor of Vernon H. Nelson* (Nazareth, Pa.: Moravian Historical Society, 2003), 121–40.

35. The so-called "Sifting Time" has been the subject of much discussion among spe-cialists in Moravian history. See Atwood, *Community of the Cross*, 11–19. Paul Peucker, "'Blut auf unsre Grünen Bändchen': Die Sichtungszeit in der Herrnhuter Brüdergemeine," *UF* 49–50 (2002): 41–94. PT 227.

36. For discussion of Moravian finances, see Edmund de Schweinitz, *The Financial History of the American Province of the Unitas Fratrum and of its Sustentation Fund* (Bethle-hem, Pa.: Moravian Publication Office, 1877). See also J. Taylor Hamilton and Kenneth G. Hamilton, *History of the Moravian Church: The Renewed Unitas Fratrum, 1722–1957* (Beth-lehem, Pa.: Moravian Church in America, 1967), 34–59, 76–81, 140–42; and Otto Ut-tendörfer, *Wirtschaftsgeist und Wirtschaftsorganisation Herrnhuts und der BrüderGemeine von 1743 bis zum Ende des Jahrhunderts* (Herrnhut: Missionsbuchhandlung, 1926). For dis-cussion of Herrnhaag and the sifting time, see Hans-Walter Erbe, *Herrnhaag : eine religiöse Kommunität im 18. Jahrhundert* (Hamburg: F. Wittig, 1988).

37. W. R. Ward, "Zinzendorf and Money" *Studies in Church History* 24 (1987); 283–305; Spangenberg quotation, 302. Uttendörfer, *Alt-Herrnhut: Wirtschaftsgeschichte und Religionssoziologie Herrnhuts während seiner ersten zwanzig Jahre* (Herrnhut: Missionsbuchhandlung, 1925), 144 ff. John R. Weinlick, *Count Zinzendorf: The Story of His Life and Leadership in the Renewed Moravian Church* (New York: Abingdon Press, 1956), 109.

38. Edmund De Schweinitz, *Financial History of the Northern Province*, 5–9. Hamilton and Hamilton, *History of the Moravian Church*, 94–113. For the war in Saxony, see De Watteville to Spangenberg, 9/20/1757, Broderson to Spangenberg, 10/8/1757, SPBG III.

39. Circular Letter, section B, 10/17/1759, Box: Economy Period: Letter and Accounts (with Europe).

40. Spangenberg to Zinzendorf, 7/6/1758, R.14.A.20.7.16, UAH.

41. Letter to the Directorial Collegium, 1/13/1759, BethCong 425. This letter and its accompanying appendices can also be found in Herrnhut, UVC.X.145, UAH.

42. Spangenberg to Zinzendorf, 7/6/1758, R.14.A.20.7.16, UAH.

43. Letter to the Directorial Collegium, 1/13/1759, BethCong 425.

44. Johannes to "Allerliebster Geschwister," 12/8/1759, De Watteville Collection, Box 2.

45. Johannes to "Allerliebster Geschwister," 12/8/1759, De Watteville Collection, Box 2.

46. Spangenberg to Zinzendorf, 6/11/1760, R.14.A.20.7.29, UAH.

47. Levering, 376. See also Weinlick, *Count Zinzendorf*, 219–34.

48. Craig Atwood argues that Zinzendorf's death and the subsequent end of the Moravian Church's commitment to his "Religion of the heart" provide the most important marker for understanding Bethlehem's religious evolution. Atwood, *Community of the Cross*, 224–27.

49. Quoted in Hellmuth Erbe, *Bethlehem, Pa.: Eine kommunistische Herrnhuter Kolonie des 18. Jahrhunderts* (Stuttgart: Ausland und Heimats Verlag, 1929), 128.

CHAPTER 6. TWO REVOLUTIONS: ENDING THE OECONOMY AND LOSING THE MISSIONS

1. Raths Conferenz, 7/7/1760, 7/16/1760, R.6.Ab.44, UAH.

2. It should be noted that whatever the precise combination of pressures resulting from the Oeconomy's size, the Unity's debt load, and Zinzendorf's death, Bethlehem's communalism did not end because of a basic failure to meet the material needs of the people who depended on it. See Annual Extracts, MAB, and also Hellmuth Erbe, *Bethlehem, Pa.: Eine kommunistische Herrnhuter Kolonie des 18. Jahrhunderts* (Stuttgart: Ausland und Heimats, 1929), 124–26.

3. Johannes de Watteville to Spangenberg, 7/15/1760, R.14.A.20.7.31, UAH.

4. Spangenberg to Johannes de Watteville, 11/11/1760, R.14.A.20.7.33, UAH. Erbe also

discusses Spangenberg's letter at length, placing Bethlehem's leader in opposition to David Koeber in Herrnhut (Erbe, *Bethlehem, Pa.*, 127–36). That reading, in this author's opinion, overplays Koeber's role and underestimates Spangenberg's longer-standing concerns about the Oeconomy. One particularly interesting document for assessing Koeber's role from Spangenberg's perspective, as well as the broader situation, is a collection of quotations compiled by Spangenberg. Titled "bey einer, mit gottes hülfe, intendirten Veränderung der gemein-oeconomie in Bethlehem u. auf Nazareth wird folgendes zur Uberlegung gegeben," the document is a list of quotations taken from communications with Europe on the subject. The citations include notes from the Directorial Conference Minutes, Raths Conference Minutes, and letters from Johannes de Watteville. None of them specifically came from Koeber. Of course, the document also provides insight into what Spangenberg thought the key issues were, and this analysis follows that lead. Box: Termination of the Economy.

5. Spangenberg to Johannes de Watteville, 11/11/1760, R.14.A.20.7.33, UAH.

6. Spangenberg to Johannes de Watteville, 11/11/1760, R.14.A.20.7.33, UAH.

7. Spangenberg to Johannes de Watteville, 11/11/1760, R.14.A.20.7.33, UAH.

8. Protocol of the Directorial College, 2/12/1761, UAH. Principal among problems discussed was Bethlehem's legal ownership. For years, Father David Nitschmann had held the deed. Upon his death his daughter Anna, Zinzendorf's second wife, inherited, but her death in 1760 necessitated further action. Nathanael Seidel became the next owner, as he had already agreed to relocate to Pennsylvania. The details of this transfer, complicated by the need to conform with British land laws, required a great deal of discussion. See Edmund de Schweinitz, *The Financial History of the American Province of the Unitas Fratrum and of its Sustentation Fund* (Bethlehem, Pa.: Moravian Publication Office, 1877), 14–18. The Herrnhut discussions are recorded in the Protocol of the Directorial College, 1759–1762, UVC Records; and the Raths-Conferenz, R.6.Ab.44, UAH. See also R.14.A.41.b.3; R.14.A.41.b.5; R.14.A.41.b.6; and Summarischer Aufsatz, UVC X.141, UAH.

9. Johannes to Spangenberg, et al., 6/11/1761, PHC Misc. Corr., mostly from Europe, 1760–1847, Box 2, Folder 10.

10. Johannes to Spangenberg, et al., 6/11/1761, PHC Misc. Corr., mostly from Europe, 1760–1847, Box 2, Folder 10.

11. Spangenberg to "Unsern L. Brrn," 12/14/1762, SP A VI, SPBG.

12. Dietrich Meyer, *Zinzendorf und die Herrnhuter Brüdergemeine, 1700–2000* (Göttingen: Vandenhoeck & Ruprecht, 2000), 63–78; Spangenberg to "Lieben Geschwister," 1/4/1763, PHC Misc. Corr., mostly from Europe, 1760–1847, box 1, folder 1. Chief among the conservative turns of the era was a turn against women in leadership positions among the principal governing men. See Paul M. Peucker, "Gegen ein Regiment von Schwestern: Die Stellung der Frau in der Brüdergemeine nach Zinzendorfs Tod," *UF* 45–46 (1999): 61–72.

13. "Original Constitution & Instructiones für die Missions-Deputation," R.15.A.4a.7c, UAH

14. R.6.A.b.47.c, 4/10/1764, UAH.

15. Enge Conferenz to Bethlehem Oeconomats Conferenz, 4/26/1764, contained within M. Dep. I.1. p. 26 ff, UAH.

16. ECM, 8/21/1764.

17. Nathanael to Engen Conferenz, 8/25/1764, R.3.B.4.b.6. item 44, UAH.

18. Annual Extracts, 1761, 1762, 1763. One last aspect of the transition that warrants mentioning is the relationship between Bethlehem and Nazareth. Before 1762, the two towns shared one integrated economy. While Bethlehem's transition occurred in that year, Nazareth and the other "upper places" continued to live communally for another year or so, under the guidance of the church, merely to simplify the transition. Despite this fact, 1762 marks the division of the towns into separate entities. Their histories, though integrally linked, began to diverge from that point.

19. Directorial College to Spangenberg et al., 3/31/1761, PHC Misc. Corr., mostly from Europe, 1760–1847, Box 2, Folder 10. These lists are included in Spangenberg's set of excerpts.

20. Account Extracts, 1763, 1763, 1764, 1765.

21. MCT; see also proposed contracts in folder IV, Box: Schriften das Oeconomicum Betreffend.

22. 1762 Tannery inventory; MCT.

23. MCT. For more on Andreas, see Daniel B. Thorp, "Chattel with a Soul: The Autobiography of a Moravian Slave," *PMHB* 112 (1988): 433–51.

24. MCT.

25. MCT.

26. MCT.

27. Bookkeeping instructions; MCT.

28. MCT. The soap boiler faced a different situation entirely: he earned an annual salary of £40, and no share of any profit. In fact, during the first years of the new system, he was prohibited from selling his own wares to outsiders and restricted to selling all his produce to the town store. His total earnings were thus controlled far more than either those of the independent artisans, or those of individuals like the millers and storekeeper. Christiansen's biography appears in Carter Litchfield et al., *The Bethlehem Oil Mill, 1745–1934: German Technology in Early Pennsylvania* (Kemblesville, Pa.: Olearius Editions, 1984), 21–22.

29. Johannes to Spangenberg, et al., 6/11/1761, PHC Misc. Corr., mostly from Europe, 1760–1847, Box 2, Folder 10. BD Memorabilia for 1761. For descriptions of the German Choir system see Otto Uttendörfer, *Wirtschaftsgeist und Wirtschaftsorganisation Herrnhuts und der Brüdergemeine von 1743 bis zum Ende des Jahrhunderts* (Herrnhut: Missionsbuchhandlung, 1926), 188–356. See also Gillian Lindt Gollin, *Moravians in Two Worlds: A Study of Changing Communities* (New York: Columbia University Press, 1967), 67–109.

30. Single Brother's Tisch Buch, BethSB 149; Diacony Ledger E, Accounts for Single Sisters and Single Brothers, for example Folio 89.

31. John Arbo's Commonplace Book, BethSB 7, 2; "Projects and Proposal for the intended change . . . re Single Brethren," Trans.

32. For discussion of the Single Sisters' Choir, see Beverly P. Smaby, "Forming the Single Sisters' Choir in Bethlehem" *TMHS* 28 (1994): 1–14; and "'No one should lust for power . . . women least of all': Dismantling Female Leadership Among eighteenth-century Moravians," unpublished paper presented at Wake Forest University, "German Moravians in the Atlantic World" conference, 2002. For shifting attitudes of Moravians toward gender in this period, see Peucker, "Gegen ein Regiment von Schwestern," 61–72. For discussion of the gendered division of labor in Pennsylvania and early America more broadly, see Adrienne D. Hood, *The Weaver's Craft: Cloth, Commerce, and Industry in Early Pennsylvania* (Philadelphia: University of Pennsylvania Press, 2003); Joan M. Jensen, *Loosening the Bonds: Mid-Atlantic Farm Women, 1750–1850* (New Haven, Conn.: Yale University Press, 1986); Jeanne Boydston, *Home and Work: Housework, Wages, and the Ideology of Labor in the Early Republic* (New York: Oxford University Press, 1990), and Laurel Thatcher Ulrich, *Good Wives: Image and Reality in the Lives of Women in Northern New England, 1650–1750* (New York: Knopf, 1982).

33. "Projects for the intended change of the Bethlehem Economy, re: Single Sisters, 1761," Trans.

34. "Aufsatz dessen, was die Led. Schw.n bey der bevorstehenden Veränderung der *Oeconomie* hauptsächlich anzumercken haben," Box: Termination of the Economy, Folder 1.

35. For more on Herrnhut and its organization, see chapter 1. For Herrnhut's Brotherly Agreement and Manorial Injunctions, see Hans-Christoph Hahn and Hellmut Reichel, eds., *Zinzendorf und die Herrnhuter Brüder: Quellen zur Geschichte der Brüder-Unität von 1722 bis 1760* (Hamburg: Wittig, 1977), 68–80. See also Otto Uttendörfer, *Alt-Herrnhut: Wirtschaftsgeschichte und Religionssoziologie Herrnhuts während seiner ersten zwanzig Jahre, 1722–1742* (Herrnhut: Missionsbuchhandlung, 1925), 14–24; Guntram Phillipp, "Wirtschaftsethik und Wirtschaftspraxis in der Geschichte der Herrnhuter Brüder Gemeine," in Mari P. Van Buutenen, Cornelis Dekker, and Huib Leeuwenberg, eds., *Unitas Fratrum: Moravian Studies* (Utrecht: Rijksarchief, 1975), 401–63. For quotations from Bethlehem's 1762 Brotherly Agreement, see http://bdhp.moravian.edu/community_records/regulations/brotherly_agreement/batintro.html. Bethlehem's 1754 Brotherly Agreement appears in Erbe, *Bethlehem, Pa.*, 166–69.

36. Daniel K. Richter, *Facing East from Indian Country: A Native History of Early America* (Cambridge, Mass.: Harvard University Press, 2001), 191–216; Jane T. Merritt, *At the Crossroads: Indians and Empires on a Mid-Atlantic Frontier, 1700–1763* (Chapel Hill: University of North Carolina Press, 2003), 273–82; Colin G. Calloway, *The Scratch of a Pen: 1763 and the Transformation of North America* (New York: Oxford University Press, 2006).

37. Gregory Evans Dowd has argued that Pontiac's War, and particularly its Pennsylvania component, was a continental conflict over the status of Indians within British America. Dowd, *War Under Heaven: Pontiac, the Indian Nations, & the British Empire* (Baltimore: Johns Hopkins University Press, 2002), 1–4, 174–212.

38. Dowd, *War Under Heaven*, 191–95; Merritt, *At the Crossroads*, 272–77; Paul Moyer, "'Real' Indians, 'White' Indians, and the Contest for the Wyoming Valley," in William A. Pencak and Daniel K. Richter, eds., *Friends and Enemies in Penn's Woods: Indians, Colonists, and the Racial Construction of Pennsylvania* (University Park: Pennsylvania State University Press, 2004), 221–38, esp. 226–27.

39. BD 11/5/1763, 11/6/1763.

40. Psalms, 5:8–9. English translation taken from the King James Version.

41. BD 11/8/1763.

42. BD 11/16/1763. The diaries for the mission during its time in Philadelphia are found in RMM Box 127, passim. Dowd, *War Under Heaven*, 190–96.

43. Nathanael to Engen Conferenz, 12/10/1763, R3.B4.b5.35; Nathanael to Engen Conferenz, 3/31/1764, R14.A45.2, UAH.

44. Spangenberg to De Watteville, 10/2/1758, R.14.A.20.7.19; Marshall to the Directorial Collegium, 6/30/1764, R.14.A.45.4, UAH. Possibly, as Jane Merritt has argued, the jury had freed him out of the prevailing fear that a guilty decision would only lead to further retaliation from an already angry Indian population. At any rate, the incident, "rather than easing tensions between Indians and whites, helped generate a racial discourse that would limit the options for Indians throughout Pennsylvania." Merritt, *At the Crossroads*, 281.

45. Merritt, *At the Crossroads*, 264–67; Dowd, *War Under Heaven*, 83–85, 215–16.

46. Diacony Ledger D, folio 66; Single Sisters Catalogue, BethSS 24, 11; Single Sisters Diary, BethSS 2, 3/6–7/1764, MAB. Marshall to Directorial Collegium, R14.A.43, Letter 3; Nathanael to Engen Conferenz, 3/31/1764, R.14.A.45.2, UAH.

47. Dowd, *War Under Heaven*, 191–203; Alden T. Vaughan, "Frontier Banditti and the Indians: The Paxton Boys' Legacy, 1763–1775," *Pennsylvania History* 51 (1984): 1–29; Brooke Hindle, "The March of the Paxton Boys," *William and Mary Quarterly* 3 (1946): 461–86; Peter Rhodes Silver, "Indian-Hating and the Rise of Whiteness in Provincial Pennsylvania" (Ph.D. dissertation, Yale University, 2001), 327–36.

48. RMM 127/2, 6/7/1764.

49. RMM 127/2, Memorabilia for 1764.

50. RMM 127/4, 1/17/1765, 1/18/1765, 2/5/1765.

51. RMM 127/4, 1/24–1/26/1765; 3/16–3/19/1765. The text of the Indians' declaration appears on March 18 of the Moravian diary for the Philadelphia congregation, and also in John Heckewelder, *A Narrative of the Mission of the United Brethren Among the Delaware and Mohegan Indians from its commencement, in the year 1740, to the close of the year 1808* (Philadelphia, M'Carty & Davis, 1820), 91–92.

52. Heckewelder, *Narrative of the Mission of the United Brethren*, 92–122; Amy C. Schutt, *Peoples of the River Valleys: The Odyssey of the Delaware Indians* (Philadelphia: University of Pennsylvania Press, 2007), 126–34; Ralph Mark Radloff, "Moravian Mission Methods Among the Indians of Ohio" (Ph.D. dissertation, University of Iowa, 1973), 46–53.

53. Committee über die Heyden Sache, R.15.A.4a.4.8, UAH.

54. At this meeting the subject of new missions in the Southern colonies was discussed, though no Lots were pulled on that issue. Committee über die Heyden Sache, R.15.A.4a.4.8, UAH. See also Unity Directorial Collegium to Oeconomats Conference, 1/26/1765, R.14.Aa.44a, 1765 folder, UAH.

55. Protocol of the Unity Direction, 3/6/1765, R.2.B.4.e, UAH. Boehler to Nathanael, 3/7/1765, Peter Boehler Collection, Box 1, folder 3. Boehler's letter presented the Nain plan as a suggestion, not a Lot, but given subsequent communications, the fact that it had been endorsed by a Lot must have communicated in another form.

56. Bethlehem Indian Conference, R15.H.Ia.2, UAH.

57. Bethlehem Indian Conference, R15.H.Ia.2, UAH.

58. Protocol of the Unity Direction, 5/13/1765, 6/6/1765, R.2.B.4.e; 7/24/1765, R2.B.4.e, UAH.

59. Several David Nitschmanns played prominent roles in eighteenth-century Moravian history. David Nitschmann (1703 or 1705–1779) the "syndic" visited Bethlehem at this time. R.2.B.4.e; Visitation Instructions, R.14.A.49, UAH.

60. 3/10/1766, R.2.B.4.e; see also R.14.A.49, UAH.

CHAPTER 7. A CHANGE IN MISSION

1. John Adams to Abigail Adams, Baltimore, Feb. 7, 1777, printed in *Adams Family Correspondence*, ed. L. H. Butterfield, vol. 2 (Cambridge, Mass.: Harvard University Press, 1963), 154–56. Adams returned to Bethlehem later that year and attended a worship service. He noted afterward that the women, who sat as a group and dressed alike, "resembled a Garden of white Cabbage Heads." *Diary and Autobiography of John Adams*, ed. L. H. Butterfield, vol. 2 (Cambridge, Mass.: Harvard University Press, 1961), 266–67.

2. Stephen Innes, *Creating the Commonwealth: The Economic Culture of Puritan New England* (New York: W.W. Norton, 1995), esp. 107–59; Charles L. Cohen, "The Saints Zealous in Love and Labor: The Puritan Psychology of Work," *Harvard Theological Review* 76 (1983): 455–80; Ilse Tönnies, "Die Arbeitswelt des Pietismus, Erweckungsbewegung und Brüdergemeinde: Ideen und Institutionen," *Jahrbuch für die Geschichte Mittle und Ostdeutschlands* 20 (1971): 89–133; 21 (1972): 140–83. For secular attitudes toward labor, see Joyce Oldham Appleby, *Economic Thought and Ideology in Seventeenth-Century England* (Princeton, N.J.: Princeton University Press, 1978). Max Weber's influential thesis is elaborated in *The Protestant Ethic and the Spirit of Capitalism*, trans. Talcott Parsons (1930; London: Routledge, 1992).

3. For the methodology behind these figures, see Katherine Carté Engel, "Of Heaven and Earth: Religion and Economic Activity Among Bethlehem's Moravians, 1741–1800" (Ph.D. dissertation, University of Wisconsin, 2003), appendix.

4. Joseph Horsfield, Lebenslauf, MS Box 9; Christian Renatus Heckewelder,

Lebenslauf, MS Box 11. Beverly Smaby argued in *The Transformation of Moravian Bethlehem: From Communal Mission to Family Economy* (Philadelphia: University of Pennsylvania Press, 1988) that a secularization of consciousness occurred in the years after the dissolution of the economy, which she measured by a decrease in references to religious matters and to community matters in Moravian spiritual autobiographies over the century between 1740 and 1840. These findings concur with my argument that in the post-Oeconomy period individual and family meanings for work came to replace the religious value generated by the community's missionary work. See esp. chapters 5 and 6.

5. Oberlin to "Lieben Brüder," 4/26/1762, Folder 6, Box: Schriften das Oeconomicum Betreffend. Oberlin was not clear about what exactly would make the store smaller, whether it would be subdivided, or merely crowded with more goods.

6. Oberlin, April 26, 1762, Transition documents, MAB.

7. Oberlin, April 26, 1762, Transition Documents, MAB.

8. CM 6/18/1762. For early American apprenticeships more broadly, see W. J. Rorabaugh, *The Craft Apprentice: From Franklin to the Machine Age in America* (New York: Oxford University Press, 1986); Lawrence W. Towner, *A Good Master Well Served: Masters and Servants in Colonial Massachusetts, 1620–1750* (New York: Garland, 1998), 23–49.

9. CM 7/10/1762.

10. CM 7/10/1762.

11. CM 10/19/1762; 9/4/1762; 1/28/1768.

12. Annual Extracts, MAB.

13. Annual Extracts, MAB. For the farms, see Smaby, *Transformation of Moravian Bethlehem*, 35.

14. Annual Extracts, MAB.

15. For the evolution of customary economic controls in early America, see Simon Middleton, "'How It Came That the Bakers Bake No Bread,': A Struggle for Trade Privileges in Seventeenth-Century New Amsterdam," *WMQ* 58 (2001): 347–72. Middleton argues that such controls should not be read merely as part of a binary transition to capitalism, but rather as part of complex economic strategies that drew on both competitive and customary practices. Mary M. Schweitzer argues in *Custom and Contract: Household, Government, and the Economy in Colonial Pennsylvania* (New York: Columbia University Press, 1987) that Pennsylvania's economic policies, including the branding of flour, were effective in promoting its economy, even as the economy retained traditional, custom-bound characteristics. See especially chapter 6. Studies detailing the role of government in economic promotion include Margaret Newall, *From Dependency to Independence: Economic Revolution in Colonial New England* (Ithaca, N.Y.: Cornell University Press, 1998) and Innes, *Creating the Commonwealth*. See also John J. McCusker and Russell R. Menard, *The Economy of British North America, 1607–1789* (Chapel Hill: University of North Carolina Press, 1991), 331–48. For collective economic action in early America, see Barbara Clark Smith, "Food Rioters and the American Revolution," *WMQ* 51 (1994): 3–38; Middleton, "'How It Came That the Bakers Bake No Bread'."

16. Digitized original, transcription, and translation of the 1762 Brotherly Agreement appear at http://bdhp.moravian.edu/community_records/regulations/brotherly_agreement/batintro.html, accessed April 1, 2003.

17. CM 9/30/1767; 5/30/1774; Annual Extracts, 1762, 1763; DCM 3/9/1763.

18. CM 2/18/1775–4/3/1775; quotation 4/3/1775. ACM 1/17/1781; 1/31/1781; 5/2/1781. See also William C. Reichel and John W. Jordan, eds., *Something About Trombones and The Old Mill at Bethlehem* (Bethlehem, Pa.: Moravian Publication Office, 1884). Digitized at http://bdhp.moravian.edu/art/architecture/oldmill.html, accessed April 1, 2003.

19. CM 6/6/1774.

20. "Herrschaftliche Gebote und Verbote," reprinted in Hans-Christoph Hahn and Hellmut Reichel, *Zinzendorf und die Herrnhuter Brüder: Quellen zur Geschichte der Brüder-Unität von 1722 bis 1760* (Hamburg: Friedrich Wittig Verlag, 1977), 68–80, quotation p. 71.

21. CM 5/25/1762; Schultze, "The Old Moravian Cemetery of Bethlehem, Pa., 1742–1897," *TMHS* 5 (1899), 100.

22. CM 9/13/1762.

23. CM 9/13/1762. See also CM 12/13–20/1762; 1/3/1763; 1/24/1763; 2/18/1763; 2/28/1763. Digeon's mental health did not improve. In March that year he was caught setting fires and his problems only worsened from there. He died in 1777.

24. CM 3/17/1772; 2/9/1773.

25. CM 8/28/1770; 5/20/1771. Although Poppelwell and his family were asked to leave Bethlehem, he died suddenly within a few months of the request and was buried in the town cemetery. His widow, who received assistance because her husband left her impoverished, remained in Bethlehem until her death forty-one years later in 1812. Schultze, "The Old Moravian Cemetery," 101, 169.

26. CM 8/30/1762.

27. CM 3/28/1763; 3/18/1765; 4/28/1765.

28. DCM 6/7/1762; CM 1/12/1767; 9/30/1767; CCM 3/5/1767; 4/2/1767.

29. CM 2/24/1765, See also CM 7/23/1764; 8/25/1766.

30. CCM 5/29/1767; 2/5/1767.

31. CCM opening document.

32. Innes, *Creating the Commonwealth*, 160–91. CCM 12/11/1766. The Commercial Council, quite unusually, kept its minutes in English for a brief period before switching to German for the duration of its two-year tenure.

33. CM 7/24/1762; 7/12/1762; CCM 4/2/1767; 5/1/1767; 8/21/1767.

34. CCM 6/26/1767; 7/23/1767.

35. See, for example, CM 9/20/1763; 7/30/1764; 5/15/1765; 1/28/1768; 6/10/1771.

36. For German assimilation into British American society, see Aaron Spencer Fogleman, *Hopeful Journeys: German Immigration, Settlement, and Political Culture in Colonial America, 1717–1775* (Philadelphia: University of Pennsylvania Press, 1996); A. G. Roeber, *Palatines, Liberty, and Property: German Lutherans in Colonial British America*, 2nd ed. (Baltimore: Johns Hopkins University Press, 1998), 243–310.

37. BD 12/21/1765; ECM 9/28/1774.

38. Liam Riordan, *Many Identities, One Nation: The Revolution and Its Legacy in the Mid-Atlantic* (Philadelphia: University of Pennsylvania Press, 2007) argues that the experience of the Revolution diverged in the various areas of the Mid-Atlantic. See also John B. Franz and William Pencak, eds., *Beyond Philadelphia: The American Revolution in the Pennsylvania Hinterland* (University Park: Pennsylvania State University Press, 1998), esp. introduction; William Pencak, "The Promise of Revolution," in Randall M. Miller and William Pencak, eds., *Pennsylvania: A History of the Commonwealth* (University Park: Pennsylvania State University Press and Pennsylvania Historical and Museum Commission, 2002), 101–52; James H. Hutson, *Pennsylvania Politics, 1746–1770: The Movement for Royal Government and Its Consequences* (Princeton, N.J.: Princeton University Press, 1972); Fred Anderson, *Crucible of War: The Seven Years' War and the Fate of Empire in British North America: 1754–1766* (New York: Knopf, 2000), xv–xxiii.

39. I would like to thank Daniel K. Richter for drawing my attention to the parallels between Herrnhut's action and the Proclamation of 1763. Kenneth Gardiner Hamilton, *John Ettwein and the Moravian Church During the Revolutionary Period* (Bethlehem, Pa.: Time Publishing Co, 1940), quotation, 148 n. 22. Colin Podmore, *The Moravian Church in England, 1728–1760* (Oxford: Clarendon Press, 1998), 228–65. Ronald Hoffman, Thad W. Tate, and Peter J. Albert, eds., *An Uncivil War: The Southern Backcountry During the American Revolution* (Charlottesville: University Press of Virginia, 1985). For North Carolina Moravians during the Revolutionary War, see Jon F. Sensbach, *A Separate Canaan: The Making of an Afro-Moravian World in North Carolina, 1763–1840* (Chapel Hill: University of North Carolina Press, 1998), 74–102; Elisabeth W. Sommer, *Serving Two Masters: Moravian Brethren in Germany and North Carolina, 1727–1801* (Lexington: University Press of Kentucky, 2000), 168–69; Hunter James, *The Quiet People of the Land: A Story of the North Carolina Moravians in Revolutionary Times* (Chapel Hill: University of North Carolina Press, 1976).

40. Riordan, *Many Identities, One Nation*, 68–81; Anne M. Ousterhout, *A State Divided: Opposition in Pennsylvania to the American Revolution* (New York: Greenwood Press, 1987); Eugene R. Slaski, "The Lehigh Valley," in Franz and Pencak, eds., *Beyond Philadelphia*, 46–66; Francis S. Fox, *Sweet Land of Liberty: The Ordeal of the American Revolution in Northampton County, Pennsylvania* (University Park: Pennsylvania State University Press, 2000).

41. Johannes Ettwein, Lebenslauf, BD January 1802. See also Hamilton, *John Ettwein and the Moravian Church*, 17–46.

42. Hamilton, *John Ettwein and the Moravian Church*, 131–40; Peter Brock, *Pacifism in the United States from the Colonial Era to the First World War* (Princeton, N.J.: Princeton University Press, 1968), 285–329; Aaron S. Fogleman, "The Decline and Fall of the Moravian Community in Colonial Georgia: Revising the Traditional View," *UF* 48 (2001): 1–22; Richard K. MacMaster, "Neither Whig Nor Tory: The Peace Churches in the American Revolution," *Fides et Historia* 9 (1977): 8–24.

43. Hamilton argues for the importance of Ettwein's leadership in *John Ettwein and the Moravian Church*, 135–37.

44. Fox, *Sweet Land of Liberty*, 73–96; Ousterhaut, *A State Divided*, 192–94; Benjamin Franklin, *The Papers of Benjamin Franklin*, vol. 22, *March 23, 1775 Through October 27, 1776*, ed. William B. Wilcox (New Haven, Conn.: Yale University Press, 1982), 56–58. The best source on Bethlehem during the Revolutionary era is Joseph Mortimer Levering, *A History of Bethlehem*, 441–505. Ettwein wrote a history of the conflict in 1781, which has been translated and annotated by Kenneth Gardiner Hamilton and appears in *John Ettwein and the Moravian Church*, 131–233.

45. See, for example, SBDT 10/19/1776, 12/21/1776, 2/13/1777, 2/15/1777, 4/11/1777, 5/13/1777, 6/10/1777, 8/18/1777.

46. SBDT 6/18/1777; 7/3/1776; 7/6/1776; 8/29/1776; 9/1/1776; 12/31/1776.

47. Levering, 451–56.

48. Levering, 464–82; SBDT 9/20/1776, 9/21/1776.

49. ECM 4/3/1778. Levering, 496–500.

50. Johann Christian Till, Lebenslauf, MS Box 10.

51. Hamilton, *John Ettwein and the Moravian Church*, 131–233.

CHAPTER 8. UNRAVELED STRANDS

1. There is a large literature on religion during the era of the early republic. For works that emphasize the growth of denominational institutions, see Philip N. Mulder, *A Controversial Spirit: Evangelical Awakenings in the South* (New York: Oxford University Press, 2002); Dee E. Andrews, *The Methodists and Revolutionary America, 1760–1800: The Shaping of an Evangelical Culture* (Princeton, N.J.: Princeton University Press, 2000); Nathan O. Hatch, *The Democratization of American Christianity* (New Haven, Conn.: Yale University Press, 1989).

2. Beverly Smaby, *The Transformation of Moravian Bethlehem: From Communal Mission to Family Economy* (Philadelphia: University of Pennsylvania Press, 1988), 41–42, 179–95; Hatch, *Democratization of American Christianity*; Paul K. Conkin, *Cane Ridge: America's Pentecost* (Madison: University of Wisconsin Press, 1990); William G. McLoughlin, *Revivals, Awakenings, and Reform: An Essay on Religion and Social Change in America, 1607–1977* (Chicago: University of Chicago Press, 1978); Paul Douglas Newman, *Fries's Rebellion: The Enduring Struggle for the American Revolution* (Philadelphia: University of Pennsylvania Press, 2004); Levering, 564–65, 536–82, passim.

3. For discussion of the Unity's financial situation, see Edmund de Schweinitz, *The Financial History of the American Province of the Unitas Fratrum and of its Sustentation Fund* (Bethlehem, Pa.: Moravian Publication Office, 1877). For broader histories of the Unity in this period, see Dietrich Meyer, *Zinzendorf und die Herrnhuter Brüdergemeine, 1700–2000* (Göttingen: Vandenhoeck und Ruprecht, 2000); J. Taylor Hamilton and Kenneth G.

Hamilton, *History of the Moravian Church: The Renewed Unitas Fratrum, 1722–1957* (Bethlehem, Pa.: Moravian Church in America, 1967), 163–86.

4. The records of the 1764 and 1769 Synods show a great deal of discussion of these issues. In addition to those records (R.2.B.44.11; R.2.B.44.1.C.1–C.2; R.2.B.44.1.C.1; UAH), the discussions of the subcommittee appointed by the 1764 Synod to discussion commercial issues is also important (R.4.A.51.1b, UAH).

5. R.2.B.45.2.a, V.1, UAH. 1749 marked the end of the "sifting time," which probably explains Zinzendorf's reluctance to ruffle feathers at that time.

6. R.2.B.45.2.a, V.8, UAH.

7. R.15.A 4a.7 c, UAH.

8. R.15.A.4a.7 c, UAH.

9. Missions Deputation Protocol, 1765–1769, UAH. Laura M. Stevens, *The Poor Indians: British Missionaries, Native Americans, and Colonial Sensibility* (Philadelphia: University of Pennsylvania Press, 2004), 22–29; Jon F. Sensbach, *Rebecca's Revival: Creating Black Christianity in the Atlantic World* (Cambridge, Mass.: Harvard University Press, 2005), 236–39; August Gottlieb Spangenberg, *An Account of the Manner in which the Protestant Church of the Unitas Fratrum, or United Brethren, preach the Gospel and carry on their Missions among the Heathen* (London: H. Trapp, 1788); J. C. S. Mason, *The Moravian Church and the Missionary Awakening in England, 1760–1800* (Suffolk: Boydell Press for Royal Historical Society, 2001).

10. Richard White, *The Middle Ground: Indians, Empires, and Republics in the Great Lakes Region, 1650–1815* (Cambridge: Cambridge University Press, 1991), 387–396. David Zeisberger, *The Moravian Mission Diaries of David Zeisberger, 1771–1781*, ed. Hermann Wellenreuther and Carola Wessel (University Park: Pennsylvania State University Press, 2005), 21–37; John Heckewelder, *A Narrative of the Missions of the United Brethren among the Delaware and Mohegan Indians from Its Commencement in the Year 1740 to the Close of the Year 1808*, ed. William Elsey Connelly (Cleveland, Ohio: Burrows Brothers, 1907), online facsimile edition at www.americanjourneys.org/aj-120/, accessed June 19, 2006.

11. Heckewelder, *A Narrative of the Mission*, 385, 422–23; Wellenreuther and Wessel, *Diaries of David Zeisberger*, 33–37.

12. Heckewelder, *A Narrative of the Mission*, 416–33, recounts the massacre in detail. See also R.14.A.a.44.a. item 144, p. 441–2, UAH. For a recent interpretation of the event, see Rob Harper, "Looking the Other Way: The Gnadenhütten Massacre and the Context Interpretation of Violence," *WMQ* 64 (2007): 621–44.

13. Jane T. Merritt, *At the Crossroads: Indians and Empires on a Mid-Atlantic Frontier, 1700–1763* (Chapel Hill: University of North Carolina Press, 2003), 169–97; Collin G. Calloway, *The Scratch of a Pen: 1763 and the Transformation of North America* (New York: Oxford University Press, 2006), 66–111; Collin G. Calloway, *The American Revolution in Indian Country: Crisis and Diversity in Native American Communities* (Cambridge: Cambridge University Press, 1995), 108–128; 272–91.

14. BD 11/25/1755.

15. ECM 4/5/1782.

16. ECM 4/5/1782, 4/11/1782.

17. For Zeisberger's life, see Zeisberger, *Diaries of David Zeisberger*, 72–74; Amy C. Schutt, *Peoples of the River Valleys: The Odyssey of the Delaware Indians* (Philadelphia: University of Pennsylvania Press, 2007), 170–71.

18. Kenneth Gardiner Hamilton, *John Ettwein and the Moravian Church During the Revolutionary Period* (Bethlehem, Pa.: Times Publishing, 1940), 88–128. The founding of the Moravian Society for Propagating the Gospel is also discussed in Katherine Carté Engel, "Bridging the Gap: Religious Community and Declension in Eighteenth-Century Bethlehem, Pennsylvania," *1650–1850: Ideas, Aesthetics and Inquiries in the Early Modern Era* 11 (2005): 407–42.

19. "State Rules of the Society of the United Brethren for Propagating the Gospel Among the Heathen (Philadelphia, n.d.); Ettwein Papers, 1373, MAB.

20. See Hamilton, *John Ettwein and the Moravian Church during the Revolutionary Period*, 114–28; Maia Turner Conrad, "Stuck in Their Hearts: David Zeisberger's Moravian Mission to the Delaware Indians of Ohio, 1767–1808" (Ph.D. dissertation, College of William and Mary, 1998); American State Papers 030, Public Lands Vol. 3, 17th Congress, 2nd Session, Publication No. 374; accessed online, Readex *American State Papers, 1739–1838*.

21. Quoted in Hamilton, *John Ettwein and the Moravian Church during the Revolutionary Period*, 119 n. 85.

22. *Newport* [Pennsylvania] *Herald*, 8/6/1789; *Federal Gazette, and Philadelphia Evening Post*, 4/11/1791, 11/9/1793.

23. Alan Taylor, *The Divided Ground: Indians, Settlers, and the Northern Borderland of the American Revolution* (New York: Knopf, 2006), 249–59, 270–73.

24. Gemein Nachricten, 1792, Part 1, Quartal 2, Item II, MAB.

25. Gemein Nachricten, 1792, Part 1, Quartal 2, Item II, MAB.

26. Jeffrey B. Long, "The Development of 18th-Century Moravian Church Architecture," May 18, 2006, unpublished manuscript in author's possession.

27. Mabel Haller, *Early Moravian Education in Pennsylvania* (Nazareth, Pa.: Moravian Historical Association, 1953), 13–32; Levering, 569–73.

28. *The Mail*, 8/9/1791, reprinted from the *Massachusetts Magazine*; *Pennsylvania Mercury*, 5/8/1788, reprinted from the *New-Haven Gazette*; *Federal Gazette*, 8/20/1790.

29. Gemein Nachricten, 1792, Part 1, Quartal 2, Item II, MAB. See also William C. Reichel, *A History of the Rise, Progress and Present Condition of the Bethlehem Female Seminary* (Philadelphia: J.B. Lippincott, 1858), 97–105. Walter Pilkington, ed., *The Journals of Samuel Kirkland: 18th Century Missionary to the Iroquois, Government Agent, Father of Hamilton College* (Clinton, N.Y.: Hamilton College, 1980), 245.

30. Engel, "Bridging the Gap: Religious Community and Declension in Eighteenth-Century Bethlehem, Pennsylvania."

31. ACM 9/28/1791, 2/15/1792, 4/24/1792; 5/21/94; *Newport* [Pennsylvania] *Herald*,

9/11/1788; *Independent Gazetteer,* 11/6/1788; Philadelphia *Mail,* 10/10/1792; *Dunlap's American Daily Advertiser,* 6/29/1792.

32. ACM 6/13/1792, 10/31/1792, 1/15/1794.

33. ACM 5/15/1793; 5/22/1793; 6/19/1793; 2/19/1794.

34. ACM 3/30/1791; 5/2/1791; 12/21/1791; 3/28/1792; 1/16/1793; 1/15/1794.

35. ACM 3/30/1791; 4/13/1791; 4/27/1791; 5/2/1791; 5/11/1791; 5/25/1791; 7/6/1791; 3/28/1792.

36. ACM 3/16/1791; 5/16/1792; 11/7/1792; 11/21/1792; 5/4/1794; 9/24/1794; Gemein Nachrichten, 1794, Part 1, Quartal 1, Number 2; Single Brethren's Diary BethSB 5, Memorabilia for 1794. The Single Brethren's diary lists the year's final count at 39 rather than 42, and it may have been compiled later in the year.

37. Gemein Nachrichten, 1792, Part 1, 3d Quartal, #2, MAB.

38. John C. Ogden, *An Excursion into Bethlehem and Nazareth in Pennsylvania in the Year 1799* (Philadelphia: Charles Cist, 1805), 1.

INDEX

ACKNOWLEDGMENTS

A project like the one contained in these pages relies on help from many quarters, financial, scholarly, and personal. I am grateful for the generous support I've received in all these respects. In the first category, I would like to take this opportunity to thank the McNeil Center for Early American Studies, the Library Company of Philadelphia's Program in Early American Economy and Society, and Yale University's Center for Religion and American Life. Each provided for a year of dedicated research and writing. Each also introduced me to the wonderfully fruitful intellectual environments they foster. Texas A&M University and the German Academic Exchange program (DAAD) also provided important assistance for dedicated research. The Melbern G. Glasscock Center for Humanities Research provided a very useful publication grant.

This project has taken many forms over the years, and its development was shaped by the many folks who have talked about it with me, in formal and in informal settings. At a critical moment, two scholars asked insightful questions which had far-reaching results for how I conceived of Bethlehem's history. Jeanne Boydston asked, upon reading the completed dissertation, why Bethlehem's story could only have happened in the eighteenth century. Around the same time, Craig Atwood wondered why the Moravians did not build another Bethlehem in the Ohio Valley in the 1780s. I have spent the past four years attempting to answer those questions, and I remain deeply grateful to my interrogators, and to the many others who knowingly or unknowingly guided this study.

The community of historians and researchers in Bethlehem and in the larger Moravian world is both warm and welcoming. Members of that community were unfailingly generous with their sources, their ideas, and their time. Craig Atwood, Otto Dreydoppel, Sue Dreydoppel, Katie Faull, Aaron Fogleman, Jon Sensbach, Paul Peucker, and Beverly Smaby all deserve particular mention. Vernon Nelson and Ralph Schwartz provided a wealth of valuable information, and their companionship made my many months in the Moravian Archives a pleasure. Julia Maynard Maserjian has been a faithful friend and support throughout, bringing key sources to my attention and opening her home to me whenever I needed a place to stay. Rachel Wheeler has been a wonderful friend and sounding board over the years; she has done much to sharpen arguments, and saved me from many errors. I would also especially like to thank the staffs at the Moravian Archives, Bethlehem, and the Unity Archives in Herrnhut, particularly Rodiger Kroeger and Lanie Graff.

As a piece of writing and argument, this book has been through many versions, and I want to thank those who pushed it along. Charles Cohen shepherded the project in its early days and urged me to craft its arguments carefully even as he encouraged me to think broadly. Cathy Matson has been a good friend and kind mentor through the years, and she offered many insightful comments and suggestions on early drafts. Daniel Richter read multiple renditions of the manuscript with great attention to details and argument, and his editorial attention substantially improved the whole. Bob Lockhart and the staff at University of Pennsylvania Press gave excellent feedback and advice, and moved the project along steadily. Melissa French read the whole beast at a late date, as did Ben Engel. Frances Kolb provided excellent research support, and Rebekah Weinel helped with some difficult German translations. My colleagues, first at Rutgers University, Camden, and then at Texas A&M University, have been equally supportive. Special thanks go to Howard Gillette, Shan Holt, Margaret Marsh, Walter Buenger, Troy Bickham, Carlos Blanton, Lauren Clay, Walter Kamphoefner, Andy Kirkendall, and Brian Linn. Cyndy Bouton, April Hatfield, Sylvia Hoffert, and Rebecca Hartkopf Schloss provided the best sounding board and advice an author could ever hope for. The project was much improved, and the writing of it made enjoyable, by their collegial support. Thanks are also due to Ted Bromund and Ann Carter-Drier of Yale University's International Security Studies, which gave me a home to hammer out the manuscript one last time.

Most of this book's initial arguments were born in long and treasured conversations with my brother, Adam Carte. He also spent hours helping me with the intricacies of twenty-first-century spreadsheets and eighteenth-century currencies. Special thanks are also owed to Trish Carte, Miyoko Sato, and David Johnson, as enthusiastic and loving a family as anyone could ask for. My grandmother, Doris Bishop Huddell, first introduced me to the Pennsylvania Germans when she took me to visit the Ephrata Cloister as a child. She has always nurtured in our family a deep respect and love of history. I hope the result meets her high standards. My in-laws, Lory and Toby Engel, have supported me in innumerable and loving ways over the years. They hosted dozens of trips to Philadelphia, with child, cat, and only occasionally husband in tow. My extended family, Sidney and Rafi Feinstein, Melissa and Jonathan Webster, Marilyn Huddell, Akio and Uta Miyabayashi, Ben Engel, Josh Engel and Laura Struve, and Eleanore Rodney, provided me with much love and support over the years.

Much life happens while a book percolates, and I want to take this opportunity to thank the dear friends who have made the last decade so much fun, particularly Constance and Ben Kim-Gervey, Geoff and Melissa French, and Andrew Preston and Frances Patrick. Jennifer Turner pulled off an impossible task of modern life, and she made the last major round of revisions in New Haven possible. She and the rest of the Turner-Pittenger clan also made our time there fun. We have found in College Station, Texas, a wonderful community of dear friends. Bies-Egans, Schlosses, and Simaneks, have all helped us take pleasure in the joys and pitfalls of academic life and parenthood.

My parents provided me with a home full of love and a deep respect for both faith and rigorous scholarship, and this book is written in their honor and memory. My deepest thanks go to my husband and my son. Jeffrey has been my companion since the week I turned in the first dissertation proposal. Without his love, his friendship, his enduring intellectual partnership, his deep devotion to hyperbole, his ability to turn a terse phrase into a lengthy paragraph, and his truly outstanding chicken paprikash, nothing would have been written. Marshall is a newcomer to the family, but he cheerfully and insistently ensured that academic prose shared time with Peter Rabbit, the Wild Things, Babar, Mike Mulligan, and the Cat in the Hat, and for that I am most grateful of all.